Elementary Classroom
Management

For
Ryan and Tyler

Elementary Classroom Management

A Student-Centered Approach to Leading and Learning

Kerry Curtiss Williams
Wayne State College

Los Angeles • London • New Delhi • Singapore • Washington DC

For information:

SAGE Publications, Inc.
2455 Teller Road
Thousand Oaks, California 91320
E-mail: order@sagepub.com

SAGE Publications Ltd.
1 Oliver's Yard
55 City Road
London EC1Y 1SP
United Kingdom

SAGE Publications India Pvt. Ltd.
B 1/I 1 Mohan Cooperative Industrial Area
Mathura Road, New Delhi 110 044
India

SAGE Publications Asia-Pacific Pte. Ltd.
33 Pekin Street #02-01
Far East Square
Singapore 048763

Printed in the United States of America

Library of Congress Cataloging-in-Publication Data

Williams, Kerry C.
Elementary classroom management: A student-centered approach to leading and learning/Kerry Curtiss Williams.
    p. cm.
Includes bibliographical references and index.
ISBN 978-1-4129-5680-2 (pbk.)
   1. Classroom management. 2. Education, Elementary. I. Title.

LB3013.W526 2009
372.1102′4—dc22   2008024295

Printed on acid-free paper

08 09 10 11 12   10 9 8 7 6 5 4 3 2 1

Acquiring Editor:	Diane McDaniel
Editorial Assistant:	Leah Mori
Production Editor:	Sarah K. Quesenberry
Copy Editor:	Melinda Masson
Proofreader:	Joyce Li
Indexer:	Rick Hurd
Typesetter:	C&M Digitals (P) Ltd.
Cover Designer:	Candice Harman
Marketing Manager:	Christy Guilbault

Brief Contents

Preface   xiii

Acknowledgments   xix

SECTION I. A VISION FOR CLASSROOM MANAGEMENT   1

  1. Autonomy, Belonging, and Competency for Children   3

  2. Creating Democratic Communities   31

  3. Motivation and Classroom Management   61

SECTION II. STRUCTURES AND TOOLS FOR CLASSROOM MANAGEMENT   87

  4. Pedagogical Structures for Managing Learning   89

  5. Creating Thinking Classrooms   119

  6. Leading and Learning With a Whole Group of Students   141

SECTION III. CREATING CLASSROOMS THAT MEET THE NEEDS OF
        INDIVIDUAL CHILDREN   167

  7. Recognizing, Accommodating, and Advocating for Children
      With Special Needs   169

  8. Language and Literature as Classroom Management Tools   195

  9. Asking Students, Parents, and School Resources for Help 219

Section IV. Making a Classroom Management Plan Your Own
          Inside and Outside   247

    10. Creating a Classroom Arrangement That Promotes Autonomy, Belonging,
        and Competency   249

    11. Managing Beyond the Boundaries of the Classroom

    12. Making the Classroom Your Own: A Beginning   305

Glossary   331

References   337

Index   349

About the Author   369

Detailed Contents

Preface   xiii

Acknowledgements   xix

SECTION I. A VISION FOR CLASSROOM MANAGEMENT   1

Chapter 1. Autonomy, Belonging, and Competency for Children   3
    Reflection Tool Number 1: What and Why   6
    Reflection Tool Number 2: Prior Beliefs About Classroom Management   9
    Reflection Tool Number 3: Thinking About the Future   10
    Autonomy and Its Impact on Students   11
        What Is Autonomy?   12
        What Is an Autonomy-Supportive Classroom?   13
        Why Do We Need Autonomy?   16
        What Does Autonomy Cost?   17
    Belonging and Its Impact on Students   17
        What Is Belonging?   18
        What Is a Belonging-Supportive Classroom?   19
        Why Do We Need Belonging in Our Classrooms?   21
        What Are the Costs of Belonging?   21
    Competency and Its Impact on Students   22
        What Does It Mean to Be Competent?   23
        What Is a Competency-Supportive Classroom?   24
        Why Do We Need Competency?   26
        What Are the Costs of Competency?   26
    SO . . . WHAT?   28
    GET READY FOR . . .   28
    ACTIVITIES TO TRY   28

Chapter 2. Creating Democratic Communities   31

Knowing Students   33
     What Does Knowing Students Mean?   35
     What Knowing Students Does Not Mean   36
     Why Do You Need to Know Your Students?   38
     How Can I Get to Know My Students?   39

What Is a Democratic Classroom?   41
     Three Kinds of Classrooms   41
     What Does Having a Democratic Classroom Mean?   44
     What a Democratic Classroom Is Not   46
     Why Have a Democratic Classroom?   49

How Do I Create a Democratic Environment in My Classroom?   51
     Believing in Democracy for the Classroom   51
     Developing Community as a Process for Democracy   51
     What Does It Mean to Develop Community?   52
     What Community Development Is Not   55
     Why Develop Community?   55

So . . . What?   57
Get Ready For . . .   58
Activities to Try   58

Chapter 3. Motivation and Classroom Management   61

Influences on Motivation   63
     The Brain   63
     Self-Efficacy   73
     Attribution   74
     Relationships   77
     Tasks and Topics   81

Demotivational Influences   83
So . . . What?   84
Get Ready For . . .   85
Activities to Try   85

Section II. Structures and Tools for Classroom Management   87

Chapter 4. Pedagogical Structures for Managing Learning   89

Connections Between Pedagogy and Management: If, Then   91
     Cooperative Workshops   93
So . . . What?   116
Get Ready For . . .   116
Activities to Try   116

Chapter 5. Creating Thinking Classrooms   119

Thinking Models   121
     Three Pieces of Thinking   122

Thinking in the Classroom   123
    Students in Thinking Classrooms   124
    Teachers in Thinking Classrooms   125
Thinking Routines   130
    Plan-Do-Review   132
    Collect-Categorize-Connect   136
    Think-Pair-Share   137
    Know-Want to Know-Learned   138
    Body Models   138
Thinking Routines as a Piece of Classroom Management   139
So . . . What?   139
Get Ready For . . .   140
Activities to Try   140

Chapter 6. Leading and Learning With a Whole Group of Students   **141**
What Is a "Whole" Group?   143
    "Whole" Groups Include All of the Children   144
    "Whole" Groups Have and Work on Common Goals   145
    "Whole" Groups Do Things Other Than Academic Work Together   145
    "Whole" Groups Celebrate Learning   146
Hot Tools for Facilitating a "Whole" Group   147
    Class Meetings   148
    Data Collection Tools   151
    Whole Class Service Activities   157
    Group Energizing Tools   161
Managing a "Whole" Group   163
    The Spaces of "Whole" Group Work   164
    Timing of "Whole" Group Work Is a Key to Success   164
    Visions of "Whole" Group Work Need to Be Developed and Revisited   164
    Juicy Problems Make "Whole" Group Time Worthwhile   165
So . . . What?   165
Get Ready For . . .   166
Activities to Try   166

**Section III. Creating Classrooms That Meet the
Needs of Individual Children**   **167**

**Chapter 7. Recognizing, Accommodating, and
Advocating for Children With Special Needs**   **169**
Knowing Students With Special Needs   171
    Development   172
    Physical and Mental Disabilities   176
    Cultural Differences and English-Language Learners   178
    Environmental   181

The Teacher's Role   184
    Be There   184
    Reflect Toward the Future   184
    Accommodate Individuals   185
    Advocate   186
    Collaborate   186
    Be Creative/Be a Learner   186
Structures and Tools for Struggling Children   187
    Something to Care About   187
    Peer Interactions   189
    Technology   190
    Movement   192
So ... What?   192
Get Ready For ...   193
Activities to Try   193

Chapter 8. Language and Literature as Classroom Management Tools   **195**
Managing With Language (and I Don't Mean Swearing!)   197
    Questions Versus Statements   198
    Stories Versus Lectures   200
    Empathy Versus Anger   201
    Assessment Versus Evaluation   203
    Times to Be Directive   204
    Effective Single Words   204
    Body Language   205
Management With Children's Literature   207
    What's a Good Book?   208
    How to Use Literature as a Management Tool   208
    Books to Use and How to Find More   210
Writing Stories Together   214
    When to Write a Story   214
    Writing a Story With a Child   215
So ... What?   216
Get Ready For ...   218
Activities to Try   218

Chapter 9. Asking Students, Parents, and School Resources for Help   **219**
Help Wanted: Children Who Help in the Classroom   221
    Children Can Help You With Jobs Around the Room   221
    Children Can Help With Assessments   223
    Children Can Help You Communicate With Parents   225
Help Wanted: Involved Parents/Caregivers   226
    Good Relationships With Parents Provide Opportunities for Help in the Classroom   227
    Help Parents Feel They Can Contribute   230
    Parents May Need Multiple Kinds of Invitations   231

Help Wanted: Resources Inside School   232
    When Do I Ask Another Teacher for Help?   234
    When Do I Ask a Principal for Help?   234
    When Do I Ask a Secretary for Help?   236
    When Do I Ask the School Nurse for Help?   236
    When Do I Ask a Student Assistance Team for Help?   237
    When Do I Ask a Special-Education Teacher for Help?   237
    When Do I Ask a Speech Language Pathologist for Help?   237
    When Do I Ask a Reading Specialist for Help?   238
    When Do I Ask an Occupational Therapist for Help?   238
    When Do I Ask a Counselor for Help?   238
    When Do I Ask a School Psychologist for Help?   239
Help Wanted: Resources Outside of School   240
    Internet Sites Can Be a Resource for You and for Children   240
    Professionals in Your Community Can Be a Resource for Children   243
    Organizations in Your Community Can Be a Resource for Children   244
So . . . What?   245
Get Ready For . . .   246
Activities to Try   246

**Section IV. Making a Classroom Management
    Plan Your Own Inside and Outside**   **247**

**Chapter 10. Creating a Classroom Arrangement
    That Promotes Autonomy, Belonging, and Competency**   **249**
The Classroom Setting   250
    Room Arrangement   251
    Materials   259
    Aesthetics in the Classroom   263
Planning Tools for Classroom Settings   267
    Reflection Tools for the Future   269
    Reflection Tool for the Present   275
    Reflection Tools for the Past   275
So . . . What?   277
Get Ready For . . .   278
Activities to Try   279

Chapter 11. Managing Beyond the Boundaries of the Classroom   **281**
Managing Adventures Inside the School Building   282
    Technology   282
    In the Hallways   287
    In and Out of the Bathrooms   291
    In the Cafeteria   292
    Assemblies   292

Managing Adventures Outside the School Building   293
    The Playground   293
    Outside Lessons   296
    Sending Students Home   299
Managing Adventures Off School Grounds   301
    Field Trips   301
So ... What?   302
Get Ready For ...   302
Activities to Try   303

Chapter 12. Making the Classroom Your Own: A Beginning   **305**
Classroom Management Autonomy   308
    What Are Your Core Beliefs About Classroom Management?   308
    What Is "Out of Bounds"?   310
    Withitness   311
    Making Classroom Procedures Your Own   314
Classroom Management Belonging   317
    Colleagues   319
    Friends and Family   321
    Children   322
Classroom Management Competency   323
    Knowing How Children Learn   323
    Knowing the Content   326
    Knowing Yourself as a Teacher   327
The End?   328
So ... What?   328
Activities to Try   329

Glossary   **331**

References   **337**

Index   **349**

About the Author   **369**

Preface

Welcome to *Elementary Classroom Management: A Student-Centered Approach to Leading and Learning!* This book provides an introduction to student-centered classroom management practices and the theories that support them. It was written with preservice teachers in classroom management and methods courses in mind, as well as for inservice teachers who are working to improve their classroom management practices. The ideas in this book, however, can be applied to a variety of settings. After all, the purpose of classroom management and therefore this book is to create classroom spaces that facilitate academic and social learning, as well as dispositions that foster lifelong learning.

Classroom management, a great influence on students, is a main reason many new teachers get out of the classroom early in their careers. Indeed, our schools and students deserve teachers who know content but also pedagogy, classroom management, and how to work with children who present special needs. Preservice teachers are often taught "tricks" to use for certain management problems rather than to understand the issues of the classroom and school, the students as individuals, and the pedagogical choices that profoundly influence their academic and social success. Tricks often work for a few days or months, and then the teacher is left reacting to problems that could have been prevented. This book is designed to help teachers think about and reflect on why things happen in classrooms, understand the connections between classroom management and learning, begin to utilize pedagogical structures that facilitate success and thus management, and finally design classrooms that work for students who may need something extra.

Many current textbooks on classroom management follow a model of telling readers what to do in specific instances, emphasizing what to do *to* students when they _____ (fill in the blank), or a model of sharing many different theories on classroom management. This book provides readers the opportunity to understand classroom management theories through research, stories, and cases and then asks them to construct their own philosophy of classroom management and begin to apply it in the classroom. Just as we cannot teach students by merely pouring information into their heads, we cannot ask teachers to implement effective classroom management plans by merely reading about theories or trying to memorize what to do in specific instances. Teachers must have the opportunity to understand the theories that shape students' academic and social learning; to think, reflect, and try strategies, structures, and tools and make them their own; and to realize that constructing a classroom management plan that works requires continued learning even after they are finished reading the textbook. In other words, constructing classroom management plans is about constructing meaning through knowledge, experience, and reflection.

Goals of the Book

There are five main goals that create the framework of this book:

1. **Thinking and reflecting about key issues of classroom management, such as autonomy, belonging, competency, democratic communities for learners, and motivation.** To create effective classroom management plans, teachers must understand *what* they are doing and *why* they are doing it. In my experience, many teachers think classroom management is about controlling behaviors. Instead, this book focuses on why students behave the way they do and encourages readers to pay attention to and address these needs with a variety of structures, strategies, and tools.

2. **Thinking, reflecting, and designing pedagogical structures and classroom procedures that, when used, address the key issues of classroom management in very practical and innovative ways.** In some ways, the education field is asking new and veteran teachers to teach in ways that they have never experienced. Indeed, many of us grew up in classrooms where our names were put on the board with chances for three checks before we had to go to the principal's office. It is very difficult to break out of what we have experienced. This book was designed to help readers resee classroom management, students with individual needs, and what it means to learn in general by providing examples of flexible structures that can be transformed into their own creations yet still promote the key issues described in other chapters. Some of these include cooperative workshops, thinking routines, and classroom meetings.

3. **Thinking and reflecting about individual children, including those with needs that require something special in the classroom, so they can be socially and academically successful.** New and veteran teachers are often the most worried about

students who may need them to try something different in the classroom. It is very easy to worry about disruptions, students who are seemly unable to learn, and being out of control. This book was written to help readers understand and learn about individual students in the classroom, as well as to give them unique strategies and structures, such as language and literature, that will assist them. Perhaps most important, it provides an entire chapter dedicated to working with colleagues, parents, and outside resources when the strategies they are trying don't work. I hope this book encourages teachers to know individual students' needs, to create exciting opportunities for all students to learn, and to ask for help when they need it.

4. **Thinking and reflecting about how managing the physical classroom, as well as the spaces outside the classroom, influences learning.** There are many influences on academic and social learning, including the physical classroom itself and the procedures used to manage all of the various spaces in which students learn throughout the day. Once again, it is not enough to tell teachers what to do. Instead, this book was designed to help readers ask questions and reflect on where they will put items in the classroom, how they will help students walk down the hall, and who will be in charge of materials.

5. **Thinking and reflecting about creating a classroom management plan that reflects the teacher's beliefs and philosophies so the plan doesn't change with each new problem or issue.** We often behave like windblown flowers in the world of education. We bloom every time the latest, greatest trick comes out yet blow away when any problem arises that the trick doesn't fix. I hope teachers who read this book will develop some roots that will help them continue to bloom even when the wind comes. Teachers must understand what they believe about classroom management and how students learn and then create a plan that reflects those beliefs. I put reflection tools in each chapter and then created an entire chapter that addresses readers' core beliefs, their boundaries, and opportunities to keep learning.

Pedagogical Features of the Text

Learning about classroom management requires understanding the key issues that influence classroom management; actively experiencing practical strategies, structures, and tools; and thinking and reflecting in the past, present, and future. The pedagogical features of this text were designed to assist readers do all three.

Stories, Cases, Research

Throughout the text, stories from real classrooms are connected to the latest research on topics influencing classroom management. In addition, cases are included for readers to grapple with and think about what they might do. Key words are bolded and put into a Glossary.

Practical Strategies, Structures, and Tools

There are practical ideas throughout the text that readers can immediately take into classrooms and use. These practical ideas are connected with helpful questions that readers can answer as they begin to use these ideas.

Collections

I encourage all teachers to keep collections of everything from lesson ideas to brain tools they might use. In addition, I have included some collections for readers to take and make their own, including Internet sources, children's literature, and thinking routines. Some charts are also included so readers may begin creating their own collections. For example, Chapter 11 includes a chart they can use to list their school district's policies.

Activities to Try

At the end of each chapter, a section of activities to try is included. Readers may want to try these activities on their own or in classes. Each activity to try includes a mini action research project so they can continue to look at classroom management issues systematically and deeply.

Reflections

Throughout the text, there are questions helping readers go beyond their own experiences and think further about key issues and stories. There are also reflection tools, such as an opportunity to write a classroom management biography in Chapter 1 and a relationship diagram in Chapter 10, that will help them reflect on where to place learning areas in a classroom.

Letters From Master Teachers

Twenty-four master teachers took time to write friendly, supportive advice letters for this book. They are real teachers who really do the things discussed in this book. I hope they provide a sense that these ideas truly can be realized.

Organization of the Text

Section I. A Vision for Classroom Management

This section consists of three chapters on key ideas influencing academic and social learning that will allow readers to create a vision for classroom management. I put this section at the beginning because it is important for teachers to understand the influences on learning and classroom management before creating a plan that works for them. These chapters will become the readers' base for a philosophy that they will come back to throughout the book. Chapter 1 introduces readers to the "what" and "why" questions of classroom management, as well as the need for all children to have autonomy, belonging, and competency in the classrooms they attend. Chapter 2 introduces readers to democratic communities in the classroom and the notion that, rather than trying to change students, we need to change classrooms so learners are successful. Many people have misconceptions about democratic classrooms, and this chapter will help readers see what it is and is not. Chapter 3 is devoted completely to motivation, a topic often left out of classroom management texts yet one of the most important ideas to understand when it comes to creating a classroom where students are motivated to learn rather than create problems.

Section II. Structures and Tools for Classroom Management

This section includes three chapters on pedagogical structures that will help teachers give all students autonomy, belonging, competency, motivation, and an opportunity to belong to a democratic community. Why put pedagogical structures in a classroom management book? Classroom management must be about all ideas that help children learn and succeed socially. Pedagogical structures that provide opportunities for the key ideas listed above are invaluable in creating classrooms where learners are successful. The first structure, included in Chapter 4, is called a cooperative workshop and will allow teachers to design lessons and units within a flexible structure, providing "juicy" problems and meaningful group work. It can also be used to develop differentiated stations. Chapter 5 introduces a pedagogical structure Ritchhart (2002) calls a thinking routine. Sometimes we forget that classrooms should be places where students are thinking rather than just looking busy, quiet, and good. Thinking routines help create thinking classrooms. Chapter 6 is all about pedagogical structures that help teachers manage a whole classroom of students. Class meetings, data collection, and graphing are some examples of structures mentioned in this chapter.

Section III. Creating Classrooms That Meet the Needs of Individual Children

This section includes three chapters on working with students who need something special to succeed in the classroom. This might be a student who is just having a bad day, who doesn't speak English, or who is physically or mentally handicapped. The important idea from this section is that teachers should work to do something different that may help the learner succeed. Chapter 7 is about identifying what individual children need. Sometimes we get stuck on labels, and this chapter encourages teachers to really know their students and find creative solutions to help them. Chapter 8 is all about language and literature that teachers can use to help students who struggle in the classroom. Sometimes using a story or just a different way of phrasing something can help students. Chapter 9 is about all of the resources teachers have inside and outside of their buildings that can help them when a student has a special need that they just aren't able to provide. I hope this chapter encourages especially new teachers to ask for help when they need it.

Section IV. Making a Classroom Management Plan Your Own Inside and Outside

This section is about making a plan for classroom management inside and outside of the classroom. Instead of giving them "right" answers, this section really works to help readers answer "right" questions. Chapter 10 is about the physical nature of the classroom and setting it up so all of the ideas in previous chapters can be achieved. Several questions about room arrangement, materials, and aesthetics will help readers determine the design of the classroom. Chapter 11 is about managing all of the places children go outside of the classroom. Whether it is the Internet, the playground, or a field trip, readers will begin to create plans for each place. Chapter 12 is about making a classroom management plan that works for the individual reader. Although it is the last chapter of this book, it is really the beginning of the journey into creating a classroom management plan. Readers will come away with their core beliefs and boundaries, as well as ways to have their own autonomy, belonging, and competency in the classroom.

Ancillary Materials

In addition to the text, ancillary materials further support and enhance the learning goals of *Elementary Classroom Management: A Student-Centered Approach to Leading and Learning*.

Instructors' Resources CD

This CD offers the instructor a variety of resources that supplement the book material, including video clips (also included on the Web-based student study site) with discussion questions, PowerPoint lecture slides, and test questions. Additional resources include teaching tips, sample syllabi, and Web resources. To obtain a copy of this CD, please contact Customer Service at 800-818-7243.

Web-Based Student Study Site

www.sagepub.com/kwilliamsstudy

The Web-based student study site provides a comprehensive selection of resources to enhance students' understanding of the book's content. The site includes study materials such as video clips, practice tests, flashcards, and suggested readings. Other resources include "Learning From SAGE Journal Articles," and additional activities created by the author.

Acknowledgments

In my opinion, one needs three things from others to write a book: inspiration, support, and love. I was fortunate to have all three throughout this process and sometimes more than one at a time. I want to thank everyone for bringing this book to life!

Inspiration

Even though he is gone now, I must acknowledge Dr. Robert Egbert because he taught me all of this through his stories and questions. I can only hope to do the same for my readers. Thanks to George Veomett who believed I was a good writer and taught me about lifelong learning for real. Thanks to all of the Wayne State Learning Community teachers and facilitators for inspiring and learning with me throughout this process. Blair I, Blair II, Fremont II, and Fremont III, all I can say about this book is that it is my sandwich! Thanks to inspirational teachers Rae, Chad, Julie, Mary, Cheryl, Deanna, Jim, Pam, Tom, Brian, Jill, Deann, Mary Jo, Josh, April, Zonna, Jenny, Denise, Kevin, Dene, Lisa, Durkhany, Kelly, and Carla for writing master teacher letters! You are the ones who make classroom management look so easy! Thanks to John Weaver for teaching me about autonomy, belonging, and competency. Thanks to Jesse Kiefer for his wonderful art! The cartoons really help me tell this important story! Thanks to Lisa, Rubi, Laura, Donna, and Kelsey for providing such wonderful first experiences with school for my sons. I often thought of you as I wrote.

Support

So many people were interested and supportive of me during this process. First, thanks to Cheryl Larmore and Mary Trehearn, who were my best cheerleaders. They read every word—sometimes twice—and always gave me great feedback. Your compliments and enthusiasm kept me writing. Thanks to Dawn Hanneman, Stacie Wall, Gina Smith, and Shelly Taylor for inviting my boys to come and play when you knew I really needed some time to work! Thanks to Diane McDaniel and Leah Mori at SAGE Publications for a smooth and wonderful journey.

Love

You can't write a book without unconditional love from those who mean the most to you because they often have to sacrifice things they need in order for it to be finished. Thanks to my mom and dad, who provide me with inspiration, support, and love every day and who allowed me to experience democracy and many other things in this book through their parenting. Thanks for being so proud and for loving me no matter what. Thanks to Jen, Mike, Bob, Kay, and all of the Williams family for all you do for me and especially for caring about my various projects. Thanks to Ryan and Tyler, my sweet boys, who have love in their eyes each day, even when I am sitting at the computer again. And thanks to John. I can't imagine how I could do much without you, your patience, and your love.

Reviewers

Finally, I would like to acknowledge the hard work and helpful comments of the following reviewers. Their suggestions and ideas were invaluable in writing this book.

Alda M. Blakeney-Wright, Kennesaw State University

Angela Humphrey Brown, Piedmont College

Kellie J. Cain, University of the Pacific

Richard H. Costner, Coastal Carolina University

Laura Latiolais Duhon, Texas State University–San Marcos

Mona C. Majdalani, University of Wisconsin–Eau Claire

Sam A. Marandos, National University

Sarah S. Marshall, Georgetown College

Patricia E. Murphy, Arkansas State University

Lois B. Paretti, University of Nevada–Las Vegas

Beverly Schumer, University of Michigan–Flint

Linda Schwartz Green, Centenary College

Cindy Shepardson, Keuka College

Judy Carrington Shipley, Hardin-Simmons University

Jennifer L. Snow-Gerono, Boise State University

Anita S. VanBrackle, Kennesaw State University

Kim Wieczorek, Nazareth College

E. Cam Willett, Laurentian University

Carolyn H. Wilson, Virginia State University

A Vision for Classroom Management

Look beyond the obvious and see the possible.

—Brooks, 2002, p. 7

Classroom management comprises many important pieces, all of which are discussed in this book. The physical classroom, the routines and structures, and the concepts and tasks all require attention when thinking about managing a classroom effectively. Missing from the list above (and often missing altogether from classroom management plans), however, is vision—your vision—involving not what tricks or programs you follow, but what you believe about children and how they learn best. How will you manage your classroom even when the going gets tough? The first three chapters of this book will help you create a vision for classroom management, including what all children need for success, what type of classroom environment will fulfill those needs, and how you, as a teacher, can influence motivation. Although many ideas in these chapters are meant to push your thinking, you must create your own vision for classroom management, which will help open your mind to new ideas but keep you grounded in your beliefs.

As you read these first three chapters, consider your past experiences with classroom management, reflect on how they fit or don't fit with the information you read, and be open to previously unexplored possibilities. The best kinds of classroom management begin with teachers who know what they believe about children and learning and who understand that their actions must reflect these beliefs. As you read, begin to form a vision statement about classroom management. Although it will change with each new chapter and experience, having a vision is vital as you work to help children learn.

Chapter 1 discusses your vision for your students and their needs. You may be thinking, "Just give me some techniques or ideas!" But how can you have techniques if you don't know your beliefs about what children need? In addition to helping you reflect on what you believe and why, Chapter 1 will help you understand that classroom management is about managing not students but the classroom to meet students' needs.

Chapter 2 discusses your vision for the classroom environment. Much more than a physical structure, the environment in a classroom includes the feelings that arise when you enter it and how you make it attractive to both yourself and children. Day to day and year to year, Chapter 2 will help you begin to design a classroom that meets all students' needs. It will also help you understand that classroom management is about fixing not the students but the place they visit every day.

Chapter 3 discusses your vision of motivation and how you as a teacher can influence it. If you understand motivation and what influences it positively, you can better create a classroom where children get what they need and where they want to be. Chapter 3 will help you understand that teachers cannot motivate children because motivation comes from within. You can, however, do everything in your power to create a classroom where motivation thrives.

Don't worry. This book provides a lot of structures, strategies, tasks, and tools, but if you have a vision first, they will make much more sense, and you will be able to use them wisely. Happy reading!

CHAPTER 1

Autonomy, Belonging, and Competency for Children

As I sit down to write this chapter, I hope my computer doesn't break or malfunction in any way. I will be fine if everything works correctly, especially the buttons, and if the formatting doesn't change while I write. I know how to word process, create margins, and style words in bold or a different color, but if something suddenly doesn't work, I will be in trouble. If I can't save the document or the printer won't print, I will not know what to do except yell at or plead with the computer to work. You see, I know how to use a computer, just not how it works. If something were to go awry, I would not understand enough about the computer to troubleshoot possible solutions.

This metaphor may also apply to teachers in their classrooms. Management programs that teachers can implement with ease certainly exist. Just as computer programmers have made using computers a cinch, researchers trying to make classroom management easy have packaged products for every kind of problem (and some have made a lot of money as a result). There are character education programs, behavior management programs, discipline programs, and so on, and, like the computer story above, we often use these programs without understanding enough about them or how they affect the students in our care. When a problem occurs that the program does not address, it is easy to yell, plead, or resort to something that, in the long run, may not help anyway.

In addition, particular students may need something a management program can't give them. An art teacher I know once implemented a program in her classroom that

Jesse Keifer

Just as it is easier to work with a computer we fully understand, we must understand children and their needs to create classroom management plans that work.

advised being a "broken record" when students wouldn't do what they were supposed to. For those of you too young to know what a record is, that simply means repeating and rerepeating what you want the student to do. The art teacher tried this and noted, "The student really had a valid point, and I was so busy being a broken record that I didn't listen." Students don't need managers but teachers who know them and what they need to ensure success.

This chapter is about knowing what students need and why, about managing not the students but the classroom and the structures therein. What's the difference? When we manage students, we do things to them, and when we manage classrooms, we create places where students can become caring, competent, and self-directed. What do students need to learn successfully? What does the classroom look like when those needs are fulfilled? By the end of this chapter, I hope you have:

- Reflection tools that help you understand your management choices

- An understanding of your own management experiences and beliefs

- An understanding of the importance of **autonomy, belonging,** and **competency** and how support of these three concepts affects students

LETTER FROM A MASTER TEACHER 1.1

Autonomy, Belonging, and Competency in a Real Classroom

I learned about the importance of autonomy, belonging, and competency the ninth year I taught. That was the year of the "dirty dozen" plus one. My principal assigned me 13 students who were labeled the worst of the worst in sixth grade that year. I panicked! How was I going to manage this class of students? The first day I had placed large ceramic pots full of plants on bookshelves, and within 2 hours the pots were broken and plants, dirt, and shards of ceramic pieces littered the area. My face flushed, and I knew I was about to punish these students. As I looked at them, I realized that they were as frightened as I was angry. Tentatively, I asked them what needed to occur. They looked at me and very quietly said that it needed to be cleaned up. And so they set about doing so.

These students struggled to work with the designed sixth-grade curriculum and lashed out at each other, at the class, at the school, at the world, and most of all at me. One morning we began conversing about what they wanted the class to be like, what they were interested in, and what they thought they needed to know in order to live well and happy lives. They brainstormed issues that were meaningful for them. One of many themes that emerged was how one gets the best deal on products. We studied advertisements and flyers from grocery stores, and so on. They read and analyzed complex issues. Does the lowest price mean the best deal? What does weight have to do with getting the best deal with foods? The point is that these obnoxious, less-than-intelligent hooligans began to feel competent. Slowly throughout that spring semester, behavior issues became manageable and typically were managed by those 13 individuals.

The next year I could have returned to a law-and-order classroom. But those "dirty dozen" plus one taught me more in that semester than I had learned over 9 years of teaching and professional development. I learned that we teachers often "take over" students' learning, believing that we know what is best for each one. They taught me that curriculum, instruction, and classroom management are related and connected. They taught me that, when they became a vital part of a group, they did not have trouble with their peers and that, when they did have a problem, they needed to and could figure out how to solve their issues. They discovered they might not have learned in the same ways as the other students. I discovered that classroom management is not about control but about the children and their needs.

—Pamela Curtiss
Sixth-Grade Teacher

Reflection Tool Number 1: What and Why

As you begin reading Chapter 1, think of it as the "What and Why" chapter. What? Why have a "What and Why" chapter in a classroom management book? Good! You are already doing what you need to do to be a great teacher . . . question! You see, classroom management has relatively little to do with the often-promoted "tricks" and more to do with *what* you believe about children, learning, and learning environments—and *why* you believe what you do. These two simple words can make a world of difference in **classroom management** and therefore students' lives in school.

We have come to a time in education where information is all around us. Thousands of journal articles, books, and speakers provide research on the latest next-best strategy. As an educator, you can find research advocating just about everything. Take **rewards**, for example. Some teachers advocate using rewards in the classroom to improve the classroom experience (Alberto & Troutman, 2003; Cameron, Banko, & Pierce, 2001; Colvin, 2004; Kauffman, Mostert, Trent, & Pullen, 2006), and some believe rewards damage students' learning (Deci, Koestner, & Ryan, 1999; Kohn, 1993). Some veteran teachers believe that rewards are necessary in classrooms, and some do not use them at all. Many school-wide management systems use rewards, and at some schools individual teachers create their own reward systems. As an educator, you must be able to sort through all of this information and decide what is best for you and your students. Otherwise, you may tumble from one trend to another without really understanding what you believe and why. Ask yourself, "Why give rewards? What are the benefits of giving rewards? What are the costs? What are my experiences with rewards? What do others say?" If you can answer those questions in some depth, you are ready to make decisions about using rewards in your classroom. If your only answer is that teachers around you use rewards or that you do not know how else to manage a classroom, it will be hard to create a consistent, safe environment for children.

"What" and "why" questions can be intimidating. I supervised a student teacher named Kevin who, during my observation, had his students clean out their desks. My feedback consisted of one list of observations and one list of questions, including, "Why did you have the students clean out their desks?" Just as students often erase their math problems if the teacher probes them about their answer, Kevin worried that I was unhappy that he had the students engage in this task. In reality, I merely wanted to know if he was thinking deeply about his choices. What was the purpose of cleaning desks? Why was it important for the students to have clean desks? What were the costs of taking the time to clean desks? Kevin actually had very good reasons for the activity and knew exactly why he had chosen it. He had thought about the activity and wasn't just doing it to do it. He had a purpose, but whether he consciously understood this prior to receiving my probing questions I don't really know.

It is very easy to go through the daily teaching routine without stopping to think about why we do things. "What" and "why" questions help you reflect on children, learning, and the learning environment you create. Indeed, you will not be able to ask what and why for every daily decision you make. However, **reflection** is a key ingredient in great instruction and learning to teach more effectively. Many researchers have described the importance of reflection in continual professional growth and successful teaching (Cruickshank, 1985; Dewey, 1933; Gore, 1987; Kraus & Butler, 2000; Lowery, 2002; Schon, 1987; Valli, 1997). In reflecting, good teachers not only think about whether or not events in their classrooms are working; they also struggle through reflection to find out why (Jay, 2002).

I knew a teacher who taught young children. At the beginning of the year, the students in her classroom tattled on each other—as many young children do. To curb this behavior, the teacher pinned a fluffy, pink, feathery scarf (a tattle tail) to the students' pants when they tattled. She raved to others about how wonderfully this worked and noted that students never tattled in her room. As I reflect on this strategy, I think this teacher probably understood what she was doing and why . . . because it worked. I also think, however, she did not take the time to reflect on the costs of this strategy. What were her students learning? What were they feeling? What other options did she have? Just because something "works" does not mean it is respectful of or appropriate for students. Reflecting at the surface level (does it work or not?) isn't thinking deeply enough about the decisions you will make in your classroom. You must go deeper (see Figure 1.1).

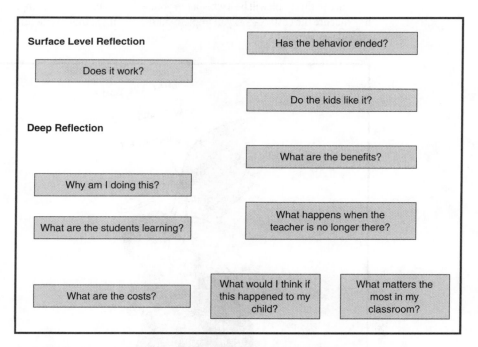

FIGURE 1.1   Deep Reflection About Management

When reflecting on classroom management strategies, I hope you will dive deeply into questions that will help you determine if the strategy is really working for long-term success of the child and the classroom.

Reflection does not necessarily involve knowing a right answer but rather thinking about the question and possible answers. There are no right answers in classroom management, but management decisions still have consequences. Eleanor Duckworth (1996) wrote, "Of all the virtues related to intellectual functioning, the most passive is the virtue of knowing the right answer. Knowing the right answer requires no decisions, carries no risks, and makes no demands. It is automatic. It is thoughtless" (p. 64). The "pink scarf" teacher believed she had the right answer for tattling because it created the desired behavior. She did not reflect deeply enough to see the whole picture. A chance to move beyond "right" answers toward thoughtful reasoning and wondering, reflection is anchored in experience and provides a vehicle into learning (McAlpine & Weston, 2000). It requires you to understand what you are doing and why rather than mindlessly doing it without considering all of the issues involved.

Using the many tools, structures, and strategies in this book will help you develop a classroom. Certainly not "right" answers, instead they are areas in which to begin. In the end, you must design, use, resee, and revise your classroom management plan based on experiences, understandings, and deep reflections of classroom management results. I hope the first tool, the "what" and "why" questions, will stay with you as long as you teach. I hope my voice in this book will be a whisper in your ear—"What are you doing? Why are you doing it? What are the costs?"—as you implement management tools, structures, and strategies in your classroom.

Jesse Keifer

As you work with students in a classroom, be sure to hear my whispers in your ear!

Reflection Tool Number 2: Prior Beliefs About Classroom Management

This "what" question is important to think about as you begin to create a classroom management plan. Although you may not think you know much about classroom management, in reality all teachers—and anyone else who once attended school—have beliefs about classroom management that influence how they teach. Our beliefs about education, learning, and teaching come from many environments and various experiences, personal and vicarious, that we have tucked away and, most importantly, not reflected on. Difficult, if not impossible, to disregard, beliefs and experiences about the past can directly impact what we learn and choose to do in the classroom (Holt-Reynolds, 1992).

"To most adequately address the needs of other learners, a teacher must first understand him/herself as a learner" (Canella & Reiff, 1994, p. 27).

Dewey (1934) called this **continuity of learning.** Ideas considered in the present may not click until connected with future learning, and ideas from the past may be connected to the present and the future. "The junction of the new and old is not a mere composition of forces, but is a re-creation in which the present impulse gets form and solidity while the old, the 'stored,' material is literally revived, given new life and soul through having to meet a new situation" (Dewey, 1934, p. 60). In other words, what we can learn for use in the future very much depends on what we believe about our past and present understandings.

While prior experiences and beliefs can be helpful, they can be powerful and misleading as well. We sometimes dismiss ideas that are contrary to our experiences, and we use personal histories to test our choices (Holt-Reynolds, 1992). We often make classroom choices that work best for us as learners without considering that students may learn differently (Knowles & Holt-Reynolds, 1991).

"Good" or "bad" teachers from our past also influence us in making and defending classroom choices (Holt-Reynolds, 1992; Smith, 1991). For example, if one of your teachers used **cooperative learning** and you hated it, you may not be open to using cooperative learning as a structure for your classroom even if you can understand that it might be effective.

Beliefs and experiences can also act as obstacles to reflection. The number of decisions, the variety of tasks, and the demands of teaching in general create an instinctive reaction to problems. This causes us to revert to what worked for us in the past. Hectic situations foster information overload, so instead of being influenced by students, we revert to what we have experienced (Schempp, Sparkes, & Templin, 1993).

As you can see, your prior beliefs are quite important in this journey. Take some time before reading the rest of this chapter to sort through your beliefs based on your prior experiences (see box below). I am not advocating that you get rid of your beliefs but rather that you understand those beliefs in relation to developing ideas about how you will manage a classroom. It is important to identify them so you can better understand the choices you make and where they come from. You may end up developing a classroom management plan that you have never before seen or experienced. You will, however, be open to this only if you first examine your past beliefs and experiences.

Classroom Management Autobiography

Use the space in the reflection journal at the companion Web site for *Elementary Classroom Management*, www.sagepub.com/kwillamsstudy, to write about your prior experiences with classroom management.

What do you remember about classroom management when you were in elementary school, high school, or another stage of your education? How did the management styles you experienced make you feel? Which teachers had the best strategies? What made them work? Which teachers had the worst strategies? What made them the worst?

Reflection Tool Number 3: Thinking About the Future

Take a moment to think about the future (see box below). In 30 years, what will people need to know and be able to do both socially and academically? What does this mean for schools right now? What should we teach children to ensure their success now and in the future? Beyond that, what should we teach children so they have the ability to take care of themselves and one another? Remember that the children you teach will someday help make decisions about your life. What do you want them to understand? What do you want them to experience? What does your list mean for classroom management?

What Should Students Know and Be Able to Do in the Future?

Take some time to think about what students will need to know and be able to do 30 years from now. How will your classroom management facilitate this?
    In 30 years, my students will need to know and be able to:

As a part of my master's degree program, I spent time with a principal, Dr. Weaver, in the school where he worked. I was comparing and contrasting different styles of leadership and came to observe him. As I sat in his office one day, I noticed three words on the white board in his office. Almost stained on the board, like they had been there for quite a while, the three words—*autonomy*, *belonging*, and *competency*—looked used and worn. They glared at me and made it difficult to see anything else in the office. When Dr. Weaver came in, I asked him about those words and why they were there, and he explained his belief that all people need those three things. So, when anyone—a student, a faculty member, or a parent—came into his office, he wanted to remember the words as they solved problems together. And as I watched him that day, autonomy, belonging, and competency became evident in how he worked people, how he helped others help themselves solve their problems, and how the school worked. I have come to believe that those three words are the basis for any good classroom management plan and can help teachers develop structures, strategies, and tools that will facilitate much-needed learning now and in the future.

Autonomy and Its Impact on Students

Dr. Weaver spent time in the cafeteria and on the playground during his day, and I followed along. On the playground, two young boys got into a fight. I waited, presuming that the boys would be taken to the office, as that was what my prior experiences had taught me would happen next. Instead, the two boys, bundled up in their snow gear, came and stood next to their principal. After a few moments of cooling-off time, Dr. Weaver asked if they were ready to solve the problem. They said yes and explained what had happened without interruptions from Dr. Weaver. After a while, one of the boys looked up at him and said, "Dr. Weaver, why does the snow sparkle?" The two boys spent the rest of recess together experimenting to figure out why snow sparkles. And so I ask you . . . is this autonomy?

Sometimes autonomy involves giving students time to discover the world around them, whether that is a big icicle on the playground or how to solve a problem on their own.

What Is Autonomy?

Ryan and Deci (2002) refer to autonomy as "the perceived origin or source of one's own behavior (p. 8). In other words, autonomous people perceive that their decisions and behavior are based on their own ideas and beliefs. Kamii (2000) writes that autonomy is the opposite of heteronomy: "Heteronomous people are governed by someone else, as they are unable to make judgments for themselves" (p. 57). Autonomous people, then, make their own judgments and believe they can do so effectively.

Think about people you believe are autonomous. What qualities do they possess? At first, you may think of very independent people or those who do only what they want, but do not confuse autonomy with independence. Autonomous people often rely on others' opinions and direction. They are not, however, coerced by others' opinions and directions. The difference, while perhaps difficult to distinguish, is hugely important as we begin uncovering classroom management. Autonomous people look to and learn from others but are difficult to manipulate (Ryan & Deci, 2002). They think for themselves, know who they are, and know what they believe and why.

The same can be said for **freedom**. You may think of autonomy as freedom in the classroom. Autonomy is not freedom of action, however, but seeing connections between personal goals and ideas (Assor, Kaplan, & Roth, 2002). Not necessarily about getting to do whatever you want, autonomy is about seeing relevance in what is done and having a voice in problem solving and decision making.

It is difficult to be autonomous in schools today—even for teachers. Schools are full of manipulation for the sake of quiet classrooms and orderly lines. Teachers often fear the dreaded "uncontrolled classroom," and students understand at an early age that they should do what the teacher says and learn what the teacher wants. Students accept academic and social rules that they don't understand because their autonomy is not fostered. Haven't we all learned something and not questioned it even if it didn't make sense?

Were the boys in the above story autonomous? You might say yes because they solved their own problem. They had a voice; the outcome depended on their decisions; and they had a resource in Dr. Weaver and certainly could not do whatever they wanted. They were not allowed to fight. On the other hand, you might say we do not know if the boys were autonomous because they never really found a solution. Time to ponder may have affected the result. Certainly, the snow distracted them and became a type of solution to the problem. Indeed, the case above is not cut and dried. Classroom management never is. The issue of autonomy for young people is not about whether or not they have it but about whether or not they have opportunities to move toward it. Most likely, your list of students' needs for the future doesn't include them relying on you for every decision or problem. Most likely, you thought of such qualities for students as self-motivation, conscientiousness, and decisiveness. Kamii (2000) states that people learn to make decisions by making decisions, but we cannot expect children to become autonomous by watching others be autonomous. Teachers who want autonomous students provide **classroom management structures** that support autonomy.

What Is an Autonomy-Supportive Classroom?

For material related to this concept, go to Clip 1.1 on the Web-based Student Study Site.

Autonomy in the classroom? I can hear it now: "That would be chaos. If I let students choose, they would choose not to do anything. How will I cover the standards if everyone is doing something different?" Autonomy can frighten teachers because they believe they will need to give up power and control, and all of us need a sense of control (or autonomy) over our lives and our spaces in the world. Autonomy support, however, does not mean minimizing the teacher's presence but making that presence useful for students who strive to realize their personal goals and interests (Assor, Kaplan, & Roth, 2002). Autonomy-supportive classrooms are very structured but in a way that promotes autonomy (Reeve, 2006). Indeed, based on providing opportunities for autonomy, belonging, and competency, this book provides strategies, structures, and tools to help you begin. First, though, try to think about autonomy support from two different perspectives of classroom management:

1. The teacher's perspective

2. The students' perspectives

Autonomy From the Teacher's Perspective

One of my favorite metaphors for autonomy-supportive classrooms is a theater. A theater has a director, but he or she is "behind the scenes," not out front telling the actors what to do. The director may, however, have opportunities to give input and ask questions. Certainly, some directors are controlling, but when actors talk about good directors, they usually say that the director let them act and did not control every movement. After agreeing on the script, the actors and director collaborate toward the best solution to uncover its meaning.

Autonomy support means a teacher or another authority figure tries to understand the student's perspective, acknowledges the student's feelings, provides opportunities for choice, and minimizes the use of pressure and demands (Deci & Ryan, 1985). The teacher helps students solve problems. In other words, the teacher is behind the scenes but still an active part of students' activities and learning. Strachota (1996) says this is like setting up a party so the students *and* teacher will like it. Alfie Kohn (1993) advocates using a chart (for example, see box below) to determine whether a solution to a problem is controlling or supports autonomy.

Reeve (2006) lists instructional behaviors that support autonomy:

1. Listening carefully

2. Creating opportunities for students to work in their own way

3. Providing opportunities for students to talk

4. Arranging learning materials and seating patterns so students manipulate objects and conversations rather than passively watch and listen

5. Encouraging effort and persistence

6. Praising signs of improvement and mastery

7. Offering progress-enabling hints when students seem stuck

8. Being responsive to students' questions and comments

9. Communicating a clear acknowledgment of students' perspectives (p. 230)

Reeve also lists instructional behaviors that inhibit autonomy:

1. Keeping possession of and monopolizing the learning materials

2. Physically exhibiting worked-out solutions and answers before students have time to work on the problem independently

3. Telling students the right answer instead of allowing them time and opportunity to discover it

4. Uttering directives and commands

5. Interjecting "should," "have to," "must," or "got to" statements in the flow of instruction

6. Using controlling questions (e.g., Can you do what I showed you?) as a way of directing students' work (p. 231)

Indeed, implementing these instructional behaviors is difficult because of our prior experiences. We revert to what we know when situations become difficult. In addition, you

TABLE 1.1   Autonomy-Supportive Versus Controlling Classroom Management

Take some time to consider the following issues and how teachers could approach them. Think of what teachers could do to provide autonomy and then how they could control the situation.

Issue	(Autonomy-Supportive) Working With Students	(Controlling) Doing to Students
Students being unkind to others		
Students talking when someone else is speaking		
Student having trouble understanding math		
Student stealing		

must really believe the underlying principle that people and young children need autonomy. If you understand your prior experiences and believe that autonomy is needed, working toward autonomy-supportive instruction will be productive.

Autonomy From the Students' Perspectives

Let's look at the students' perspective of autonomy support. What do "actors" do with the director behind the scenes for support? Movie actors usually need good scripts, lighting and props that work well, other actors to help them improve, and opportunities to make mistakes and try again. Many scenes are repeated until everything comes together with input and feedback from all involved.

The same occurs with students in a classroom. Students do not necessarily need tasks that are personal favorites, but they do need **authentic** and relevant tasks (Assor, Kaplan, & Roth, 2002), which Strachota (1996) calls "juicy problems" (p. 27). Everything we teach doesn't necessarily have to be exciting or fun, but teachers and students need to understand why they are undertaking a task—and not just to meet standards.

Students need materials they can actually use, as well as time to work with others and flesh out their ideas, but they often do not receive materials that help them make sense of their learning. If educators provide students with time, resources, and the

Engaging students with interesting problems and materials helps them want to be in the classroom.

autonomy to be creative, they will have "wonderful ideas" (Duckworth, 1996, p. 1). I find it strange that in this day and age of wanting every student to, in effect, be the same, know the same things, and pass the same tests and of school districts' insistence that every teacher teach the same thing at the same time, we also look for creativity to solve global problems. How will adults ever create unique solutions to our world's social needs, energy needs, and economic issues if they haven't been given opportunities to solve real problems?

Although writing these autonomy-supportive actions on paper is easy, I understand that implementing them is not as easy. This is not the last time you will hear about autonomy in this book. The following chapters are full of specific ways to create an autonomy-supportive classroom while teaching the curriculum, maintaining classroom structure, and managing behaviors that arise.

Why Do We Need Autonomy?

Perhaps you wonder why autonomy is so important. Check your list of students' future needs for anything that requires autonomy. Perhaps you listed problem solving as a skill important for students. How does autonomy relate to problem solving, creativity, and decision-making skills? Perhaps you would like students to be honest and have other values that make strong community and family members. How does autonomy relate to values? I bet many of the qualities you listed require autonomy, but beyond that, and more pressing, is that students thrive in autonomy-supportive classrooms.

Autonomy-supportive classrooms are associated with students having better **conceptual understanding** (Grolnick, Ryan, & Deci, 1987; Williams, 1996), being more creative (Amabile, 1985; Koestner, Ryan, Bernieri, & Holt, 1984), and having a more **positive affect** (Ryan & Grolnick, 1986). Students in autonomy-supportive classrooms show a greater belief in their competence (Deci, Nezlek, & Sheinman, 1981; Ryan & Grolnick, 1986), higher mastery motivation (Ryan & Grolnick, 1986), a preference for challenge over easy success (Boggiano, Main, & Katz, 1988; Pittman, Emery, & Boggiano, 1982; Shapira, 1976), greater engagement (Reeve, Jang, Carrell, Barch, & Jeon, 2004), enhanced well-being (Black & Deci, 2000), better academic performance (Boggiano, Flink, Shields, Seelbach, & Barrett, 1993; Miserandino, 1996), and academic persistence. This means that fewer students may drop out of school (Vallerand, Fortier, & Guay, 1997). Finally, Skinner and Edge (2002) found that children's perceived autonomy is a significant predictor of their ability to cope with problems and issues in their own lives. For you as a teacher, this means that if you provide an autonomy-supportive classroom for students, they will do better academically and socially and not need the "management of students" strategies often promoted. On the other side of the coin, students who do not have autonomy support can become disengaged. "Children who are taught what to do, who learn to work within limits and toward fixed objectives determined by adults, and who develop little personal investment in these activities develop a sense of separation from school" (Weikart, 1989, p. 28). Autonomy support is necessary for all grade levels and ages of students (Assor, Kaplan, & Roth, 2002).

What Does Autonomy Cost?

Returning to our reflection questions—what, why, and at what cost?—note that we have begun to uncover the what and why of autonomy but not the costs, and I can think of a few: First, autonomy support can be slow. We often want quick fixes to classroom issues and problems. Supporting a child who needs autonomy takes more time than a controlling reaction. It would have been quicker for Dr. Weaver to send the students who were fighting on the playground to the office. He could have given them consequences, told them never to fight again, and been done with it. Second, behaviors and actions are much easier to measure than perceived autonomy. Indeed, we could have measured how many more times the boys fought on the playground after the consequences to see if the solution "worked." It is difficult to know what the boys learned by having to solve their own problem. Finally, people often get upset when they believe there are no consequences in the name of fairness. The boys' parents and teachers would probably want to know what happened to them because they fought. They might be upset to know that the boys merely learned to work together. Another question is whether they continued to work together or to fight.

You should definitely consider these issues, as well as the costs of a more controlling student management approach. It is easy to lose sight of the goals of education, especially those you wrote earlier. Is making children stand in a line by means of manipulation (punishments or rewards) worth their loss of self-reliance? Is it more important to punish children for fighting or to help them learn to solve problems in other ways?

Belonging and Its Impact on Students

Dr. Weaver's school, like every other, had its share of unengaged students: the children who played alone on the playground, worked alone in the classroom, and merely existed day in and day out in school. One such student, third-grader Kyle, often was angry and hurt other children on the playground and in the classroom. He didn't understand how else to have a place in school. Because of his actions, Dr. Weaver had Kyle check into the principal's office every day at 12:30 shortly after his class went to recess. Instead of recess, Kyle went to a kindergarten room each afternoon to collect information about how the children there treated each other. You might initially consider this punishment; after all, Dr. Weaver was keeping Kyle from recess. Intended not to punish him, however, this gave him the opportunity to gain experience with his need to belong. In the kindergarten room, Kyle took notes on a clipboard about what the children did to help each other and what they did when they were not helping each other. Then Dr. Weaver and Kyle discussed Kyle's findings about students' behaviors in the kindergarten room.

Something more happened, though. Kyle became an important presence in the kindergarten room. The kindergarteners needed—and asked for—his help. Even though Kyle decided he was ready for the playground after a few weeks, he continued to visit the kindergarteners whenever he could. What do you think might have happened if Kyle had been sent to in-school suspension for his fighting?

Students need opportunities to feel as though they belong to a cohesive group in school.

What Is Belonging?

You may think I have just created a **paradox**. Do children need autonomy or belonging? Aren't they opposites? That's one way to look at the two words, but in fact, as you unpack them, they become integral to each other. My husband, an Air National Guard pilot, for example, must be able to make decisions and judgments while flying his plane. He has a great deal of autonomy because he is in so many different situations—be it a different country or refueling different planes. Yet his sense of belonging to the guard and his mission guides his decisions and judgments. His autonomy is not freedom in the sense that he can fly the plane wherever he wants (to Hawaii, all the time!) but is guided by the notion that the other people in his unit and, in a sense, everyone in the United States depends on him and what he does in that plane. We need to be autonomous so we can make necessary decisions, and we also need to be a part of something larger than ourselves so those decisions we make are meaningful for us and others.

Instead of belonging, Ryan and Deci (2002) call this need **relatedness**. "Relatedness refers to feeling connected to others, to caring for and being cared for by those others, to having a sense of belongingness both with other individuals and with one's community"

(p. 7). *Webster's New Collegiate Dictionary* defines *belonging* as follows: "To have a proper, appropriate, or suitable place; to be naturally associated with something; to fit into a group naturally." Where and at what kind of place do you feel care? Where do you care about others? Why? In many cases, perhaps because of love or unconditional support, people feel a sense of belonging within their families, but there are many other places and groups where people feel they belong. Think about students. Sometimes, they feel they belong nowhere and to no one, and school can be a refuge for that need—that is, *if* we make belonging a goal. If students feel part of a safe, secure classroom, their brains are allowed access to higher levels of functioning, and real learning can take place (Sprenger, 2007).

Indeed, many researchers have identified belonging as important for humans in general. Glasser (1986) believes belonging is an important basic need written into the human genetic structure. Sapolsky (2004) believes social support is necessary for coping in stressful situations. Seligman (1995) and Benard (2004) listed social support and caring relationships, respectively, as integral to **resiliency** in children. Note that feeling you belong involves not merely believing that someone will help you when you need it, although that is important, but also the sense that you are needed as well. Many teachers, caring and kind, "would do anything for students." They may not, however, have a classroom where each student feels he or she has a purpose and that, without him or her, it wouldn't work well.

People try to belong very early in life. Young children—and sometimes all of us—try to belong by imitating those around them, as well as through contagion. **Contagion**, or when students act like others because it is "contagious" or everyone is doing it, can be harmful at times because students may sacrifice autonomy for contagion. Hopefully, belonging comes through identification. Students who identify with others and feel as though they have a voice belong to the group (Brothers, 1997).

Belonging occurs when teachers help students feel special and important (Furrer & Skinner, 2003). Often, schools do not meet children's needs for belonging (Schaps & Solomon, 1990). Children who fail in school often have the cognitive skills necessary for success but feel detached and isolated from others (Beck & Malley, 1998). When this occurs, young people must get their sense of belonging from another source. For example, students recruited to gangs often have no other place to belong. Gangs become popular because they provide students with a sense of belonging (Burnett & Walz, 1994). We might learn important social issues from gangs, which have powerful strongholds on their members. What do gangs do to help members feel they belong? What would the positive version of that look and be like in classrooms?

What Is a Belonging-Supportive Classroom?

Students are not born with social skills but must be taught (Jensen, 2005). We often work arduously to help students read, but if a student seemingly doesn't belong or struggles socially, we write it off as a bad childhood or strange behavior. If we want students to belong and to understand the importance of belonging for others, we must include social skills in our lessons and curriculum. Students without a sense of belonging must develop skills that invite others to belong rather than make them feel like outcasts. It is critical that teachers not give up on this important skill if one strategy does not work. We must still teach reading, math, social studies, science, and writing, albeit in a way that incorporates and supports belonging for everyone.

I once taught a student named Zach who had Asperger's syndrome and therefore unique behaviors and ideas that caused trouble for him socially. One day he was upset that other children were chasing him during recess even though they were playing tag. After I worked to help him understand the game, the next day after recess he was upset because the other children had not chased him. To help him belong, we gathered a group of students who knew Zach and became his mentors. We taught them how to help him if he needed it, and they learned to include rather than leave Zach out. Who learned more: the students, Zach, or I?

A vital role for you as teacher is students' experiences with belonging in the classroom and the school. Your relationships with students might give them their first sense of belonging and support. This requires really knowing who they are and what they care deeply about. "Once you have the knowledge about the children—once you really see what they care about—then you can do a great deal for them" (Senge, Cambron-McCabe, Lucas, Smith, & Dutton, 2000, p. 122). You can't know a child if you only know him or her as a student. Knowing students' outside interests as well as what their home lives are like affects how you create a relationship with them. Connecting personally to students' interests can make a huge difference. Providing personal attention, support, and encouragement to all students and eliminating failure, rejection, and humiliation from the classroom is vital to the student and the classroom context (Charles, 1999). A sense of belonging will not develop in a stressful classroom. Long (1997) found that classrooms in which there was a sense of belonging had teachers who promoted and provided continuous acts of kindness. You may be that one person who helps a student gain a sense of belonging.

Teacher-student relationships are vital, but students must also be actively involved in the classroom (Beck & Malley, 1998). It is important to help students contribute positively to their classrooms to allow them a connection to what happens there (Albert, 1996). Having jobs to do around the room enhances student involvement in improving their classroom environment. Having multiple "right" answers promotes active involvement and thus a sense of belonging. Such classroom structures as cooperative learning, think-pair-share, workshops, simulations, unstructured social time for discussions, and play are all great ways to incorporate social learning and help children feel needed and wanted in their classrooms. Play is children's work (Jensen, 2005). In addition, such structures as reader's theater, puppet shows, and other kinds of plays or performances can help create a sense of belonging because of the various roles and the fact that students can share with other classes or parents. Jensen recommends balancing social and individual events to allow students opportunities to belong as individuals and not always group members. I will explain all of these ideas in detail in the coming chapters, but I want you to connect to belonging before you get there.

In addition to teacher-student relationships and active involvement in classrooms, children need to gain a sense of belonging through work with other students. We need to allow them to help each other learn. (Remember the child who "taught" the kindergarten students?) There must be a sense that it is important for all students to do well. Individual competition and vying for exclusive opportunities in the classroom negate any true sense of belonging. If one student must beat another to feel that he or she belongs, how does that affect

For material related to this concept, go to Clip 1.2 on the Web-based Student Study Site.

other students and the classroom environment? Glasser (1986) recommends having learning teams take care of one another in the classroom. Gorrell and Keel (1986) advocate cross-age tutoring, especially for students who, for whatever reasons, have difficulties with their own peers. Beyond that, students need opportunities to have discussions and share their ideas and thoughts with each other. Silent classrooms in which everyone works alone do not promote belonging.

Why Do We Need Belonging in Our Classrooms?

Look back once more at your list of students' future needs. Which items require belonging? Difficult but hugely important to humans, belonging doesn't always stand out when we make this kind of list; however, belonging is very important to being successful parents or successful in an occupation, both of which you may have listed. When students feel they belong, they have an enhanced sense of worth and increased self-confidence (Crandall, 1981). In addition, students who feel they belong are more motivated, have higher expectations of success, and value their academic work (Blum, 2005; Goodenow, 1993). On the contrary, students who feel isolated invest energy into looking for belonging rather than caring about academic issues (Beck & Malley, 1998).

A sense of belonging also helps students within the classroom, where it really does matter how students feel. It matters for cognitive development, and it matters for behavior. Brain research shows us that stress and emotions are vital to the functioning brain (Jensen, 2005; Sousa, 2006; Sprenger, 2007). "Animal studies suggest that position within a social group may influence brain chemistry, which, in turn, affects behavior" (Jensen, 2005, p. 98). "It's much less likely that youngsters will lash out at teachers who know them well and who have established relationships with them" (Haberman, 1995, p. 4). "A feeling of belonging and contributing motivates children to abide by and uphold the norms and values that the school community has decided are important" (Schaps & Solomon, 1990, p. 39).

What Are the Costs of Belonging?

Perhaps the biggest cost in helping students gain a sense of belonging is that it requires you to trust them. We don't often trust students to tell us what they need; yet in whatever language they can muster, they are telling us, and we need to listen. If they tell us they don't know how to work in a group by shying away from or acting out in groups, we need to listen and help them. If they tell us they feel they don't belong by not speaking at all or by hiding in the back of the room, we need to listen and help them. If they tell us they are just fine but need some time away from the group by finding a quiet spot in the room, we need to listen and help them. Trust can be difficult, but helping students belong requires our trust. Nancy Lockett (personal communication, February 10, 2008) described her son as very introverted, bright, and quiet. He went to school with the goal of seeing how many days he could go without saying a word. What was he learning about school? What were the costs to his sense of belonging?

Competency and Its Impact on Students

Teachers often sent misbehaving students to Dr. Weaver's office when they needed help. In most schools, this "help" refers to punishment. For example, I once sent a student who needed some time away from the other children to the principal's office in my school. Unfortunately, the principal punished her behavior by having her copy words from a dictionary, undermining my attempt to help her see writing as a positive endeavor. Sending a child to the principal's office in Dr. Weaver's school, however, meant something different. Per the words on his white board, Dr. Weaver intended not to punish but to do research. Genuinely interested in what the student and the teacher needed, Dr. Weaver talked to the child, played basketball with the child, or took him or her on walks. He listened and gathered information.

One student Dr. Weaver worked with, Sam, came to his office quite regularly at the beginning of the year because he was misbehaving in his fourth-grade classroom. Dr. Weaver spent time with him and finally figured out that Sam couldn't read. What was missing? Competence. During their conversations, Dr. Weaver also figured out that Sam, who lived on

Helping students become competent means giving them opportunities to make sense of their experiences.

a farm, liked and knew a lot about snakes. With that in mind, Dr. Weaver and Sam spent time together every week working on reading and writing about snakes. Sam began to be able to read books about snakes and research snakes on the computer, and he ultimately wrote a book called *Snakes*. What was present? Autonomy, belonging, and the beginnings of competency. Sam's behavior problems in the classroom decreased, *and* he learned to read.

Indeed, the teachers were fortunate to have a principal willing to go to such great lengths. You may or may not have that kind of support in the school where you teach. The point of the story, though, is quite important as you construct your ideas about classroom management. If your students feel competent, for the most part they will want to be in the classroom. Students who want to be in the classroom may have few, if any, serious behavior problems, and vice versa.

What Does It Mean to Be Competent?

"Competence refers to the need to experience oneself as effective in one's interactions with the social and physical environments" (Skinner & Edge, 2002, p. 301). In other words, it feels good to understand something and be able to share it with (teach it to) others. Think about a time when you felt competent. What made you feel that way? How did you react in that situation? Think about a time when you felt incompetent. Again, what made you feel that way, and how did you react? Most of us have at one time felt competent or incompetent. I don't know about you, but when I feel incompetent, I do extraordinary things, such as raising my voice or trying to slink away. Sometimes I act silly or try to make jokes. I might blame someone else or even lash out at whatever or whomever made me feel incompetent. Students feel this way as well.

You may think the feeling of competency is enough, but if people only needed to feel competent, we would just tell our students how well they are doing and everyone would behave. To truly feel competent, however, one must *be* competent. Students know when they do not understand something. For example, I learned every rule and procedure about decimals in multiple math courses. I could divide, add, and multiply decimals, all because I was able to memorize the procedures. Not until my undergraduate elementary math methods course did I learn what decimals really are. Was I competent in math? The teachers thought so. I was not a behavior problem, and I turned in my homework—not because I was competent but because that was expected at home. I aced my math classes and even got a math award once (I wonder how my peers felt about that?). I was not competent, however, and I knew it. You may be able to fake competency with other people, but you cannot fake it for yourself. Much more than memorization, fact finding, and answering questions with right answers (Glasser, 1989), competency is feeling you are worthy of having an opinion. It is understanding at a deep level.

Do we have to be competent in everything? I hope not. Considering the meaning of education, Alfie Kohn (2004) wrote of his wife, a talented physician, who evidently hasn't read many of the "classics" and who doesn't speak in grammatically correct sentences. I certainly am not competent in mechanical issues or chemistry, but I am a competent person overall because I feel very competent in certain areas. Indeed, all of us feel incompetent in certain areas. Competency does not mean understanding everything there is to know. In fact, isn't it good that we all have different competencies? Dewey (1964) believed that the goal of education is more education. To be competent, then, is to have the desire and the means to make sure that learning never ends (Kohn, 2004). Do our students feel competent at something in the classroom? Do they feel they can and want to continue to learn? How can teachers help them develop competency?

What Is a Competency-Supportive Classroom?

One of the best ways to develop a competency-supportive classroom is to create worthwhile and meaningful tasks that cause students to take risks. Strachota (1996) called them "juicy problems," and Brooks (2002) called it doing "original research" (p. 84). Kohn (2004) wrote about having students do problems and projects and asking questions rather than memorizing facts, skills, and disciplines. Glasser (1989) wrote about tasks with value. Whatever you call them, competency comes about when we want to learn something, when the issue, problem, or task is intriguing. The task need not necessarily be fun, but it must be engaging, meaningful, and important to the students doing it. "Our schools' tasks are to create educational contexts that are engaging enough to prompt students to show up and follow directions, and also to design, create, plan, devise, propose, build, produce, generate, and engage in all the other activities. Showing up and following directions are just pieces of a larger puzzle" (Brooks, 2002, p. 69). Classrooms that support competency are classrooms where students engage in worthwhile tasks.

Engaging, fun, and intriguing can be different for each individual student, perhaps causing you to wonder how one teacher can possibly handle this. Many strategies, structures, and tools presented later in this book will help you create a classroom that invites competency. For now, let's think broadly about this kind of task. Think about books you like to read versus books you do not. Think about studying something in science—say, rocks. Would you rather read about rocks and answer questions or collect rocks and try to figure out how they were made? Would you rather do 50 similar math problems or work on one problem that requires some struggle and manipulation but for which there are multiple answers? Engaging tasks require thought, manipulation, and creativity. In the name of competency, we often give students the answers or the procedures—never allowing them to experience the wonderful feeling of figuring something out. In his book, *Teaching With the Brain in Mind* (2005), Eric Jensen writes:

> Our brain is highly effective and adaptive. What ensures our survival is adapting and creating options. A typical classroom narrows our thinking strategies and answer options. Educators who insist on singular approaches and the "right answers" are ignoring what's kept our species around for centuries. Humans have survived for thousands of years by trying out new things, not by always getting the "right" tried and true answer. That's not healthy for growing a smart, adaptive brain. (p. 16)

Teachers do not assign engaging tasks to keep students busy; rather, engaging tasks keep students busy on their own. Some teachers assign engaging tasks only to students who are gifted or finished with the "real" work, but all students need to feel competent. Withholding an engaging task from a student who cannot understand a particular problem or perform a particular task will not make him or her feel or be competent. All children deserve worthwhile tasks that connect to their prior experiences (remember Sam?). Such tools as concrete learning materials, computers, pictures, and peer helpers can help students who struggle.

"Children can learn almost anything if they are dancing, tasting, touching, hearing, seeing, and feeling information" (Maguire, 2001, p. 1).

Competency need not be competitive. All students are competent in some areas. Have you ever taken a course where the instructor's mission was to "weed out" a number of students? Often instructors in these courses give out a specific number of A's even if many students do exemplary work. This does not promote competency but hard feelings among students. In addition, it destroys their willingness to learn from and with each other, disrupting the classroom community. The grade then becomes the goal rather than the learning.

Competency-supportive classrooms also require multiple attempts at learning. One does not become competent in something by doing it once or twice. "As teachers, I think one major role is to undo rapid assumptions of understanding, to slow down closure, in the interests of breadth and depth, which attach our knowledge to the world in which we are called upon to use it" (Duckworth, 1996, p. 78). Competency requires experiencing, reflecting, sharing, questioning, and experiencing again and again. Competency, not a linear process, is spiral in nature. You might assume that saying students need to experience something multiple times means they need rote training, but this is definitely not the case. It merely means that to become competent, we need to uncover (Duckworth) or unpack (Ball, 2000) the concept instead of skimming over it with multiple practice sessions. Students need valuable tasks and multiple ways to uncover them. It certainly took me more than one try to write this book. With each new iteration, I became more competent at thinking deeply and writing.

That reminds me: I definitely did not write this book on my own. Many editors, my parents, other teachers, and my husband read and gave me suggestions and things to think about before this reached your hands. Competency-supportive classrooms allow students and teachers to work and learn together. It is very difficult to learn alone (Glasser, 1989). Classrooms should be full of opportunities to share, converse, and debate (Jensen, 2005). Teachers and students should have opportunities to try out their ideas with each other. "Activity settings in schools need to create and support instructional conversations. To converse involves assuming the learner has something to say beyond answers, engaging learners in the discourse. Too often classroom discourse shuts down students through interrogation instead of dialogue" (Hausfather, 1996, p. 6). Teachers need to be genuinely involved in conversations rather than merely looking for right answers.

I mentioned earlier that in some cases it is easy for students to fake competency. In a competency-supportive classroom, the teacher must know the students and what they understand. Teachers must assess students constantly to find out where they are in their thinking, what they can do, and then how to proceed. I taught second grade for a number of years, and many students could fake reading. They could say the words but did not understand a bit of what they read. In individual conferences every 2 weeks, the students and I discussed the books they were reading, which allowed me to really know what they understood and to create meaningful tasks that would help them with reading comprehension. You cannot support competency if you do not know your students.

As you begin to know where your students' competency starts, you can begin to help support them by **scaffolding** experiences. "Scaffolding means changing the level of support over the course of a teaching session, with the more skilled person adjusting guidance to fit the child's current performance level" (Santrock, 2000, p. 261). The more skilled learner—in many cases the teacher—needs to design appropriate experiences, ask guiding questions,

For material related to this concept, go to Clip 1.3 on the Web-based Student Study Site.

and, at times, develop tools for students so they can learn more effectively. Scaffolding might mean breaking down a task into simpler steps or helping students organize their thoughts and learning. Once again, the teacher does not give information but instead finds out what the students understand and helps them construct new ideas based on past experiences and understandings. Just as we know when we have faked competency, we also know when we haven't done something for ourselves. Just ask my 4-year-old: When I try to do something for him and pass it off as something he did, he says, "But you did it for me."

Why Do We Need Competency?

Perhaps the obvious answer to this question is that students go to school to become competent. We often forget, however, that we are not helping robots learn. We are helping human beings with emotions that affect how the brain processes information (Freeman, 1995). Our psychological need to be competent matters in school. "When we feel stressed, our adrenal glands release a peptide called cortisol. Chronically high cortisol levels lead to the death of brain cells in the hippocampus, which is critical to explicit memory formation" (Jensen, 2005, p. 53). That is a technical way of saying that we can't learn if we are too stressed. Being incompetent in front of peers or a teacher can be stressful. Teachers must start where students are competent but where there is enough stress to engage them and move from there. All other learning stems from where students are competent. If we start from where students are incompetent, relatively little new learning will occur.

Competency is also important in developing democratic citizens. Look at your list of students' future needs. Does competency apply to any of your listings? I suspect many of you put technology somewhere on your list. My list always includes something about understanding different cultures and monetary issues, all of which have to do with competency. For our democracy to work, it is vital to have (among other things) competent voters, workers, and parents.

Competency and behavior are connected. Considerable evidence suggests that learning and behavior problems go hand-in-hand (Halonen, Aunola, Ahonen, & Nurmi, 2006; Hinshaw, 1992; Kauffman & Davis, 2001; McGee, Williams, Share, Anderson, & Silva, 1986; Roeser, Eccles, & Strobel, 1998). This makes sense, doesn't it? If you feel incompetent and inferior, behaving inappropriately can take attention away from your deficit, help you save face in front of your peers, and signal that you need help. In addition, when we provide competency-supportive tasks, we promote appropriate behaviors. Traynor (2002) notes that "if the material itself is engaging and meaningful, there is far less likelihood of other competing classroom stimuli triggering inappropriate behavior" (p. 496).

What Are the Costs of Competency?

Were there any costs to Dr. Weaver's interactions with Sam? Perhaps. Being "behind the scenes" creating meaningful opportunities for students—that is, helping them achieve competency—takes time and effort, a lot of listening and following rather than telling and leading, and knowing students and where individuals' competency starts. Finally, I think teachers must know where they are competent and where they need to continue to learn. This all takes time. I believe that in the long run, however, teachers will not have to deal with many behavior issues.

I really tried to come up with costs of competency to students but couldn't think of any. There may be some costs, but for the most part meaningful tasks, engaging learning, and a beginning competency make everyone, including the teacher, feel good. Sam, in the story from above, felt better about himself as a learner and became open to being in the classroom. Teachers want students to want to be in school, yet sometimes we make school unkind and embarrassing. My mom always says, "We adults can leave places or circumstances that make us feel incompetent or embarrassed. Children have to be in classrooms day after day after day no matter what."

LETTER FROM A MASTER TEACHER 1.2

Autonomy, Belonging, and Competency in Any Setting

I am a music teacher. My music classes are often very large. In the case of my bands or choruses, numbers approaching 100 learners are typical. Give each of these 100 learners a noisemaker, and one can suppose that I am facing a difficult management problem. I might choose to be very structured and controlling in dealing with the behavior of my students. I might make strict rules and treat learners as cogs in a machine that I control with an iron hand. However, I believe that excellent musical performance and learning require that learners feel a sense of ownership and creativity that would be inhibited in a classroom like that.

Meaning and full understanding of music depend on performance. Even when there is just one performer and some number of listeners, there needs to be a connection and an emotional commitment between the performer and the audience. This connection requires trust and a sense of belonging. Cooperation and teamwork are every bit as important as they are in athletics. Each member must feel that his or her contribution is honored and valued. Everyone, from the solo performer to the clarinet player at the end of the row, must feel this. I believe that this sense of belonging is seldom found in an environment where learners are coerced, bribed, and strictly managed. When I take on this difficult project with my 100 learners, I am almost certainly doomed to failure. Someone will always feel slighted or picked on. On the other hand, if everyone regards his or her contribution as necessary to the success of the group, management becomes a different problem altogether.

I try to foster in my performing groups a feeling of interdependence that relies on the competence and autonomy of each member. That clarinet player needs to believe she is able to contribute importantly to the success of the group. By the same token, she needs autonomy to judge for herself both the ability she has to make that contribution and the nature of the contribution itself. In other words, she needs to know where she fits and where she belongs.

So, when I encourage learners to use their own intuition and feelings, a sense of belonging is fostered. This, in turn, leads to willing cooperation and fewer management problems.

—Jim Curtiss
Music Teacher

So . . . What?

Beth Doll (personal communication, December 10, 2006) told a story about a principal who said that people always come to his school to "fix the fish" when they really need to "fix the water." Classroom management needs to be about fixing the classroom, not the students. We need to make sure the students get what they need. A classroom that allows them opportunities for autonomy, belonging, competency, and reflection is the place to launch everything else—a good fish bowl, you might say. And:

People of all ages need autonomy, belonging, and competency.

When a problem occurs in a classroom, teachers need to ask themselves what is missing: autonomy, belonging, or competency?

Teachers must reflect on what they do, why they do it, and at what cost.

Teachers must reflect on their prior beliefs and experiences so as to move forward.

Teachers must remember that they are not managing students but instead managing the classroom environment to address all students' needs both individually and collectively.

Get Ready For . . .

The next part of this journey is about fixing the water. How might we create classrooms where autonomy, belonging, and competency are present? How might we create classrooms where democracy and community thrive?

Activities to Try

✎   Go to your autobiography and make notes about autonomy, belonging, and competency within it. Were there times when you experienced these three things? Were you missing some? Which ones? Why?

✎   Within the autonomy, belonging, and competency sections, we discussed creating a classroom that supports each of those needs. Go through them and see if any ideas cross over. In other words, could any suggestions in the autonomy support section also be recommended for the competency section on support, and so on?

✎   Gather and analyze some classroom management programs. Look for strategies that could promote autonomy, belonging, and competency and those that could hinder them.

✎   **Make a collection!** Buy some folders and label them with each subject or perhaps each standard that you teach. Begin collecting "juicy problems" that would engage students and slip them into the folder. Don't worry if they are not grade-level appropriate or if you don't know if they would be. You can adapt them for whatever grade level you need.

✎   **Conduct action research!** Interview one student about things he or she dislikes and likes about his or her current classroom. Connect his or her answers to this chapter.

Student Study Site

The companion Web site for *Elementary Classroom Management* can be found at www.sagepub.com/kwilliamsstudy.

   Visit the Web-based student study site to enhance your understanding of the chapter content. The study materials include video clips, practice tests, flashcards, suggested readings, and Web resources.

CHAPTER 2

Creating Democratic Communities

As you think about creating a classroom environment, take a moment to consider what it will feel like—not what it will look like physically but how it will feel. How would you like students to feel when they think about going to school? How would you like them to feel when they get there? Why do you want them to feel that way? What kind of environment would best support these feelings?

Nel Noddings (1995b) believes that we want students to feel cared about when they come to school—that teachers care not only about them as students but about all aspects of their lives:

> Caring is not just a warm, fuzzy feeling that make people kind and likable. Caring implies a continuous search for competence. We want to do our very best for the objects of our care. To have as our educational goal the production of caring, competent, loving, lovable people is not anti-intellectual; it demonstrates respect for the full range of human talents. Not all human beings are good at or interested in math, science, or literature. But all can be helped to lead lives of deep concern for others, for the natural world and its creatures, and for the preservation of the human-made world. All can be led to develop the skills and knowledge necessary to make positive contributions, regardless of their occupation. (p. 1)

When we care about students, we know them in deep ways. We care about their talents, even if they lie outside of the school curriculum. We care about their circumstances, their needs, their goals, and their futures. In other words, we care enough about them to know what they have experienced, who they are, and what they want to become. To know students in this way, we must create an environment in which they can access autonomy, belonging, and competency and care about themselves and others.

Educators want motivated, well-behaved, and caring students. We expect them to care about their grades and topics in class. Yet we often we create environments where it is difficult for them to care about anything (Kohn, 1996). New teachers are told not to smile for the first few months of the school year so they don't give up too much control. Children are expected to like reading but have no opportunity to read something that interests them. Students learn to walk down the hall in straight, quiet lines—perhaps not because they care about the people learning in other classrooms but because the teacher said so. What do those things feel like? Is caring a part of the above processes? According to Noddings, "We have to show in our own behavior what it means to care. Thus we do not merely tell our students to care and give them texts to read on the subject; we demonstrate our caring in our relations with them" (1995a, p. 190). How will your classroom environment promote caring about autonomy (self), belonging (others), and competency (curriculum)? See box below.

> ### Reflections on Caring Teachers
> Write about a teacher who cared about you. What did he or she do to get to care about you? Why do you think he or she did these things? What happened as a result?

You may be thinking, "How do I care about *all* of them? Do I need to come up with a management plan for *each* and every student? Yikes!" Once again, we have come to a paradox. How can we create a single environment for a classroom of students that is individualized enough to meet their needs? How can one teacher care deeply about a whole class? The answer may lie in the water (i.e., the classroom environment) that we create for the fish (i.e., the students). The metaphor from Chapter 1 about fixing the water and not the fish is central to the ideas in this chapter as well. We cannot change what happens to children outside of school, but we can change their inside-school environment (Doll, Zucker, & Brehm, 2004).

Jesse Keifer

Our goal as teachers should be creating an environment where children want to be and learn.

We do not want to change who students are but rather help them reach their full potential. Chapter 1 discussed students' need for autonomy, belonging, and competency; however, these needs will not magically appear. We cannot have just any old water (i.e., classroom) sustaining their needs. As teachers, it is our job to work with students to create a caring environment for all of us who spend time there. If we want students to reap the benefits of autonomy, belonging, and competency, we must consciously create places where these needs are nurtured and where students nurture others.

By the end of this chapter, I hope you have:

- Ideas about how to deeply know your students and how to use that knowledge

- An understanding about and strategies for creating a **democratic classroom**

- An understanding of and strategies for creating classroom communities that nurture individual students

Knowing Students

For material related to this concept, go to Clip 2.1 on the Web-based Student Study Site.

Bronfenbrenner (1991) said, "Every child needs at least one adult who is irrationally crazy about him or her" (p. 2). To care (or be crazy) about students, you must know them. Knowing someone—and in many classrooms around 28 someones—is not an easy task, yet it is vital to classroom management and the world in which we live. Caring about and knowing the students in your room doesn't mean keeping track of everything about their lives. It means opening the environment and yourself so you can know each other when the opportunity arises.

Children come to school with a variety of experiences, ideas, and values that influence how and what they learn. Right now I could list statistics about how many students live in poverty, how many come to school from abusive homes, and how many experience depression, but they would just be numbers to you—important numbers, but just numbers nevertheless. Along with the pressured children who are not poor and the children whom teachers and schools ignore because they are "just fine," those numbers leave out what is really happening to children. You don't need these statistics to help you create a classroom environment where autonomy, belonging, and competency thrive. You need to know and care about the children in your classroom. You need to know that Sonya sucks her thumb in class because her mom agreed to put her in a foster home instead of leaving her husband who sexually abused Sonya. You need to know that Derek's mom works nights and that might be why Derek is late for school every day. You need to know that Michael steals from other children because his family often steals to get what it needs. You need to know the whole story rather than just the behaviors that accompany them. "Once you have the knowledge about the children—once you really see what they care about—then you can do a great deal for them" (Senge, Cambron-McCabe, Lucas, Smith, & Dutton, 2000, p. 122).

LETTER FROM A MASTER TEACHER 2.1

Democratic Communities Require Acknowledgment of Every Child's Effort and Contributions

It was my first class as a teacher. Those bright, shining faces were looking up at me, waiting to learn. Wait, what was that? Who was sitting in the trashcan? How did he somersault himself onto the wall? How could he possibly get nothing done all day? I didn't know a notebook of paper could get cut into so many pieces in such a short amount of time. Was there a point in the day that he ever sat still? I always thought that bouncing off the walls was a metaphor, but not for this child.

As the months went on, however, I got to see him as a person, not just his behavior. He knew more about animals and aquatic life than anyone else I know. He could add and subtract like crazy in his head. He just couldn't get it down on paper, and when I went to fill out his report card, it looked like he wasn't very successful at school. By the standards set by the state and the district, he was a struggling student. I knew he was incredibly smart, but I had nothing that could prove that to him or his parents.

I then knew that I had to do something. I couldn't let students pass through my classroom without letting them know that they were special and unique and had something to offer. I wanted them to know that they counted.

As soon as I started highlighting this student's achievements and celebrating his strengths, asking him to help other students when it came to his knowledge in animals, I began to see a change. He started to work on the things that he wouldn't even try before. Students began to treat him as part of our class instead of a huge disruption.

When this student began to feel important, he began to behave like he was important. He no longer had to gain attention through other avenues. The students began to work as a team to help each other. It was amazing to see what could happen when the students knew that their efforts were meaningful. This student's grades never got to where they should have been, his report card wasn't perfect, but I hope he and the other students left my room knowing that he counted.

I hope you will let students know that their effort matters—that while their grades might not be perfect or they might not be the best athlete, a drama star, or a musical wonder, they still have something to offer. I hope every student who walks through your door will learn to feel successful as a person.

—April Broderson
First-Grade Teacher

What Does Knowing Students Mean?

You may think this section is a no-brainer. Of course we need to know our students. As you begin to unravel what it means to know students, however, it becomes more complex than just knowing their names and perhaps their interests. Knowing students is not just about the surface-level information that comes from being together for some time; rather, it involves a constant, conscious effort to figure out why they do what they do both academically and socially, working with them to figure out what they need in their environment to move forward, and celebrating who they are and as they grow. Knowing students at a deep level can have a huge impact on their lives even though it may not seem so at the time.

Case Study 1: Chris

Chris was a student of mine who, in second grade, struggled to read. Funny, hardworking, and friendly, he was not a behavior problem and was well liked by his classmates. I knew, though, that if his reading struggles continued, his need for competency would erode his attitude. I cared about Chris and his struggles to read.

Sometimes, as teachers, we try to solve problems without really knowing why they exist. Asking a "why" question can help save time, ease frustration, and help us truly solve a problem. In Chris's case, I listened to him read, asked him what he thought about his reading, and asked some of his past teachers what they thought. I knew Chris struggled with fluency. He could decode the words, but it took him so long to read a sentence that he forgot what he was reading. Finally, I talked to his parents, and we decided that Chris's eyesight had not been checked in a while—one bit of information we didn't have. Chris's parents had his eyesight checked and discovered that one of his eye muscles contained a small stutter. In other words, Chris's eye moved slightly back and forth, causing blurry vision. Reading fluently or smoothly would be fairly difficult if your eye moved back and forth. Chris did exercises to help his eye, and we continued to work on reading together.

Let's take a moment to analyze this story. How did I get to know Chris? What did I do first? Who was involved in this process? What do you think would have happened if I had not gotten to know Chris? Indeed, Chris's story turned out to have a "happy ending." Knowing someone is not necessarily about fixing him or her; sometimes the solution is beyond our capabilities. Knowing someone is about caring enough to wonder and reflect, think through all of the possibilities, and create an environment where children open up to you. Chris felt safe enough to read aloud to me and was able to choose both appropriate and interesting books. I welcomed other teachers' and his parents' help in getting to know Chris better. He wasn't pulled into another room to work on reading.

Case Study 2: Emzie

At times, teachers encounter children who are not easy to care about. Their behavioral issues may get in the way of knowing them. Although caring is tough in these situations, it is important that we find support and work to know these students as well. Emzie, a child I will never forget, was from Nigeria. Bigger than the other children in my fourth-fifth combination room, he spoke English, though not very well, and loved to draw superhero cartoons. He was very quiet in our classroom and didn't always smell very good. Emzie often punched his classmates at recess as they played soccer. No matter how I asked or how much time I gave him, Emzie only shrugged his shoulders when asked why he behaved this way. The other children who played soccer and I talked together with Emzie about what was happening. I tried assigning a peer to help him on the playground, but nothing seemed to work. One day after school, I noticed Emzie's mother picking him up. I ran out to meet her and invited her to the classroom for a moment. She accepted, and I told her that Emzie was fighting on the playground. Was there anything we could do to help him? She proceeded to punch Emzie with a closed fist right in front of me. Emzie cowered behind me, and I told his mother to stop. I told her that everything would be OK and that she need not be upset with him, and they left. I called Social Services, which got involved for a while, until Emzie and his family moved the next month. On his last day before they moved, he was late, and I panicked that we would not get to say goodbye. However, he came late because he had waited until the stores opened to get me a present—a purse that I know his family couldn't afford. I know he felt cared about and often wonder what happened to him.

Emzie's story does not have a happy ending, at least that I know about. So why did I choose to tell it? Sometimes knowing students happens by chance. In this case, Emzie was never going to tell me that he hit because he was hit. He probably didn't realize it. However, that piece of information was crucial for me to know Emzie. As a teacher, you must be open to the information that comes your way. Emzie's story also highlights the fact that we often live and know from our experiences and our cultures. I do not believe that Emzie's mom was abusing him. In her culture, hitting may be what happens to students in trouble at school. That doesn't mean I let it continue, but it helped me understand and begin to know where to go and what to do. Knowing a student takes time, and though in Emzie's case I didn't have enough, I continue to learn from him even to this day, and he has helped me know other students along the way.

What Knowing Students Does Not Mean

First, knowing students so you can care about them does not mean you are the only one who cares. Classrooms need to be designed so the students can care about each other. Students need opportunities to get to know each other academically and socially. This means working on juicy problems together, helping each other when needed, and understanding that everyone has stars and wishes (things they do well and things they want to do better). This means they must have opportunities to talk to each other and celebrate each other's accomplishments.

Second, you have to live in the "water" too. Your values, ideas, and needs are just as valid as those of any other member of the class. Let the students know you. Tell them what you worry about. Tell them when you feel sick, and let them care of you. Ask them for help on a management problem. For example, "The teacher next door says we are too noisy. I don't know what to do. How can we solve this problem?" Classrooms need not be about perfect people and behaviors but rather about knowing each other well enough to help each other become better each day.

Third, knowing students doesn't mean letting them get away with unacceptable behaviors. This is not about poor Emzie, whose mother hits him, so we are just going to let everything slide. If you lower your expectations because of students' past experiences, you are not helping them gain autonomy, belonging, or competency. On the other hand, punishing them for actions that may need more diverse solutions is not acceptable either. Knowing children is not about justification but about understanding and then smart problem solving. I would certainly be able to fix my computer (which, by the way, hasn't caused me any fits yet) if I knew more about it.

Speaking of fixing, *knowing students is not about fixing them.* Computers can be fixed, problems can be solved, but students can't be fixed either. Knowing students needs to involve helping them learn about interesting topics, themselves, why they do what they do, and caring for others. Only students can change their own behaviors. You can't. If you know them, however, you can create an environment where they have the tools and strategies to do so.

Finally, knowing students is not about getting them to the next grade level. Knowing students means learning about their whole lives, not just caring enough to teach them fractions so they can pass fourth grade. You must know the students so they will be good citizens, have happy lives, and continue to learn. If you help them do that, they will succeed in fourth grade.

Mr. Johnson listens carefully to a student share her ideas.

Why Do You Need to Know Your Students?

Knowing your students deeply will help you develop an environment, lessons, and assessment tools that will help them become competent. We do not learn from present experiences alone but instead through connecting past, present, and future experiences. Jensen (2005) reports that the frontal lobes of our brains hold new data in short-term memory for only 5 to 20 seconds. Irrelevant, trivial, or not compelling enough, most of the new data are thrown out and never get stored. In other words, if we want students to learn a particular idea or concept, it must be relevant and compelling and connect to something else they know or want to know. It is much easier to help students make connections if you know them.

In Chapter 1, Dewey's (1933) idea of continuity was highlighted as integral to the connections between your past experiences with classroom management and your future actions. "An everyday **inquirer** draws on her past experiences and knowledge in order to make sense of a problematic present situation" (Schutz, 2001, p. 270). Dewey was convinced that understanding something involves seeing how it connects with other things and events (Schutz). Knowing students helps us begin to scaffold lessons for them. For example, think about all of the skills necessary for learning measurement. One must understand that the units of measurement should be the same, what the different standardized units of measurement are, and when to use different units of measurement. Knowing your students will help you determine what kinds of lessons to create. Stiggins (2005) calls this assessment *for* learning.

When issues exist and a child is having difficulty learning a concept or struggling with competency, you need to know him or her well enough either to find out why he or she is struggling or to find different ways to help him or her learn. I once had a student who could not spell words for spelling tests correctly when writing them on paper. Together, we discovered that she could spell them if she said them aloud. She had been practicing her words with her mother in the car every morning and did not write them down. She took the tests verbally until we figured out how to use her effective strategy for spelling through a different medium. Students learn in many different ways, and we need to realize and use them.

We also need to know students for social and emotional reasons. Sometimes we treat young people as subhuman. I, for example, complain to my mom that my 4-year-old son is awful on particular days, and she says, "Well, you have grouchy days too. Give him a break." Just as I expect my son to always be happy and energetic, we often expect our students to come to class each day with attitudes fit for learning. If you think about it, though, students' out-of-class experiences affect them just as ours do. They have grouchy days for no reason apparent to us. How would you want to be treated if you had a bad morning and walked into a classroom? Indeed, we cannot make our classrooms places where students don't have to learn if they had a bad morning. We can, however, create environments where we all care, wonder, and understand.

How Can I Get to Know My Students?

There are certainly many different ways to get to know students. You will probably come up with better ones than I did. After you read my suggestions, brainstorm for some more. One way to spark your brainstorm is to look back at the piece you wrote about a teacher who cared about you. How did that teacher get to know you? Why did he or she care? How did you know that he or she cared?

The main thing to remember about getting to know students is that it is important. Time getting to know students is time well spent. Many of these same ideas will be fleshed out in later chapters in ways that will help you plan and implement them; however, it is important to see these strategies as learning tools as well as ways to know students.

Be a researcher who collects many kinds of data.

- Collect data about what children do and do not understand. This can be as sophisticated as a pretest, a journal entry, or filling out a KWL (Know-Want to Know-Learned) chart together. It can be as simple as asking students to show you with a finger scale how comfortable they are with the material (one finger indicates struggling; five indicate the students have got it).

- Assess students using many different formats. For example, have them draw pictures, write stories, make concept maps, do skits, do projects, make posters, develop their own tests, and verbally explain what they know to show what they understand about a concept.

- Take pictures (with permission from parents) of happenings in your classroom. Pictures are powerful evidence of learning and growing, as well as a fun way to get to know students. Sometimes, let the students have the camera.

- Write down students' verbal statements and questions in class (I did this on a computer whenever I had a chance, and then student quotes became evidence of learning on their report cards).

- Take class surveys and share the results with the class. For example, 10 out of 28 children think they understand division well enough to teach it to others, 5 out of 28 think they need a lot of help with division, and 13 out of 28 think they understand division but need more practice.

- A **portfolio** is a great way to know students. Unfortunately, portfolios take a lot of time. I suggest letting the children keep track of their portfolios. Have them decide what pieces go in and how they will look.

Ask and then listen.

- Sometimes we try to know children without talking to them. Instead of jumping to conclusions or making assumptions, we should just ask students what they think or are going through (Noddings, 1992).

- We need to have conversations with children and not interrogations. This applies to both social and academic interactions. Instead of asking children what answer they got to see if they are right or wrong, ask them because you really want to know their perspective. Instead of asking them why they fought on the playground so you can punish them, ask so you can help them solve their problem.

- Get in on the conversations about juicy problems. Pull up a chair while children are working and wonder with them or just listen to their conversations. "Teachers can create an ethos of caring in the classroom by engaging in ongoing, frequent conversations with their students" (Doll, Zucker, & Brehm, 2004, p. 17).

- Sometimes, sit at the lunch table with children.

- Sometimes, sit at groups of tables or desks and purposefully get off the subject . . . just for a minute.

- When you see students outside of class, stop and talk to them, even if you're in a hurry.

Think outside the box.

- Open your mind to new ideas. Sometimes the craziest ideas work. I have heard of teachers putting stationary bikes in their rooms for children to peddle while they read because sitting still wasn't working. I also know a father/teacher who is studying different diets for his young son who has been diagnosed with **ADHD (attention-deficit/hyperactivity disorder).**

Ask others to think outside the box with you.

Let students have choices.

- You can learn a lot about students from their choices of books, science topics, whom to work with, and materials. Having many choices around the room will help you know your students immensely.

- Schedule times during the day where students choose what they will do. **Plan-do-review** is one great **thinking routine** that will allow for a lot of choice (Williams, 2004).

- Let students pick appropriate music to play during work time.

Create opportunities to get to know children all year, not just in the beginning.

- Have opening-circle time each day where you ask students to answer the same question—for example, what they like to do best when it snows. You could also ask them something about learning, such as what they remember about insects.

- Sometimes, take your whole class to the playground when no one else is there and play a game with the whole class.

- Create writing or other projects that help you learn more about the students.

Know your students' parents or caregivers.

- Invite parents and caregivers to the classroom often. Invite them to plays, to science fair activities, or to the classroom for a special activity. I invited parents to see the projects their children made for our human body unit. We set it up fair style, and they wandered the room looking at all the projects. I just chatted with them.

- Ask parents with all kinds of special talents to visit your room and teach children. I invited seamstresses to teach any children who wanted to know how to sew. I invited a father, a chemical engineer, to show the students what happens when different chemicals are mixed. Sometimes, parents just wanted to help in the classroom whenever they were available, and I didn't require them to call ahead of time.

Let your students know you.

- Share your life with your students. Show them pictures of your children or dog. Tell them you are moving or getting married, and so on. Let them celebrate with you.

- Commiserate with them about problems you have experienced. For example, I always told children whose parents were getting divorced that my parents were divorced.

There are many, many ways to know students. These are just a few to get your mind going. Before you begin reading the next section, review my suggestions as well as your own ideas for getting to know students. If you categorized them, what themes would emerge? What do they have in common?

What Is a Democratic Classroom?

Three Kinds of Classrooms

For me, the strategies above all relate to how a classroom environment is balanced. There are basically three kinds of classroom environments, and the differences have to do with the balance of power and control.

As the diagrams in Figure 2.1 show, two of the environments are unbalanced (the **autocratic environment** and the **permissive environment**), and one is relatively balanced (the **democratic environment**). The differences in management among them are striking. "An autocratic teacher is one who lays down the law in the classroom, feels a strong need to

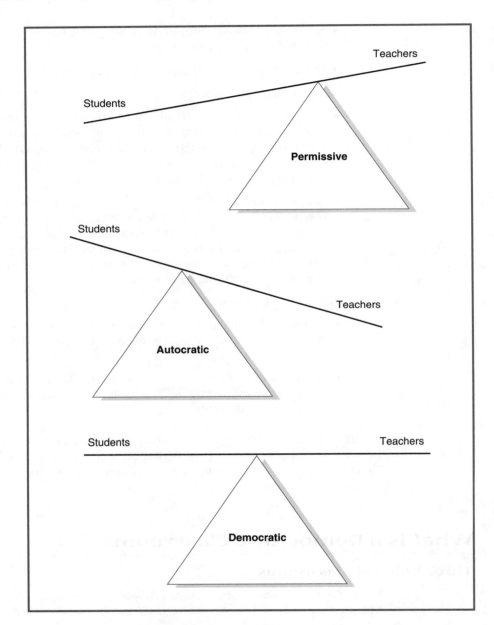

FIGURE 2.1   **Kinds of Environments**

These three diagrams show the different levels of control students and teachers have in three different environments including permissive, autocratic, and democratic environments.

be always in charge, and doles out harsh consequences when rules are broken" (Charles, 1999, p. 44). On the other hand, "A permissive teacher is one who fails to insist that students comply with reasonable expectations. Permissive teachers do not help students realize that freedom must be linked to responsibility" (Charles, 1999, p. 45). Before we discuss democratic classrooms, let's think about how autocratic and permissive classrooms look, sound, and feel (see Table 2.1).

In addition, think about how you would get to know your students in autocratic and permissive classrooms. Would the strategies for getting to know students work in autocratic and permissive classrooms? Would students have opportunities to gain autonomy, belonging, and competency in these environments?

I suppose I should spend more time on autocratic and permissive classroom environments, but I think we all know what those are like. Think back to a classroom you would label autocratic. What do you remember? I remember my fifth-grade math teacher held "question time" right after every lecture, and we were not allowed to ask any questions outside this window of time. Even as a fifth grader, I didn't know what questions I had until I started to work on the problems. Autocratic environments have rigid rules with no flexibility for individual needs.

TABLE 2.1   Autocratic and Permissive Classroom Environments

In autocratic or permissive classrooms, you might see, hear, and feel such things as these.

	Autocratic	Permissive	Democratic
Looks Like	• Students sitting in rows • Teacher at the front of the room • Behavior charts on the wall • Lots of rewards and punishments	• Students all around the room • Teacher at his or her desk or nowhere to be found • No sign of any structure	• Students working on projects with support from teacher • Structures that promote cooperation and learning
Sounds Like	• Very quiet with only teacher talking • Teacher making all decisions	• Noisy • Each student talking about whatever he or she wants	• Productive noise • Students and teacher solving problems together
Feels Like	• No control • Stressful	• No control • Boring	• Self-control • Interesting • Safe

We've all been in permissive classrooms as well. What do you remember about a permissive classroom? I remember my sixth-grade music teacher really just wanted us to like her. She tried to make lessons fun, yet they had no purpose. She didn't really care what we did as long as we were doing something. Permissive environments don't promote mutual respect and learning but force children to find their own way.

I could spend more time on these kinds of classrooms, but I would rather use this book to discuss classroom environments that you may not have experienced and that we desperately need: democratic classrooms.

What Does Having a Democratic Classroom Mean?

I once visited a truly democratic school. Children and teachers worked together to make everything work—and I mean everything. The children made decisions about lunch based on the food pyramid, served each other, and cleaned up after each other. The students made the phone calls when they wanted to set up a field trip, helped each other understand concepts, and made sure everyone participated in discussions. They cared about their school and each other. Teachers in this school helped students make decisions by asking them questions, wondering aloud, and creating a rich learning environment full of materials, juicy problems, and plenty of student-teacher interaction. Considering the main ingredients in this democratic school, I think of a cause larger than self, shared decision making and responsibility, voice, choice, and shared values.

In democratic classrooms, there is a cause larger than self (Glickman, Gordon, & Ross-Gordon, 1998). I like this definition because it encompasses many of the things that come to mind when we think of democracy—namely, voting, responsibility, and freedom—and takes them farther. To work on a cause larger than self, classroom members must do their best for each other, and in turn, everyone will grow individually. A cause beyond self does not have to be a big project where students do something for the whole school or community, although those projects are important as well. A cause beyond self might mean making sure each member of a group understands the concept being studied or understanding why it is important to walk down the hall quietly or to help others learn. Shared decision making, problem solving, and **individual accountability** thrive in classrooms where students are a part of something that goes beyond their grade. In democratic classrooms, then, the students do their best to benefit the class, the community, and, in turn, themselves.

In democratic classrooms, students and teachers make decisions together and feel responsible for one another. "The opportunity to make decisions is a responsibility: it means students have an obligation to participate in figuring out how things are going to be done in the classroom rather than leaving everything to the teacher" (Kohn, 1996, p. 141). We often complain that students are not responsible, yet they have no experience with responsibility. You might argue that handing in homework is a responsibility, but most homework has no purpose other than making children practice something over and over that they don't understand or that they understand and shouldn't have to study any longer (Kohn, 2006). Experience with responsibility needs to be about caring: for other people, about learning, and about concepts. Children need the opportunity to make decisions and to be responsible for things they believe are important and that affect them and their classmates. "To summarize Thomas Jefferson, public education has two corollary purposes: (1) to provide for an educated citizenry to participate in decisions about promoting the future good of our democratic society and (2) to allow for leadership in a democratic society to develop from the merits, abilities, and talents of the individual" (Glickman, Gordon, & Ross-Gordon, 1998, p. 452). These two ideas cannot be accomplished without opportunities to make and learn from decisions.

For material related to this concept, go to Clip 2.2 on the Web-based Student Study Site.

In democratic classrooms, all voices are heard. This means voting at times, as well as listening to the minority. "Our democracy is not a process of decision making always predicated on the rule of the majority. The rule of the majority can by tyrannical. We balance the rights of the majority with the right of the minority" (Glickman, Gordon, & Ross-Gordon, 1998, p. 456). Students must experience coming up with solutions that are good for everyone involved instead of merely voting and not bothering to think about the minority. Having a voice means having the right to ask why and to disagree respectfully. It means having an opportunity to share different ways of getting an answer and to attack problems in ways that make sense. Often, students in classrooms are voiceless, required to sit and listen for hours. Being respectful often means not saying anything.

Democratic classrooms make it possible for individual students to choose what they do best. I find it interesting that in many classrooms we try to make students be good at the same things. Everyone must do well on tests, write well, and be on the same page of the same book. In our world, we really need people who are good at different things and who are willing to share their talents for the betterment of society. "Effective schooling, Dewey argued, must begin with the interests of the child, using them as resources to develop problems for the child to grapple with, something that requires constant and careful planning on the part of teachers" (Schutz, 2001, p. 270). We must still encourage students to try new things, but we needn't keep them from things they do well. Compose a list of things you don't like to do or don't do well. Now imagine doing those things every day for 6 hours. Wouldn't you start to misbehave or try to disappear? The subjects we teach in schools are vital to every concept and idea. You might think there are certain skills that every child should know and be able to use. I agree but would add that those skills are important in a wide variety of topics. Why does it matter what topic we read about as long as we learn to read and comprehend? Wouldn't conversations in social studies be rich if we all studied a big concept from different angles? Choice, infused into everything we do, makes learning valued and interesting.

Finally, in democratic classrooms, there are common values. This might seem frightening at first. Voices in your mind might scream that teaching values in school is not OK because parents should do that at home. Let me clarify. In democratic classrooms, there are common *classroom* values. In other words, no one has to give up his or her values or adopt values he or she doesn't believe. Instead, students and teachers must agree on what kind of classroom they want to have. You need not necessarily call them values; call them rules, goals, beliefs, whatever, but know your classroom needs them. If each member of a classroom decides that he or she wants kindness as a value, it can be a cause to work for beyond oneself. The members of the classroom must define values and expect them for and from every member. Broad values are the glue that holds the members together, even when times are tough.

Miss Kraus's class values, written on this poster, include each student's handprint reaching for the stars.

What a Democratic Classroom Is Not

Democratic classrooms are not places where there are winners and losers. I have been in many classrooms where teachers try to get students to behave by making some children "good" and some children "bad." Sometimes it is subtle, as when some students get to choose an activity because they finished an assignment early while others struggle and never get that opportunity. Sometimes it is overt, as when students sit in a group and the teacher hands out stars/stickers/classroom cash, and so on, to students who are sitting still and acting like they are listening. Those who are "bad" get nothing. We must get it out of our heads that there are good children and bad children. Children are innately good when in an environment with autonomy, belonging, and competency. You may have experienced these techniques as a student. Think about other management techniques that divide students into winners and losers, bad children and good children. What do these techniques teach the winners? What do they teach the losers? In democratic classrooms, there are no winners and losers, only children who can sometimes help and who sometimes need help.

Democratic environments inspire students to be good at some things and to improve others with support and appreciation for trying something difficult. If a child does something wonderful, you must celebrate in a way that doesn't make others into losers. If a child does something not so wonderful, you must help him or her in a way that doesn't turn others into winners. You may think the U.S. democracy thrives on competition with winners and losers or that students need to learn how to become good winners and good losers. As Brooks (2002) reminds us, however, "Childhood need not mimic adulthood in order to help youngsters prepare for it. It's true that effectively dealing with disappointment and loss helps people live longer and happier lives. But it's not familiarity with loss that helps adults cope with death, abuse, neglect, and various other negative experiences; rather it's the internal strength that comes from a childhood that has known the warmth of safety and the comfort of community" (p. 51). Young children will have plenty of opportunity to compete in their lives. Let's not make learning a competition. Learning for everyone benefits everyone. Democracies don't survive if their citizens cannot think and make decisions, be good family members, and be good neighbors.

Democratic classrooms are not manipulative or coercive. If we create classrooms where students have a cause beyond self, opportunities to make decisions, voice and choice, and common values, manipulation and coercion are unnecessary.

> Children who are genuinely and continuously cared for usually turn out to be reasonably good people. Thus when things go wrong or threaten to do so, we have to reflect on our own actions and beliefs. It is not just a matter of tightening up the rules, getting tougher, being consistent about penalties, teaching "them" what's right. It is more a matter of bringing relations into caring equilibrium, balancing expressed and inferred needs, and helping children understand both our actions and their own. (Noddings, 2002, p. 154)

Letting go of manipulation and coercion as tools for behavior management can be frightening. Remember that democratic classrooms are not perfect. Instead, they are places to learn. I have certainly had children get out of hand during a lesson. I remember one time we were testing peanut butter to see if it was a solid or a liquid, and the children got carried away. It was loud, students weren't working on their experiments, and it couldn't go on. I stopped them, brought them to the front floor where they would be close to each other and me, and told them I was concerned that class members were not doing what they were supposed to and were thus taking away from learning in the classroom. I asked the students if they could continue the experiment or if they needed to stop for a while. They needed to stop, but as they calmed down, they continued their experiments. Though honest about my feelings, at the same time I gave my students a voice. Manipulation may work for the short term. Handing out prizes for good behavior certainly works in the moment, but in the long run children who are manipulated into doing what's right don't really understand what "right" is (Kohn, 1993). "Right" can become whatever the teacher says, and although that may sound good in a moment of chaos, do we want children who don't know how to act when the teacher is not there? If we have to coerce children into doing something, is the activity appropriate?

In democratic classrooms, teachers do not force values on others. Democracy is not about believing in the same things as everyone else. In a democratic classroom environment, students and teachers can have meaningful conversations about what is important to them and what they need for success. In addition, democratic environments help students understand that they must be willing to give others what they need as well. "As teachers, we [must] concentrate on establishing conditions that will call forth the best in students, that will make being good both possible and desirable" (Noddings, 2002, p. 2). Those conditions and that environment depend on the people involved in the conversation. Even preschool-aged children have the ability to talk about kinds of classrooms that meet their needs.

In my second-grade classroom, we created a living community (Curtiss & Curtiss, 1998) so that students could construct meaning about living in a community. They built buildings, roads, and houses for the community and then dealt with problems that developed. At one point, the second graders decided they needed laws, so we talked about kinds of government. At first, they wanted me to be a dictator because it would take less time. After I talked to them about what that would mean, they began to value their voice and ability to choose what would happen in the community. They, as a group, came up with laws (values?) that they wanted for their community. I was a part of it, but only a part. Although I was only one voice in our classroom, my voice had experience behind it. I was able to ask questions and guide the students, but I didn't force them. If they had decided to go with a dictator, I would have been one. We would have learned a lot, and then I hope they would have changed their minds.

In democratic classrooms, choice is not an absolute. Slipping into a permissive state is easy when thinking about democracy. The students in a democratic classroom don't make all of the decisions. Learning concerns, safety concerns, and social concerns must be considered. Students should not be able to choose to bother others who are trying to learn. Students should not be given the choice to hurt or bully anyone in the classroom. They should not be able to choose to exclude a classmate from a game or an activity. Indeed, you need to determine what you will and will not accept in a classroom and then be consistent. The things you will not accept, however, must revolve around a caring environment and not necessarily around what is best or easiest for you.

Democratic classrooms are not chaotic. If I had a nickel for every time someone said that democratic classrooms have no structure, I would be rich. Democratic classrooms may look different from other kinds of classrooms, but they have a definite structure that children in democratic classrooms know as well as their responsibilities. Movement of the students may make democratic classrooms look more chaotic than others. Students may be working on the same project yet be in different places in the room, or they may be working on different aspects of the same problem. Students may be working alone or in small groups. In democratic classrooms, the structure is flexible and there are choices, but clear directions, time management procedures, and juicy problems also keep students engaged.

If you are in a classroom that feels chaotic, stop for a moment and try to figure out why. Is there really chaos (i.e., neither the students nor the teacher have focus or direction), or are you merely not used to seeing a classroom where children make decisions, talk together, and work on projects of their own design? If you kneel down with a student and ask him what he is doing and he can tell you not only that but when his time is up and what will come next, there is no chaos in the classroom. We have grown so used to the routine of the teacher telling the students what to do that when something looks different, we perceive it as chaos. Sometimes quiet is optimum for learning, but at other times group work is optimum. As a teacher, you must work behind the scenes so the structure promotes the best environment for learning. You must give clear directions that include opportunities for choice. You must teach children how to work in groups effectively, and you must help them learn to manage their time. Finally, when management becomes an issue, you must include students in the problem-solving process to fix the issues.

Why Have a Democratic Classroom?

You might think there are some benefits to autocratic or permissive classrooms, and indeed there are, depending on what you hope to achieve. Researchers have studied the three types of classrooms to determine the benefits and limitations of each. We will look at one particular study because it provides insight into how the environments we create for children affect them, not just in the moment but for a lifetime. Before you read about the study, think about the benefits and limitations of autocratic, permissive, and democratic classrooms on your own.

The aforementioned study is valuable because it is longitudinal, meaning that the researchers followed the participants for more than 30 years. Since it is so long, the study sheds light on long-term benefits and limitations of different classroom environments. Beginning in the 1960s, researchers with the High/Scope Educational Research Foundation studied preschool curricula and environments, but any grade-level teacher can gain perspective from the study.

The Curriculum Comparison Study examined the High/Scope Curriculum (democratic) and two other common models of the time—nursery school (permissive) and direct instruction (autocratic). Three groups of preschool children were formed through random assignment, each group experiencing a different curriculum model. The main difference in orientation of these three models related to the amount of teacher control: "These approaches differ[ed] with respect to the degree of initiative expected of the child and the degree of initiative expected of the teacher—whether the child initiated much or little or whether the teacher initiate[d] much or little" (Schweinhart & Weikart, 1997, p. 119). On a continuum of control, the three approaches were at very different points. The traditional nursery-school approach was nearest to control by the child. "The traditional nursery school was a child-centered approach in which children initiated activities and the teachers responded to them" (Schweinhart & Weikart, 1998, p. 58). Direct instruction, represented in the study by the DISTAR (Direct Instruction System for Teaching Arithmetic and Reading) program, was at the other end of the continuum, with the teachers doing most of the initiating. "Direct instruction was a scripted approach in which the teacher presented activities and the children responded to them. Teachers clearly defined academic goals in reading, arithmetic, and language" (Schweinhart & Weikart, 1998, p. 58). When the study began, many people believed that lower-achieving students would learn best by direct instruction. The High/Scope Curriculum tended toward the child-centered end of the continuum but added a framework of teacher support and involvement. "The High/Scope Curriculum was an open-framework approach in which teacher and child planned and initiated activities and worked together" (Schweinhart & Weikart, 1998, p. 58).

The majority of the children in the three groups had similar household situations. For example, these children's parents had no significant differences in level of income, education, or work status. The three groups of preschool students spent the same amount of time in preschool and went to kindergarten at age 5.

The students' progress was monitored until each turned 23. Researchers collected data periodically from the students, the school, the community, and social services records. Thus, they examined not only participants' academic success but their social success as well.

The Curriculum Comparison Study showed strong positive results for all three preschool curricula. Each substantially improved young children's intellectual performance, with the average IQ rising 27 points (Weikart, Bond, & McNeil, 1978). Over time, however, major differences among the three approaches emerged. The High/Scope Curriculum's effectiveness for creating a disposition to continue to learn, as well as promoting **self-regulation** and academic achievement, stood out in the results. "The curriculum study's most recent data suggests that there are important social consequences to preschool curriculum choices" (Weikart, 1988, p. 37).

At age 27, most of the High/Scope Curriculum participants had completed high school, earned $2,000 a month or more, owned a home, and were married. In addition, only a small percentage of the High/Scope group had five or more arrests, received welfare payments as an adult, and had children out of wedlock (Schweinhart & Weikart, 1993). These amazing results suggest that curriculum is important to both social and cognitive development. The study magnifies the importance of who initiates learning in the classroom. "The results of this study suggest that children in developmentally appropriate and child-initiated programs—who plan, who have responsibility of their own making, and who initiate their own work—develop the capacity to work independently of adults" (Weikart, 1989, p. 28). The components of the High/Scope Curriculum provide children opportunities to initiate learning and to construct their own understanding with adult support. In doing so, children develop cognitively and socially in a way that lasts beyond their school years.

The High/Scope program highlights the importance of a curriculum that is cognitively oriented, encourages child initiative and choice, and promotes a disposition to learn. In addition, the High/Scope approach produced unanticipated benefits related to socialization and self-regulation. The students learned much more than facts and ideas. They learned how to initiate learning, how to regulate themselves, and how to ask questions, and they discovered that they could achieve in school and throughout their lives.

The effectiveness of the High/Scope program was also studied at the elementary level. Three different sites—Leflore County, Mississippi; Okaloosa County, Florida; and Public School 92 in Manhattan—adopted the High/Scope Curriculum. Researchers found that students using the High/Scope approach scored significantly higher on achievement tests than students in comparison classes and comparable national norm samples. In addition, High/Scope students wrote longer, more descriptive, and more effective reports with richer vocabularies. They spent more time working in small groups, talking with adults, and working with adults individually. Finally, they initiated reading and writing activities more frequently and had better attitudes toward reading and writing than students in non–High/Scope classrooms (Schweinhart & Wallgren, 1993). "If the High/Scope Curriculum has the same effects for elementary-aged children that it has for similar preschool-aged children, it is reasonable to expect that the High/Scope children will engage in less crime and achieve greater school success and later socioeconomic success" (Schweinhart & Wallgren, 1993, p. 54).

These studies show that if we want classroom environments that promote only cognitive growth, any of the three kinds of classrooms will work. If we are looking for classroom environments that promote cognitive growth as well as decision-making abilities, creativity, dispositions to continue to learn, and social/emotional health, however, we must create democratic environments. "All students deserve rich educational experiences that will enable them to become active citizens in a democratic society" (Noddings, 2006, p. 5).

It is important to note that this study began in the 1960s. We are almost 50 years beyond that, and our world continues to change. The children in that study are now in their 40s. Do you think the democratic curriculum that was created taught the students about computers? Did the students in the study learn all of the information we now use in the 21st century? Did they learn that the world would, in a sense, shrink and that they would need to be able to work in a global economy? No. But they did discover that they were able to make decisions, learn, and be creative. They learned that their voices were important and to care for each other. We do not know what our students will encounter in the next 50 years. We are teaching for a future we cannot see. Do we really want adults who can only follow specific directions, who can answer a multiple-choice test but not be creative or solve problems, who cannot work together, or who only care about getting ahead in the world and not about their fellow citizens?

How Do I Create a Democratic Environment in My Classroom?

Creating a democratic environment will not happen the first day and will not be finished on the last day. About always moving toward democracy, even if you never get there, creating a democratic environment is like aiming for the bull's-eye on a dartboard. Sometimes you hit it, other times you get close, but you are always aiming for it: a cause larger than self, shared decision making, choice, voice, and shared values.

Believing in Democracy for the Classroom

The first step in developing a democratic environment in your classroom is belief in its importance. If you do not believe, it will be hard to implement and even keep aiming. The environment must continue to evolve as its members grow and change. The second step is to continually reflect on what you have attempted, what happened, and why. Creating a democratic environment requires support. Find someone who believes in you and what you are doing, and ask for support in your aim to create a democratic environment. Finally, creating a democratic environment requires a process of continual renewal within a community.

Developing Community as a Process for Democracy

We have a lot of ingredients now for creating a democratic environment. The "water" requires a teacher who knows and cares about the "fish," a cause beyond oneself, shared decision making, choice, voice, and values. Indeed, those ingredients are vital; however, the classroom environment cannot be a packaged product but must be developed with processes that help use those ingredients. We as teachers cannot just put those ingredients into a classroom and expect great things to happen. As with learning, the students must be a part of the processes of developing that environment.

If we stick with the fish and water metaphor a bit longer, the water pump on fish tanks that clean the water, provide oxygen, and keep things moving could represent the processes needed to create movement in the classroom, or community development. Some would call this community *building*, but I like *development* better because it connotes learning and growing. Indeed, community development processes must exist for any democratic environment to thrive. Without them, classroom environments are just places where students go to get knowledge and then go home. With them, the environment becomes a place to care about others, about content, and about themselves.

What Does It Mean to Develop Community?

Classroom communities are developed through stages of communication. If students are to benefit from a democratic environment, they must be able to communicate. You might think that learning to communicate means teaching them listening skills and how to be articulate. The process of communication within a group of people, however, is about developing through stages just like a baby develops the ability to talk or walk. We don't teach babies sounds, syllables, and then words. We talk, read, and play with them. In developing the ability to communicate in a classroom environment, people go through stages as well. Peck (1987) identified four stages of developing communication within a group: pseudocommunity, chaos, emptiness, and true community.

In pseudocommunity, members communicate to get along and emulate true community. They try to avoid conflict, ignore individual differences, and try not to offend anyone else. Pseudocommunity resembles wearing a mask. What is really under it?

In the chaos stage, however, problems begin to emerge. No one really listens, but instead everyone tries to get his or her ideas out, creating a lot of talking but no listening or understanding. In chaos, people try to fix each other or convert others to their beliefs. Although this may sound bad, it really provides a way from pseudocommunity to true community. Trying to avoid problems in the classroom, teachers often stay in pseudocommunity, which is easier and less messy and causes no bad feelings. Though less pseudo, the communication in chaos is still nonproductive, like being on a phone that doesn't connect to anyone. Working through this stage rather than pushing it under the rug or returning to pseudocommunity is important.

In the emptiness stage, perhaps the hardest part of reaching true community, members "empty themselves to barriers to communication" (Peck, 1987, p. 95). This means that members must stop; look at their expectations, needs, and prejudices; and get rid of them so they can be open to new thoughts coming in. In a sense, whatever was blocking the phone call from getting through is eliminated, and the lines of communication are open. Listening closely to others when you disagree or when the experience is contrary to yours is difficult. Really listening, though, is about emptying out anything that might keep you from hearing the message.

Developing community is not merely about being together in the same room.

True community may be the last stage on this page, but it is not last as we try to help members of a classroom work together and communicate. True community comes and goes. In this stage, members can communicate effectively, are honest in their conversations with others, and work together toward a common goal. Just as the water in a fish tank may become dirty even after it is cleaned, communities can fluctuate among periods of pseudocommunity, chaos, and emptiness. The stages of communication are more like a circle than a line.

For material related to this concept, go to Clip 2.3 on the Web-based Student Study Site.

Classroom communities develop within goal-setting and problem-solving processes. Without something to work toward, students really have no reason to come together. They must develop a sense of connection to each other and understand that they are a part of an "us" (Kohn, 1996, p. 101). Many communities outside of school come together because of a crisis (Peck, 1987), and though there is no need to set up a crisis for students in a classroom, they do need a cause beyond themselves and those juicy problems to develop a community. Goal-setting and problem-solving processes are similar. Whether it is in small groups or a large group, whether the students or the teacher comes up with the problem, and whether it is academic or social, students need a process for solving problems and making and obtaining goals. For example:

- Identifying the problem or goal
- Previewing the problem or goal
- Assembling resources
- Analyzing resources and plans
- Selecting and implementing the plan
- Monitoring the process
- Assessing the solution (Williams & Veomett, 2007, p. 122)

As with the stages of communication, students need to go through processes to solve problems and set goals. You may help them with a thinking routine, but you also might let them develop their own processes for solving problems and setting goals. In the process of doing so, they will experience juicy problems, shared decision making, voice, choice, and values. They will also go through the stages of communication in a group and make the environment a place they want to be, where they believe in each other and themselves.

Classroom communities develop within processes where students to get to know each other. We talked earlier about ways you, as the teacher, can get to know children deeply. Equally important is that the students in your classroom get to know each other. Many times teachers just expect students to be able to work together without giving them any processes to learn about and from each other.

Such processes as classroom meetings (Murphy, 2002), cooperative learning (Wentzel & Watkins, 2002), whole-class service activities (Elias, 2003), "Tribes" activities (Gibbs, 2001), and class maps (Doll, Zucker, & Brehm, 2004) have all proven to strengthen peer relationships and to help students know and thus care about each other in the classroom. I will detail these processes in later chapters. Certainly, if you know someone's situation and where he or she is coming from, it is much easier to understand and accept him or her. Teachers should not try to control whom students like or with whom they choose to play (Gibbs, 2001). In this type of situation, Gibbs believes that the teacher's responsibility is to live up to the facilitator role— reminding the students of how to include others, what they have learned about inclusion, and what you expect of them as community classroom members.

Processes to get to know each other must also include sharing and celebrations. Not necessarily full-blown parties, processes of celebration can be as simple as students reading their writing in an author's chair to the class or sharing a new way to solve a math problem. Nancy Lockett (personal communication, February 10, 2008) calls tests "celebrations of knowledge." All cultures have celebrations (Deal & Peterson, 1999), and your classroom needs them as well.

What Community Development Is Not

Community development is not led by a dictator. "A healthy classroom community exists when students feel included in the group, know they have influence in how the community functions, and trust they can be open with their feelings, abilities, and opinions" (Obenchain & Abernathy, 2003, p. 60). The teacher does not push students through the stages of communication but instead determines the group's position and helps the students move forward through questioning, juicy problems, and reflection. Nor does the teacher drill problem-solving skills or come up with goals for the students; instead, he or she encourages students to go through the problem-solving routines and reflect on what works for them, as well as to come up with goals and work together to achieve them. The teacher does not coerce students into doing projects and lessons because there will be a celebration. Celebrations are not used as bribes.

Community development is not phoo-phoo. With all of the accountability expectations and talk of rigor in education lately, it is easy to think that processes of community development take too much time and are not worthwhile. Killion and Simmons (1992) discuss the importance of going slowly to go fast. If you take the time to help children develop as a community, know each other, and work on problem solving together, learning will be easier and more productive. "Taking the necessary time to create a supportive classroom community where students accept each other's differences and support each other's learning is a crucial issue for teachers" (Harriott & Martin, 2004, p. 49). Community development is as important as learning math facts, yet we need not have one without the other. Academic work can be learned within community processes. "It is not an add-on, something extra to make time for, but rather an integral part of the day's planning and curriculum" (Kriete, 2002, p. 9).

Community development is not problem-free. I once worked with a teacher who was implementing some community development processes in her classroom. I think she expected that once she implemented the processes, everything in her classroom would be perfect. Quite disappointed at first, after a while she found that the students really valued the processes and were getting to know each other in meaningful ways. The key to community development is that it is a work in progress. Communities don't just happen. "Building community is a deliberate process that a teacher or leader facilitates over a period of time" (Gibbs, 2001, p. 88). Note that problems will help rather than hinder developing community. Problems show us the strategies we already have, where we need work, and who needs help. Community processes should be just that: processes rather than products.

Why Develop Community?

"Once a group has achieved community, the single most common thing members express is: 'I feel safe here'" (Peck, 1987, p. 67). We often talk about how classrooms need to be safe, but that usually means physically safe or safe from a harsh teacher. The safety that comes from community development is more a safety from within, a feeling students get when they have control over their lives and know that they can solve problems.

LETTER FROM A MASTER TEACHER 2.2

Building a Classroom Community

One of the most valuable things a teacher can do is instill a sense of community. Make the classroom feel like it is the students' learning home for the year, and tell them so. Send out "Welcome to School and *Our* Classroom" notes the week before school begins in the fall, make family stick pictures to help students introduce their families during the first week, or put everyone's handprint on the door. In this way, you will get to know your students better, and they will feel a connection with you and everyone who'll be sharing that room for the year.

For many, the democratic classroom includes actual elections and meetings. You can set up formal class meetings that include electing class officers who learn parliamentary procedures. This provides a way for students to propose ideas for change, for action, or for continuation of sameness. Class meetings foster a structure for doing things, making decisions, and supporting each other. Students will learn how they can disagree with each other without being disagreeable; they can see that there are other opinions besides theirs to be heard. Children are shown how to appropriately applaud when the election results are announced; they are guided how to offer a word of care or encouragement to a class member who wasn't successful in this election. All of this supports each person in the room and offers a way to make positive change.

In a classroom where community is nurtured, where students feel connected to their teacher and each other, they learn how to deal with each other in a genuine way, how to allow for differences among themselves, and how to open their senses to the excitement of learning. In these classrooms, the teacher is not seen as the center of the classroom with all students joining hands around the outside circle. Rather, the teacher is one of the members of the group joining hands in a circle.

Whether or not your classroom community includes parliamentary procedures or class officers, work toward a goal of efficacy. Picture how you can impact the students' experiences so that as adults they will be problem solvers, have consideration for others, and develop skills to make positive contributions to their families, their communities, and the world.

As Dr. Haim Ginott said, "I have come to the frightening conclusion that I am the decisive element in the classroom. It's my daily mood that makes the weather." Think about what kind of classroom you want to have and what elements you want to incorporate into your day.

—Rae Brown
Fourth-Grade Teacher

Community processes make the classroom interesting, fun, and social. Doing the same thing day after day is tiresome. Routines, especially thinking routines (see Chapter 5), are important, but learning about each other through an interesting morning question or while playing a game livens the classroom and makes coming to school exciting rather than dull. Students need not dread learning. "When students experience a feeling of community they become more willing to take on tough tasks because they expect to succeed; absenteeism drops; and their attitude toward the course [becomes] more positive" (Hamby Towns, 1998, p. 69).

How Do I Develop Community?

 Having come full-circle now, we must go back to the beginning to make some connections. You develop community by making sure your students have opportunities for autonomy, belonging, and competency; by ensuring the environment has a teacher who cares and who knows the children, opportunities to think about a cause beyond self, shared decision making, voice, choice, and shared values; and by encouraging students to go through such processes as the stages of communication, problem solving, and goal setting. You may think you want some practical ideas about how to develop community, and many will indeed come later in this book. It is up to you, however, to make these ideas your own, and you can't do that until you understand why they are important and where they come from. Wouldn't it just be easier to sit the children in rows and pour the knowledge they need for the test into their heads? Probably, but what would you and your students be missing?

So . . . What?

We have thought a lot in this chapter about the environment of a classroom. Not just about furniture placement or the routines put in place for movement or behavior issues, the environment you help create is also about feelings of care, control, and safety.

In democratic environments, students gain autonomy, belonging, and competency.

To create a democratic environment, you need to know your students at a deep level and care about them as whole people.

To create a democratic environment, you need five ingredients:

1. A cause beyond oneself

2. Shared decision making

3. Choice

4. Voice

5. Shared values

To create a democratic environment, you need to develop community within three processes:

1. Communication stages

2. Problem solving and goal setting

3. Opportunities for children to know their peers

There are many ways for an environment to support democracy, and you need to tailor your classroom environment to meet your students' needs.

Get Ready For . . .

Motivation! We have talked throughout this chapter about why you must get to know your students, why you need a democratic classroom, and why processes that develop community are so important. One answer for each of those questions might be motivation, and the next chapter is all about motivation from within. Unless you understand the ideas surrounding motivation, including environment, the brain, and relationships, more than likely you will end up motivating students extrinsically, or from an outside source. What's wrong with that? Check out the next chapter and find out. Are you motivated to do so? Why or why not?

Activities to Try

Although we have not discussed the physical classroom yet, begin thinking about what physical pieces would support a democratic environment. Where would the furniture and supplies be? Why? What would be on the walls? Why?

In Chapter 1, we talked about the teacher being "behind the scenes." What would this mean for developing a democratic environment? What would you need to plan? What would you need to gather?

Interview a child about what he or she most wants in his or her classroom. How do his or her answers connect to this chapter?

Make a collection! Gather activities that would help you and your students get to know each other throughout the year.

Conduct action research! Find an environment that you think is democratic. Spend some time there talking to people, and consider how the evidence you collect relates to this chapter.

Student Study Site

The companion Web site for *Elementary Classroom Management* can be found at www.sagepub.com/kwilliamsstudy.

Visit the Web-based student study site to enhance your understanding of the chapter content. The study materials include video clips, practice tests, flashcards, suggested readings, and Web resources.

CHAPTER 3

Motivation and Classroom Management

Tonight, before I started to write this chapter, I made dinner for my family. I detest cooking, but I have to do it to feed my family. When I patiently asked my son to set the table, he said—and I quote (in a snotty tone)—"Why do I *always* have to set the table?" A myriad of responses came to my mind: "Because I said so," "Just *do* it," and "Your life depends on it," for example. I didn't say any of these, however. Instead, I told my son he was a part of the family and setting the table was his family job. He rolled his eyes and then set the table. And now, I must begin to write a chapter on motivation. Ironic, isn't it? Why was I motivated to cook but my son was not motivated to set the table? I am not always motivated to cook. Sometimes I make my husband do it or take me out for dinner. Do I cook out of guilt, because my family depends on me, or for another reward?

We in education sometimes connect **motivation** with simple **stimulus-response** behaviors when, in fact, motivation is quite a complex feeling related to many things besides stimulus. Even if I am motivated to do something, I might not do it, but why? Of course, that is the million-dollar question for educators because we need students to be motivated to learn and succeed academically.

Our complex brains are connected to motivation in intricate ways. Maybe my 4-year-old son's brain is not capable of making the complex leap from setting the table to helping his family. Choices can greatly affect our motivation. My son did not have a choice in the matter. He had to set the table, and he really didn't even have a choice in how he went about setting it. Our previous experiences with a task can influence motivation. Maybe my son is just sick of doing the same job night after night or doesn't see its importance. Other people influence motivation as well. I am certain that I influenced my son's motivation to set the table, even if it was not in a positive manner. As you begin to uncover motivation, think about a time you were very motivated to do a task, a time when you were not motivated at all but did the task anyway, and a time when you were not motivated at all and did not do the task (see Table 3.1).

Motivation cannot be completely controlled within others. Certainly, without something as severe as harsh punishment, you cannot be motivated to do or believe certain things. Although we can control others' behavior with extreme measures like punishment, we cannot control others' feelings about those behaviors. You may wonder why we, as teachers, should care whether or not students are motivated as long as we obtain the desired behavior. In other words, why think about motivation if we can come up with strategies that *make* children do what we want?

We need to care because we want students to persist and to continue to use what they learn with us. In other words, we want them to do more than learn. We want them to gain dispositions to continue to learn. If students can only learn or use what they learn until the test, are they really learning? If students don't care about what they have learned or are not motivated to continue to learn, are we successful? We need to care because we are dealing with human beings whose lives do not begin when they enter the "real" world after school. We want them to have happy, engaged lives prior to school. Upon entering school, many hours of those lives are spent in classrooms, and they should not be drudgery. We need to care because motivated students will make our classrooms easier, more relaxed learning environments. Teaching motivated students is fun and exciting because such students find learning easier and worthwhile. Finally, we need to care because sometimes we will do everything "right" but still fail to motivate our students. We need to understand motivation well enough to realize that this occurs and then move on.

TABLE 3.1   Motivation Chart

What motivates you? Think about deeply motivational and demotivational tasks.

	Highly Motivated and Completed Task	Not Motivated and Completed Task	Not Motivated and Didn't Complete Task
What are the characteristics of the task?			
Are you always motivated or not motivated to complete this particular task? Why?			
When the opposite is true, what things are influential?			
Besides the task, what was motivational?			

The last two chapters discussed, respectively, the students and the classroom environment. This chapter is about you, the teacher, and how you can help your students stay motivated to learn. Helping students stay motivated may be different than you think, however. It is not about giving them rewards or entertaining them in the classroom but rather about understanding what influences motivation and demotivation and then teaching in a way that uses those influences.

By the end of this chapter, I hope you have:

- A deep understanding of why motivation matters as you construct a classroom management plan

- An understanding of how the brain, self-efficacy, attribution, relationships, and tasks and topics influence motivation

- An awareness of demotivational aspects of classrooms

- An awareness of the many tools available to strengthen student motivation

Influences on Motivation

The idea that motivation is connected to academic success is a chicken-and-egg question. Which came first, motivation or academic success? Do the students in our classrooms need motivation to help them find academic success, or does their academic success motivate them to learn? And then, should we as teachers work to improve motivation or academic success? Of course, there are no "right" answers to these questions, but they are worthy of your reflection as you develop a management plan.

You could certainly argue that academic success will more than likely follow motivation. Many times teachers use that argument when they justify using rewards to help children learn. They believe they can jump-start students' motivation, and once the students become more motivated to learn, the rewards can be taken away. You could also argue that students with past academic success are motivated because they have been successful. This argument doesn't give much room for students who struggle in school. Again, we have made the complex concept of motivation too simple for there are endless numbers of influences on motivation. Teachers who are engaging or motivating do not rely on one mechanism for motivation but instead rely on many different mechanisms (Bogner, Raphael, & Pressley, 2002; Dolezal, Mohan Welsh, Pressley, & Vincent, 2003). I have chosen five influences to discuss in this book. Although others may exist, these five—the brain, self-efficacy, attribution, relationships, and curriculum—seem to have great implications for teachers. We cannot control students and their motivation, but in our classrooms we can influence motivation in a positive manner.

The Brain

Recently, there has been an explosion of resources on brain-based learning and teaching (Fogarty, 2001; Jensen, 2005, 2000; Sapolsky, 2004; Sprenger, 1999, 2007). Some believe,

This child is motivated to complete his work with stamping patterns. Why is he motivated?

however, that brain research should complement rather than replace traditional educational research (Bruer, 1998; Goswami, 2004). For example, there is a plethora of educational research about young children and their need for manipulatives to help them make sense of mathematics (Kamii, 2000; Labinowicz, 1980), and now that idea has been supported through brain research as well. "Neural areas activated during finger-counting (a developmental strategy for the acquisition of calculation skills) eventually come to partially underpin numerical manipulation skills in adults. If this were the case, then perhaps finger counting has important consequences for the developing brain" (Goswami, 2004, p. 8). Indeed, it is important that, as with any research, we consume brain-based research with caution, however difficult it seems to ignore similar ideas from many different sources.

Much of the brain-based research coming out actually helps us improve classrooms and teaching by enhancing what educational studies have shown for many years. We may not know for sure that all of the brain studies give us "truths" about teaching and learning, but we do know that it sparks changes in how classrooms are designed and how teachers think about teaching and learning. Sprenger (2007) calls this "changing institutions that encourage students to have classroom-compatible brains to institutions that encourage teachers to have brain-compatible classrooms" (p. 5). Brain research helps teachers see the value in making classrooms **child-centered** rather than **teacher-centered**.

Counting on your fingers is a good thing. Why might it be motivational?

How does brain research relate to motivation? In my opinion, *brain-friendly* is synonymous with *motivation*. We don't have very many absolutes in the classroom because children are so different. The large individual differences between brains (Goswami, 2004) make brain research very difficult to generalize. We know, however, that motivated children can accomplish a great deal (Linnenbrink & Pintrich, 2002; Morgan & Fuchs, 2007; Pintrich & Schunk, 2002) and that teachers can influence student motivation by using many of the suggestions that derive from brain research (Jensen, 2005). We may not have bulletproof evidence that the ideas coming from brain research directly help students learn, but brain-based changes in how we manage, design, and implement instruction are, at the least, motivational. Indeed, many ways to motivate students are now supported through brain research (Sprenger, 2007). Let's look at a few examples.

Our brains can be motivated if new ideas and tasks are in the classroom. Neuroscientists have found that novelty appeals to the brain (Carper, 2000). In studies of motivational classrooms, teachers encouraged curiosity and suspense, stimulated appropriate cognitive conflict, and encouraged students to try a wide range of strategies to accomplish tasks (Dolezal, Mohan Welsh, Pressley, & Vincent, 2003). This does not mean

For material related to this concept, go to Clip 3.1 on the Web-based Student Study Site.

that you must change your entire schedule every day; rather, you should add new topics, ideas, and strategies throughout the school year. Many teachers rely on routines in an effort to make students feel safe; however, some routines can cause boredom and fatigue. Have you ever been in a class where every day you graded the homework, listened and took notes during a lecture, got an assignment, and left? Although repetition is good for the brain when a concept is novel, if a task becomes boring, repetition is no longer effective (Jensen, 2000). You must find ways to have routines but also bring in new ideas and tasks (see Figure 3.1).

FIGURE 3.1   Novelty

Here are some ways to bring newness into a classroom.

Motivating the Brain

Ways to bring newness into the classroom:

- Find interesting problems that go with content you're uncovering in class.
- Make the walls of your classroom look slightly different with new posters or student work, or hang from the ceiling any items that connect with topics you're studying.
- Have students share their ideas in different ways, such as skits, drawings, poetry, and so on.
- Invite speakers to come in and talk about a topic you're studying.
- Invite students to share ideas and items that connect to topics you're studying.
- Rearrange the seating arrangement or classroom.
- "Do unusual experiments." —Gerald Brand, Master Teacher
- "Share cultural and traveling experiences with your students." —Liana Whipking, Master Teacher

Our brains can be motivated if we are physically active in the classroom. Movement has been found to be key in increasing attention, focus, and thinking skills (Jensen, 2005). "Physiologically, movement is essential for learning. It is vital for nerve net development, and adequate development of the heart and lungs. This development is necessary for support of brain function" (Hannaford, 1995, p. 158). Indeed, keeping young children from moving is like asking them not to breathe (Hohmann & Weikart, 1995). We have all felt tiredness after sitting for a long period, yet in many classrooms, students sit in desks the entire day. Many school districts have limited physical education and recess to allow more time for academics (Jensen, 2005). While this may seem like a good idea, in reality exercise improves classroom behavior and academic performance (Dwyer, Sallis, Blizzard, Lazarus, & Dean, 2001). Movement and exercise are important for **special-needs students** as well. Children with dyslexia were found to have improvements in dexterity, reading, verbal fluency, and semantic fluency when participating in exercise-based programs (Reynolds, Nicolson, & Hambly, 2003). Teachers often fear they will lose control if students are moving around the room (Sprenger, 2007). Many movements, however, work well in classrooms and can easily be incorporated into a good classroom management plan. Try some of the suggestions in Figure 3.2, as well as within the many resources listed below.

Figure 3.2   Physical Activity

Here are some of the many ways to bring movement into a classroom.

Motivating the Brain

Ways to bring movement into the classroom:

- Do cross-crawl and lateral movement exercises before you begin class (Dennison & Dennison, 1994).
- Have students go on a walk and talk about a problem.
- Have students build a model.
- Have students go on a gallery walk to see others' work.
- Let students choose where they would like to sit, lie, or stand while reading.
- Go on a scavenger hunt to find things around the school that you are studying.
- Put some tape in the hallway so that students can do a "balance beam" on the way to lunch.
- Let students who are having trouble sitting in desks stand at the back of the room on one foot and then switch to the other.
- Get some exercise balls for students to sit on rather than chairs.
- Make sure students have time for recess.
- "We play lots of games—board races, alphabet knockout, sparkle, stand-up/sit-down activities, individual white board activities, vocabulary races using pictures." —Stacy Hagemann, Master Teacher
- "When my kids don't seem to be responding or able to concentrate, I have them stand up, and we do brain-friendly stretches. It really seems to help the students come alive." —Amanda Petersen, Master Teacher
- "We do an 'order of operation' movement activity in math." —Kathie Leach, Master Teacher
- "I have a brain box, and at the beginning of class a student selects an activity from the box. The activities consist of stretches designed to get the blood moving." —Tarah Jansen, Master Teacher

Our brains can be motivated if we have healthy snacks and plenty of water. We have known for a long time that students with poor nutritional habits struggle in school. "Students who come to school hungry, sick or hurt are unlikely to be motivated to seek knowledge and understanding" (Woolfolk, 1998, p. 384). Although this is not always the case, some brain research now concurs with this evaluation. "Diet affects the brain. A child whose diet is poor will not be able to respond to excellent teaching in the same way as a child whose brain is well nourished" (Goswami, 2004, p. 2). Water is also a key to students' motivational success. "The brain, the control center for learning, needs energy, oxygen, and water to operate. Electrical transmissions in the nervous system depend on water. This neurological transfer of information through water is important for learning" (Fahey, 2000, p. 60). We cannot go into the homes of our students and feed them, but we can provide healthy snacks and water throughout the day.

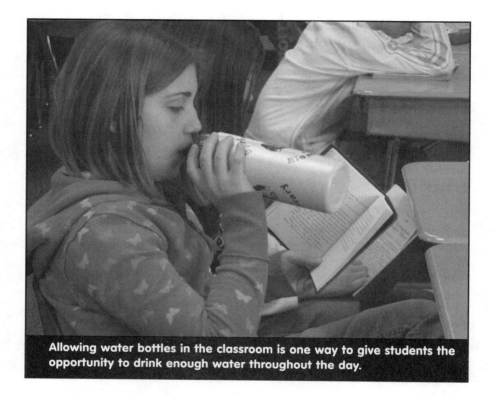

Allowing water bottles in the classroom is one way to give students the opportunity to drink enough water throughout the day.

Even though water and healthy snacks can improve students' experiences in classrooms and in learning, some critics believe they disrupt learning and management. Teachers do not want children eating and drinking in the classroom because of the mess and distractions they may cause. Instead of completely ruling out snacks and drinks, however, think outside the box (see Figure 3.3). How can you integrate snacks into your routine? What jobs could you assign students with regard to snacks and drinks that would help keep the room mess-free? What kind of water bottles or containers would be appropriate and easy? One teacher I know grew tired of having water tip over onto papers. Instead of banning water, she collected half-gallon milk jugs, cut the bottoms off of them, and attached the handles to the back of students' chairs. These milk jugs became water bottle holders and helped solve her water problems. Important for learning, water and healthy snacks shouldn't be used as rewards or punishments, and they should be welcomed rather than tossed. Your students will feel better, and we all know people who feel better learn better, behave more appropriately, and love coming to school.

Our brains can be motivated if we have time to make connections and reflect about learning. Learning connections require time and maintenance. "The brain has several systems and structures, such as the hippocampus that actually inhibit higher speeds of processing" (Jensen, 2005, p. 42). In other words, we cannot continue to pretend that we can stuff a large amount of learning into children's heads and make it stick. Students need sense-making time—time to

Figure 3.3   Diet and Water

Here are some ways to bring a healthful diet and water into a classroom.

Motivating the Brain

Ways to bring healthy snacks and water into the classroom:

- First, make sure you know if children in your class or the school have allergies.
- Snacks don't have to be a whole bunch of food. A few pretzels, carrots, or raisins will do.
- Ask parents to take turns supplying snacks.
- Purchase ingredients for snacks, and make them with students.
- Ask local stores to provide snacks.
- Have individual students bring their own snacks.
- Make snack time when students are reading or writing.
- Let students get a drink of water whenever they need one.
- Let students bring water bottles.
- Have water breaks throughout the day.
- Make water containers out of milk jugs and attach them to each student's chair so that water stays off of desks.
- "I organize a snack schedule for my classroom with nutritional snacks for the month." —Nadine Poulos, Master Teacher
- "Food and drink are OK in my classroom as long as they don't disrupt anyone." —Doug Smith, Master Teacher

grapple with ideas and play with productive wrong answers. Eleanor Duckworth (1996) advises, "As teachers, I think one major role is to undo rapid assumptions of understanding, to slow down closure, in the interests of breadth and depth, which attach our knowledge to the world in which we are called upon to use it" (p. 78). To help students truly understand something, to appreciate their wonderful ideas, and to help them love learning, we must get past this notion that the right answer is the only good answer. Our brains don't construct such knowledge.

We seem to understand that concept for adult learners and our youngest learners, but we still expect children in school to learn without time or productive mistakes. Consider that for a minute. Do you think someone will be able to tell you how to parent? Someone who has done it before might be able to give you advice or reassure you, but he or she certainly can't give you the "right answers." Babies are given time and plenty of opportunities to learn to walk, talk, sit up, and eat. It's funny to think about a baby eating correctly the first time. My 18-month-old son goes up and down the stairs and ramps, and I can see him trying new things and working on balance. He knows to do this without any coaching from me. Every once in a while, he needs me to hold his hand or pick him up, but mostly he swats my helping hand away. This is the same kind of time we must give our students (see Figure 3.4). They need to work with numbers over and over again in different ways; to read and reread interesting books, act them out, and draw pictures about them; and to experiment with rocks, water, microscopes, and light bulbs. They may never get the right answer, but they will get a great base on which to build knowledge and motivation to continue to learn.

Figure 3.4   Reflection

Here are some ways to help students slow learning so they can retain it.

Motivating the Brain

Ways to slow learning in the classroom:

- Take all of your objectives and fit them into several themes. This way, you are not only doing all of the objectives but also connecting them.
- Think-pair-share throughout the day. Ask a question, ask your students to think about it or even write an answer down on paper, and then ask each student to share his or her answer with someone near them (or far from them if you want some movement too). Then ask your students to share their ideas with the whole class.
- Take time to make connections with unique assessment tools like concept maps, plays, body models, drawings, and so on.
- "I have students talk to each other about what they learned." –Brian Johnson, Master Teacher

Our brains can be motivated if we are in an appropriate emotional state. We talked earlier about the importance of movement and physical activity to get brains going. Sometimes, though, students get so wound up or are under so much stress that instead of getting brains going, we need to calm them down. For example, after children come in from recess, it can be difficult to get them ready to learn again. Just as you can use exercise and movement to reinvigorate tired brains, you can use music, lighting, and brain tools to help get children into an optimum state for learning (Swanson, 2007). See Figure 3.5 for ideas.

Our emotions greatly influence learning. "Emotional states run our lives, including how we think, feel, remember, act, and dream" (Jensen, 2005, p. 77). One emotion, stress, seems critical for optimum learning. Occasional or moderate stress is, for the most part, a healthy state. A brief period of stress enhances memory (Jensen, 2005). For example, you might remember a time in school when you were more moderately stressed than on most days. High stress, however, is not good for learning; it has been shown to kill brain cells (Sapolsky, 2004) and keep students from participating fully in class. "If the classroom is a fearful, unpredictable place and students seldom know where they stand, they are likely to be more concerned with security and less with learning" (Woolfolk, 1998, p. 384). Fear and stress are demotivators, and punishment and public reprimand negatively affect students' academic motivation (Dolezal, Mohan Welsh, Pressley, & Vincent, 2003).

In addition, outside events that trigger emotions can influence motivation. If students are aware of disrespect toward culture or ethnicity, they can become demotivated (Jensen, 2005). Students' home lives, their friendships, and incidental events can all tip motivation into demotivation. "You never know what happens in the hallways. At the start of class, students could still be reeling from an insult, a breakup with a close friend, a fight, or the loss of something valuable" (Jensen, 2005, p. 111).

You will not be able to—nor do you want to—keep emotions out of your classroom. Lack of emotion is just as bad as uncontrolled emotion. Instead, work to avoid both extremes. Just as we've seen with stress, moderate amounts of any emotion can enhance learning (Jensen, 2005). Teachers must provide students with the tools to control their emotions. Children, if taught, can learn how to self-regulate their own emotions using these tools. It is important that they know when and how they can help themselves become better learners.

For material related to this concept, go to Clip 3.2 on the Web-based Student Study Site.

Current brain research, though valuable as you plan strategies for classroom management, is not a cure-all that will make children perfect angels who gobble up knowledge each day. Instead, the little bit of brain research cited here and the multitude of research to come is another piece of the puzzle helping you be the best teacher possible. Brain research and the implications that stem from it require some action research on your part as well. Make it your mission to plan, try, reflect, and revise as you go. Making your room brain-friendly and motivational is not difficult. It only requires that you think about what makes learning easy. It's not hard to believe that being comfortable, having a drink of water, having time to think, and being able to get up now and then will enhance learning. Perhaps the Golden Rule applies here: Treat your students as you would want them to treat you.

Figure 3.5 Emotions

Here are some ways to help children deal with emotions in the classroom.

- In addition to oxygen demand, slow, deep breathing has been said to release tension in muscles, which is very useful for relaxation and stress reduction (Hannaford, 1995).
- Get some stuffed animals and remove their stuffing. Replace the stuffing with beans or sand and sew the animals back up. You can also put beans or sand in gloves and sew them up. These are called heavy hands, and when children are feeling stressed, put them on their shoulders or their heads. Try it; it feels great.
- If you don't have stuffed animals or gloves, just putting your hands on children's shoulders can help.
- When children come in for recess, have them put their heads on their desks and dim the lights. This is not to punish them but instead to help the pressure points in their brains calm down.
- Make some discovery bottles, and let children put them at their desks when they need to.
- Make or buy some brain tubes, and let children put them at their desks when they need to.
- Turn on music that is 60 beats per minute.
- When you need children's attention, say and have them say, "Shh, shh, shh" while bringing your arms down (like an airplane) and crossing them over your chest.
- "I have a box of brain toys in my room including stress balls, glitter wands, Legos, and other hand manipulatives that the students are welcome and encouraged to play with during class." —Tarah Jansen, Master Teacher
- "Early on I let the students know they can trust me and I will listen to them without judgment. I try to be their sounding board in private and keep our talks confidential." —Vicki Brabec, Master Teacher

LETTER FROM A MASTER TEACHER 3.1

Using Brain-Based Strategies in the Classroom

I decided to become a teacher because I wanted to be a positive, encouraging influence on children while they were learning and growing. As soon as I found out I was going to be an "official" teacher of students in the first grade, I called everyone who would listen to tell them my good news, and then I went shopping! I knew that one of the keys to unlocking children's brains and opening the doors to learning was to surround them with an enriched environment that allows them to be engaged in every "sense" of the word.

For my students to grow and mature socially, emotionally, and academically, I knew that they needed to be surrounded by a secure, nurturing, caring, and stimulating environment. I felt it was very important to provide an atmosphere that was not only safe but also supportive of each of my students' beliefs and ideas. My students needed to feel they were a part of something big and that they were more than just a number or a body in a chair. They also needed an environment optimal for learning, an environment that engaged all the senses. I incorporated some brain-based strategies into my teaching by creating a "Brain-Friendly" classroom with brain tools that included Brain Gym exercises (Dennison & Dennison, 1994). After I incorporated brain tools into the classroom, my students discovered that there were tools to not only help them focus and concentrate but also help them handle their own fears and anxieties.

A student could choose to use a squish ball to help him or her think, or a student could choose to perform a few Brain Gym exercises as a way to help release his or her feelings of stress, nervousness, frustration, or anxiety. When my students started to realize the benefits of performing the Brain Gym exercises, their enthusiasm soared, and then I could be their coach and their number-one fan.

Because my students were in an environment that was positive physically, socially, and emotionally, they could allow themselves to feel secure enough to enjoy and celebrate learning. The enthusiasm and excitement that came from my students showed me that they were motivated. They not only enjoyed learning; they celebrated it. I will continue to incorporate brain-based activities into my classroom for future years to come. I highly recommend that you incorporate brain-based activities into your classroom to enhance the environment of your students. For teachers who wish to discover an exceptional way for their students to learn, engage the senses; it just makes sense!

—Julie Duff
First-Grade Teacher

Self-Efficacy

If you think about it, there are probably tasks and topics that you like to study and some that you would be willing to trade for going to the dentist. I like to read and study educational **pedagogy** (methods of teaching), and I like to garden and snow ski. I would rather go to the dentist every day for a month, however, than take a chemistry class. List the tasks or topics that you like or are motivated to do on most days, and list some you really hate to do. How do they compare? One common thread might be whether or not you feel successful doing the task. I, for example, can't do chemistry, don't understand chemistry, feel stupid when someone asks me about it, and actually don't even really care that I don't know it; in other words, I do not have **self-efficacy** within the chemistry field. (Luckily, others in this world love and understand chemistry. Diversity is good.)

Self-efficacy describes people's judgment about how well they feel they will perform on a task—that is, whether they perceive themselves as capable or incapable (Bandura, 1977, 1993). Self-efficacy is different from self-esteem in that it is task-specific (Linnenbrink & Pintrich, 2002). I can be efficacious about gardening and not about chemistry but continue to have high or low self-esteem.

Self-efficacy is an important construct for you as a teacher because it affects motivation and, in turn, student achievement (Bandura, 1993; Pintrich & Schunk, 2002; Seifert, 2004). Students with high efficacy are more likely to be self-regulating, strategic, and able to engage in difficult or challenging tasks while students with low efficacy avoid challenging tasks (Bandura, 1993; Dweck, 1986; Schunk, 1984). High self-efficacy is positively related to higher levels of achievement and effort and increased persistence (Pintrich & Schunk, 2002). For example, because I have high efficacy in gardening, I often spend a great deal of time in the garden and won't give up if a plant or two dies.

On the other hand, if one does not feel efficacious about a topic or task, he or she may exhibit behaviors that signal motivational issues. "If students perceive themselves incapable of performing well (low self-efficacy), they may become motivated to protect perceptions of competency, for if they can convince themselves and others they could do well, they will be able to maintain some sense of worth or dignity" (Seifert, 2004, p. 144). In other words, if a student feels he or she will do well on a task, he or she may not study or try to do his or her best. When students don't give much effort to a task, it is easy to explain poor performance. Students would rather not work and feel guilty than work hard and fail, which may cause them shame (Covington, 1984; Seifert & O'Keefe, 2001).

Feelings of efficacy need to be at or a little above actual skills (Pintrich & Schunk, 2002). If a student's efficacy is too high relative to his or her actual abilities, he or she may take on tasks that are too difficult and struggle until feelings of efficacy deteriorate. I feel good about my gardening skills in my backyard, but I could not write a gardening book and would not want an expert to inspect my handiwork.

Stop reading for a minute and reflect on one of the topics you listed as something you are least efficacious about doing. How could a teacher help you feel efficacious about that topic or task at an appropriate level? How could a teacher help me feel efficacious about chemistry?

"In terms of instructional implications, self-efficacy is best facilitated by providing opportunities for students to succeed on tasks within their range of competence and through these experiences actually develop new capabilities and skills" (Linnenbrink & Pintrich, 2002, p. 316). To feel efficacious about chemistry, I would need to relearn it in a way that is within my range of competence. In my case, that would mean making chemistry more concrete because I have trouble visualizing something that abstract. I would also need opportunities to step to harder concepts incrementally as I understood them. In other words, chemistry would need to be scaffolded, which might mean breaking it down into simpler steps or building onto what I already know. I would need to find and build from the point where I understand chemistry, and I would need someone I trust to help me make sense of it. I would need this person not to tell me what he or she knows but rather to find ways to help me understand. "For their part, teachers must find ways to understand students' viewpoints, propose alternative frameworks, stimulate perplexity among students, and develop classroom tasks that promote efforts at knowledge construction" (Glasson & Lalik, 1993, p. 188). Opportunities to work with others and share ideas promote efficacy as well (Linnenbrink & Pintrich, 2002).

Lev Vygotsky (Bee & Boyd, 2007) referred to this "range of competence" as the **zone of proximal development (ZPD)**. Vygotsky believed that this optimal zone for learning was unique for every individual. "Each child, in any domain, has an actual developmental level and a potential for development within the domain. The difference between the two levels is what Vygotsky termed the zone of proximal development" (Hausfather, 1996, p. 3). Learning takes place within the ZPD because the material is challenging yet attainable. "It is important that educators calibrate tasks and assessments so that success is attainable" (Linnenbrink & Pintrich, 2002, p. 316). Vygotsky believed that to operate successfully in the ZPD, learners need to interact socially with peers who have a greater understanding of the subject (Hausfather, 1996).

Teaching within this "range of competence," or ZPD, means knowing what students already understand, helping them by scaffolding onto what they already know, and providing support through peers and the teacher. Students can develop self-efficacy both by learning and by supporting others.

Attribution

Researchers have found that motivation declines as students get into higher grades (Eccles, Wigfield, Harold, & Blumenfeld, 1993; Gambrell, Codling, & Palmer, 1996; McKenna, Ellsworth, & Kear, 1995). This may be because children begin to show differences in abilities and place more emphasis on competition in upper grades (Guthrie & Wigfield, 2000). Students begin to understand that others may have higher abilities in certain areas than they do. A key to influencing motivation is how you, as a teacher, deal with those realizations.

If students begin to think that they don't have the ability to succeed at a task, they may decide not to try. For example, I ran in track and wanted to run the sprints, the short, fast races. My friend Soni, who also ran the sprints, was much quicker than I was, and I distinctly remember telling her that I would never be able to run as fast as she could, that my body just wasn't made for running sprints. A kind friend, she tried to encourage me, explaining that if I just tried harder, I would be able to run faster. I, however, attributed my failure in track to my ability rather than my effort or strategy. I continued to run track but without much motivation to improve. **Attribution** theory suggests that when a failure or success occurs, students analyze the situation to determine its perceived causes (Weiner, 1985). This theory is important to motivation and you as a teacher, because if students believe that they can never improve at a task or that their innate ability keeps them from obtaining a goal, they won't be motivated to continue (Linnenbrink & Pintrich, 2002). My niece, a fourth-grader, has already decided that she isn't good at math. Many teachers with whom I work, having decided that they can't teach science, don't. What are the implications for my niece? What are the implications for the students in classrooms where teachers don't teach science?

If we want to motivate students, we need to help them understand that ability is only one factor in successful learning. "Students need real evidence that effort will pay off, that setting a higher goal will not lead to failure, that they can improve, and that abilities can be changed" (Woolfolk, 1998, p. 395). Some researchers recommend that teachers promote **effortful strategy** use rather than merely effort (Carr, Borkowski, & Maxwell, 1991; Licht, 1983). Effort alone will not help many students succeed, and all students need strategies for learning and success. I have a problem with losing keys—OK, my husband would call it a disease, and he might add my cell phone, my planner, my purse, and so on. At any rate, effort alone is not going to help me with my issue. I can try really hard not to lose my keys, but I really need a strategy to help me, just like a struggling student would. Simply telling your students to try harder is not good enough. You must help them gain strategies for future success (Linnenbrink & Pintrich, 2002).

Try not to think of strategies as giving students the answers or "tricks" for performing pseudowell. There is a difference between helping students become competent with strategies and helping them pass tests. Instead, strategies need to be tools students can use to think, plan, reflect, and comprehend. For example, if students don't believe they can do mathematics, I might help them develop the strategy of drawing a picture of the math problem. If students are struggling with reading, I might give them a bookmark that helps them remember what to do if they can't figure out a word: Sound it out, look at the picture, replace it with a word that makes sense, and so on. Many students who are successful in school already use these strategies automatically. By the way, strategy use isn't good just for motivation but for learning as well.

Teachers also can help set **mastery goals** for students who attribute success to ability. "Mastery goals orient learners to developing new skills, trying to understand their work, improving their level of competence, or achieving a sense of mastery based on self-referenced standards" (Ames, 1992, p. 262). In contrast, **performance goals** are more competitive and encourage students to focus on their ability by outperforming others in achievements or grades (Ames). Mastery goals have been shown to help students become self-regulating and self-determining and to foster cognitive development (Seifert, 1997). "When students are focused on trying to learn and understand the material and trying to improve their performance relative to their own past performance, this orientation will help them maintain their self-efficacy in the face of failure, ward off negative affect such as anxiety, lessen the probability that they will have distracting thoughts, and free up cognitive capacity" (Linnenbrink & Pintrich, 2002, p. 321).

On the other hand, performance goals can be demotivational. Students pursuing performance goals, or goals measured in relationship to other students' performances, are likely to believe that their ability caused their success or failure and that intelligence is a fixed entity, to view difficulty as failure, and to engage in less sophisticated strategy use. Such students make more negative self-statements and attribute success to uncontrollable factors (Dweck & Leggett, 1988; Nolen, 1988; Seifert, 1995).

Ames (1992) recommends teachers create lessons that engage students in hands-on, applied activities and help them see how what they learn in school relates to things outside of school. In addition, teachers should use a variety of tasks and allow students to choose among them to keep social comparison to a minimum. Teachers can also promote mastery goals by developing opportunities for autonomy and belonging (Ames).

Teachers' reactions to students can also influence attributions. For example, if a teacher pities a student who does poorly, he or she may attribute the failure to low ability (Linnenbrink & Pintrich, 2002). You can help students feel they can improve by reacting in a way that suggests this and by giving them feedback and strategies to do well (Pintrich & Schunk, 2002).

The kinds of assessments you use also influence attribution and thus motivation (Linnenbrink & Pintrich, 2002). Rather than focusing on students achieving absolute standards, focus on individual progress (Dolezal, Mohan Welsh, Pressley, & Vincent, 2003). It is important to note here the connections between attribution and assessment. To do so, let's look at assessment versus evaluation and progress versus growth (Lockett, 2006).

According to the *Merriam Webster New Collegiate Dictionary*, the Latin root of the word *assess* is *assidere,* meaning "to sit beside, to sit alongside a judge." Although it may be difficult to distinguish assessment from evaluation, this root helps. **Assessment** means to *work beside* students, facilitate their learning, and plan the next step in the learning process—that is, to tell them what is right, what is wrong, and how to fix it (Lockett, personal communication, February 10, 2008). In contrast, to evaluate means to *judge* how well a student (teacher, school, or school system) performs relative to a standard or to others' performance. Nancy Lockett distinguishes between assessment and evaluation with a metaphor comparing assessment to being a coach and evaluation to being a referee. A coach watches and then helps players improve by giving them strategies, things to work on, and so on. A referee just tells players how well they did in the game and doesn't give suggestions or help them improve. We can't give students a grade (evaluation) and expect it to motivate them. We can, however, tell them what is right and wrong and give them strategies to fix it (assessment), which will allow them to get better. In other words, we need to do a lot more assessing and a lot less evaluating.

Lockett (personal communication, February 10, 2008) also believes that teachers need to understand the difference between progress—how well a student did in comparison to others in the class—and growth—how well a student did in comparison to his or her past work. For example, if a student gets a C grade, that tells us something about how he or she did in comparison to his or her classmates. If the student got an F on a previous test, however, he or she has grown tremendously. Motivating students requires measuring and celebrating both progress and growth.

Relationships

Perhaps one of the most important things we can do as teachers to help students enjoy school and become motivated to learn is to create relationships with them. Strong evidence suggests teacher-student relationships influence students' social and intellectual development from preschool to high school (Davis, 2003). The quality of relationships between teachers and students also influences learning problems, retention (Pianta & Steinberg, 1992), competence with peers, tolerance of frustration, academic and social skills (Pianta & Steinberg, 1992), concept development (Pianta, Nimetz, & Bennett, 1997), and behavior problems (Marachi, Friedel, & Midgley, 2001).

I bet you can name a teacher who made you feel good about yourself and believed in what you had to say. As an undergraduate student, I had a teacher who thought I would be the best elementary teacher in the world. In fact, *every* student who took his classes believed he or she would be the best elementary teacher in the world. The relationship this teacher formed with me and probably hundreds of others motivated us to be the best teachers we could be. He believed in us, and we believed in him.

Relationships with students don't have to be mushy or stringy. In other words, you don't have to buy students things, tell them they are great, or try to be their friends. You don't have to see them outside of school or stay in contact with them forever, but you should let them know that they are worthy, truly believe that they matter, and be willing to support them on their journey of learning.

I once asked a group of 50 experienced teachers of all levels and subjects to name one tool they use to help manage their classroom. Most of the teachers named behavior charts, stoplight cards turned from green to yellow to red with poor behavior, and referral cards to go to the office. A usually quiet teacher named Karla spoke up after a while and said, "I ask them what is wrong and wonder how I can help them"—a powerful statement from a special education teacher who probably deals with more behavior problems than most. Karla's students know they can count on her and that she cares. In turn, they work hard and do their very best. "Teachers who are perceived as being nurturing, supportive, and helpful will be developing in students a sense of confidence and self-determination which will be translated into the learning-oriented behaviors of the intrinsically motivated student" (Seifert, 2004, p. 148.). Teacher-student relationship is a critical factor in fostering a sense of competence and autonomy (Seifert & O'Keefe, 2001).

Although positive relationships sometimes keep problems from occurring, they are not the answer to every problem. There is a difference between having a relationship with students and using relationships to get them to do what we want. I am reminded of teachers who talk to children in sugary-sweet voices but who say things that are really coercive. "I like the way Ryan is sitting so quietly," even in a sweet voice, may motivate some students to sit quietly, but it makes Ryan into a goody-goody and doesn't address the problem. We don't want a group of children who are motivated to learn because they like the teacher. We want children who are motivated to learn because they are interested in the topic, have the tools to be competent, and realize the importance of learning. One seventh-grade teacher told me he

Miss Laura takes the time to let Tyler share his project with her.

puts a question on the board that students work on as they come into his room each day. He came to me frustrated because on a particular day he had stepped out of the room for a moment to talk to a parent and, when he came back to the room, many of the children were not doing the question and instead were "messing around." He told me how he doesn't have any trouble with them usually, but he couldn't believe how awful they were being that day. I am guessing that this teacher and his students have a relationship where they do things to please him rather than because they believe they are important or worthwhile. I wonder if he ever spoke with them about the questions he poses at the beginning of class, genuinely listened to why they were having a problem answering them, and discussed with them how it could be solved.

While we don't necessarily want students to do things to please us, relationships certainly create opportunities to work out problems rather than sweep them under the rug. A third-grade teacher, Christine, had a student who threw a fit after math one day. Instead of sending him to the office or assigning him time out, she sent the rest of the children to music and let him calm down for a bit. Then she walked by and asked him if he would like a juice box. He said yes. Christine let him drink the juice box for a while and then asked him why he was so upset. The child told her he didn't understand the math, and together they came up with ideas about asking for help and how she could help him. The simple gesture of asking him if he would like a juice box was compassionate, created a trusting relationship, and helped the student find other ways to get help. Strachota (1996) calls this "allying with children" (p. 30).

This is the part where you wonder how the student in the story above could possibly be motivated to do math or behave appropriately with the thought of extra teacher time and a juice box after throwing a fit. You might think the child should have been punished, ignored, or given a logical consequence (like having to stay after school to get math done) so he wouldn't ever want to throw a fit again. As you wonder about ideas like this, reflect on what you believe about the nature of children in general. "We need to be on the lookout for profoundly negative theories about the motives and capabilities of children, which frequently animate discussions about classroom management" (Kohn, 1996, p. 2). Is the child just inherently bad? Was he trying to get something? Probably not. Children inherently want to do well, to be kind to others, and to be generous. When they are not, they may be unaware of the effects of their actions or unable to act otherwise (Kohn). Remember that self-efficacy and self-worth are important constructs in motivation. Instead of teaching the child that he is bad or that you don't care whether or not he understands math, why not give him time to calm down, let him know you have had a similar experience and that throwing a fit isn't a good way to solve problems, and work together with him to find a solution? Children want to do a good job in school both academically and socially. We need to help them do so by listening rather than telling, understanding rather than judging, and being a part of the solution rather than denying there is an underlying problem. Isn't that how the best relationships are created?

Relationships cannot be created when there is fear. "The simple truth is that most classrooms today are managed by one thing and one thing only: fear. The teacher is afraid: afraid of looking bad, of not being liked, of not being listened to, of losing control. The students are even more afraid: afraid of being scolded and humiliated, of looking foolish in front of peers, of getting bad grades, of facing their parents' wrath" (Esquith, 2007, p. 5). Although fear may get children to do what you want, it will not help them learn, help you learn, or get them to do what they need to do when you're not there. If we form relationships so children can be good human beings and not just good students, we must help them understand productive, positive relationships rather than relationships of power and fear.

Finally, it is important to form relationships with parents as well. Researchers have found that teachers who make contact with parents have highly motivated students, especially if those parents are invited into the school as volunteers (Dolezal, Mohan Welsh, Pressley, & Vincent, 2003). Just as you need to build relationships with students, you also need to let their parents know that they are important in your classroom. This means having an open-door policy at all times, asking parents to volunteer whenever they can, and regularly providing notes, newsletters, e-mails, and so on, about what you are doing in class. A cooperating teacher of mine once told me it was important to stop and talk to parents wherever you are and wonder how they are doing. I agree.

LETTER FROM A MASTER TEACHER 3.2

Building Relationships With Students

Ours is the most important profession in the world, because from the fruits of our labor come all other professions. Moreover, we influence how people relate to others and solve problems. We have the capacity to evince great changes in people. We can help create an avid love of learning, an intense fear of failure, or absolute apathy.

Motivating students is possible only if we understand them and truly care about them as fellow human beings. In other words, we must start by building relationships with them. How? Treat each student as if he or she is your favorite. Greet your students every day with a welcoming smile, whether you feel like it or not. Laugh with them. Give them choices. Respect them and show and mean it. Tell them you're proud of them when they show progress, creativity, tenacity, and empathy for others. Help them when they feel discouraged. Listen to them. Play with them. Let them explore. Be patient with them. Be brave enough to gently guide them into finding their own answers to their questions. Know when to hold back. Let them ask, "Why are we doing this?" Help them see purpose in all they do. Tell them you're thankful for them. Promise them you will always do your best for them. Tell them you expect the same. Remember they are strong but unbelievably fragile. Promise them a safe environment free of threat or ridicule. Let them experience the sheer joy of learning. Ask for their ideas. Tell them you expect to learn from them as well. Ask them how you can help. Tell them about yourself. Ask them about their likes, dislikes, dreams, and fears. Never lie to them because once they find out, they'll never fully trust you again. Trust them. Let the classroom be their home away from home. Consider what makes a home, and include all of those elements still practical for a classroom that you possibly can for the children who so openly trust and depend on you to guide them in their pursuit of knowledge. Create a room rich with color, music, plants, good smells, and inspirational quotations. Provide comfortable places to sit and read, think, reflect, and collaborate with their peers. Commemorate your journey with them, and memorialize even the small moments with pictures.

I wish you much happiness as you continue on this profound journey with the hundreds of children whose lives you'll touch. Use your heart in making decisions that will affect them, and hold what's best for your students above all else. May you hold on tight when challenges arise, and may you touch the heart of every child you meet in some small way. The world needs you. Thank you for making education your vocation.

—Mary K. Trehearn
Ninth-Grade English Teacher

Tasks and Topics

For material related to this concept, go to Clip 3.3 on the Web-based Student Study Site.

The tasks we ask students to do and the topics we ask them to learn about influence motivation. "It is not difficult to see how learning flourishes where there is interest, confidence, and understanding and how it withers under boredom, trepidation, and confusion" (Smith, 1998, p. 85). Unfortunately, motivation usually rests with the child who doesn't do what he or she is asked and never with what he or she has been asked to do (Kohn, 1996). To help motivate students, then, we need to be mindful of the tasks and topics we ask them to do. I once observed a student teacher who had first-graders sit on the floor for more than 45 minutes while she read and reread an inappropriately difficult book. Supposedly learning vocabulary, many of them started to get restless, others started playing with materials around them, and several sat patiently with glazed looks in their eyes. As things started to get out of control, instead of considering the task, the teacher gave out tokens (to spend at a class store) to those who were sitting still "listening." All the children shaped right up in a matter of seconds but quickly resorted to keeping their minds and bodies occupied after a while. What did these children learn that day? Some learned they are unworthy of tokens because their way of keeping their minds and bodies active isn't as appropriate as staring into space quietly. Some learned that being a good person is about mindlessly doing whatever the teacher says. None learned that reading is exciting and fun or that vocabulary comes from many different places and can help tell stories. My student teacher learned the importance of planning meaningful tasks rather than planning how to control children. I learned that tasks, topics, and their level of difficulty matter.

As teachers, we should work to motivate children by manipulating the tasks and not the children themselves. "It is a great irony that in any discussion of motivation, the one factor that is almost universally overlooked is student interest" (Clark, 1997, p. 41). Manipulating tasks and topics means taking an objective and fleshing out all of the possible topics that will help students meet the objective, creating opportunities for choice in the classroom, and scaffolding content so it connects to students' prior experiences. Wiggins and McTighe (2005) agree, saying, "Motivation is increased when the work is of obvious value, has intrinsic interest, and provides transfer" (p. 206).

When students are interested in the topics they are studying, they have fun in the classroom.

In this day and age of standards and teaching so that every child is on the same page at the same time, it may seem difficult to manipulate tasks to keep students interested and motivated. Many argue that teachers who teach the same thing as their counterparts in other schools help students who transfer schools regularly. That solution, however, seems only to mask a bigger problem and at the same time prevents all students from being interested and engaged in learning. No matter how hard we try to keep students the same, they will always be unique, and I am glad about that. Our classrooms should support rather than squelch that uniqueness. How can we use objectives to help us construct meaningful tasks and topics?

First, we need broad rather than narrow objectives. For example, if our goal is to help all students learn about life cycles, many different tasks and topics can help them, but if our goal is to help all students learn about the life cycles of mealworms, we cannot integrate as many interests. Does it matter if students learn about life cycles of frogs, insects, cats, or humans? Is the conversation in a classroom not richer if many life cycles are studied and compared? Smith (1998) tells us, "Learning is most effective when we voluntarily participate in an interesting activity" (p. 84). If our objectives are broad, students will be able to find something that interests them and everyone will be exposed to the objective. It is your job as a teacher to do the "behind the scenes" work of determining all the different topics that might fit under an objective, which ones would work best for students, and how they fit together. In my district, we had to teach life cycles, and if I had used the textbook, students would only have learned about life cycles through insects. One year, however, a couple of my students were extremely interested in frogs. So I ordered some frog eggs to go along with our life cycle unit on insects. Were the children motivated? Yes. Did they have a broader understanding of life cycles? Yes. Did they have behavior issues? No.

Second, students need to have choices within the broad objective, in how they learn the objective, and in how they demonstrate what they know about the objective. Choice is a huge motivator as well as a deterrent for inappropriate behaviors. Cordova and Lepper (1996) found that choice produced dramatic increases in students' depth of engagement in learning, how much they learned, and perceived levels of competence. A study by Powell and Nelson (1997) indicates that choice may help teachers manage behavior in general education classrooms and reduce undesirable behavior. Jolivette, Wehby, Canale, and Massey (2001) found that opportunities to make choices can positively influence behavior of students with emotional and behavioral disorders.

Third, students need content that builds off of their prior experiences. My sister, a molecular biologist, once had me read a paper that she wrote. I was motivated to read it because I have a great relationship with her and wanted to provide some good feedback. I am somewhat efficacious about biology, although not at that level. It was a meaningful task; I had enough water, and so on. In other words, my motivation was influenced positively in many ways. I started to read the paper but then found myself thinking about something else—not because it was boring or repetitive but because I couldn't understand it. I didn't have the language to read it. In fact, I found myself looking for a sentence that I *could* read. Finally, after a little while of struggling, I found myself unmotivated to continue. With every motivational construct in place but prior experience with the topic, I became unmotivated. How often do we do this to children? We give them a topic that they have no experience with and expect them to stick with it until they get it. It would not have mattered if someone had given me a reward for reading the paper; nor would it have mattered if I was kept in for recess. I still wouldn't have been motivated to read the paper. Understanding that paper would have taken me forever, even with a biology dictionary. We must start our tasks and topics where students have experience, or keeping them motivated will prove very difficult.

Content can be too easy at times as well. Students may avoid classroom activities if they see no reason for them. They may find little challenge, stimulation, satisfaction, or meaning in the work, so they just do the minimum to get by (Seifert, 2004). If a student knows how to do something or knows a topic well, it may be difficult to keep him or her motivated. I often feel unmotivated to play trains with my sons. I love them, but choo-chooing for hours gets really old. It's OK if I get to help build the track because figuring out how to make tunnels and bridges is a puzzle that keeps my mind engaged. We need to do the same in classrooms. Students must have opportunities to stretch their brains.

Finally, we should use many kinds of materials to motivate students in the classroom (Dolezal, Mohan Welsh, Pressley, & Vincent, 2003). Technology, games, manipulatives, and music all help motivate students. Teachers often save these materials as a way to motivate students to do not-so-engaging things. For example, a teacher might say that after students get their worksheets done, they can have 10 minutes to work on the computers. Why not have them use the computers to learn the task on the worksheet? Traci, a master teacher I know, studied special-needs students and technology. She had them do graphs on paper and then showed them how to do it on the computer. Motivated because of the tool they were using, the students loved it and continued to make graphs on the computer all the time. Technology, games, manipulatives, music, and many other tools are good for motivation because they help children understand in engaging ways.

Demotivational Influences

Just as teachers need to be aware of influences that positively affect motivation, they also need to be aware of influences that negatively affect motivation. Almost all of the influences listed above have demotivational opposites. For example, fear, mindless tasks, performance goals, and low self-efficacy all influence motivation negatively. These influences hinder rather than help students in classrooms.

Why think about demotivators? Interestingly, many demotivators look like motivators if framed in different ways. For example, you may believe that fear is a motivator because it gets students to do what you want. This is similar to performance goals. Many teachers believe that comparing children or schools is motivational because it makes tasks competitive. I cannot argue with these statements, but I can argue that many practices used to motivate students and people in general only work for a brief period, require direct supervision, and do not promote learning. In other words, demotivators shape behaviors but not long-term dispositions. Let's look at one example more closely: rewards.

Rewards are demotivators (Jensen, 2005; Kohn, 1993). Although rewards have traditionally been touted as motivators, in reality they merely get children to comply or motivate them to get more rewards. Because the brain requires novelty, students given rewards will need and want an increasingly higher level of reward each time (Jensen). Children who frequently get rewards tend to be less generous than their peers (Fabes, Fultz, Eisenberg, May-Plumlee, & Christopher, 1989; Grusec, 1991), don't perform as well as their peers, tend to lose interest in tasks, and often choose the easiest possible tasks (Kohn). Internally motivated students develop increased persistence, engagement, and academic achievement (Pintrich & Schunk, 2002).

Teachers use rewards (i.e., stars, stickers, extra time at recess, the opportunity to do a special project) for many reasons, and I hope you will consider why you would use them. I believe that many teachers use rewards because they fear the unknown. They wonder how they would get children to do what they want without rewards. Hopefully this chapter has given you some ideas about how to motivate children without using rewards and in ways that promote learning dispositions. Some teachers have only experienced motivation through rewards, which are commonplace in schools everywhere. I am asking you to try something new and to try again if at first it doesn't work exactly as planned. It will be worth it. Other teachers believe that there is no harm in using rewards. If you are one of them, I encourage you to gather some research on rewards and see for yourself.

As you probably guess, I didn't give rewards when I taught elementary school. I did, however, celebrate both individual and class accomplishments. What's the difference? Celebrations are not meant to be coercive. I didn't tell the students that we would have a pizza party if they all read a certain number of books. They read books because they got to choose the books they were interested in reading, to make cool projects to go with their books, and to share their books with friends. I didn't announce some children's names over the intercom because they were "good" in my eyes. I did, however, eat lunch with my students when *we* felt like that was a good thing to do; celebrate at the end of a unit all that we had learned by inviting parents to come in and see our projects, our play, or our demonstrations; and write notes home about things we did well that week. Everyone got a note because everyone deserved one.

At the beginning of this chapter, I told you my son wasn't motivated to set the table. You may have screamed into the book (like I often do to the television) that if I gave him money or a treat, he would set the table. I could probably even "help" him get rid of that snotty voice by threatening to take the treat away. But what would he learn, and how long would it last? Instead, I will help him understand the importance of the task, create opportunities for him to set the table creatively (yikes!), and sometimes let him do other tasks than setting the table. Perhaps when he is a bit older he will understand that families need each other and that we need him. As an adult, he will have a job that pays him to do things, but I hope he feels it is so important and he is so vital that he would do it for free. I'll let you know how it goes.

So . . . What?

Motivation is key to classroom success for you and your students. The good news is that you can influence motivation in several ways:

The brain likes novelty, physical activity, nutrition and water, time to reflect, and low levels of stress. Treat students as you would like them to treat you.

Self-efficacy and self-worth are important influences of motivation. Help students feel efficacious by providing appropriate tasks and by scaffolding material at their ZPD level.

If students attribute their success or failure to ability, they won't be very motivated. Help them by providing effortful strategies rather than telling them to try harder. Provide opportunities for them to set up mastery goals rather than performance goals.

Your relationship with students needs to be genuine and not coercive. We don't want relationships that create pleasers or brown-nosers. We want students to know they are cared for and that they matter.

The tasks and topics that you design matter with regard to motivation. Connect them to students' prior knowledge, interests, and competency levels.

Don't be fooled. Rewards are demotivators. If you use them, you will end up with children who need more rewards rather than have the dispositions to keep learning.

Get Ready For . . .

The first three chapters of this book were all about beliefs. What do you believe about students' needs, the environment where students go to school, and teachers' role in helping students do well in school and in life? If you believe that all children need autonomy, belonging, and competency; that the environment in classrooms should foster democracy and community; and that a teacher can influence motivation in positive ways, you need to design a classroom management plan with structures that will help you create that place. Many teachers tell me, "I just can't [blank]," and I tell them they can, but they just don't have the necessary structures. They often try to give students autonomy without such structures as class meetings, belonging without cooperative learning, and competency without workshops. They often try to eliminate rewards without replacing them with structures. When teachers don't have structures that support their beliefs, they end up not believing any longer. The next three chapters, all about structures, will help you plan a classroom that is good for students and for you.

Activities to Try

 I purposefully did not define motivation in this chapter. Think about past experiences when you were motivated and not motivated in relation to the chapter and write a definition of motivation.

These first three chapters are full of ideas that will help you determine how you will plan for classroom management. Take some time before moving to the next section to make connections among all of the ideas. In a sense, the concepts presented depend on each other. Can teachers help students have autonomy, belonging, and competency without democracy? How about motivation?

If you were given the assignment of teaching fifth-grade students a unit on machines (or any other topic), how would you motivate them? How would you begin? How would you incorporate the ideas from this chapter?

Make a collection! Collect some exercises you can do in the classroom to get students moving and learning.

Conduct action research! Try this on yourself. Pick something you really want but are unmotivated to do (like cleaning the kitchen, exercising, or losing weight). Give yourself a reward every time you do it. Keep a log of what happens throughout the research.

Student Study Site

The companion Web site for *Elementary Classroom Management* can be found at www.sagepub.com/kwilliamsstudy.

Visit the Web-based student study site to enhance your understanding of the chapter content. The study materials include video clips, practice tests, flashcards, suggested readings, and Web resources.

Structures and Tools for Classroom Management

Classroom management is all about perspective. In a sense, the last three chapters advised putting on different lenses to "see" classroom management from different perspectives. In Chapter 1, you looked through a filtered lens to see children's needs. In Chapter 2, the lens was shaped so you could think about the classroom environment. In Chapter 3, the lens focused inward so you could see how you influence student motivation. And now, combining all three lenses for a clear view from multiple perspectives, we can begin to look at strategies, structures, and tools used in classroom management. Without these three lenses or perspectives, the structures and tools you use in your classroom might look good but still be missing pieces of the picture.

As promised, the next three chapters are full of ways to help individuals and whole groups learn and be happy at school. These structures and tools provide children with multiple opportunities to develop autonomy, belonging, competency, and motivation in democratic ways. Although they may be different from what you are used to as a student, that's OK. Compare and contrast them to what you have experienced as you begin to design a draft of your beliefs about classroom management.

Chapter 4 is about a structure called cooperative workshops, which are easy to plan and provide multiple opportunities for different types of learners to learn in the same room. A lesson plan form is included, as are many ideas about how to design and implement cooperative workshops.

Chapter 5 is about thinking routines, which will help you develop young thinkers. Sometimes we forget that classroom management needs to enhance learning, not just force children to comply.

Chapter 6 is about working with whole groups to create communities of learners. Students learn much more effectively if those around them are supportive and fun. The structures and tools in this chapter will help you bring students together into a community and give each child a voice within a large group of students.

Enjoy these chapters as you begin to look through new lenses at what classrooms can and should be. Play with the ideas here, and try to wonder and dream. In your classroom, wonderful things can happen when children can safely be themselves and when everyone can learn.

CHAPTER 4

Pedagogical Structures for Managing Learning

W hen I was a third grader, my class went to a district-wide assembly that included a magician who, during his act, asked for a brave young lady to be his assistant. To my horror, my class nominated me by waving and pointing wildly, and I was chosen. I reluctantly went on stage where my arm was put in a contraption that minutes earlier had sliced a potato in half. Rest assured, when the magician pointed his magic wand at the contraption and the blade fell, my arm came out whole. After the assembly, my classmates asked me how the magician had done it, knowing that it wasn't really magic. I did not know the answer to their question, and to this day I do not know why my arm wasn't sliced in two.

Classroom management isn't magic either, no matter how magical a classroom where the children and teacher work merrily without distractions may seem. Since we know it isn't magic, we may assume that the children in such classrooms are from good homes, yet scores of teachers have created classrooms where even the "hardest" children excel (Clark, 2004; Collins, 1992; Esquith, 2007; Littky, 2004;). Classroom management is not magic for any kind of student. Just as the magician I encountered as a third grader used a special structure and tool in his act, great teachers use structures, strategies, and tools (pedagogies) to make their classrooms look like magic.

If only I could wave a magic wand from my computer at you and make classroom management magically take place. I wish I could just give you tricks to implement in your classroom that would help all children succeed every year, but it doesn't work that way.

Jesse Keifer

Classroom management is not about magic but purposeful pedagogy.

I have no tricks up my sleeve; however, I do have some structures that will amaze you. How brave are you?

I am talking about **pedagogical structures**. "The word pedagogy stems from the Greek word paideutike, meaning 'the art of teaching the young'" (Senge, Cambron-McCabe, Lucas, Smith, & Dutton, 2000, p. 207). Pedagogy is the "how" of teaching. In other words, pedagogical structures are like skeletons holding up the meat of the lessons. You may choose among unlimited numbers of pedagogical structures as you begin thinking about lessons and classrooms. The choices you make with regard to how you teach are vital to learning and classroom management. Indeed, you must make purposeful and artful pedagogical choices.

Some may wonder why pedagogy is in a classroom management book. Doesn't pedagogy belong in a methods text? Certainly, some pedagogies work well in specific subjects. General structures, however, help children learn any subject and can simultaneously help you manage your classroom. We often think of management and facilitating learning as two different entities, but some structures bring the two together.

"Experts" often promote autonomy, belonging, competency, democracy, and motivation but do not show teachers how to move toward them. If we want to create classrooms that meet students' needs, where democratic communities are formed, and where motivation is positively influenced, we need pedagogies that support those things. We can't expect them to magically appear. We must plan purposefully (with a conscious effort to use structures and strategies that promote the ideas we believe in) and artfully (with creativity and novelty in mind).

By the end of this chapter, I hope you have:

- An understanding of how pedagogical structures influence classroom management

- Pedagogical structures, strategies, and tools that promote autonomy, belonging, competency, democratic communities, and motivation

- An understanding of pitfalls to avoid that may cause you to go back to teaching as telling
- Reflection tools that will help you know what to do next

Connections Between Pedagogy and Management: If, Then

If you believe that students' needs, democratic communities, and motivation are important in creating well-managed classrooms, then the structures you use to set the stage of learning must align with those things. For example, you cannot expect to have autonomous students if you tell them what to do and give them the right answers. You cannot expect to motivate students with an everyday routine of checking homework, giving an assignment, and watching them do problems. If you believe that students need the concepts we talked about in the first three chapters, your actions must speak louder than your words. The pedagogy you use, the tasks you create, and the expectations in your classroom must promote those concepts.

If students show signs of poor motivation, if they misbehave, or if they are zombies merely existing in your classroom, then before you do anything else, look at the pedagogy, the materials, and their appropriateness for struggling students (Center, Deitz, & Kaufman, 1982; Kohn, 1996). Certainly, in many cases, looking at pedagogical structures in your classroom will not be the last thing you do, but it should be the first. Looking at your pedagogy closely does not mean working to make it more fun. It means finding ways to involve the students more and help them connect with the material you are studying.

If you use structures, strategies, and tools that help students move toward the concepts in the first three chapters, then you will not need to have external classroom management programs in place. Sometimes teachers see management and learning content as two different things. In these teachers' classrooms, there is learning time, and then there is management time, during which students are either reprimanded or taught a social skill separately from the rest of the curriculum. If you use pedagogical structures that promote engaging learning and democratic communities, however, you will be teaching social skills right alongside academic goals. And, if you do need some management time, students will be able to use the pedagogical structures to help them solve problems. I am not suggesting that teachers combine management programs in the middle of their lessons. Helping a child fill out a behavior sheet in the middle of reading would be unproductive. I am, however, implying that teachers should teach social skills within academic lessons. Teaching children how to solve problems should be a social *and* an academic endeavor. McCloud (2005) says we should help children be "problem solvers instead of problem producers" (p. 46), but I say we need children to be problem producers *and* problem solvers, for without problems we cannot be problem solvers. Of course, we don't want children causing problems just to be naughty, but we do want them to feel comfortable enough to be themselves, take risks, and make mistakes academically or socially so we can work together as a community to learn to solve problems. "The strategic use, rather than the mere possession of knowledge, improves learning. Teaching students strategies not only improves their learning but also empowers them psychologically by increasing self-efficacy" (Bruning, Schraw, & Ronning, 1999, p. 102).

If you believe that pedagogical structures can be a piece of a successful classroom management plan, then you must think of the children's needs before your own and teach in a learner-centered manner that puts children first. Senge, Cambron-McCabe, Lucas, Smith, and Dutton (2000) suggest we create classrooms that facilitate "learner-centered learning rather than teacher-centered learning; variety, no homogeneity, understanding a world of interdependency and change rather than memorizing facts and striving for right answers" (p. 55). I know this is a tall order. At first it may be easier to do what is more familiar, but keep working toward using pedagogical structures that help children become lifelong learners rather than test takers. In the long run, they will be a lot happier, and so will you.

Let's look at some pedagogical structures that will help you create a classroom full of autonomy, belonging, competency, democracy, and motivation. In this chapter, we will look at one structure in particular, but there are more in the next couple of chapters as well. The structures in this book have worked for me over the years. I have not necessarily taken each of them as they came to me. I have taken the pieces that I find work best for my students and me, and I hope you will do the same. Remember to reflect on whether or not your students are getting what they need to be socially and academically successful. Remember, too, that the structures you create are meant to help you be "behind the scenes" rather than "on stage." If you often find yourself out in front, consider reexamining your structures.

When students work together, actively engaged in meaningful tasks, there aren't many management issues.

Cooperative Workshops

Cooperative workshops have evolved from two different, highly researched pedagogies, including cooperative learning (Johnson & Johnson, 1987) and High/Scope's workshops (Hohmann & Weikart, 1995). Separately, each is a great pedagogical structure for all kinds of children. I have put them together into one pedagogical structure because I like the tools that Johnson and Johnson's cooperative learning provides for problem solving, *individual account-ability*, and **interdependence**, and I like the flexibility of group size, the ability to **differen-tiate**, and the focus on projects that the structure of High/Scope's workshop provides. Combining them seems to create a pedagogical structure that works for any subject at any grade level. Together they provide a great way to incorporate all of the tools we talked about in the first three chapters that promote autonomy, belonging, competency, democracy, and motivation. Finally, combining them creates a pedagogical structure that emphasizes social and academic goals rather than goals to be taught separately.

LETTER FROM A MASTER TEACHER 4.1

Using Cooperative Workshops

I did not know a lot about cooperative workshops when I began using them. I knew I was teaching special education and had a wide variety of abilities, interests, and needs all in one classroom. Nowadays, with inclusion being the norm, almost every classroom has those same characteristics. What better way to make connections with each and every child than to use cooperative workshops!

I first began using cooperative workshops in the area of writing. Every student had the opportunity to use process writing or creative writing for his or her own purpose. I often started our writing workshop with a mini lesson, demonstrating or modeling the practice of capitalization, spacing, and much more. But when "writing time" began, my students were often spread out throughout the room and each doing their "own thing." As I facilitated the workshop, I saw everything from coloring a picture and labeling it with one word to writing a letter to a grandparent. The autonomy, competency, and motivation that this structure instilled led to learning on my part as well as the students'. Students who are able to choose tasks and who are given the time necessary for discovery, problem solving, and sharing will be motivated to learn and share their discoveries with others. When this happens, classroom management decisions are a part of the community. And when that happens, you find yourself able to confer with, question, and guide students to the learning they desire and need.

When I began teaching in a regular second-grade classroom, I used cooperative workshops for both reading and writing. Students were excited by the idea that they could read self-selected books for pleasure, for practice, for research, and for knowledge. I remember brainstorming as a class a list

(Continued)

(Continued)

what our workshops "looked like." These charts gave the students something to refer to as they used an hour of time independently. It also aided me in classroom management. The students knew what was expected of them, what they could do, and what needed to be accomplished by the end of the workshop. I was free to teach mini lessons, listen to students read, have conferences about self-selected reading, and assess student progress through observations and testing.

As I structure my day, my classroom, my lessons, and my materials, I constantly keep in mind these questions: What is my purpose? Why am I doing this? Where does this fit in with the big picture? How will I know if the students are learning? When can my students use this information? And then I let those answers and others drive my further planning for instruction. There's really nothing easy about it, but it sure can be rewarding!

—Cheryl Larmore
Second-Grade Teacher

How could one pedagogical structure be effective in so many different areas? The magic here is that this kind of structure provides stability and routine while simultaneously enabling the teacher and students to go in a worthwhile direction both as a whole class and as individuals. Cooperative workshops have some very sturdy and strong components, without which the structure of the lesson would collapse, just as a body without a skeleton would. The pieces comprising the strong, sturdy skeleton of a cooperative workshop include social and academic goals, group size, tasks, individual accountability, positive interdependence, and sharing. You must have each of these pieces to ensure that you are creating a cooperative workshop. In addition, the "meat" around the skeleton must be flexible to meet students', curricular, and teachers' needs. The structure is there, but how you chose to use it depends on your needs. Let's start using the parts of the skeleton to make some choices. As you read the section below, use the lesson plan form in Table 4.1 to help you keep track of and understand all of the choices you need to make for an effective cooperative workshop. Although you may not use it for every lesson, using this kind of form at the beginning will help you make sure you are including all of the parts. As you become more experienced with cooperative workshops, you will begin to think about these choices automatically.

Choice 1: Social and Academic Goals

One of the first choices you will need to make when using cooperative workshops has to do with your goals. Take careful note of the two separate yet intertwined types of goals in this section: social and academic. At times it is easy to get wrapped up in the students' academic progress and forget that you need to teach social goals as well (see Table 4.2 for an example of a lesson plan that incorporates both types of goals). Children don't just automatically know how to work in groups and with each other. They don't automatically know how to plan and solve problems. Each workshop must help children learn how to work with others in their community. You're probably thinking, "I don't have time to teach social goals!" but you do

TABLE 4.1   Cooperative Workshop Lesson Plan Form

Date	Subject		Objective(s)	
What are my goals?				
Academic			Social	
How will I set up the lesson?				
Problem(s)	Action(s)	Sharing	Materials	
How will I set up groups?				
	Small Groups	Stations	Individuals	
Size of group?				
Movement?				
How will I group the students?				
Plans for positive interdependence				
Plans for individual accountability				
Questions I might ask:				

when you combine them with your academic goals and incorporate them into your everyday activities. Before you choose some academic and social goals, think about the following.

Academic goals need to be scaffolded. You must begin with something that the students understand and keep connecting goals with each other from there. For example, if your curriculum says that an objective is to learn addition of two-digit numbers, ask yourself:

- What experiences would someone learning to add two-digit numbers need?
- What would be a logical order of events for those experiences?
- What do my students already know about two-digit addition?

Social goals need to be scaffolded as well. For example, what would students need to know and have experienced to be able to work in a group? If your students have not worked in groups very much, they may need to start with the simple goal of staying together. Social goals should be scaffolded according to what you and your students need in the classroom.

Think back to Chapters 1, 2, and 3. Why is it important to scaffold experiences for students? If they have nothing understandable with which to connect new content, will they feel competent? Will they be motivated? Will their brains connect the information? This applies to social and academic goals. Learning to work in a group or to add two-digit numbers isn't a one-step process. Learning must come in layers (Senge, Cambron-McCabe, Lucas, Smith, & Dutton, 2000), and goals must reflect this notion.

For material related to this concept, go to Clip 4.1 on the Web-based Student Study Site.

Have mastery goals rather than performance goals. You read about the difference in Chapter 3, but it is important to reiterate that goals should be about learning and not about meeting a certain percentage or number. Assessment is not absent, however, but needs to be about the learning, and students should be involved in deciding if they "get it" or not. When you talk about what you will be studying, do not mention grades or the number correct. For example, a performance goal might be for everyone to get 90% or better on the spelling test. A mastery goal might be for everyone to use spelling words in writing. What's the difference? Why does it matter?

Social goals should be stated as mastery goals as well. Many times teachers give stars or other tokens for "good" behavior, and then students are good to get tokens (a performance goal). A mastery goal would be working to make a classroom a good place. How can you tell the difference between a mastery goal and a performance goal? It's really easy. All you have to do is ask yourself and your students what they need to know forever and what they want and need to improve—mastery goals. Your school district will certainly have a great deal of input about the goals and objectives you choose for your students; however, it is up to you to help students value their lessons and create ways to learn more. Simply changing the emphasis and the wording you use makes a powerful difference, as does asking students to work together to meet those goals.

Choice 2: Tasks

After setting your goals based on your curriculum objectives and standards and your students' needs, you must choose tasks that will help the students move toward meeting them.

TABLE 4.2   Lesson Plan With Goals

Here is an example of social and academic goals for money.

Date 1/23/09	Subject Money	Objective(s) Students will be able to make different amounts with coins.
What are my goals?		
Academic 1. I want them to be able to see that multiple coins make the same amount. 2. I want them to know coins up to a quarter.		Social 1. I want them to have good sportsmanship during a game. 2. I want them to help without giving answers.

How will I set up the lesson?

Problem(s)	Action(s)	Sharing	Materials

How will I set up groups?

	Small Groups	Stations	Individuals
Size of group?			
Movement?			
How will I group the students?			
Plans for positive interdependence			
Plans for individual accountability			

Questions I might ask:

As you read in Chapter 3, the tasks you choose will influence learning and classroom management, and thus they matter, as does the order in which they are experienced. Sometimes we think the hard work of teaching is standing up in front of the students each day or checking papers after class, but I believe it is the thinking and collecting you must do to come up with tasks that help students find learning exciting and worthwhile. Assigning meaningful, engaging tasks with a good level of difficulty will make the work in the classroom much easier.

Choose tasks that are worthy. What is a worthy task? Although they come in many shapes and sizes, worthy tasks have three distinct characteristics. First, they are physical as well as mentally engaging. "Human cognitive development involves just as much 'body knowledge' as it does 'mind knowledge.' Learning is inseparable from action" (Senge, Cambron-McCabe, Lucas, Smith, & Dutton, 2000, p. 37). Students need to be actively involved in the tasks you choose. If the goal is to learn about different units of measurement, the task should actually involve students measuring. If the goal is to learn about contractions, students should read books containing contractions that they can actively find and share with others. If the goal is to learn about erosion, students should go outside to look for signs of it. Students should have access to materials that they can manipulate in all subjects. How can you learn about teaspoons if you don't have a teaspoon to fill and refill? How can you learn to read without reading exciting books?

Students use paper mittens as they begin to learn to measure. What might the next lesson be?

The second characteristic of worthy tasks is that they often develop out of problems. Working on a problem is much more engaging than learning something for a test. The professor who taught me classroom management, Dr. Egbert, once gave us a worksheet full of mathematics problems, which we did and turned in. Then he gave us a problem where we needed to go on a trip in a car. We got to choose where we wanted to go and which car we wanted to use. We had to figure out the mileage and the amount of money we would spend. Some of us didn't know how to figure out gas mileage, so we stopped in the middle of the problem to discuss it. We talked about the best ways to calculate gas mileage and then went on with the problem. The funny thing is, after we were finished, we figured out that we had used some of the same mathematics skills in the trip problem as we had used on the worksheet. The difference was we were much more motivated to do the trip problem than the worksheet, and we learned a lot about things besides mathematics, such as problem-solving skills, how to make decisions together, and how to budget for a road trip.

Solving problems can take several days or a few minutes. For example, the road trip problem could have taken several days to complete, especially if students needed to stop and figure out different mathematical solutions. Some problems, however, can be accomplished in one class period—for example, figuring out how many ways you can make 25 cents or coming up with an alternate ending to a story. Almost any objective or goal can be turned into a problem, and the benefits are great. If we meet goals by learning individual skills on worksheets or by listening to the teacher talk and answer questions, we may learn the skill. If we meet goals by solving problems, however, we may also learn problem-solving and social skills. Problems provide active mental and physical learning opportunities.

The third characteristic of worthy tasks is that they provide opportunities for differentiation. This means a task may have more than one right answer or way to get the answer. Tasks need to help students connect with what they already understand and rethink and revise those understandings. If students make connections and think about their answers, they are learning and moving toward the goals. I had my second graders look at drops of pond water through microscopes. The goal was to observe using tools. They drew what they observed, and we talked about what might be in the water. Some students, too young developmentally to understand that one-celled animals were moving around in the water, often pointed them out as rocks. You might say that this was wrong and they didn't meet the goal, but looking through microscopes provided many opportunities to differentiate instruction. Everyone worked toward meeting the same goal, yet the task was open-ended enough to give each student what he or she needed. I could pose the same problem for students of any age because of the endless possibilities for learning. A 4-year-old may learn how to use a microscope; a 12-year-old may learn that some animals in water are smaller than the eye can see; a 35-year-old may learn that there are many kinds of one-celled animals in different kinds of water; but everyone would experience and learn the skill of observing using tools. The microscope example may seem extreme, but any goal can fit a variety of needs. For example, a reading goal might be learning to draw conclusions. Having students read and draw conclusions about a variety of books at a variety of levels would help them meet the same goal at appropriate levels for different learners. In math, a goal may be learning to divide. By providing choices of problems to do or different tools to solve the problems, you can accommodate all children for success.

The task must provide experiences as well as reflection. To feel and be competent, students must be able to connect ideas with experiences. Ideas don't "stick" without experiences. We can certainly memorize anything for a short period; however, if our aim is long-lasting competency, students must reflect about their experiences. Learning doesn't take place in the absence of either experiences or reflection. For example, if I plan a task for social studies where students use the Internet to interview children from other countries about their customs and traditions but we don't have a conversation about what they found out, the experience won't mean as much. The opposite is true as well. If I plan a task where students define customs and traditions but do not have a chance to engage with others, they won't have the experience to come up with a meaningful definition. There are many ways to include reflection in a lesson. Sharing products, writing in journals, talking to a neighbor about findings, or presenting to the class all help children reflect on their experiences and draw conclusions from what they learned. You must plan for both experiences and reflection as you design worthy tasks.

The order of instruction makes a difference. As you begin to gather and plan worthy tasks, keep in mind the following order: *problem, actions, sharing.* Each lesson should have these components. Give students a problem that will help them move toward the goal of the lesson, have them actively use materials to solve the problem, and then ask them to share their solutions. All three parts are vital to a worthy task, and the order is as important as the components. Let's look at an example in the subject of writing. A goal in writing might be to put punctuation at the ends of sentences. This kind of goal may require many tasks, and as teachers we would need to determine what our students know about end punctuation. Indeed, most classrooms would probably contain a wide range of understandings. Let's focus on a task that would help us determine what the students know about punctuation.

- *Problem:* "Each of us has a few pieces of writing that we've been working on lately during writer's workshop, and we want to publish one of them. The problem is, we can't publish a piece of writing for others to read if there is no punctuation in the writing. We need to make sure that readers know when to stop when they are reading your sentences. We will be editors."

- *Action:* Put students into groups of two and have them add punctuation where they think it should go. Then have the editor read the writer's work out loud and see if it makes sense. Have students go back and make changes as needed.

- *Sharing:* Ask students to share their pieces of writing. Then ask questions, and have students ask questions, about the placement of punctuation and how they determined where to place it.

Notice, in that example, the problem was posed, the students worked on the actions, and then the teacher helped them make sense of the actions through questions. What would have happened if the order had been reversed and the teacher told the students how to put punctuation in and then had them work on pieces of writing? Some students probably would have been able to edit their pieces; however, the teacher would have done a lot of the thinking and thus learning. You see, we want students to come up with the strategies, rules, and inventions.

If they have the opportunity to "play" with punctuation a bit before they get the "right answers," they will understand rather than memorize and construct rather than regurgitate. That doesn't mean you shouldn't help the students come to common conclusions about punctuation or any other goal. You should, however, give them time to think about punctuation and how it works before you discuss the accepted answers.

You may wonder how students could ever just "invent" the ideas that you want them to understand. They will come to a common understanding if you assign them appropriate tasks and challenge their beliefs with good questions and opportunities to share. Some people were surprised to come into my second-grade classroom and find the students using such vocabulary words as *hypothesize* and *observe*. I think they were surprised because teaching the students such words would be difficult, but I didn't teach the vocabulary. The students experienced it. They made hypotheses, which we talked about using that word. Vocabulary is often taught first in lessons when it should be taught last or while students are learning. Wouldn't the language of a car motor make much more sense if you were removing or replacing its pieces from deep inside the car? We often take the thinking right out of lessons. We tell students how to solve math problems. We tell them how to do the science lab. We give them answers to choose from on a reading comprehension test. That's not learning. That's regurgitating. Students, with support from teachers and their classmates, need to wrestle with problems and try out their answers. The order in which you have them complete a task will make or break such wrestling.

It is important to note that teachers often leave the third step—sharing, where the construction of learning really takes place—out of their lesson plans. Sharing, the reflection and thinking part of the lesson, is important to you as the teacher because it will help you assess what students understand. Sharing helps them connect with their actions. Have you ever done something and then tried unsuccessfully to explain it? Sharing ideas helps students organize their thoughts, reflect on what they did, and make meaning. In addition, it allows you to ask questions and challenge students' thinking even further. You can't have a worthy task without sharing or conversation about what the students discovered during their actions. Sharing doesn't always have to come at the end of a task. You can walk around during tasks and ask questions that might challenge students. In teaching students punctuation, for example, I might wonder out loud if a sentence was a question or a statement. During a math lesson, I might ask students who are wrestling with a problem to prove their answer to me.

How do I come up with worthy tasks? Sources include your own experiences in the world (e.g., how did you figure out that if you are missing the half-cup, you can use two quarter-cups?), the Internet (e.g., http://www.marcopolo-education.org), other teachers, and teaching magazines (e.g., *Instructor*, *The Reading Teacher*, and anything published by the National Council of Teachers of Mathematics or the National Science Teachers Association). To keep track of worthy tasks, I suggest making a **collection**, which for me was a filing cabinet with a folder for each objective I taught (e.g., addition, space, inferences, community, houses and homes, human body, and measurement). When I found something that helped me create a task that met the needs of my students, I cut it out, wrote it on a note card, or printed it and put it in the appropriate folder. Then when I began to teach that objective, I pulled the folder out, went through it to come up with goals for lessons, put the goals in order, and began to create tasks. You may come up with a better system. The point is having worthy tasks to pull out and use as needed.

Creating a collection never ends. Look for new ideas all the time. I can't even play with my sons without coming up with a great way to use their blocks for a math lesson! If you continually search for new ideas for tasks, you will sometimes find gaps in your collections. Each year the children taught me something, and I would fill it in with another task. For example, I taught habitats for several years without doing any tasks about decomposers, producers, and consumers. Then I read an article about a teacher who made a pond in her classroom, and that year my collection included tasks on making a pond and thus the corresponding vocabulary.

You may end up in a district that requires you to use tasks from a textbook. Although not always ideal, you can certainly use those lessons. You may have to rearrange them a bit, but they will work. Try rephrasing the task as a problem and then creating opportunity for action and sharing. For example, if the students need to do a page of math problems, before you tell them how to find the answers, let them "play" with a few. Let them try to figure out the problems before you teach them the "fast" procedure. Let them share their ideas and examples. Then tell them how the book says the problems should be done. At first the students may want you to give them the answers because they may not be used to thinking that way. They will get used to it, however, and be better thinkers and problem solvers as a result. Go back to your list of things you want for students. I bet you didn't write that you want a bunch of students who can memorize for testing. Developing worthy tasks for students will help them become motivated to think and learn.

Table 4.3 will show you how to set up a lesson.

Choice 3: Group Size

Another choice? Yikes! I know this sounds like a lot of decisions to make for one little lesson. How in the world do teachers handle it? In the beginning, you will probably have to think through all of these choices with a higher level of consciousness. As you continue to use cooperative workshops, however, it will become more automatic. The third choice you need to make when planning cooperative workshops involves grouping, of which you may have three kinds: small groups, stations, and individuals. Each is unique, will work well for different tasks, and may be used in many different ways, yet all three have common characteristics as well.

Small-Group Cooperative Workshops. Small groups work well for many kinds of tasks and can be changed to meet the needs of a variety of students. They also provide many benefits beyond academic goals. According to Bruning, Schraw, and Ronning (1999), "Peer tutoring or small cooperative learning groups are an especially effective way to pool metacognitive knowledge and strategies" (p. 102). In addition, allowing students to work together has been shown to increase task-related interactions (Gillies, 2006) and improve overall academic success (Ladd & Price, 1987; Schunk, 1987; Slavin, 1995; Wentzel, 1991). Group work reinforces commitment to being in school and doing well there (Berndt, 1999; Clark, 1991).

There are many different ways to use small groups effectively in your classroom. I will give you a few examples here, but think outside the box. Among the many benefits to using small groups are a few pitfalls to avoid, but for the most part, small groups help students learn at many different levels, develop socially, and gain a sense of belonging.

TABLE 4.3   Lesson Plan With Setup

As we continue our money cooperative workshop, what do you notice about the connections between the goals and the activities?

Date 1/23/09	Subject Money	Objective(s) Students will be able to make different amounts with coins.

What are my goals?

Academic	Social
1. I want them to be able to see that multiple coins make the same amount. 2. I want them to know coins up to a quarter.	1. I want them to have good sportsmanship during a game. 2. I want them to help without giving answers.

How will I set up the lesson?

Problem(s)	Action(s)	Sharing	Materials
You will not always have the same coins in your pocket. How will you buy things?	1. Play money-trading game. 2. How many ways are there to make __ cents? 3. Assessment with me.	Hang up students' papers showing how many ways there are to make __ cents.	1. Play money 2. Dice 3. Paper 4. Crayons 5. Assessment sheets

How will I set up groups?

	Small Groups	Stations	Individuals
Size of group?			
Movement?			
How will I group the students?			
Plans for positive interdependence			
Plans for individual accountability			

Questions I might ask:

Almost any task can be used, but tasks that take longer, have multiple steps, are more diffi-cult to solve alone, or require a lot of materials are perfect for small-group work. Playing games in small groups is also effective. Let's look at a few examples. To learn about life cycles, students in my room had several critters to take care of and observe. They had mealworms, waxworms, milkweed bugs, and frog eggs. Because the task was long term, had multiple steps and mini tasks, and would require students with different strengths to be a success, it was suit-able for small-group use. Students stayed in their "bug" groups for a whole month and created calendars where they drew pictures of their insects and how they had changed. They had such different jobs in these groups as drawer, timekeeper, and caretaker (who made sure everyone was humane to their animals and each other). Everyone got to observe and share ideas.

Another good example of a task that worked well in small groups involved our genre groups. Again, students stayed in groups for several weeks while they read books from a cer-tain genre (all at different levels but in the same genre, such as myths). Each group had two weeks to read several books from the genre, or just one if it was a chapter book, and create a project to share with the class. In this case, I allowed only four people to a group, but there was often more than one group per genre. I met with each group daily and listened to the students read, asked questions, and took notes about their progress. After two weeks, they reformed groups according to their interests, and we did it again.

Small-group work doesn't always have to be within long-term projects. Small groups can work very effectively for just a class period. For example, I had students work in small groups to solve math problems all the time. I would give them a jar full of beans, and they would have to figure out how many were in the jar and then share their strategy; or I would give them paper "pizza ingredients," and they would have to make a pizza with each ingredi-ent on a different fraction of the pie.

What kinds of tasks don't work well in small groups? Small groups aren't the best solution when you want to assess each child's attempt at solving a problem or when you need the room to be quiet (for another teacher or event). For example, if you want to know how many of your students understand two-digit multiplication, putting them in groups and asking them to solve a problem together isn't going to help. In that case, you would need to use stations or individual tasks.

To tell you the truth, I had a hard time coming up with situations when small groups won't work well. They are really versatile, and students learn a great deal from their peers. Teachers often worry about using small groups, however, because when students work together, they may get out of control and become unmanageable. It is important to note here that students coming into your room won't automatically know how to work in any kind of cooperative workshop. You must teach this just as you would reading or math. Social goals are key here:

- Staying with your group
- Doing your job
- Using kind words
- Complimenting each other
- Taking turns

Those are just some examples. You will need to observe your groups and then turn whatever is keeping them from cooperating into a goal. You can teach such goals by role-playing how staying in a group looks and sounds and providing some examples of what should happen and what should not. If noise is an issue, center a class meeting on how the groups are too loud and have the students brainstorm solutions. Sometimes I took pictures of really engaged groups and then made a poster called "What a Group Looks Like." I changed the picture every so often so all my students would have a chance to be on the poster.

Choosing groups is another issue that often comes up when discussing small-group work. Again, there are many possibilities. I would suggest, for the most part, making heterogeneous groups (groups that have different levels, genders, etc.). Some people would say that students should be grouped by ability so the "high" children don't have to wait on the "low" children. In some cases, this is true, and you may want to consider it as you begin to create groups; however, also weigh the benefits of grouping the children based on interests and differing skill level. All children have strengths, and even "low" children can contribute to group work in meaningful ways.

Another issue with creating groups is knowing the students in your classroom. If you work with kindergarteners, you won't want to start out with groups of four or five—they won't be able to manage that—but you will want to start out with pairs. If some of your students are really interested in a topic, you might want to put them together. If some of your students have trouble getting along, put them together, but not all the time. If some of your students always want to be together, let them be, but not all the time.

For material related to this concept, go to Clip 4.2 on the Web-based Student Study Site.

Cooperative Workshop Stations. Cooperative workshops succeed when students move to different stations. This kind of cooperative workshop works well for goals with several like tasks that you want to accomplish or that you want children to do multiple times. Stations are also very helpful when you want to assess or work with a small group of students. The most motivating and engaging classrooms involve quite a bit of direct instruction, but it is usually done one-on-one with individual students (Dolezal, Mohan Welsh, Pressley, & Vincent, 2003), which is difficult with a classroom of children and not much time. With stations, however, it is easy to work with individual students. Stations are flexible and can help meet the needs of many different levels of students while including everyone. Let's look at some examples.

Math is a great subject for stations. For example, students could solve math problems at two or three of the stations and play math games at two or three others, and you could assess students' math skills individually at another. You could also use stations in math when you are studying goals that have more than one part, such as geometry. Each station could focus on a different shape about which students write properties. You could have measurement stations where students measure different objects, money stations at which they count money, or just different problem stations.

Science is also a good subject for stations. At the end of one class study of solids, liquids, and gases, I made six stations, five of which contained a material like peanut butter, corn meal, or toothpaste. At the sixth station—my favorite—I assessed my students' understanding of the states of matter. The students went to each station; tested the materials to see if they were solids, liquids, or gases; and wrote a rationale for their decision. At my station, I gave them a required test from the book. In this case, students didn't make it to all of the stations in one day.

They went to three, and then the following science class they finished the final three.
There are several different ways to guide movement during stations:

- Students move to stations every 15 minutes or so, depending on the number of stations.

- Students go to each station as they finish, but they need to manage their time so that they make it to all stations.

- Students choose from a menu of stations and need to complete one or several in the class period, but they need not get to all of the stations.

In the examples above, the students needed to go to every station, and I helped them keep time by shutting the lights off at moving time. Teaching time management through stations is a great social goal. Just make sure there is some accountability (i.e., something to share or hand in from each station), and students will learn to manage stations on their own.

Using stations where students have a choice makes it possible to meet many students' needs. Students can choose an activity at their own level, which helps them gain **metacognitive knowledge** about what they are learning. Choices require students to think about what stations would be appropriate for them. Let's look at an example of students monitoring their own movement. In social studies, students often learn about different states in the United States. Students could choose which stations, each representing a state, they wanted to visit and learn about qualities unique to that state. Although the students would not learn about all of the states in depth, they could share what they learned at the end of the lesson. Remember that computers can also function nicely as stations, especially if you only have a few computers in your room.

Some people say that stations are too much work. Although they may sound difficult to prepare, stations don't have to be pretty. Many teachers take time to make signs and materials, but you don't need to do that much work, unless you want to. Gather the necessary materials, write some directions on paper, and combine them in a baggie. In addition, keep stations throughout the years so you don't have to remake them. Ask your school's media specialist to help you gather different levels of books about a certain topic, and use familiar activities in some of the stations and new activities in others. Playing a math game several times is good for children, and you can always make the game harder or easier as needed. Finally, five- or six-station cooperative workshops may need to be split into two class periods requiring less planning.

Think about managing stations as you design them. How will you keep students engaged if you are not there? How will you know what is happening at each station if you are at one station assessing students? These are really good questions to consider and plan for. Once again, you must *teach* students to use stations effectively. It is important to help them understand the expectations at each station and that they should help each other. If someone is having trouble at a station, ask him or her to step out of the station until he or she is ready to go back. Sometimes, I asked parents to volunteer during a stations activity if I knew it was an especially active station day. For example, during Measurement Olympics, each station was an event, and I put parent volunteers where I thought the children might need help. At times, it is important to decide who you will put together for movement around stations. During stations where students monitor their own movement, it is also important to limit the number of students at each station. For example, if you are studying rocks and the students can choose among rock stations, many might choose the rock tumbler. You and the students would need to decide how many students would be appropriate for each station, and they would be in charge of going someplace else if the rock tumbler station was already full.

Stations probably aren't the best choice in cooperative workshops if the room needs to be quiet, if there aren't several tasks that center on the same goal, or you don't know what the students understand about the topic. For the most part, however, stations help promote autonomy, belonging, competency, and motivation because they contain so many possibilities, both social and academic. Stations also promote physical movement that the brain research you read about earlier supports (Jensen, 2005).

Individual Cooperative Workshops. We have talked a lot about students working in groups. Sometimes, however, individual cooperative workshops, such as reading and writing workshops, work better. Individual cooperative workshops work best when students have individual goals and need time to work at their own pace, when you want to give every child an opportunity to use materials to learn, when everyone needs to experience specific processes, or when you need your classroom to be quiet for a short period.

There are many examples of individual cooperative workshops. I used them a lot during reading and writing because they afforded children time to read and write individually. Each child needs a large amount of time to read and write. Therefore, putting students in groups to do these tasks probably isn't a good use of time. In addition, students need to repeat specific writing processes (planning, writing, editing, peer review, publishing, sharing), and working as individuals allows them to read and write at or above the level where they would be most successful (zone of proximal development).

Of course, individual cooperative workshops aren't just for reading and writing. Sometimes I wanted all of my students to use hundreds/tens/ones blocks to figure out addition or subtraction problems, so I put blocks where each individual student could access them. Each student had a placemat where he or she could work on the problems. For social studies, students learning about community worked individually to create a town in the classroom (Curtiss & Curtiss, 1998).

Students working as individuals can still help each other. During writer's workshop, my students would often help each other with spelling, ideas, and peer editing. If students needed help with a word, they asked; if they wanted to share an exciting part of their book during reader's workshop, they did. The purpose of individual cooperative workshops is not to take the cooperation away but instead to meet students' individual needs.

"In many classrooms, where teaching to the 'middle' is the norm, some learners are bored as they 'repeat history,' and others are lost because they don't have the background or experience they need to understand or be able to do what is expected of them" (Gregory & Chapman, 2002, p. 64). Differentiation works well in individual cooperative workshops because you can structure the workshop in many different ways:

- Assign different tasks to achieve the same goal.

- Assign the same task in its own unique way (e.g., by drawing, using manipulatives, making a poster, creating a skit, or solving a problem).

- Assign the same task but with different materials (e.g., books, manipulatives, or writing tools).

Individual cooperative workshops work well for differentiation because they allow students the safety and self-worth to work at their own pace and with the tools they need while still doing the same task. In other words, you don't need to pull a student out or give him or her something different to work on because everyone will be doing what he or she needs to do. I find it funny that differentiation is often promoted for "low" or "high" children when it really should be promoted for every child (Tomlinson, 2001). You don't have to come up with a different task for everyone, but you should allow students to choose and to do what they need. You can base different assignments on the same concept, just at varying levels of abil- ity. "Although the assignment is adjusted for different groups of learners, the standards, concepts, or content of each assignment have the same focus and each student has the opportunity to develop essential skills and understanding at his or her own appropriate level of challenge" (Gregory & Chapman, 2002, p. 58).

A good example of differentiation in an individual cooperative workshop is reading. Every student in my room read a different book at whatever level he or she needed. Some needed to listen to taped readings of books they chose (Carbo, 2007). I kept a variety of books in my room, and I borrowed many from the library based on student interest. We worked on skills with short, mini lessons, but each student practiced those skills on a different book (Avery, 1993). Every book contains skills that you must teach, such as contractions, pronouns, and punctuation. Children can learn fluency, comprehension, and making inferences from any book. This kind of differentiation can take place with a variety of tasks within individ- ual cooperative workshops.

There aren't many limitations to using individual cooperative workshops. I recom- mend, however, that you not use them exclusively. Students need to learn to work together in a classroom, and completing tasks as individuals won't always promote that. In addi- tion, leaving out social goals may be easy when planning an individual cooperative work- shop, but this should not happen. Social goals, such as how to help someone rather than give them the answers and when to ask for help, are important lessons that can be facil- itated within this structure. Finally, it is imperative that individual cooperative work- shops don't become busywork time. Tasks should continue to be worthy even if students are working alone.

Table 4.4 provides an example of how to set up groups.

TABLE 4.4   Lesson Plan With Groups

I made the activities in this workshop into stations. How might these activities look in small groups or within individual cooperative workshops?

Date 1/23/09	Subject Money	Objective(s) Students will be able to make different amounts with coins.	
What are my goals?			
Academic		Social	
1. I want them to be able to see that multiple coins make the same amount. 2. I want them to know coins up to a quarter.		1. I want them to have good sportsmanship during a game. 2. I want them to help without giving answers.	
How will I set up the lesson?			
Problem(s)	Action(s)	Sharing	Materials
You will not always have the same coins in your pocket. How will you buy things?	1. Play money-trading game. 2. How many ways are there to make__cents? 3. Assessment with me.	Hang up students' papers showing how many ways there are to make __ cents.	1. Play money 2. Dice 3. Paper 4. Crayons 5. Assessment sheets
How will I set up groups?			
	Small Groups	Stations	Individuals
Size of group?		3 stations	
Movement?		Move every 20 minutes	
How will I group the students?		Number off 1, 2, 3 Form groups within stations on their own	
Plans for positive interdependence	Students will need to play the game together. It is not a game they can play on their own. Working individually at other stations.		
Plans for individual accountability	Students will turn in papers showing how they made a certain amount of money		
Questions I might ask:			
1. What did you find out about money? 2. What is the easiest coin to trade? 3. Are there coins that cannot be traded?			

Choice 4: Promoting Individual Accountability and Positive Interdependence

You may think cooperative workshops sound like any other classroom structure. Sometimes you put the students in groups; sometimes they work individually. What's so special about that? The most important differences lie in creating tasks that require individual accountability and positive interdependence. Individual accountability exists when "the performance of each individual student is assessed and the results are given back to the group and the individual" (Johnson, Johnson, & Holubec, 1991, p. 1:12). Positive interdependence "is the perception that you are linked with others in a way so that you cannot succeed unless they do (and vice versa) and their work benefits you and your work benefits them" (Johnson, Johnson, & Holubec, 1991, p. 4:6). In traditional group work, students often end up doing all or none of it. The choices you make in structuring individual accountability and positive interdependence will help ensure your students are actively involved in the tasks.

Individual accountability won't just happen. You need to decide how you will structure tasks to promote it. In a graduate class, for example, I once had the students make pendulums to determine what would make them swing faster. To ensure individual accountability, everyone needed to create a chart and record his or her data to prove to the rest of the class that his or her answers were correct. The small groups discussed and made the pendulums and tested different ways to make them go faster, but everyone had to collect data. One student, Erica, commented to me after the lesson that, even though she had already done the experiment and knew the answer, collecting data made her more engaged. If I had structured the task so students could just complete and discuss it, Erica probably wouldn't have participated. Even graduate students need tasks that hold them accountable.

Positive interdependence was also structured in Erica's task. She couldn't create a pendulum on her own and collect her own data because there were only enough materials for the small group. She needed her group. In addition, the groups presented together rather than individually, enhancing positive interdependence, and had to discuss their data before they presented. There are many creative ways to add individual accountability and positive interdependence to your cooperative workshops. Here are just a few:

- Have students share materials and ideas, but everyone must turn in a paper.

- Tell students ahead of time that you will be choosing a reporter after the task is over.

- Assign roles (jobs) for each person, such as recorder, drawer, compliment collector, materials manager, question asker (only this person can ask a question of the teacher), reader, checker, noise monitor, or others based on the task.

- Jigsaw the task so every member has one piece that the whole group needs or so each member must become an expert on one piece and teach it to the others.

- Tell students ahead of time that they will need to come to a single solution to the task rather than several.

- Role-play what happens when someone doesn't do his or her job in a group, as well as what happens when groups don't work together.

- Create boundaries where students must sit in groups using chairs, tape on the floor, and so on.

- Have a whole-group processing time where students can share things that went well in their groups and things they need to work together to solve.

- Tell students that they must ask three other people for help before they ask you.

- Have large poster paper at each station so students can write their answers and sign their name.

- Turn in logs or answer sheets after each visit to a station.

- Assign student editors to look over work before turning it in.

This part of planning is often left out. Tremendously important, however, it will make using cooperative workshops easy and valuable.

What the Teacher Does During a Cooperative Workshop

For material related to this concept, go to Clip 4.3 on the Web-based Student Study Site.

When designing cooperative workshops, remember that your job is not over when the workshop starts. Wanting students to construct their own meaning and solve problems together, however, doesn't mean you aren't involved. Think of yourself as a personal trainer. Give enough support to stretch learners, but not so much that they are sore the next morning (Williams & Veomett, 2007). Facilitating learning in this way means asking questions rather than telling and challenging ideas rather than giving right answers. It means learning along with the learners. What should you do before, during, and after cooperative workshops?

Before a Cooperative Workshop

Before a cooperative workshop, consider your knowledge about the concepts you are teaching, the structures you will use, and the children you will facilitate. We often think of reflection as a tool to use after lessons or days; however, it is important to reflect before the lesson as well. For example, you might want to think about different situations that might come up during a lesson and how to prevent them or what you will do when they happen. One of my students, for example, never came to the front floor while the other children were sharing. He refused. So, before many lessons with him, I asked myself how I could help him. What would I do when Jerry refused to come to the front floor? The first couple of times I tried to get him to join us, he wouldn't. After a few missed attempts, I gave him the choice to sit next to me or one of his friends during sharing time. He chose his friends—a solution that might not work for every child but that worked that day for Jerry. I might not have been able to think of such a solution in the moment, so I planned and reflected for it instead.

It is important to plan for questions before your lessons as well. I have been teaching for many years, and I still write down questions that I want to be sure to ask. Many questions will come up along the way; however, the questions I write down are imperative to the goals of the lesson, and I might skip over them if I haven't thought of them ahead of time. Make sure you have materials ready and accessible; otherwise, management will not be easy. There are many strategies for this. A teacher I knew, Kelly, for example, kept stacking baskets on her desk, labeled them Monday through Friday, and used them to store each day's necessary materials. Finally, before a cooperative workshop, reflect about whether or not the workshop you planned promotes autonomy, belonging, competency, democracy, and motivation in some way.

During a Cooperative Workshop

Your role during a cooperative workshop is guide. You will guide students to the problem they will encounter, as they work through problems by asking them thoughtful questions and challenging their ideas, and toward the goals of the task. Guiding students instead of telling them the way will help them engage more fully in the task and cut down on the need for discipline (Gillies, 2006). It is difficult to be behind the scenes during a task because you have probably experienced just the opposite. Allowing students to take the lead and then challenging them and questioning their ideas, however, will be very exciting and fulfilling.

Guiding students into a problem means introducing the problem, providing directions and goals, and then making sure they understand the problem. It does not mean showing them the solutions. Remember that goals need to be scaffolded: You may not have to introduce a problem every day because you may be working on the same problem for a couple of days. Children's literature, interesting events, and unique materials provide great ways to introduce a problem. For example, if my goal is to teach children about adding and subtracting money, I could read *Alexander, Who Used to Be Rich Last Sunday* by Judith Viorst to the children, give them a certain amount of money, and then set up stations around the room where they must add up things they might buy. If my goal is to teach volume, I might set up an experiment where I put two film canisters of the same size but different weights in a pitcher of water to see which one moves the water up more (they will displace the water equally because, though they weigh different amounts, they have the same volume), and then groups of students could test other objects and determine which has the most volume. If my goal is to teach life cycles, I might bring in frog eggs and let students observe them over time. There are many ways to guide students into a problem. Be creative and have fun, but don't feel like every lesson has to be a grand show. Sometimes it is best just to give the students the problem and let them work. Sometimes the best way to introduce a problem is to let the students find it themselves.

Guiding students through problems is about questioning, challenging, and (sometimes, but not very often) modeling. Questioning is the most powerful pedagogical tool teachers have, but sometimes coming up with great questions is difficult. To help you, Penick, Crow, and Bonnstetter (1996) have developed a system of questioning called HRASE to assist teachers in probing students' thinking. Each component of HRASE—History, Relationships, Application, Speculation, and Explanation—refers to a specific type of question.

History questions help you and the students gather information about what the students did. For example:

- What did you do?
- What happened?

- What happened next?

- What did you do first?

- What procedure did you use?

- What color (temperature, weight, size) was it?

- What made you think of doing that?

Relationship questions help students look for relationships and patterns in science. For example:

- If _____ happened, what happened to _____?

- Where have you seen something like this before?

- Did any other students get these same results?

- What order does that usually follow?

- What seems to be a common element in all your findings?

- Where (when, how) do you usually find these?

Application questions are valuable in discerning what students understand. For example:

- How could you use this?

- What problems could this solve?

- Where can we find examples of this in the world?

- What machine could you build that would do this?

Speculation questions go beyond the data and information and encourage creative thinking. For example:

- What if you (changed, eliminated, added, mixed, waited)?

- What would it take to prove that?

- If you wanted to prevent that from happening, what would you do?

- If that is true, then _____?

Explanation questions help students convey their observations and conclusions. For example:

- How does that work?

- What causes that to happen?

- How would you change your explanation if I changed _____?

- How does your explanation fit this other phenomenon?

Questioning is a valuable way to encourage students to think deeply about what they have done and noticed. It also gives you insight into what students understand so you can plan additional experiences to help extend their knowledge. Using this method to help students construct content knowledge, however, requires flexibility on your part and a willingness to listen.

Challenging students during a cooperative workshop just means wondering aloud. Such challenges should not be confrontational or have winners and losers. For example, if a student shows me a correct math problem, I usually say, "Hmmm. How did you get that answer?" Sometimes the students think their answer is wrong, but after a while they begin to show me their process and believe in their answer (competency?). If a student shows me an incorrect math problem, I usually say, "Hmmm. How did you get that answer? I didn't get the same one. Did anyone else get that answer?"

Modeling is also a powerful tool. Be sure to use your power for good. Only use modeling when frustration is high enough that a student may give up or when there is another way that none of the students have thought about. Modeling used at the beginning of a lesson becomes the "right answer" and doesn't allow students to really understand their own thinking.

Guiding students to the end goal of the task requires closure. Students need time to reflect on what they have thought about and learned. This may be as quick as asking a few children what they found out during the lesson or as long as having them write a reflection. Sharing is a great catalyst for closure. For example, if you have done a cooperative workshop about machines and groups share machines that they made, asking some good questions after everyone has shared can help children draw conclusions about machines. At times, you may not have time for much closure. On these days, I asked children to tell me one thing they learned as they got in line or went home. Closure is great for assessment as well!

After a Cooperative Workshop

When you are finished with your day or have a break, take some time to reflect about the cooperative workshops that took place. Ask yourself:

- Were there any children that I need to write about (with regard to excitement or worries)?

- What experiences does this group of students need next (academically and socially)?

- What went well?

- What would I change next time?

It's not always easy to do this kind of reflection; however, if you make it a practice, you will help your students tremendously . . . and then it will be time to start your next plan.

I hope this chapter has taken some of the mystery out of great classroom management by showing you how to structure your goals and lessons into cooperative workshops. Remember that classroom management is not magic, but it is thoughtful planning, responsive facilitating, and careful reflection.

LETTER FROM A MASTER TEACHER 4.2

Preteaching Cooperative Workshops

After supervising and teaching many preservice learners, I have found that many are often afraid to teach according to the outline in this chapter. Don't we need to do vocabulary sheets to teach the common language of a unit? A recent student teacher thought so. But, as I questioned him, it became clearer that he was more comfortable with teacher-directed learning, and he was convinced that it was his insurance policy that students had indeed learned.

Most of his discomfort centered on the movement of the students in the classroom. He began using two strategies as a way of preteaching. First, before he did any activity, he asked the students: "What will learning look like?" He had them consider four consistent questions: "How long will we do this? How will you ask for help? What if you get done early? What if you show me you are not OK doing the activity?" After he explained what he expected of them, he asked students their understanding of the questions until he felt comfortable. Setting this up took a little bit of time, but it was well worth it and became routine.

As another way of preteaching in the beginning, he used the fishbowl technique to model effective group work. Using a rubric, he paired a listener outside of the fishbowl to assess one of the participants inside. The two would talk afterward about what they saw and felt during the discussion using the rubric that focused on "what they did right, what they did wrong, and how they could fix it."

Another strategy to alleviate the uncertainty my student teacher had about a classroom that seemed out of control to him was to identify the social skill(s) he hoped the students would practice while doing the activity. Our school focused on putting the day's learning objective on the board, and the principal would often check to make sure it was appropriate. So, in addition to this knowledge objective, he would write a skill objective. These often centered on social skills like "I can be OK when others aren't OK" or "I can be frustrated and ask a clarifying question." When reviewing these written objectives, he found it valuable to share about the disposition of people who are successful working with others.

A final tool this student teacher used as a way to alleviate his discomfort was to simply ask the students what they learned that day. There are many ways for students to reflect, but he focused on learners popping up one at a time to share something they learned in that period. Pair-sharing, writing, walk and talks, etc., were all used at various times. Besides the processing time for students, the reflection helped assure my student teacher that learning vocabulary does not have to happen on paper.

—Denise Knotwell
Eighth-Grade Social Studies Teacher

So . . . What?

The pedagogy you choose influences whether or not students have access to autonomy, belonging, competency, democratic community, and motivation. It matters! Cooperative workshops provide a great structure for ensuring students' access to these things. To plan cooperative workshops, you must:

Develop social and academic goals based on your objectives and students' needs. Develop mastery rather than performance goals, and make sure they are scaffolded.

Collect and implement worthy tasks that provide experience and reflection and are ordered so students can make connections.

Determine the perfect size for the task (e.g., small groups, cooperative workshops, cooperative workshop stations, or individual cooperative workshops).

Create opportunities for individual accountability and positive interdependence within the task.

Make a plan for what you will do before, during, and after cooperative workshops.

Get Ready For . . .

A cooperative workshop isn't the only magical structure in classroom management. In the next chapter, we will consider thinking routines as a way into learning, to stay in the learning, and to go deeper in the learning. Thinking routines will help you provide cues to help children learn in the classroom, as well as on their own for a lifetime. Instead of managing students to make them busy and good, we need classroom management structures that promote thinking.

Activities to Try

✎ Think about how cooperative workshops give individual students what they need.

✎ What questions do you have about cooperative workshops? How could you find answers?

✎ Use the form that I provided and write a lesson plan for an objective or for a student you know.

✎ **Make a collection!** Create some folders with different topics, and begin looking for tasks that you might use. Don't leave something out that you think might be too hard or too easy. You can modify it or save it for a student who may someday need that task.

Conduct action research! Try a cooperative workshop out on a group of students or even one student or colleague. What happened? Why? What happens next?

Student Study Site

The companion Web site for *Elementary Classroom Management* can be found at www.sagepub.com/kwilliamsstudy.

Visit the Web-based student study site to enhance your understanding of the chapter content. The study materials include video clips, practice tests, flashcards, suggested readings, and Web resources.

CHAPTER 5

Creating Thinking Classrooms

OK, we're on Chapter 5, and it's confession time. When I told some of my colleagues that I was writing this book on classroom management, they laughed. "*You* are writing a classroom management book? Really?" Yep. They probably laughed because my classroom wasn't exactly the model for busy, quiet, and good (you know the unwritten rule that if students are busy, quiet, and good, they must be learning). I don't blame my colleagues for laughing. Traditionally, good classroom management involves quiet classrooms, busy students working alone on a page of problems, and well-oiled routines that all students uniformly follow. My classroom was full of children who were scattered all around the room working together, having discussions, and using all kinds of materials. I didn't want children who were busy, quiet, and good but not thinking.

I wanted thinking and active children, children who were autonomous and competent, felt that they belonged, and were motivated to learn.

Children deserve far more than classroom management for management's sake. They deserve classrooms where management is designed to help them think, make decisions, and learn. Some may believe I am advocating disorderly, chaotic classrooms, but that is definitely *not* my intention. Deep, active thinking does not exist in classrooms where everyone is expected to do the same thing and think the same way in the name of good classroom management; nor does it exist where there are no goals, expectations, structures, or routines. In a sense, classroom management should not be an algorithm but instead a piece of art. In other words, management cannot be a prescribed system of ordered things to say and do.

What might these students be thinking about?

It must be a creative exchange of reflection and experience within flexible structures and routines. Instead of having unbendable, mindless structures and routines that treat students like robots, we need structures and routines that help students develop strategies for exploring, wondering, and uncovering. This chapter is about classroom management that will help make the classroom into a thinking place.

Why would you want a classroom where children are actively engaged in thinking? As Ritchhart (2002) says, "After the final test has been taken, when students have long since left our doorways and the chalk-board has been erased for the last time, what will stay with our students isn't the laundry list of names, dates, computations, and procedures we have covered. What endure are the dispositions and habits of character we have been able to nurture. What stays with us, what sticks from our education, are the patterns of behavior and thinking that have been engrained and enculturated over time" (p. 229). We need to use structures and routines that nurture thinking and reflecting in ways that will stay with students long after they leave our classrooms.

After you read this chapter, I hope you have:

- Your own model of what it means to think.

- An understanding of classroom management strategies that promote thinking.

- Thinking routines that you can use in any classroom with any group of children to help create a thinking classroom.

Thinking Models

I think we would all agree that we want classrooms with opportunities for thinking. Before we can create classroom management structures and strategies that promote thinking, we need to understand what thinking is. What does it mean to think? What processes are involved in thinking? What tools can be used to help someone think? What does your model of thinking look like? If you do not have your own understanding of thinking, it will be very difficult to create classroom management techniques that facilitate it. Thinking may sound like something you just do; however, deep thinking for learning is a process that children need to develop. Children between kindergarten and sixth grade have shown an inability to monitor their thinking and have difficulty describing their own cognition (Bruning, Schraw, & Ronning, 1999).

In addition, we often associate thinking with academic learning, but thinking is equally important in social learning. We want children to think about their actions and behaviors, to learn to identify purposes of tasks and determine what is important to learn, and to be deliberate rather than impulsive (Bruning, Schraw, & Ronning, 1999).

Take some time now before you read further to make a list of words or actions that relate to thinking (see Figure 5.1). What does thinking look like? How can you tell someone is thinking? What might thinking sound like?

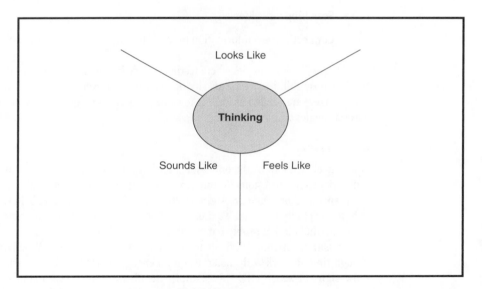

FIGURE 5.1   Model of Thinking

Use this map to help you describe your own ideas about what it means to think. Share yours with someone else. Are they the same?

Three Pieces of Thinking

Perkins, Tishman, Ritchhart, Donis, and Andrade's (2000) model has really helped me think about thinking. It is short, incorporates many aspects of thinking, works well for classroom teachers, and has three pieces or parts, including **abilities**, **sensitivities**, and **inclinations** to think. As you read about the three pieces, incorporate them into your own model of thinking.

Ability

For the most part, thinking and intellectual performance have traditionally revolved around abilities like speed and accuracy (Perkins, Tishman, Ritchhart, Donis, & Andrade, 2000; Sternberg, 1990). Good thinkers are seen as the children who finish the assignment first, who get all of the answers correct, or who can perform the procedure or memorize the best. Traditionally, children who ask question after question, take time to uncover ideas, and wonder why procedures work the way they do are not seen as good students. The ability to think, however, should not be judged or encouraged merely by speed or accuracy.

To promote the ability to think, you should also encourage children to ask great questions, struggle with hard problems, and persist when the answer doesn't come right away. Try the following thinking strategies to engage the ability to think:

- Brainstorming

- Considering hidden options

- Searching for evidence

- Connecting new information to old (Chipman, Segal, & Glaser, 1993)

We are living in an age where testing is very important, and we need to help children develop those abilities. We are also living in an age, however, where problem solvers and creative thinkers are needed as well. Take some time to brainstorm ways you could use each of these strategies within a lesson.

Sensitivity

Thinking abilities aren't the only aspect of thinking we need to manage in our classrooms. Sensitivity to the occasions for thinking is an important piece of thinking as well (Perkins, Tishman, Ritchhart, Donis, & Andrade, 2000). Perkins and colleagues believe it is not enough to have the ability to think. We must also cultivate the sensitivity to know when there is a problem, what kind of problem it is, and how we might go about thinking it through.

Sensitivity is more difficult to see or measure than ability. When we give children enough time to work with materials on an engaging problem, however, they will begin to show signs of sensitivity. For example, members of my class made structures out of marshmallows and toothpicks each year to see if they could build something strong enough to hold a dictionary. Many students would build something and then start all over even though they hadn't tried it. They were sensitive to the fact that there was a problem that needed fixing. To cultivate the sensitivity to think, we must encourage children to:

- Go back and think about what happened

- Think about what their decisions were and why they thought that way

- Reflect before, during, and after an activity

- Challenge each other's solutions

Inclination

The final piece of thinking, according to Perkins and colleagues (2000), is inclination. Thinking will not happen in the classroom if the students do not believe it is valued. I once worked with a group of seventh- and eighth-grade students who were building small cars. With limited materials and no motors, they needed to try to get the cars to go as far as they could from the starting line. I thought it was a fairly worthy problem. The children made their cars, tried them one time, and gave up. They certainly had the opportunity to work on them after a practice run, but, satisfied with their one and only attempt, nobody chose to. You can spend some time thinking about why they chose not to persist in working on their cars. Overall, though, they just didn't have the inclination to think. I know how they feel, and I bet you do too. Sometimes, I am just tired of thinking. It's hard work. Sometimes, my thinking runs amok, and I can't even go to sleep. The point is that we need to foster the inclination to think in our classrooms. The inclination to think requires:

- Worthy problems

- Choice

- Good questions

- Time to think

- The ability to use materials and processes that help children think and explore

Sound familiar? The inclination to think is about motivation. In some ways, it is a bit different, however. I can be motivated to come to class or do my best, but I might not be inclined to think if speed and accuracy are rewarded or if I know I am going to get one chance and the teacher is going to go on. What other aspects of a classroom might discourage students' inclination to think? What would make you inclined to think?

Thinking in the Classroom

As you begin to consider thinking classrooms, take some time to write about classrooms that you have attended (see Table 5.1). Were they designed as thinking classrooms? What structures made them so?

TABLE 5.1 **Classroom Experiences With Thinking**

	Thinking	Nonthinking
What did you do as a student?		
What did the teacher do?		
What routines did you follow?		

Piaget said, "The principal goal of education is to create men (and women) who are capable of doing new things, not simply repeating what other generations have done . . . men (and women) who are creative, inventive discoverers. The second goal of education is to form minds which can be critical, can verify, and not accept everything they are offered" (as cited in Elkind, 1981, p. 29). If this is the goal of education, teachers must be able to construct classrooms where students can be autonomous (Kamii, 2000), playful (Henniger, 1987), active (Elkind, 1981), and constructors of knowledge (Dewey, 1938). Students must have opportunities for conversation rather than interrogation (Hausfather, 1996), for developing wonderful ideas rather than memorizing lists (Duckworth, 1996), and for struggling through perplexities rather than coming up with right answers (Glasson & Lalik, 1993). "In effect, teaching becomes a matter of orchestrating the learners' experiences rather than of transmitting knowledge, and the teacher is more centrally concerned with attending to emerging understandings than with providing unambiguous explications" (Davis, 1996, p. 232). How does this look and sound? What are the students doing? What are the teachers doing?

Students in Thinking Classrooms

Students who engage in thinking do not seek closure as much as they do understanding (Cacioppo & Petty, 1982). In classrooms we often require children to find an answer and be done. How many times have you been in a classroom where you got to do something special if you finished your work? I remember in fifth grade racing to finish my math worksheets so I could play math games. I didn't care if I'd done my worksheets well or if I understood the math. I just wanted to be done and receive my reward: playing math games. Instead, however, teachers should encourage students who finish early to think of another possible solution or explain their answer in a different way. You might ask students who quickly finish a math problem to show you the solution in a picture, come up with a story problem that represents the numbers, or think of a job where that math problem would be used. You might ask students who finish writing and don't wish to revise to replace some of their words with pictures so they might go back and rewrite using language that describes the pictures or record their writing on a tape recorder. Take some time to think of a social or an academic goal that you could extend to encourage thinking.

Students who engage in thinking also display a skeptical and discerning attitude toward information (Cacioppo, Petty, Feinstein, & Jarvis, 1996). We often discourage students who disagree with us, and we feed them information rather than let them think. Many perceive that busy, quiet, and good children are thinking. Thinking isn't always silent, however, and in some ways we need it to be visible. We want to know what students are thinking so we can help them think further or in different ways. Students who constantly ask questions, challenge the teacher, or come up with new approaches to tasks are probably engaged in thinking. Providing opportunities for students to think requires you to support new ideas instead of looking for the one right answer. For example, ask students who believe that we have seasons because of the Earth's tilt to prove their ideas with a model. Offer readings with many different perspectives on global warming. Create cordial and safe debates among students with different opinions about whether mealworms are worms or insects. Ask students to write a position paper about why they think George Washington became our first president. Encourage questions and challenges even if you are the teacher.

Students who engage in thinking also learn skills and knowledge (Ritchhart, 2002). Asking students to think doesn't mean they won't learn skills and knowledge. Certainly, we want the thinking to come to some closure. I once worked with a math professor who debated with me about having students construct their own understandings in math. He argued that students should be taught certain mathematical procedures because each was created for ease and quickness. I agree but would add that in a thinking classroom, students are asked to figure out and tear apart math problems so they have the opportunity to think about and understand them before we teach the easy procedure. Even then, we should ask students to understand why the easy procedure works. It is the same for any skill or bit of knowledge. If we ask students to know something mindlessly, they will have difficulty connecting it to other things. Instead, ask students to teach someone else a skill, such as long division, that they have mastered. Have students write "CliffsNotes" for books they have read and understood, or have them write a song for remembering the times tables.

Teachers in Thinking Classrooms

Teachers in thinking classrooms reflect on students' thinking and not merely on how well they performed. It is easy to be fooled into thinking that a lesson went well if the students were busy, quiet, and good. After a lesson, however, you really need to ask yourself, "What did the students learn?" For example, Beth was teaching a lesson on weather to first graders. She had planned to have the students create a survey about whether they preferred rainy or sunny days, and then they were to make mobiles. Beth took out a big piece of chart paper and asked the students what questions they had about rain. The first graders came up with good questions at first. They asked things like "Why does it rain and not snow?" "Why is it cloudy when it rains?" and "What happens to the rain when it hits the ground?" So far, a lot of thinking was happening, but these were not the questions Beth wanted to hear. Thinking about her survey, she skillfully guided the students away from these kinds of questions and toward such questions as "What do you like to wear in the rain?"

Catching on to what Beth was looking for, the students began to ask questions that were acceptable to her. Next, the students made umbrella mobiles using premade parts whose color corresponded with students' answers on the survey. For example, if they liked rainy days, they

LETTER FROM A MASTER TEACHER 5.1

Fun Ideas to Help Students Think

I've been teaching for 12 years, and I can vouch for the importance of helping students think in the classroom. I like to use various ways to help students think. The first is called "I know I know, I think I know, and I know I don't know." I have students create three columns on a sheet or two of paper with each column labeled either "I know I know," "I think I know," or "I know I don't know." Students take the information we are learning and place each item in the column that best fits their situation. For instance, let's say we are studying ancient China. If a student sees that he or she needs to know three ancient Chinese inventions that are still used today and he or she knows them, they would go into the "I know I know" column. If the student cannot remember three of Confucius's beliefs on good governments, he or she would place those beliefs in the "I know I don't know column." The goal would then be to review and study until the student can move them into the "I know I know" column. This really helps get students thinking about their own learning and gets them making decisions about what they understand and don't understand. When students see how they've progressed and prepared, they become more confident. I let students know this can be used for any subject, anytime.

Another thinking strategy I like to use is a game that incorporates as many learning styles as possible (kinesthetic, musical, etc.). Students have to create a skit that requires them to be creative yet think about the material we have been studying. What makes this great fun is to incorporate serious thinking into the skits, such as creating a rap song over Queen Elizabeth, being an ESPN reporter at the Ancient Greek Olympics, holding a press conference with an Egyptian mummy, or creating/drawing an action figure or doll (including all its amazing functions) from a famous Renaissance figure—just to name a few. Not only entertaining for the entire class, it really demonstrates higher-order thinking skills and allows students to think in a social setting using teamwork.

I hope some of these ideas can help, and I wish you the best in helping students think!

—Tom Roff
Seventh-Grade Social Studies Teacher

received a green handle; if not, they received a blue handle. Not much thinking. They didn't get to decide what they would put on their mobiles. Afterward, Beth reflected on her lesson, feeling that it was a great success. She discussed many aspects of classroom management that she felt had gone well. For instance, the materials were cut out and ready, and she had guided students into asking questions she wanted to hear. Beth didn't mention anything about what the students learned about rain. She believed it was a good lesson because the children were engaged and no one caused any trouble. Classroom management was a performance to her and not about the learning that had taken place.

Certainly, thinking is difficult to find in poorly managed classrooms, but that can be only one of the many questions you ask yourself at the end of a lesson or day. After reflecting on the students' behavior, reflect on what they learned, what opportunities they had to think, and individual students' ideas. Wonder to yourself how you know they learned what they learned. If you don't have any evidence of learning (such as a quote from a student, a story about a group that shows thinking, or paper showing an idea), be sure to collect some next time. This process, by the way, is called assessment.

For material related to this concept, go to Clip 5.1 on the Web-based Student Study Site.

Teachers in thinking classrooms provide opportunities for students to be the experts. I visited a classroom recently where a tremendous amount of thinking was happening because the teacher, Mary Jo, let the children become experts on magnets. There were not right and wrong answers; there were experiences and theories, challenges and reflections.

Mary Jo had set up several stations with different magnet activities at each. The first graders went to each station and came up with experiments that they wanted to do with the magnets (i.e., they played with the magnets at each station). For this particular assignment, Mary Jo didn't give out specific directions at the stations; she just wanted the students to begin understanding magnets. The children at one station put paper clips together to see how many would stick before they fell off. At another station, they used magnets to pull shavings into different piles. And, at another station, some of the students figured out that they could make scissors turn into a magnet by rubbing them with another magnet. After the students finished, Mary Jo had them draw pictures of what they had learned about magnets. In other words, she had them think about their experiences with magnets. Then they shared their ideas and became experts on the subject. Some children disagreed because of their findings and challenged each other. A lot of thinking was happening.

We must take care to let our students experience and be expert thinkers. If we are afraid of what they might think or that they won't come up with the right answer, we will end up with nonthinking classrooms. It is your job to come up with experiences that will help nurture thinking and to help children refine their thinking through questions and stories. This may be as simple as asking students to share what they think about a topic you are studying, a book you are reading, or a problem you are solving. It may be as complex as having students become experts on one piece of a lesson. For example, you might have students become experts about one state or one chapter of a book. How else can students become experts?

Teachers in thinking classrooms use thinking tools. You can use many kinds of thinking tools in your classroom to help students think and learn. Such materials as math manipulatives, microscopes, books, and even students' own bodies can be thinking tools. These materials are often promoted as ways for children to connect their physical actions to their thinking, and, for young students especially, having something to feel, see, and manipulate can really enhance thinking. Often, however, classroom management gets in the way of these thinking tools. For example, a student teacher, Janet, understood the importance of using manipulatives and pictures to help children understand math, so she decided to use hundreds/tens/ones blocks in a lesson that I was observing. Before the lesson, Janet was

Miss Lisa lets Ryan be an "expert" by sharing something he thought about the book.

worried about the management issues with manipulatives. I could tell that she had probably had nightmares about children throwing blocks! To overcome these issues, Janet planned specific ways to help the students use the manipulatives without causing problems. For example, she put the blocks in baggies for each student, made mats where the students could put the blocks, and even let the children build with the blocks before the lesson to get that out of their systems. When she started the lesson, however, Janet put the blocks on an overhead, and the children had to do exactly what she did. She gave them problems and showed the students what to do, and they copied her. The students did several problems like that and never got to try them on their own. After the lesson, I asked Janet who was doing the thinking during the lesson, and she said, "Me." The students in the room needed to learn to solve problems using the blocks. They didn't need her to tell them the procedure.

Modeling with thinking tools is good sometimes, but we must remember that creating experiences where children think requires them to be the physical and mental manipulators rather than the copycats. As nice as just giving them all of the knowledge we have accumulated would be, we can't. Students must have experiences, just as we did, in order to learn. They must do their own thinking. How could Janet have turned her lesson into a thinking lesson and managed it effectively?

Managing thinking tools should not get in your way of using them. Although it may seem daunting to have a group of children in the room with tools that could be possible distractions or even launching items, they are important in nurturing thinking. Using thinking tools can be highly effective if you do the following:

- Teach children how to use them through the social goals discussed in Chapter 4.

- Create opportunities for students to "play" with them ahead of time.

- Organize and have them ready to hand out ahead of time.

- Have procedures for students who misuse them (e.g., putting the tools away until students are ready to use them appropriately).

Teachers in thinking classrooms utilize thinking routines. In a sense, the teachers I have described are like many in that they use intuition to help them design a classroom. They intuitively know that children need support to engage in complex thinking. The kind of support we provide, however, matters. Sometimes teachers provide so much support that children do not have opportunities to think on their own. Sometimes teachers provide too little support, and children struggle in their thinking and give up. We have learned from Lev Vygotsky (Berk & Winsler, 1995) that young thinkers need tools like language and questions from more experienced peers or adults to help them engage in the abilities, sensitivities, and inclinations to think.

When I was a preservice teacher, I worked with a teacher named Tish whose classroom had wonderful opportunities for thinking because she used routines that enabled students to think all day. When they first arrived at school, the routine was to get a poetry folder and read their favorite poems to each other until everyone arrived. Tish did not put the poems in the folders; the students chose the ones they wanted. The class had a calendar routine that students serviced and led. Students in the class had a routine for taking lunch count and figuring out how many children were missing. There were routines for every subject as well. The children also had a time when they could choose whatever they wanted to learn, a structured routine called plan-do-review (Hohmann & Weikart, 1995). They needed to plan what they wanted to do, do it, and then write a reflection about what they did and learned. The children knew what was expected and what was coming next, yet the routines they participated in helped them think. I remember one time in the classroom I got up to help some children who were struggling to determine the lunch count. As soon as my rear left the chair, Tish said, "They can handle it"—a good reminder that fixing problems for children doesn't help them think.

A lot of teachers use routines in their classrooms, but some routines don't facilitate thinking. For example, many teachers have students follow a schedule. I bet you've been in a class with this routine: Grade homework, listen to a lecture about a new skill, do some seatwork, and get a new homework assignment. Indeed, thinking could be involved in that routine. The teacher could ask great questions during the lecture, or the seatwork could be very engaging. This kind of routine, however, only encourages abilities to think; it does not promote sensitivities and inclinations. Round-robin reading, another example of a routine often used in schools, doesn't promote thinking either. Sitting and listening to others read does not encourage students to wonder or create. These kinds of routines are mindless habits that do not encourage or actively support students' thinking or mental engagement. "Routine action is guided by impulse, tradition, and authority, whereas reflective action aims at active, persistent, and careful consideration of any belief or supposed form of knowledge in light of the grounds that support it and the further conclusions to which it tends" (Dewey, 1933, p. 9).

Routines like Tish's are great tools to develop and use in your classroom. Students need these kinds of opportunities to think ahead of time about tasks and processes. They need reasons to think about what they are doing and why, and they need time afterward to reflect about what happened. In classrooms, we should see "students who are learning about learning while they are learning" (Levine, 2002, p. 334). Routines that facilitate these things will help you manage your classroom *and* help children develop the disposition to think. Called thinking routines (Ritchhart, 2002), these kinds of routines are described in detail below.

Thinking Routines

For a moment, imagine a diver ready to dive into the ocean with the desire to get as deep as possible to see the spectacular sights waiting under the water. What would the diver need? First, he would need a way into the ocean, like a boat or perhaps just wading toward the deep water. Then he would need something to help him stay in the water, like a wetsuit or a snorkel. Finally, he would need something to help him go down farther, like a weight belt, flippers, or an oxygen mask. Diving into the ocean is a great metaphor for what we want for learners in our classrooms.

We want them to have a way "into" the thinking, we want them to actively participate to "stay in" the thinking, and we want them to go as "deep" as possible within their thinking (Williams & Veomett, 2007).

Thinking routines help give students opportunities to learn how to think deeply (Ritchhart, 2002) and are like most other routines in the following ways:

- They consist of a few steps.

- They are accessible to all learners.

- They are easy to teach and learn.

- They are easy to support.

- They get used repeatedly.

Thinking routines are different from most other routines as well:

- They provide a structure for thinking rather than merely giving directions for a specific task or problem.

- They guide mental actions rather than behaviors.

Just like a diver in the ocean, we want students to think deeply.

- They create opportunities for deeper understanding.

- They facilitate making connections and generating new ideas and possibilities.

- They activate prior knowledge.

- They make students' thinking visible, increasing their awareness of what goes into creating, communicating, organizing, and acting on knowledge (Perkins, 2004).

Many routines developed throughout the years could be considered thinking routines, even though they are not necessarily labeled that way. For example, in the early 1900s, a philosopher named Kilpatrick proposed a problem-solving routine that included "purposing, planning, executing, and judging" (Kliebard, 1995, p. 141). Kolb (1984) developed a learning cycle that includes engaging, exploring, explaining, extending, and evaluating. Wasserman (1988) created a routine for young children involving playing, debriefing, and replaying. Do you see any similarities in these thinking routines? We will look at four different thinking routines in depth here, but I hope you will begin to develop your own as well.

Plan-Do-Review

For material related to this concept, go to Clip 5.2 on the Web-based Student Study Site.

Most likely, you have probably been using the plan-do-review thinking routine for much of your adult life. When you go on vacation, what do you do, and in what order? You plan your trip (even at the last minute), you go on your trip, and you reflect on what happened. The thinking routine is similar when you cook a meal. You plan for ingredients, you make the meal, and then you decide if it was good. We don't often allow children these kinds of experiences. We just expect them to be able to think deeply. It is easy to forget that we have developed the ability, sensitivity, and inclination to plan, do, and review. "Nature seems to have been playing a trick on adults since the beginning of time. We quickly forget what it was like to be a child. Instead we create arbitrary expectations of what children should be like and assume we were that way as children" (Labinowicz, 1980, p. 19). Children have to experience thinking to develop good thinking skills.

The High/Scope Educational Research Foundation developed plan-do-review as a part of a curriculum for preschool children (Hohmann & Weikart, 1995). It has been used at many different levels of education, however, because it has so many benefits for thinking and learning. For example, plan-do-review has been shown to help reduce frequency and intensity of challenging behaviors and to increase quantity of work completed (Feeney & Ylvisaker, 2006); to aid in parent involvement in school due to increased ability to bring in the culture from home within planning time (Bridge, 2001); to increase children's initiation, responsibility, creativity, divergent thinking, independence, cooperation, and self-confidence; and to increase resiliency, verbal skills, autonomy, social competence, and problem-solving skills (Peyton, 2005). Plan-do-review helps all ages of learners develop abilities, sensitivities, and inclination to think deeply (Williams, 2004), and there are several ways you can use this thinking routine in your classroom.

Plan-do-review can be a time of day. Many teachers realize the importance of giving students opportunities to initiate their own projects and solutions to problems. Our discussions in the first three chapters show that choice and autonomy in classrooms are vital to school success, but these same teachers don't want to manage or see the benefit in "free time." I agree: Free time is not a good use of learning time. Students, however, do need time to explore and take their ideas in a direction that interests them. We all need that. What if you didn't have any "free time" throughout your day?

Plan-do-review provides a routine (where students know what to do and how), a structure (with expectations and accountability), and time to work on something of interest while developing habits of thinking. Plan-do-review was always my students' favorite time of day, and they often preferred it to going out for an extra recess. In fact, whenever I see former students, they don't say what a wonderful teacher I was or how they loved the room. Every single former student I have met has talked about plan-do-review time.

To use plan-do-review as a time of day, you need to plan, do, and review! You must plan for the planning phase of this routine, and the students will need to somehow let you know their plan for the time. Plans can be as simple as "I want to play a math game" or "I want to go to the lightbulb station," or they may be more complex. For example, students in my room wanted to learn about archeology, so they planned to create fossils and bury them in an archeology pit (the water table) where they could go on "digs." Some ways to help students communicate their plans include creating a plan-do-review sheet for students to fill out, creating notebooks where they write their plans and reviews, and handing out loose paper for writing their plans and reviews. Remember that you are working to help them think before they initiate action. Planning may take some time and good questioning before young students really become good planners—like my husband planning for an outing with our two young boys (he goes over every possible scenario several times before he really makes a plan!). Also remember that you can create your own way to help students plan. I have seen teachers of young children do everything from attaching a clothespin to a wheel containing all of the choices to sitting in a circle with the children and having them use an unplugged phone to tell everyone their plan. Be creative!

You will also need to plan for students' choices during plan-do-review time. Some teachers (within reason) don't limit what the students can plan, while others allow the students to choose from only a few categories. My students could plan whatever interested them. We had all kinds of projects going, and some plans were just to read. I have seen plan-do-review time, however, where students can choose to visit the computer lab, the writing center, the science center, and so on. Make sure that every once in a while you bring in something new that might spark an interest. Sometimes I asked parents to share a skill during plan-do-review time; one parent, for example, taught some of the children to sew.

Doing time is just like it sounds: Students do whatever they planned to. Sometimes, students will change their minds about their plans, or their plans will evolve. I believe that is a good thing—my students were learning that plans evolve with good observation and reflection skills—so I didn't make them go back and change their plans. This is something you will have to decide. Doing time is also an important time for you. As students carry out their plans, you can ask great questions, wonder aloud what they will do next, and assess any skills they might demonstrate.

Reviewing time, hugely important in this thinking routine, happens when children have the opportunity to make connections between their actions and their thoughts or when children can think about social issues as well as ways to fix any problems with plan-do-review time. At first, children may just give you a synopsis of what happened. For example, I worked at the water table, and we tried to get the water through the pipes across the room to the sink. The idea with a review is to help children think about what they did, so at first you may need to provide them with some thinking tools. I used to put questions on the board: What did you do today? What did you find out? What will you do differently next time? What's going on here? What do you see that makes you say so (Tishman, 2002)? What made it fun to do? Why did you choose this activity? Who helped you? Sometimes I would challenge the students to write a review that would stump me from having any questions.

Some children may not write well enough to get their thoughts on paper. There are, however, a lot of ways to review: drawing pictures, talking about their ideas and experiences with a friend or into a tape recorder, and so on. The idea is to get them reflecting about their past experience. Remember that sharing is very important for accountability and self-worth. Make sure to let the children share their reviews, whether with a partner or the whole group. I had students come to the front of the classroom when they finished writing, and when several students were finished, they took turns reading their reviews. We made sure it wasn't a race to get finished by putting each name on a popsicle stick and pulling one out of a "have not shared" jar to see who got to share next. If the student whose name was drawn wasn't done reviewing, we drew another. Each student who got to read put his or her stick in the "have shared" jar. When all of the sticks were in that jar, we put them all back in the "have not shared" jar.

Plan-do-review time can seem like a lot of time taken out of your schedule. Indeed, planning, doing, and reviewing do take a chunk of time. Although I advocate everyday plan-do-review, even once or twice a week is good. Sometimes, plan-do-review as a time just doesn't work, and there are many other ways to use this thinking routine in your classroom. Check out Letter From a Master Teacher 5.2; Brian took plan-do-review and really molded it to fit his needs.

Plan-do-review can be a routine used during a lesson. Although High/Scope advocates plan-do-review as a time, it can also be utilized with great success within lessons for any grade level. For example, if you give your students a worthy problem to solve, make one of the actions planning, one doing, and another reviewing. My students, for example, worked together to create a game that would help children practice their math facts. They had to make a plan, make the game, and then try it to see how it worked. Plan-do-review works well when students are working in groups because it slows them down and requires them to think before diving right into the solution. At first, groups in my room had to show me their plans for solving a problem before they could get materials, not so I could check their plans but rather so they were sure to make plans. After a while, I didn't even include planning in the lesson because students would automatically make plans without my prompt. Reviewing also becomes more automatic with time. We often don't take enough time to review during lessons, but reviewing should be involved to some extent in each lesson, even if it is just a short whisper to a partner or 10 minutes to write about what they learned.

Plan-do-review can also be used for social goals within lessons. For example, you may have the students plan who will do which roles in groups or how much time they will need to complete a task. Students can also review how well they worked together, if they used their time wisely, and so on. Individuals can plan-do-review their work at stations. They can decide how they will monitor their time at each station or plan the order of stations they will do. Reviewing can be a great individual activity for assessing students' work at stations. Ask them to review how their plans worked and what they would change next time.

Plan-do-review can be used as a routine for large projects. At times, you will probably have your students work on projects that take more than one class period. Plan-do-review is a perfect thinking routine for these times. Having students plan a project over time and then monitor progress throughout is a very important skill. One year, for example, students

LETTER FROM A MASTER TEACHER 5.2

Student Choices Help Them Think

When I first began teaching, I wanted my students to be able to think for themselves, to be independent. I wanted to be able to spend time teaching and getting to know these children as individuals. When I thought of an independent student, I pictured someone who knew what to do and the best time to do it. I pictured a child who did not ask questions because he or she was independent. What I was picturing, however, was not really a child but more like a robot. It was a student who would go through the motions of the school day without thinking too much.

As I have developed my classroom environment over the last several years, I have worked hard to help students realize they do not have to be independent. In the "real world," we seldom do everything by ourselves. When we are baffled by something, we ask for help. When we are excited about learning something new, we tell someone. I have worked to help students in my classroom become independent thinkers. One of the best methods I've used to encourage students to become independent thinkers is thinking routines.

A thinking routine I used often in first grade was plan-do-review. I was able to use it each day while I met with small groups during my reading instruction time. Instead of sending students to ready-made centers to do the same activities week after week, I gave them choices. Some of the choices were similar week-to-week; others were not. At the beginning of choice time each day, students planned what they would do with their time and then did it. At the end of this block of time, we would review what they had done, some students would share, and we would talk about what they would do the next day.

Children, no matter their age, are able to think. The key is trying to understand how they think and how you, as their teacher, can help them use their own way of thinking to help them learn. Thinking routines provide students the opportunity to engage in thinking while at the same time accomplishing tasks that can meet important curriculum topics and standards.

As you prepare to teach, bear in mind that students can—and will—rise to almost any challenge you present. Thinking routines will challenge students in the best way possible. Within the limits you set to keep students safe and provide the best possible learning, they will take charge of their own learning, become autonomous, and display a sense of motivation you never knew they had.

—Brian Johnson
First-Grade Teacher

in my room made large wall-sized murals of different habitats. I gave each student enough paper to cover one wall in the classroom, and as groups they planned what animals and plants would go on the mural, keeping in mind the requirement that each animal and plant must have a source of food, water, shelter, and space on the mural. Students planned both academically and socially before they started. They did research to find out what animals needed, and they worked to figure out who would do what. They even needed to plan for time issues as their mural had to be finished within an allotted time. Throughout the process, we stopped and reviewed to see how we were doing and if we needed to revise plans. The students began to see that plan-do-review isn't really a linear task but a 'round-and-'round routine.

If we are working toward creating classrooms where students become independent learners, think, plan, and make revisions, we need to create classrooms with thinking routines. "For students to be successful as independent learners, they must be aware of their own cognitive processes and be able to identify purposes of tasks, determine what is important to learn, acquire information, and monitor the success of their learning" (Bruning, Schraw, & Ronning, 1999, p. 214). Simple, easy to implement, and very motivating for students, plan-do-review is one of the best things you can use in your classroom right now. Sometimes, however, plan-do-review probably isn't the best thinking routine to use. Keep reading and you will find some other thinking routines that will work in different situations.

Collect-Categorize-Connect

Collect-categorize-connect can be used for social or academic goals and serves as a way to better understand problems before starting to solve them. At times in classrooms, we try to work on problems before we really understand them. We see children fighting on the playground or not understanding a social studies unit, and we try to fix it immediately. This thinking routine will help children get at the true nature of the problem so they can come up with meaningful solutions.

Plan-do-review can help children think about almost anything!

First, students need to collect information. Whether it is a social problem or an academic problem, collecting information is an important first step. This might mean creating a survey, doing a short quiz, or having a conversation as a group. The main idea is to get some good information that children can categorize. For example, if children have problems at recess and come in angry and upset, you can help them collect information by asking them what the possible problems might be and then making those problems into a survey. If many children are struggling in social studies, you might give them a short quiz about the topics and make a chart showing which ones were missed most often. Note that you should not conduct this kind of quiz to punish those who do not understand but rather to help the students and you gather information about what needs further uncovering.

Next, students need to categorize the information. If students create a survey, they will need to organize the information they collect into a graph or show it another way, which won't require a lot of time. Simply tallying ideas or putting them on sticky notes and categorizing them works. The main idea is for the children to think about the information they collected and organize it so they can understand it better. For example, you might have children working on a rock unit collect many different rocks from home and the playground and organize them into categories. You might have children list ways they could solve a "too noisy" problem on sticky notes, hand them in, and then categorize them.

Finally, students can connect to the information. This means that they take the time to think about and connect to the information presented. What does it mean? What are the options? What might happen if we try to solve the problem in that way? The connection phase might occur in a class meeting (Chapter 6), but it might also occur individually in a journal or reflection piece. For example, individual children could collect the math problems they missed, categorize them, and then connect to why they missed them, and you could have them share with you in individual conferences. Individual children could also collect information about what they would like to do for the school secretary on Administrative Professionals Day, categorize the ideas, and then have a class meeting to connect to the information and make a decision.

Think-Pair-Share

Another great, easy thinking routine you can use in any level of classroom is think-pair-share. This thinking routine gives students time to think before participating, allows those who take more time or do not always share in large groups the opportunity to think, and helps those who come up with ideas quickly and participate often to slow down and think through their ideas. Think-pair-share is just as it sounds: You ask a question to the group, give them time to think about it, and perhaps even have them write their answer. Then they turn to a partner and share their ideas. Finally, students can share with the whole group what they came up with or what their team decided.

This thinking routine is easy to use all day. For example, when students come in the door in the morning, they might have a think-pair-share question to do. They would need to spend some time thinking about the question, talk to another person about their answers, and then be ready to share answers with the whole group when everyone arrives. Think-pair-share can also be used as a reflection tool at the end of a lesson. You might close the lesson by asking what everyone learned and have the students think-pair-share their answers. This thinking routine can take quite a bit of time or be a short ending piece.

Know-Want to Know-Learned

For material related to this concept, go to Clip 5.3 on the Web-based Student Study Site.

You may have used or seen this KWL chart before. It is a fairly popular tool but not always called a thinking routine. Great for the beginning and end of units, a KWL chart helps children think through their prior knowledge, consider what they would like to learn, and reflect on what they learned about a topic. It is also a great tool for you as a teacher to understand where the children are in their thinking about a topic. You can discover any misconceptions they have as you begin to plan cooperative workshops. For example, begin a unit or topic by posting a large piece of chart paper with sections for Know, Want to Know, and Learned. Ask the students what they know about the sun, the Civil War, or multiplication. Write all of their answers in the Know column even if they aren't what you believe to be correct. Then ask the students what they want to know about that subject, and write their answers in the Want to Know section (later, it is important that you incorporate some of their questions into your cooperative workshop lessons). Finally, after the unit is over, talk as a class about what the students learned, and write those things in the Learned section. A great tool for differentiating what children will study and helping them plan, this thinking routine can be used individually as well.

Body Models

Body models provide a great thinking routine because they require movement. A perfect thinking routine during times of reflection and sharing, body models can be made by individuals or groups. For example, the students in my room made body models of solids, liquids, and gases. For solids, groups stuck themselves together tightly. For liquids, they held hands and "flowed" out of the "container." For gases, they individually floated around the room. Another time, we studied metamorphic, igneous, and sedimentary rocks. Whenever anyone in the room said the word *sedimentary*, everyone smashed their hands together to show the pressure that creates sedimentary rocks. When someone said *igneous*, we all stood up and made our bodies into volcanoes to show that is where igneous rocks are born, and so on. Body models can be used in any subject. We made body models of shapes, angles, and addition and subtraction problems. We did pantomimes of different books, and other children guessed what they were. We even body modeled punctuation at the ends of sentences.

There are thousands of thinking routines and many more that you can create. Remember that you want children to think in your classroom. To facilitate this, you must create an agenda of thinking, provide opportunities for students to look at multiple sides of topics, and initiate thinking occasions (Ritchhart, 2002). Thinking routines will help!

Thinking Routines as a Piece of Classroom Management

It's funny that we call leading a group of students "management" because the goal should be not to manage them but to lead them to thinking. We want students to think about where they'd like to live, the kinds of ideas they want to remember, and how they want to be treated and treat others. Management implies that we want them to work mindlessly, but we want classrooms to be thinking places. Otherwise, we will teach students that learning is passive and boring.

How do thinking routines relate to classroom management? I don't know any research that has shown that thinking routines will make the students in your room well-behaved or your classroom more orderly. Thinking routines will, however, help your students develop abilities, sensitivities, and inclinations to think (Ritchhart, 2002; Williams, 2004). If your students learn to think about social and academic goals, you will certainly be better able to have a classroom that meets everyone's needs.

As you create a classroom where the future moms, dads, workers, leaders, lawmakers, caretakers, and community members learn, I urge you to provide opportunities for them to think and learn to think. Our world needs people who are busy, happy, and good and who can solve problems, learn, troubleshoot, design, and—most of all—think.

So . . . What?

On the outside, many classrooms look and sound like great places to learn. They are calm, have quiet children doing work, and have children who get "right" answers quickly. This kind of classroom is not good enough for the young people who reside there. Classroom management must facilitate thinking as well. To create a classroom where management creates opportunities for thinking:

Create a list or a concept map of what it means to think. Make sure your ideas about thinking aren't just about abilities. Sensitivities and inclination to think are important as well.

Create a vision for a thinking classroom. Thinking classrooms have management that facilitates learning, have many experts and right answers, help students be physically and mentally active, and utilize thinking routines. How do these things look and sound to you?

Utilize tools like thinking routines throughout your day. Thinking routines can be used for any grade level and any subject. They help children think in the moment and also give them internal structures that will help them continue to think beyond their time in school.

Some effective thinking routines you might try include plan-do-review, collect-categorize-connect, think-pair-share, KWL, and body models.

Try to develop thinking routines that meet your students' needs.

Get Ready For . . .

In this section, so far you have learned some magic and some ways to bring thinking into the classroom. Not bad! The next chapter is full of tools and structures that will help you work with whole groups of students to develop a community of learners. You might say it contains the "whole enchilada" when it comes to structures and strategies for classroom management.

Activities to Try

- Write a reflection about how you think thinking has changed in the last 10 years. How do you think it will change in the next 10?

- How does a thinking routine promote autonomy, belonging, and competency?

- Let's say you have a student who is struggling to do a story problem in math and has brought the problem to you for help. Come up with as many ways as you can that will help the student think.

- Draw a classroom where thinking takes place. What is on the walls? What materials are present? What are the children doing? What are you doing?

- **Make a collection!** Collect thinking routines.

- **Conduct action research!** Find several people who work outside and inside the education field and ask them how they go about thinking when a problem arises. Then categorize and connect to their answers. What do they mean for your classroom and what the children in your classroom need to know and be able to do? Next, try the same piece of research with a group of students.

Student Study Site

The companion Web site for *Elementary Classroom Management* can be found at www.sagepub.com/kwilliamsstudy.

Visit the Web-based student study site to enhance your understanding of the chapter content. The study materials include video clips, practice tests, flashcards, suggested readings, and Web resources.

CHAPTER 6

Leading and Learning With a Whole Group of Students

One of the first years I taught, I had a class of 28 children. We had a room with only three walls and an opening to the hallway. It was crowded and difficult to get all of our "stuff" on the walls and in the room. The group of children included special-education students. There were two children who had been put into foster homes after suffering abuse. There were children who struggled in reading, some who excelled in math, and some who were really only interested in studying frogs. In other words, there was a good mix of students as always. At the end of the year, it was tradition in the school to send the children to the teacher they would have next year so that everyone could meet ahead of time. As I was splitting my children up and telling them where they would be next year, Thomas looked up at me and said, "Why can't we just all stay together?" The other children shook their heads in agreement and looked at me for answers. I can't remember what I said to them—probably something about how they would meet new friends and that it would be OK. In that moment, though, I knew they had become a community.

This group of students had worked with and for each other all year. They had helped and stood up for Zach at recess when he couldn't figure out the games children were playing because of his autism. They befriended Sonja who often smelled of urine, sucked her thumb, and wore unusual clothes. They took turns making towers with Jason because that's what he planned to do every day. They fought together, solved problems together, made cards together when someone was sick, and celebrated any small success together. You may think this must have been an unusual class, but I have seen many like it. You may think I *made* the children do those things, but I only facilitated them with structures and tools that would help them come together.

We have talked a lot about teaching "whole" children in this book. Teaching the child as a whole means not merely focusing on competency but also feeding autonomy, belonging, and motivation. Chapters 4 and 5 described structures and tools that will help you provide those needs for the children in your class. In doing so, however, we mustn't forget to make the group "whole" as well. Individuals cannot be whole if the group they are a part of is not. Robert Reich said, "In America's best classrooms the emphasis has shifted. Instead of individual achievement and competition, the focus is on group learning. Students learn to articulate, clarify, and then restate for one another how they identify and find answers. They learn how to seek and accept criticism from their peers, solicit help, and give credit to others" (Gibbs, 2006, p. 7).

The saying "the whole enchilada" comes from the idea that all the ingredients of a traditional enchilada must be present for it to be a real enchilada. For me, the metaphor of a whole enchilada is helpful when thinking about working with a group of students. Making a group "whole" is like bringing all of the individual children together into something special—rolling up all the ingredients, if you will. The great thing about the metaphor is that if one single ingredient is missing, the enchilada is not as good. It's the same in the classroom. We need all of the children and their personalities, needs, and talents to make a great "whole" group.

You will spend a great deal of time with all of the students each day in a fairly small space. You will need to develop routines and structures (like cooperative workshops and thinking routines) that help individual students, but you will also need to develop routines and structures that bring children together for support, risk taking, friendship, and commitment. The routines and structures you use to manage a group of students will help them become either a "whole" group or just a group of 28 children. "Whole" classrooms end up like the one I described above. The children aren't perfect, there are good days and bad days, and it doesn't happen overnight.

Jesse Keifer

When working with a whole group of students, you need to bring all of the individual students together into something special, just like the ingredients in an enchilada.

In the end, however, the students know each other, learn together, lean on each other, and love each other. They are a true community, and to me, that's the whole enchilada.

By the end of this chapter, I hope you have:

- Your own definition of a "whole" group

- Structures and tools to use in your quest for the whole enchilada, including class meetings, data collection tools, classroom service activities, and group energizers

- Management strategies for whole group activities, including technology, games, and classroom conversations

There are so many ways to bring a group of children together into a wonderful "whole enchilada." The ideas in this chapter only scratch the surface of the possible. The main idea, however, is that bringing children together as a "whole" group matters, in their academic learning as well as for their well-being.

What Is a "Whole" Group?

Have you ever experienced classrooms where you felt you were a part of a "whole" group? These were the classes that offered a cohesive sense of community and an opportunity to take risks, where students worked together to meet goals and could count on each other for support, and where you knew more about the other students than just their names and whether or not they were good students. What did the leader of the class do to facilitate this "whole" group?

I can think of several times that I was a part of a "whole" group. One group in particular stands out. I was in college, and it was a writing class, a normally unusual place to find a "whole" group in a classroom. The professor sometimes let us meet at the coffeehouse where we read our writing to each other. There was a huge mix of people in the class. Some were nontraditional students, some were from other countries and just learning to write in English, and others were just starting college. That summer, I experienced my first car accident, a high school classmate dying, and a boyfriend breakup. The people in that class gave me advice, let me talk, helped me get my car fixed, and so on, and I helped them with various issues. We helped each other figure out what the professor's comments meant on our papers, and we edited and rewrote together. I learned a lot about writing that summer because I was motivated to help the people who were helping me. I enjoyed sharing my writing with them because they cared. There were other classes I took that summer where I felt like one number in a row of others. That feeling didn't have anything to do with the number of people in the class, the mixture of students, or the topic we were studying. It had to do with how the class was managed.

I am not suggesting that you spend a great deal of time having students work as a whole group, especially if that time is for lecture or seatwork. It is important, however, to have times when you come together to solve problems, support each other, and celebrate the learning that has taken place. Creating opportunities for positive peer relationships and a sense of caring and support promote enhanced academic learning, stronger motivation to learn, fewer behavior problems, and greater social understanding (Good & Brophy, 2000; Lewis, Schaps, & Watson, 1996). Alas! Taking time to help students know each other and be a part of a community is actually time well spent. Students' learning is enhanced in this kind of setting. Think of a class that you were a part of that seemed "whole." How was it managed?

Certainly, there are many ways to define a "whole" group, and there is no right answer. It is important, however, to think about what your definition is so you can begin facilitating its development on the very first day of class and collecting ideas to help you do so. What do you believe are the characteristics of a "whole" group? Below are four beginning ideas to think about on your quest for the "whole enchilada."

"Whole" Groups Include All of the Children

This may seem obvious at first. To have a whole group, all of the children must be involved. As you begin to think about a "whole" group, however, the idea of including all children becomes a little messier. Some of the techniques teachers use to manage students can often leave students out of the whole. Students who are constantly sent to the office or into the hall are not in the "whole" physically or mentally. When students are sent away often, other students may ostracize them instead of working to help them. When students are reprimanded in front of the whole group or are shamed into behaving, the environment becomes one of ridicule instead of care. We send a lot of messages to individuals with the kinds of management tools we use as teachers. For example, we hear teachers say, "This is our classroom," but the teachers make all the decisions. We hear, "You are in charge of yourself," but lots of rules are on the board. We hear, "Everyone is special," but culture and ethnicity are ignored. We hear, "No one is favored," but the smart children are called on more. We hear "Creativity is important," but the approach is already defined (Gibbs, 2006, p. 3).

Some students have a hard time becoming a part of the "whole" group. For whatever reason, they may have difficulty being friendly, or they may have different mannerisms or customs. Sometimes students just don't know how to be social. We can't make students befriend one another, but we can help them see value in each person. It may be as simple as letting students shine at what they are good at. For example, I had a student named Daniel who really struggled in school. When others could do math problems in their heads, he needed to count with manipulatives. When others were reading chapter books, he was still reading picture books. The children noticed, and he started to withdraw from our class. I knew, however, that he was a really good skateboarder. He could do all of the ramps and jumps on a skateboard. So, when we sat down for a class meeting one day, I explained how some children are good at school things and some children are good at things that we don't learn in school. We all talked about things that we were good at that we didn't get to learn in school. Daniel told us about his skateboarding. I commented again that if skateboarding was a subject in school, some of us would be very good at it, and some of us would not. We had a long conversation about how everyone is good at something and that we should value all of those things. I had Daniel bring his skateboard to school and got special permission for him to show us some of his moves. I think that conversation helped Daniel and some of the others as well. The moral of the story?

Each child must be seen as and believe he or she is a valuable member of the group. Management must support each child to become a part of the "whole."

"Whole" Groups Have and Work on Common Goals

It isn't enough to just value each other, although that will go a long way in creating a "whole" group. Coming together is about working together toward something. If a group doesn't have a purpose, its members will have difficulty staying together and working hard for each other. Goals might be academic, social, or communitywide; however, students should agree on them. In other words, the teacher should not come up with the goals. Making sure everyone understands the social studies unit or has a friend to sit by at lunch helps children come together even if they have differences.

I have talked about several of my classrooms for this book because I was in seven different rooms the first 6 years I taught! One room happened to be next to a teacher who liked it quiet. The school was very open, and only moveable walls separated rooms. My class had issues with noise because the students moved around a lot and worked on projects together. When the teacher next door to me complained that my class was giving her headaches, our class suddenly had a reason to work together. In a class meeting, we talked about the noise and why the other teacher was upset. It was a major goal because no one wanted to stop doing projects or working in groups. We brainstormed ideas and then came up with a plan to keep the noise down, involving mini stop signs and quiet keepers (students whose job was to monitor the quiet). The moral of the story? If you let students work together to achieve something important, they will come together as a "whole" group.

"Whole" Groups Do Things Other Than Academic Work Together

With all of the standards and expectations put on students these days, it is difficult for teachers to make time for anything but academic work. I hear it from teachers in every class I teach. "We don't have time!" "I have to get through X amount of standards before the end of the year." I realize there is a lot of pressure to get high scores, but I hope you will consider that doing academic work all day without any whole group support or brain rest won't help your students learn the material and that, even as adults, we need time to rest and revive. We need time to think and reflect. Killion and Simmons (1992) use the phrase "Go slow to go fast," which is good to think about when working to create a "whole group." If you take some time to do a few things that aren't necessarily considered academic and the students are awakened, it will be easier for them to learn what they need to learn.

Student teachers often ask me what I did when the children in my rooms were having a bad day or just couldn't seem to settle down to work. My answer often surprises them. I think they expect me to say I made my students sit at their seats and do a worksheet as punishment. However, I usually took the students out for recess. "But . . . doesn't that teach them that misbehaving gets them a reward?" I guess it would be a reward if you believe children are trying to be disruptive, but most likely when whole groups of students are having trouble settling down or are lethargic, they just need a couple of minutes to relax. When a whole group is having trouble, punishing the students won't help. Would punishment make you want to buckle down and work harder when you feel frustrated? I usually find, if I am having trouble working, a walk around the block or something to drink helps me focus. Students who are struggling may need something different for a few minutes. Indeed, whole group brain exercises, playing a quick game together, and doing an **energizer** are helpful ways to go slow to go fast.

Sometimes "whole" groups need to come together to do something beyond academics so they can get to know each other. Children can certainly get to know each other while working in cooperative workshops, but sometimes it is important to facilitate getting to know each other with activities meant specifically for that purpose. Once again, time spent on such activities as class picnics, opening or closing circle, and other social events will prevent you from wasting time addressing behaviors and fighting. I had a couple of master's degree students who transformed their entire school with other-than-academic activities. They had all-school learning pep rallies and mixed up lunch days so buddy classrooms could eat together. Although this took time out of the academic day, they found that their school was a much more positive place and, in their action research study, that grades went up. The moral of the story? We must treat students like human beings. We can't expect them to work the entire school day and do well; nor can we expect them to come together as a democratic community if we do not give them the opportunity. Lewis, Schaps, and Watson (1996) said, "Students work harder, achieve more, and attribute more importance to schoolwork in classes in which they feel liked, accepted, and respected by the teacher and fellow students" (p. 18).

"Whole" Groups Celebrate Learning

For material related to this concept, go to Clip 6.1 on the Web-based Student Study Site.

We often forget this one, but it is fairly important. When students do projects together or have done something spectacular that needs to be shared, there should be opportunities for celebrations. I know what you're thinking: Isn't that a reward? Perhaps, but it isn't a coercive reward (e.g., "If you all pass the reading comprehension test, I will buy pizza for the whole class"), which students may believe is the only reason to do well on the test. If students work really hard on wall-size habitat murals and decide to invite parents and other classrooms to view them (with a few cookies for sustenance), however, students are sharing their learning with others. They are proud of their accomplishments and want to celebrate. My favorite "whole" group celebration happened the year my students learned about the seven defensive weapons that keep germs out of your body (Gelman, 1992). To celebrate that learning, we did the book as a play for parents and other classrooms. The children made paper costumes and were transformed into mucus, cilia, earwax, and stomach acid. It was a wonderful celebration, and we learned something too!

It is important to celebrate learning and hard work and to let students know that their work is valued. "Whole" groups celebrate individuals' accomplishments as well. Learning should not be a competition. Instead, students should have an opportunity to share things they are proud of, and students and teachers should show their appreciation. At times in my classroom, I made children who had really learned something that they were struggling with stand up and jump up and down. The other children sometimes got up and jumped with them. Sometimes, we put paper on everyone's back and wrote compliments. Sometimes at class meetings, we went around and each person gave another a compliment. The moral of the story? Celebrations bring students together and, in the process, create positive memories of school.

Simple celebrations, such as getting up and jumping up and down after doing something well, don't take much time and are meaningful to children.

Working to help children become a part of a "whole" group seems like a simple act in some ways. Making sure that all children are valued, are making and achieving goals together, get to know each other in meaningful ways, and have opportunities to celebrate can happen with a few structures and tools. Some of them are described below, and they will be helpful as you work to bring children together to learn. The important thing, however, is that you create opportunities for the students in your classroom to have a sense of belonging, a sense that they matter. Sometimes the best things for children are simple, just like the structures and tools below.

Hot Tools for Facilitating a "Whole" Group

Just like you need an oven to transform the tortilla, cheese, and meat into an enchilada, you need some hot tools and structures to help a group of students transform into a "whole" group. Remember that slow cooking is best—this transformation won't happen overnight—and that there are many kinds of ovens. Find the tools that work for you.

Class Meetings

Class meetings are one of the easiest ways to help a group of students come together. They fit into the tiniest openings in a day, and you can accomplish a great deal in a short amount of time. Providing a safe environment for students to solve problems, practice effective communication skills, and resolve conflicts (Frey & Doyle, 2001), class meetings have been shown to increase acceptable classroom behavior and students' positive self-concept (Sorsdahl & Sanche, 1985), as well as to improve overall social competence in children (Briggs, 1996). Finally, programs like class meetings have been recommended as ways to decrease bullying (Dake, Price, & Telljohann, 2003). You can use class meetings for a variety of purposes, as detailed below.

For material related to this concept, go to Clip 6.2 on the Web-based Student Study Site.

Class meetings can be used to help children get to know each other. Once a day, either in the morning or the afternoon, children can sit in a circle so they can see each other, and each of them can answer the same question. For example, ask children to name their favorite book, their best skill, or the person they would most like to resemble, or have students compliment others, say something they are worried about, or name something that makes them happy. Frey and Doyle (2001) recommend teaching young children the difference between inside compliments and outside compliments as well as how to accept a compliment when using class meetings for this purpose. Sometimes teachers ask students to come up with class meeting questions and find that the children really come up with great ones. There are a couple of keys to using a class meeting in this way:

- Everyone must be a part of the circle. In other words, someone can't be finishing his or her work or be at the office, and so on. Everyone has to be there.

- Students can pass if they need to. Be sure to come back to them at the end and ask if they would like to share.

- Students are not allowed to comment on others' replies.

- Use a speaking stick (something for children to hold when talking) to illustrate that only that child should be talking.

- Children need to understand that they should not use the information as gossip material and why.

My experience with using classroom meetings in this way has been very positive. My students and I have learned a lot about each other and laughed and sometimes cried together. If there is trust, children will tell you important things during this kind of class meeting. Be sure to listen.

Class meetings can be used as a way to solve problems. Don't forget that the students in your classroom are people just like you and me. They will have issues, fights, and disagreements with each other. Some problems will come from outside your classroom, and some problems will be about materials. Having a voice in the process of solving those problems is valuable for two reasons (you can probably think of more): First, when children solve problems together, they learn how to solve problems. Second, when children solve problems together, they often feel that the problem has actually been addressed.

Solving problems within class meetings can take some time, so I wouldn't do this every day. I might do it once a week or when something is bothering many of the children. There are several keys to problem solving during class meetings:

- Make sure the problem to be addressed is a class problem and not a two-person squabble. If it is a two-person squabble, have the two people handle it in a similar way, but not with the whole group.

- Teach the children how to state the problem. They should be able to tell you what the problem is and why it is a problem (e.g., "We have a problem at recess because a lot of children are fighting. This is a problem because when we come in from recess, we talk about recess and don't get our work done"). Particular student names should not be used.

- Discuss the problem, but limit this discussion with a timer. You will need to determine how children discuss the problem. Will they raise their hands? Will you go around the circle with those who don't need to talk passing? Will you just have them talk as they need to without interrupting?

- Have students figure out ways to solve the problem and list them on the board. Vote on the different solutions if needed. As sometimes more than one solution can be implemented at a time, however, it may be useful for each member of the class to state the solution he or she will use.

- Take some time to make sure there aren't any objections to solutions, and remember that you have a voice in the class too. If a solution isn't appropriate, be sure to say so.

- Revisit the problem at another meeting to see if solutions are working.

In my experience, using class meetings to help children solve problems has been very effective. Remember, however, that it takes time to help children learn how to solve problems in this way and requires some patience at first. Data collection will help you determine what issues need to be resolved; check it out in the next section.

Class meetings can be used to help develop and maintain a vision for classroom life. Often, teachers post and go over their classroom rules on the first day. Sometimes, teachers even come up with classroom rules with their students, have everyone sign them, and then hang them up. In my evolution as a teacher, I have done both of these things; however, I have come to believe that rules aren't the way to go. Certainly, classrooms need to be safe and respectful of teachers and students . . . but how? Rules seem to create reasons to tattle and compete. Students become the rule police instead of working together to maintain a safe, fun classroom for everyone. In addition, rules make it difficult for a teacher to help individual students. They connote the black-and-white rather than gray areas we need to see as teachers.

What might be right for one student may not be right for another. In other words, fair doesn't always mean equal. Class meetings can be a way to create a **vision** for the classroom where all students can be successful, respected, and respectful.

You may think this kind of class meeting takes place only once, but it really needs to be maintained and updated regularly. A classroom vision can't collect dust but needs to be constantly revisited and changed as problems occur and as we learn what we really want. For example, at the beginning of the year, students often want things like recess time and parties. As the year progresses and things happen in the classroom and on the playground, however, they discover that they want kindness and opportunities to shine. The vision changes as students reflect on what is important for learning. The vision also needs to be revisited when things happening in the classroom don't reflect the classroom vision. For example, if kindness is part of the classroom vision and children are being unkind, that needs to be recognized aloud in a class meeting. There are several keys to creating a classroom vision during a class meeting:

- Your first class meeting is a great time to begin work on your classroom vision.

- Voting is absent during the vision-making process because everyone must agree on the classroom vision. If you think back to Chapter 2, democracy doesn't necessarily mean voting. We don't want minority rights to be left out in the classroom.

- Instead of voting, I recommend using a process where every voice ends up in the final vision. One such process utilizes multiple groupings to get to the final work on the classroom vision. The students first think individually about what they need and are willing to give in their classrooms. Notice that it is not just what they need but also what they are willing to give. That is important. We can't have the "whole enchilada" if children aren't willing to give what they need. Have students write individual ideas on sticky notes, or write smaller children's ideas on the board. Next, have students get into small groups and categorize their ideas, using the smaller sticky notes to define the category. Combine those groups and have them repeat the process. They may have some of the same categories and, in that case, can combine their sticky notes to define the category. Finally, put all of the categories together, and write their categories and definitions as a vision statement (e.g., The children in our classroom need and are willing to give kindness, help, fun, quiet when someone needs it, and sharing).

- Post your vision somewhere in the room. I recommend keeping the sticky notes underneath the statement words because everyone's voice will be represented.

- Have as many categories as needed. Don't try to limit children to only five categories. I know it isn't as "clean" when a vision has 18 parts; however, it is important that it is the students' vision.

- You have a voice in this process. Make sure you make sticky notes as well and participate in groups.

- For smaller children, you may do the categories as a whole group and put them together, making sure to ask students if that is what they mean.

Although a vision statement and rules may seem similar, the process and differences in language are important. What's the difference between having rules in a classroom and telling a student, "Hey, you broke this rule" and having a vision and telling him, "Talk to me about how your actions support our vision. I don't want to be in a classroom where people are unkind"?

Class meetings are powerful tools in creating a "whole" classroom. Using them will help you know your students, help your students know each other, and help you create a classroom where creating a vision and solving problems help each student belong to something bigger than him- or herself.

Data Collection Tools

Working to become a "whole" class requires structures that help each class member become a researcher. In other words, teachers and students must use **data** to help assess what is really happening in the classroom. As teachers, we often think we know what is going on in our classrooms, but without meaningful opportunities for data collection, we really have only a beginning idea. Quiet students or students who work to please the teacher and superficially seem to be doing well don't always have a voice in the larger group context (Reay, 2006). In other cases, students who appear to have behavior problems may have different issues. "In the past, efforts at classroom reform have suffered from a myopic (narrow minded) emphasis on the perspectives of the teachers in the classrooms, or of outside observers who were not classroom participants. The perspectives of the students who learn in the classrooms and the students' families are sadly overlooked" (Doll, Zucker, & Brehm, 2004, p. 45). To help children succeed, we must understand their perspective and help them understand the perspective of others.

Data collection tools are one of the best ways for teachers and students to have solid information about their classrooms. I once worked with a teacher, for example, who wanted to implement class meetings and community building activities in her classroom. She worked on it for several months and collected data from surveys and interviews to see how these activities were affecting her students. Before she had analyzed her surveys and interviews, however, she came to me believing that the activities hadn't had any effect. As we sat and looked through the students' comments and made graphs about what the students said they were learning, her attitude changed. She said, "Oh my gosh. I had no idea they felt this way." The teacher thought she knew her classroom, but until she had data, she only had her own lens to look through. With data from her students, she had many lenses. There are many easy ways to collect meaningful data; share them with your students, and use them to help make the classroom a better place. Surveys, 5-minute writes, and tally charts will be described here.

Before we begin, a few words of advice: A researcher I know once described research/data collection as wisdom but not truth. This idea is important as you begin to dig deeper into what happens in your classroom. Though valuable, data collection is only a tool;

"Mr. Kraus, we have some problems. A few of us [fourth-grade classmates] think we need one of our circles." These students seemed to be on a mission and quickly found themselves positioned in a circle on the floor at the front of our room.

We had spent a great amount of time at the very beginning of the year discussing what community was; where, why, and how it existed; and if there was any parallel between outside school communities and communities that could exist inside the school or even inside our very own classroom. We had done community-building activities. We had consistently talked about each of us as individuals, as well as about the need and desire to be a "whole" for, as they liked to say, "the greater good of 4K."

This was one of several meetings that we had throughout the year where concerns were addressed, feelings were shared, and problems were solved. In this particular meeting, several things were bothering the students at lunch and lunch recess. Some were large concerns that the students drafted out and invited the principal into the classroom to discuss with them. Others were smaller and simply got talked out right then.

I remember the meeting well because it was extremely powerful, as the students took a great deal of pride in what they had been part of. I also remember thinking how great it was that at this early stage of the year, these students were already pulling together and really looking out for one another. Not that we didn't have our share of difficulties: We had several. Our classroom community, just like any true community, drifted in and out of phases and stages, but we continued to take and make time for our community throughout the year as our needs changed. At times, the whole community was in disarray. At other times, only certain individuals were at different stages. Most important was that at no time did we lose the desire to remain connected and work toward "the greater good."

I don't believe there is a "cookie cutter" model of what a community looks and feels like inside a classroom. I do believe that true community can exist in any environment where individuals and leaders take the time to foster community. Use tools that let students discuss, share, empathize, and celebrate together to make the classroom a fun, safe place for them to learn. You will never regret the time and attention spent on community, as it deepens and strengthens the learning and connections to students' worlds and each other.

—Kevin Kraus
Fourth-Grade Teacher

it is only another piece of information to analyze. If data are telling you something, you may have to ask another question, listen a little closer, or observe from another angle to get at what is really happening. Never use data for rewards or punishments. Use data to make a classroom better, to help students understand more about their learning, or to gather more information to help a student. Finally, data collection should be collected *with* students. They need to be "in on" whatever you are collecting. The tools below will help you gather data with your students and use those data in a way that will move you toward the "whole enchilada."

Surveys and Graphs

Giving surveys and then graphing the results can help the members of a classroom see and hear all voices about various social issues that are important for children. You can make up your own surveys; however, I recommend using Class Maps surveys, from the book *Resilient Classrooms* (Doll, Zucker, & Brehm, 2004). Such statements as "I know other children will not tease me, call me names, or make fun of me" (Doll et al., 2004, p. 130) can be very helpful in beginning classroom conversations about problems children have but may be afraid or unwilling to talk about. Students can answer yes, sometimes, or no to the statements, which then can be graphed so everyone can see the compiled answers. As a class, then, students can look at the graphs and begin to figure out where there are problems. A lot of "no" and "sometimes" answers might mean that many children are being teased in the classroom, which might be something for the class to address and work to solve in a class meeting. In addition, if there are only a handful of "no" and "sometimes" answers on the graph, students can still see them. As a teacher, I might say, "Gosh, a few children feel like they are being teased and made fun of in our classroom. How could we solve this problem?" This would give the children being teased the opportunity to have a voice, but since the survey is anonymous, they would not be singled out in front of the others.

After you have analyzed the graphs, it is important to talk to students about how they will fix the problem, as well as to discuss what the graphs show they feel good about. Do this in a class meeting as discussed above. After solutions are formed and implemented for some time, it is important to go back and resurvey the students to see how well they are doing. In other words, has the solution changed the graph?

You may wonder why it is necessary to go through all the trouble of doing a survey and making a graph just to find out that some children are teasing or that a couple of people feel like they don't have friends to play with at recess. You may be able to determine this without doing the surveys. Although this process may take a bit of time, it is a powerful tool that you and your students can use periodically. The visual picture of how everyone in a classroom feels is key to helping students understand their classrooms. In addition, students become partners in implementing classroom interventions rather than merely taking the blame for incidents and trends in the classroom. "Students who are involved in a collecting data and understanding it help create a better classroom and at the same time enhance their autonomy and self-determination" (Doll, Zucker, & Brehm, 2004, p. 83). Surveys and graphs are a wonderful tool that you can use to help bring all members of a class together into a "whole" (see Figure 6.1).

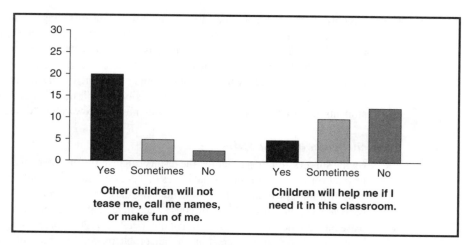

FIGURE 6.1   Example Survey Graphs

Putting this kind of data in front of students can help them determine issues and help each other solve them. What is your analysis of the graphs above?

5-Minute Writes

Sometimes numbers and graphs don't tell the whole story of the students in a classroom. Students may have more to say about bullying, the lunchroom, or how they feel in the classroom than merely yes, no, or sometimes. To bring out important stories that may hover silently in a classroom and keep a class from being whole, you can use what I call **5-minute writes**, which are just like they sound: Give the students a small piece of paper and ask them to write about a question for 5 minutes (see Table 6.1 on p. 156). This form of data collection may not work for small children who cannot write well, and in that case, it may be important to take some time to interview them briefly. The point is not to take too much time and to get some good meaty data that will help you and your students understand happenings in the classroom. For example, you might ask the students to write about their experiences at recess: What do you like about recess? What bothers you about recess?

After the students have written, collect the papers and put their statements on strips of paper that everyone can see. Make sure students know that you will be sharing their statements with the class and have a procedure ready if a student wants to write something to you privately. You don't have to use every bit of the writings, but make sure to use a part of each student's piece. Pick out small parts that you think are meaningful. Put the strips of paper on the board, and during a class meeting, have the students sort them into categories or themes. Just as recommended with the surveys, have the students analyze the data and come up with conclusions. Then have conversations about the issues and how they can be addressed.

Meant to encourage reflection and help students see others' perspectives, 5-minute writes do not need to be posted each day or week. I suggest putting them up when you need to address an issue causing problems in the classroom. For example, if you have observed some children standing alone at recess, asking the questions above might be a way into that issue. You could have children do 5-minute writes more often and use them for your own reflection purposes as well, a great way to learn what children understand academically and socially. For example, you might ask them to write for 5 minutes about clouds, mealworms, Jamestown, or whatever you are studying.

Once again, it is important that you establish a procedure for 5-minute writes that promotes trust. Children should be able to turn in their writings anonymously, and you should never use their writings for punishment or rewards. They should not be graded. As you begin to collect data to help children develop a "whole" classroom, remember that data are meant to provide an information tool. You and your students are collecting information so you can better make sense of happenings in the classroom.

Tally Charts

A **tally chart** can be used to show patterns in classroom happenings (see Table 6.2 on p. 157). Sometimes we get so absorbed in the activities and the hustle and bustle of the classroom that we can't see what is really taking place. Other times, we assume something takes place all the time when really it is isolated. I have used tally charts for a variety of purposes, both individually and for the entire class. I once had a student named Josh, for example, who really struggled behaviorally. His dad had been put into prison, and he was an angry young man. Instead of lashing out, however, he played mean pranks on other children. He locked them in the bathroom by putting a chair up against it, or he tipped over students' chairs as they were about to sit down. In other words, he disrupted class with his antics. At first, I believed his actions took place all the time throughout the day—when someone is disruptive, it can seem as though there is never a moment of peace! So, I decided to make a tally chart for Josh to see if there were times of day when he was playing his pranks and if, with that information, we could figure out why. I made a tally chart that listed each subject, including lunch, recess, and transition times, with room to make tally marks beside it. I put it on a clipboard, and it traveled with me. Every time I thought Josh was being disruptive, I put a tally mark on the chart. Of course, the students wanted to know what I was doing, so I just told them I was collecting data. They knew what that was, and I didn't explain further. After doing the tally chart for Josh for a while, I found that the tally marks were high when we were doing something that required him to sit on the carpet area (reading a book to the whole class, sharing plan-do-review sheets, getting directions, etc.) and when there was not a structured activity (bathroom breaks, walking down the hall, etc.). I also found that there were not very many tally marks when he was working on something alone or with a small group and when he was out at recess. The tally marks were fairly regular but changed from time to time as other issues came up in his life. On some days, he really struggled, and on others, he hardly had any tally marks.

After a couple weeks of tallies, I showed Josh my chart. I want to make it clear that I didn't show him the chart for any other reason than to help him analyze and understand his actions. I did not say, "Josh, if you can make fewer tally marks, I will give you a prize" or "Josh, you had better get fewer tally marks, or I will have to call your mom." Instead, I just let him look at it and asked him what he thought. He and I analyzed it and came up with some ways to help him during the times he struggled. The tally chart was a tool that helped us into a conversation.

TABLE 6.1   5-Minute Write Example

Think about the conversation you might have with the students who wrote these statements. What would you ask them?

Prompt: Why do you think we are having trouble keeping the bathrooms tidy?

Some children think it is funny to make spitballs and throw them on the ceiling. I think we should ask for help when it happens. I don't like it.

One or two students are doing it. I think there are too many children in the bathroom.

There are too many children in the bathroom at once, and it is hard to throw things away. I do not have enough time.

The bathroom is gross. There are spitballs all over, and no one throws the paper away. I think we should tell if someone does that. There are lots of children in the bathroom at once.

Some children think it's funny to throw spitballs.

There are too many children in the bathroom.

There are too many children in the bathroom.

It's hard to throw things away.

There are spitballs in the bathroom.

There are too many children in the bathroom.

There are a lot of children in the bathroom.

Tally charts can be useful for the whole group or small groups. You and your students can keep track of everything from compliments in a small group to which items on a test children have trouble understanding. Individual children can keep tally charts for individual goals, and you can use them to help the entire group resee a goal or problem.

You may wonder how a tally chart can bring a group of students into a "whole." Tally charts and every other kind of data collection help children understand the issues and problems that creep up and often go unaddressed. These tools help give children a voice and a visual picture of a cause beyond themselves.

TABLE 6.2   Tally Example

Using a tally chart can help you see some patterns when working with students.

	1/23	1/24	1/25	1/26
Opening Circle	|||			||	|||
Reading Workshop				
Story					||	||
Bathroom Break								
Math				
Lunch						
Recess				
Writer's Workshop		(During sharing time)			(Sharing again)			
Science				
Plan-Do-Review					
Closing Circle								

Whole Class Service Activities

Dissecting really strong, committed communities of people reveals that they often come together in crisis or time of need (Peck, 1987). After the attacks on 9/11 in New York City, for example, even very large groups of people came together to help one another. Even though we do not wish for crisis in a classroom to develop "whole" groups, we can help bring children together to work on a cause beyond themselves through service learning projects. **Service learning** has been shown to improve academic success (Vogelgesang & Alexander, 2000) as well as social skills and behavioral problems (Tannenbaum & Brown-Welty, 2006).

LETTER FROM A MASTER TEACHER 6.2

Using Data in the Classroom

As educators, we need to take a hard look at how we are trying to motivate students. Are we using grades, test scores, and even popcorn parties to elicit the effort and performance we desire? What do these practices do to the feelings of community that we work to create in our classrooms? Rewards or grades may work in the short term, but they do not have lasting effects on student motivation. Allowing students to learn for the sake of learning can result in incredible progress. Furthermore, giving students a visual representation of that learning can be a powerful motivator.

While teaching reading in a Title I classroom, I gave second-grade students quizzes over a random sampling of their high-frequency words. Then we graphed their results, individually and collectively. The students were excited to take the quizzes and watch their graphs grow throughout the school year. They weren't trying to get an A or pass a test; they truly wanted to learn and watch that graph go up. Students also understood how they were an integral part of the whole. They knew everyone had to continue to learn words to make the graphs go higher. On quiz days, they encouraged each other to do their best; on graphing days, they cheered for their peers' accomplishments.

I have used graphs in various classroom settings for various purposes. Students of all ages understand the graphs and what they are displaying. In my kindergarten room, students were blurting out and interrupting teachers and classmates. We started coloring a square on a graph if someone blurted out. The students were able to see how many times it happened each day and realized they could affect how many squares were colored. After a few weeks, we were able to proudly hang our descending graph on the wall with a sign that read, "We remember to raise our hands!" They weren't rewarded or punished. They merely used data to understand the problem and celebrate its solution.

Graphing behaviors or learning gives students a visual reminder of what they are working toward. They can tell how their actions can influence the class and feel a great sense of accomplishment when they see positive growth on a graph. No extrinsic rewards are necessary when students are motivated by their own progress.

–Zonna Betz
Kindergarten Teacher

Projects that involve service for others provide students with opportunities for belonging and competency. They bring children together to do something worthwhile and meaningful.

I read about a classroom of children studying history who went to a nursing home and interviewed residents about their experiences. At the same time, they made cards for the residents, sang them songs, and visited with them. Students learned history but also about the elderly, planning, and many other social skills. The residents of the nursing home had visitors and a chance to help young people see history from another perspective (Parker, 2006). I asked some of the master teachers I know about service learning projects as well. Josh talked about how his students once made a path for one of the 4-H campsites and often picked up trash around the school. Rae told me that her children had written letters to the troops and collected cans of food for the food bank. Lisa let her special education students plan and develop several service learning projects that included visiting a senior center and collecting needed items for the Humane Society. There are a gazillion different service projects you can do with your students; you just have to seek them out and allow the students to determine what is best. Think about the following things as you plan for service learning.

Miss Donna helps Lily make a blanket to take to the Humane Society. What is this child learning?

Service learning can be tied to the curriculum. You will most likely need to attach some academic learning to the project you choose. Luckily, connections between service learning projects and subjects are prevalent. "Much more than just an opportunity to do good for others, service learning projects provide an essential link between the academic skills that students are developing and the real world contexts that give these skills value" (Coulter, 2004, p. 20). Many service learning projects have math skills, writing skills, speaking and listening skills, and so on, connected at every point. I once observed a classroom where students decided they wanted to collect pennies for the Red Cross. They had been studying weather and got into natural disasters. The Red Cross came up when they were making sense of how people got relief from different storms. The students decided they wanted to know more about this and called the Red Cross to ask a speaker to come to class. When I say the students called, I mean it. The teacher didn't make the phone call but instead taught the students how to introduce themselves on the phone and ask for what they needed. After the speaker came, the students decided to collect pennies for their local chapter of the Red Cross. One day, as everyone was busily working, two students stood up and rang a bell. Everyone was quiet, and they announced that they had counted the pennies and they had reached their goal. All of the children cheered and clapped. Then they, as a "whole" group, made plans to get the money to the organization. The project was tied to many academic and social areas, including weather, counting, money, writing, speaking, and listening. Most important, the students were proud and came together to do something that would benefit others.

Service learning must be student-driven. Perhaps it would be easier to tell children that they have to do a service learning project and plan it for them. However, that would not help children come together, understand a cause beyond themselves, or become independent learners. It would only be one more thing to do to please the teacher. That doesn't mean you can't help students be aware of possibilities for service learning projects. Bringing in news clippings and having students do the same or reading books with social issues can spark ideas for social learning projects. Coming up with the idea for a service learning project isn't the only aspect of this process that needs to be student-led. Students should be in charge of calling, collecting, organizing, and implementing projects. You can help by asking questions and creating committees. You may also need to provide a voice of reason when a project gets too big or inappropriate. You must discuss feasibility of a project. For example, if students want to collect coats for a homeless shelter, they should not go door-to-door to collect them.

Special-education students are often service recipients rather than service providers. This often hinders attempts to encourage students' independence. Service learning projects that fully include students help those who traditionally receive services (Abernathy & Obenchain, 2001).

Service learning projects need not be too complex or competitive. Projects can be as simple as doing something for the school or a family within the school. Projects need not always center on collecting either. Students can write letters, draw pictures, clean, or sing songs. There are many ways to serve others. Many times, service projects become ways to win prizes. The prize for doing a service learning project should be the good feeling one gets when helping others.

Group Energizing Tools

"Whole" groups need to laugh, play, and celebrate together. Remember that learning is emotional and physical, and if we leave out those things that promote a sense of well-being, we leave out learning. Gibbs (2006) defines six outcomes achieved through the use of energizers:

- The energy of the classroom is revitalized.

- People's attention can be drawn back to the classroom after time away for activities like recess and lunch.

- Different types of academic learning activities can be bridged, renewing energy and concentration.

- People can feel connected again with one another and the whole community.

- Multiple intelligences can be reached and engaged.

- They add to the fun of learning and being together (p. 197).

For material related to this concept, go to Clip 6.3 on the Web-based Student Study Site.

At times, academic learning can be integrated into these kinds of energizers, and at other times, it is just good to give children time to rest and reenergize. I have listed some energizers below and organized them according to when you might use them. Once again, I encourage you to make a collection of energizers to pull out when you need them. One invaluable source for great energizers is Gibbs's (2006) book, *Reaching All by Creating Tribes Learning Communities*.

Some energizers can be used every day. These kinds of energizers are quick, get students moving, and can be used in many different situations in or out of the classroom. For example, if you have students stand in line and they must wait for some time, a great silent energizer is to have them hold their right index finger out parallel with the ground and point their left thumb toward the sky. Then have them switch so that the left index finger is out parallel and the right thumb points toward the sky. Have them try to switch back and forth as fast as they can. This is a great brain exercise as well. If students have been sitting, have them go around the room, give five people a high-five, and tell them they are glad to see them. You might implement a joke of the day that children can write on paper and read to the class at a dull moment or when you are transitioning between subjects.

Some days you might tie an energizer to academic learning. For example, I had children do multiplication tables by drawing number lines outside with sidewalk chalk and then jumping by 3s, 4s, and so on. I also like the idea of asking students to write their answers to questions on paper and then wadding the paper up and having a "snowball" fight with it to music. When the music stops, everyone has to pick up a paper and read the answer aloud. This can also be done with a beach ball. You can write different questions on the beach ball and have students throw it back and forth. They have to answer the question on the part of the ball where their index finger lands. Body models are also good academic energizers. Having students make models with their bodies of letters, shapes, punctuation, and so on, is a lot of fun and can energize a group. Finally, one other energizer to use on some days is a walk and talk. Students get a partner and walk on the playground reflecting about whatever they are learning. When they come back, ask one of the partners what they discussed.

You might use some energizers weekly or monthly. You may want to have children go outside or to the gym and play a class game. This can be for social purposes or to help learn something academic. For example, I used to take the children out and play kickball sometimes just for fun. Other times, we played games that went along with an academic lesson. We played a predator/prey game where students hit in a designated area and the predator had to call out the names of people he or she could see. This is valuable because it teaches children about camouflage and gets them up and moving around. At times, my class also went on scavenger hunts. They had to find things around the building like different shapes or evidence of erosion.

Some teachers designate students of the month who get to bring artifacts about themselves to share with the class. This is an energizer as well as a way to know students better. One teacher I knew took a different approach. She made a long bulletin board on which each student was assigned one square where he or she could hang anything he or she wanted. Some hung pictures, and others hung artwork and papers they created.

Changing some things around the room can also energize a class and help the students become "whole." Josh, a fifth-grade teacher, described how he had his children submit desk arrangements at the beginning of the year. Then the class would have to follow the map and create the design with the desks while being timed. Whenever they moved the desks away from that design, he would time them again and note if their time got faster. This is a great energizer, as well as a way to help children work together. I often had my students decorate the room according to science themes. We made habitat murals for the room, measured and tacked up wallpaper that had Saturn on it, and created life-size drawings of ourselves to hang around the room as we studied similarities and differences in people.

You will want to begin some energizers at the beginning of the year and then continue them throughout the year. The beginning of the year should be a time of really trying to put your children on a path of becoming "whole." Anything you can do to help them come together and be energized about working together will help the entire year go smoothly. You might have students design class flags or create a class motto. One teacher I know, Tom, had his students create a class mascot. It needed to be something that everyone could draw, and students submitted ideas and then voted on it. Some of the mascots from Tom's room have included Tuffy the Tapeworm, Burrito Man and his sidekick Potato Olé, and Krusty the Crab. After each test, the children in Tom's room turned their paper over and drew the class mascot interacting with something from the test. Another cool energizer for the beginning of the year is to measure everyone's height, add the heights together, and then do the same thing at the end of the year to see how much the students have grown.

Here is Burrito Man as a Greek god, drawn as the students in Tom's class reviewed for a test.

You can come up with many energizers or get them from resources like the Internet or books. I encourage you to have your students create energizers as well. They will keep your classroom lively and bring children together as a "whole."

Managing a "Whole" Group

Using tools and structures to help a group become "whole" is not the only whole you need to think about as you begin working with groups of students. You must begin thinking about how to manage 28 children all at once. Although you will be working with students much of the time within small groups, sometimes you will need to facilitate whole group activities, such as classroom conversations, technology, and many of the activities discussed in this chapter. Remember that managing whole group times doesn't mean losing the ideas in Chapters 1–6. Children need autonomy, belonging, and competency even when they are working within a whole group. The idea when leading a group of students is to make it as comfortable, safe, and fluid as possible. Think about the following when your students are working as a whole group.

The Spaces of "Whole" Group Work

Although we have not talked a lot about the spaces involved in good classroom management (more in Chapter 10), it is important to think about the spaces you occupy when working as a "whole" group. What are the benefits and limitations of having students at their desks during a conversation in the "whole" group? What are the benefits and limitations of having students on a carpet in a corner of the classroom? If you want a "whole" class discussion or conversation, will it work better if you are in front of or mixed in among the children? What are the benefits and limitations of having pillows or other things on the floor for children to sit on or near? All of these questions will be helpful if you take the time to think them through.

You need to consider the purpose of the work and then determine the space that would fit best. For example, if you want children to have a conversation about a math problem that everyone worked on solving, you might want to call all of the children to the front of the classroom so they can work on the board and show their examples. If you want to have a class meeting to discuss ideas, you might want to have children sit in a circle so they can see and hear everyone. Finally, if you are having a debate, you might want children to stand or sit in opposite parts of the room. You have many decisions to make, and while this may seem like a small one, spaces where children engage in learning are important, especially when working as a "whole" group.

Timing of "Whole" Group Work Is a Key to Success

As you begin to plan for things like class meetings and whole group sharing sessions among others, be sure to consider what students will be doing before and after. If students have whole group time after whole group time after whole group time, they may become restless and disengaged. If students have been sitting on the floor while you read them a book or other children are sharing, you may need to insert an energizer before moving to another whole group activity. If students have just come in from recess and are a little crazy, you may want to plan for a whole group time to wind down a bit before beginning another activity. Planning for whole group work as well as cooperative workshops means mixing things up a bit. Try to mix some individual work with some group work, some whole group work, and energizers.

Visions of "Whole" Group Work Need to Be Developed and Revisited

As you begin planning for whole group work, be sure to include some social learning goals. You and your students will need to have a vision for how whole group conversations will look and sound. You might have a class meeting about this and ask students to come up with things they need and are willing to give when the class is working as a whole. The vision could be posted all year and changed as needed. For example, a vision might be that there are no put-downs in whole group discussions. In early grades especially, students may need to practice these things using skits, perhaps showing what the vision is and is not. The same kind of visioning would be helpful for whole group work in a computer lab.

Juicy Problems Make "Whole" Group Time Worthwhile

Whole group time can be difficult to manage at times because it requires children to be quiet and listen to each other. You can prevent some issues if you have worthwhile problems for children to discuss. My students, for example, once debated whether a mealworm was a worm or an insect for an hour. They were second graders, and I had no behavior issues. Why? I had taken care of some of the issues above. We were in a good place, and they knew the expectations of the class. Also very engaged in the problem, however, they wanted to get their ideas out and know the answer. Juicy problems are good not just for cooperative workshops but for all times of day. Reading really good books, doing interesting work on the computer, or conversing about a fascinating topic keeps children engaged. Indeed, not every problem is juicy to every student. Sharing projects or ideas can get old after about the 15th one. During such times, you can use energizers to help break up the sharing.

As you begin to think about your quest for the "whole enchilada," be sure to include yourself in the "whole." Make sure to keep yourself in good mental and physical health and ask for help when you need it. You will have much more success creating a "whole" class if you are feeling whole yourself.

So . . . What?

This chapter has been about helping a group of children come together as a community or a "whole" for learning. This kind of work may seem to take too much time and energy, but it is imperative in helping children develop autonomy, belonging, and competency. It is imperative in helping children learn. A "whole" group does the following:

- Includes all of the children there

- Works toward common goals

- Does activities together other than academic activities

- Celebrates learning together

There are many great tools for helping children become a "whole" group. Some that I have found to work include:

- Class meetings

- Data collection

- Service learning projects

- Energizers

When managing a whole group, think through the following:

- The spaces where whole groups meet

- Timing of when whole groups meet

- How the problems and topics discussed affect the group

Get Ready For . . .

You may be an expert on facilitating autonomy, belonging, and competency in your classroom. You may be a genius when it comes to motivation. You may excel at using cooperative workshops, thinking routines, and "whole enchilada" tools. It does not matter. In every class, no matter the size, shape, place, or content, some children will struggle. I think it's a law of nature. The next section is all about children who, for whatever reason, struggle in school and how you can go above and beyond normal classroom structures and tools to help them.

Activities to Try

✎   Create your own definition of a "whole" group. Share it with others and compare your definitions.

✎   Describe a group you were a part of that was, in your opinion, "whole."

✎   Make a bulleted list of things that scare you about facilitating a whole group of students. Are there things in this chapter that would alleviate those fears?

✎   **Make a collection!** Collect energizers you can use throughout the year.

✎   **Conduct action research!** Take a camera and go to some classrooms where you have permission to take pictures. Capture anything you see that you think is helping create a "whole" group. Put all of the pictures together and then sort them according to theme or category. What themes or categories do your pictures show? What is the story of your pictures?

Student Study Site

The companion Web site for *Elementary Classroom Management* can be found at www.sagepub.com/kwilliamsstudy.

Visit the Web-based student study site to enhance your understanding of the chapter content. The study materials include video clips, practice tests, flashcards, suggested readings, and Web resources.

Creating Classrooms That Meet the Needs of Individual Children

S ometimes the classroom will require more than good pedagogy, thinking routines, and whole group activities. The children coming to your room, like all of us, are individuals with different issues and needs. Some of them will need accommodations above and beyond normal classroom operations even if you manage the classroom perfectly. Your job is to figure out how to help those individuals in ways that still provide opportunities for autonomy, belonging, and competency. This section includes three chapters that address individuals with special needs. As teachers, you need to know who they are, what they need, what resources are available to you, and to whom you can turn for help when you need it.

Chapter 7 is about students with special needs in the classroom. Working with children who have developmental differences, physical or mental disabilities, cultural differences, or environmental issues requires you to understand those broad categories, as well as to know your students as individuals. Chapter 7 is all about knowing and working with children who traditionally struggle in school. It will help you understand your role as a teacher of special-needs students.

Chapter 8 is about language and literature that will help you work with all students but especially those who are struggling. It is amazing how using questions, empathy, choices, and stories will diffuse difficult situations and create opportunities for learning. This chapter provides great resources and ideas for you to try when you come upon a challenging situation.

Chapter 9 was written to help you realize that you are not alone. Sometimes, even when they are struggling, teachers stay quietly in their rooms. When you run into a problem or an issue that you don't know how to handle, use the resources listed here or those that are available inside and outside of your school for help. Being a teacher isn't easy. It requires much thinking and reflecting, as well as collaborating.

I hope these three chapters will give you the tools you need to begin working with all children in your classroom with care, high expectations, and confidence. After all, every child deserves the very best.

CHAPTER 7

Recognizing, Accommodating, and Advocating for Children With Special Needs

When I was a child, I liked to play sports. I played basketball, softball, and volleyball; ran track; and was on the swim team. I lived in a small town, so anyone could be on the team. For the most part, I went out for sports because I wanted to be around the other children. I wasn't very competitive, and although I wanted to do well, I was never willing to sacrifice the well-being of my limbs or any other part of my body to win. I remember being in the outfield of the softball field hoping and praying the ball wouldn't come my way. I never wanted to have the basketball on the last play of the game or anchor the relay in track or swimming. Almost any coach will tell you that the really good players *want* the ball to come to them and *want* to make the last play. In a sense, my attitude kept me from working to be a great athlete.

The first two sections of this book were about creating classrooms where all children could be successful. I gave you some theory, tools, and structures to help you design that classroom for all of the children you will meet. Here's the thing, though: If you are afraid, believe you won't be able to handle some children, or have visions of "bad" children disrupting your plans, the last two sections won't be very useful. Teacher attitudes regarding specific students correspond with the quantity and quality of interactions and support that teachers provide (Cook, Cameron, & Tankersley, 2007), similar to the sports scenario above. I was not a great athlete because I was afraid of what might happen if the ball came to me and I couldn't catch it, and therefore I didn't really try. I was afraid of letting my team down if I couldn't run the last leg of the race fast enough or make the basket at the last second. To be a great teacher, you have to *want* the child who everyone else thinks is difficult. You have to believe that *you* will be the best thing for a group of struggling or gifted students. Not a matter of being cocky or of thinking you don't have anything to learn, instead it is about getting rid of your assumptions about children, having tools and structures you are confident using, reflecting toward the future, and having the will to be creative and learn. Although all children are different in some ways, children are children. They all have issues and strengths and need to be valued. To manage a classroom with all kinds of children in it, you have to believe you can do it and that all of the children in your classroom are worth it. Instead of being afraid of what might happen, you must plan for what might happen. Instead of giving up on children who require something extra or different, you must work to find a way.

For the most part, the structures and tools from the first two sections will work well for all children you encounter. There is enough wiggle room in each of them to allow you to adapt for different children and classes. Each year, however, some children will need a little something special—and by special, I don't mean yucky. For some reason, when a child struggles with behaviors or academics, we make him or her do really boring or harsh things, creating worse behaviors and providing no motivation to learn. One example I read discussed students who were literally forced to sit at circle time with seatbelts on or an aide behind them so they wouldn't be able to get up. Consequently, the children coped with the stress by flapping arms, making noise, covering ears, pushing another child, or becoming more self-absorbed (Greenspan & Wieder, 1998). We forget to teach and become police officers doling out punishments, which rarely help children become self-disciplined or self-reliant and certainly don't make teachers feel like they can provide classroom management that supports all children's learning. If you believe *all* children need autonomy, belonging, competency, democratic classrooms, and motivation, you will need to know how to provide that for *all* children. Students with special needs deserve classroom management structures and tools that will move them, just like every other student, toward those things. They need teachers who are willing to keep trying even when the first tries don't work so well. This chapter is about those special children and that something special that might help them succeed. It is about helping you believe that you can help *all* children, even the special ones, with whatever needs they bring.

By the end of this chapter, I hope you have:

- An understanding of the many shapes and sizes of children with special needs
- An understanding of your role with special-needs children as a classroom manager
- Tools and structures that might help students with special needs

Knowing Students With Special Needs

Although all children are special in some way and need individual attention and experiences, some will always be **vulnerable** to the school experience for a variety of reasons. Development, physical and mental disabilities, cultural differences, and the environment in which they are growing up can affect students' abilities and thus your classroom management. Even if you are not going to teach special education, you will encounter students who need unique experiences and accommodations. Most special-needs students are being educated in **general education classrooms**, and that number is increasing (Cook, Cameron, & Tankersley, 2007; Kaff, Zabel, & Milham, 2007).

We seem to put a thousand labels on children these days—for example, ADHD, autistic, second-language learner, at-risk, mildly mentally handicapped, learning disabled, hearing impaired, developmentally delayed. Perhaps at this moment, you hope I will take each label apart and tell you exactly what to do for labeled children. Sorry. Even if I had enough room in the book to do so (entire books have been written on each label), you must remember that even with a label, children are still individuals. While finding out as much as you can about strategies that have worked within different special-needs categories is certainly advisable, it is important to understand that your assumptions about labeled children may be inaccurate. "Many children today are given labels that are misleading. Instead of pinpointing a child's unique strengths and challenges, they obscure them and unwittingly demoralize and create negative expectations on the part of parents, therapists, and teachers" (Greenspan & Wieder, 1998, p. 21).

I had a child who was diagnosed with Asperger's syndrome in my classroom one year. Some of his behaviors fit under the classic definition of the disorder. For instance, he had trouble looking people in the eye; had a hard time dealing with loud noises, such as a fire drill; and didn't understand interactions with his peers, such as game playing. He also had unique strengths, however. He was a great performer. He could sing and act. He was motivated to be

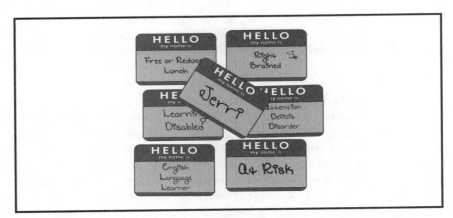

Jesse Keifer

Labels can help us begin to know students, but we need to continue to know their individual strengths and challenges as well.

able to play with his friends and worked hard to understand the games they played. Understanding a child with special needs certainly is easier if you know him or her and have access to information about characteristics that might develop. In other words, while a label can be useful for background knowledge, it must be tempered with a true understanding of the individual child. Working with Zach required me to understand the basics about Asperger's syndrome and to want him there enough to make appropriate accommodations for him individually.

Although I do not think it is worthwhile to give you a specific list of "how to work with _____ children," I do think it is valuable to discuss broad categories of special needs. Why? For you to make appropriate classroom management choices for special-needs children, you will need to know what kind of needs may arise. I also believe that the more information you have, the less afraid you will be. You must ask yourself four questions when a child behaves in a way that raises red flags in your mind. Indeed, there may be combinations of answers. As you begin to ask these questions, try not to use them to make assumptions about the child you are working to help. Use them as a way into learning about special-needs students:

- Is this a development issue?

- Is this a physical or mental disability issue?

- Is this a cultural issue?

- Is this an environmental issue?

Once again, the work we do with complex human beings becomes linear when it can't be. Indeed, some students may have issues with multiple roots. Weissbourd (1996) describes a student, Michael, who has a learning disability and also lives in poverty. The behaviors he exhibits, including the inability to pay attention and hiding under his desk, may be attributed to more than one of the questions listed above. It may take some work to be unafraid of such behaviors as Michael's or not to feel frustrated when a student exhibits them. Remember that there is a reason the child is acting that way, and it is not that he or she wants to hurt you. The questions above will help you reflect about the different issues affecting children every day in your room. This kind of reflection is vital in working with all children, including those with special needs.

Development

I had a student named Ben in my classroom the very first year I taught second grade. He was small, hadn't lost any of his baby teeth, and often acted out in class by making silly faces, giggling loudly at inappropriate times, and falling out of his seat at a constant rate. The other children affectionately called him "old geezer" because, when his blond hair was slicked back, he looked almost bald and could make his face look like a little old man with no teeth. Regularly behind the other children in his academic work, Ben was a distraction to the others because of his immature behaviors. The special-education teachers I worked with wanted to test him for a learning disability, so I needed to begin to ask myself and others the questions listed above before we could make decisions about testing. Was Ben's issue developmental, cognitive, cultural, or environmental? I believe it was developmental.

Letter From a Master Teacher 7.1

Fostering Learning for All Students

Thank you for pursuing this profession! This letter is to welcome you on a journey that is sure to bring you challenges but, more importantly, opportunities to meet people you will never forget! It would not surprise me if you know this already from your own experience. I have been working in the field of education for 30 years and enjoyed being a special-education teacher for 17 of those years.

Possibly, like me, you had an important experience in your family that influenced your decision to follow this path in education. My older brother was given medication during his first year of life that reacted horribly in his system and caused a brain hemorrhage. As a result, he lived at home until he was 11 years old, in a hospital bed, unable to achieve even the most basic of academic milestones. What my brother taught me, however, is invaluable. Jimmy taught me about unconditional love. I know some very "educated" people who are unable to give or receive that special gift.

Since you have chosen to be a teacher, I fervently hope you will offer love to each of those people who come into your classrooms! You may not like what some of those students will do to you, themselves, and others; however, if you love them, you will be able to set up an environment where they can learn. Ah, and learning is the key element to your journey, for your students and for you. Please believe that each of those children or students is able to learn. Be an advocate so each of them can grow into the adults they need to be, with their own unique gifts to offer this world. Foster inquiry, self-determination, high expectations, and pride; these attributes will hold success. This success should not be decided for them ahead of time; rather, they should assess and deem it appropriate for themselves.

Now it is your time to make a difference. You can, and you will!

—Dene Muller
Special-Education Teacher

Although there are guidelines for developmental milestones, children develop socially, cognitively, and physically at varying rates (Bee & Boyd, 2007). For example, you may have walked when you were 9 months old, but some babies don't walk until they are more than a year. For most, this seems perfectly natural. Unfortunately, educators seem to forget that children may develop at different rates. Children who aren't reading by kindergarten are sometimes seen as slow learners or perhaps even tested for learning disabilities when, really, their minds just aren't ready to read. It is the same with mathematics. We often ask second graders who don't yet understand what numbers represent to add and subtract two- and three-digit numbers. These children don't have learning disabilities. They just aren't quite ready to understand those ideas. Inappropriate behaviors can also be linked to development. We often expect small children to sit still for long periods in school when, for them, movement is like breathing (Hohmann & Weikart, 1995). It is not developmentally appropriate for them to be able to sit for a long time.

How does this relate to classroom management? Sometimes our assumptions (e.g., that every child should be reading in kindergarten, that children should be able to add two digits, or that children should be able to sit still and pay attention) cause us to have inappropriate expectations. Passed to the student, such expectations may cause them to have low self-worth, low motivation, and sometimes avoidance behaviors. This doesn't mean that we shouldn't have high expectations for students or provide experiences a bit above where they are developmentally. It merely means that children may need our support and **accommodations**. Remember that just because students can do something, they should not necessarily be doing it (Kamii, 2000). Many times, students seen as naughty or behavior problems are only trying to tell you that they don't understand.

I was driving one evening with my 5-year-old son, and he saw the moon. When he commented that it was following him, I purposefully tried to talk him out of it, telling him that it just looked like the moon was following him. I told him that we were the ones who were moving, and so on. No matter what I said, he would not believe me because the cognitive structures that help him make sense of the world aren't developed enough to allow him to fathom that the Earth is moving. He can only understand what he can see and experience. I could have *made* him change his mind, told him his answer was wrong, quizzed him until he said the right answer, or punished him until he agreed with me, but it wouldn't have mattered. He may have been able to say the right answer, but he still wouldn't have understood that the Earth is moving. And, in coercing him to say the right answer, I would have been teaching him another lesson: that his thinking isn't good. My son will figure out that the moon is not following him, just as most kindergarteners will learn to read when they are ready and if we provide opportunities for safe stretching of their thinking, experiences that will help them discover, and time to grow.

Remember that children develop by participating fully in experiences. Your job with children who may not have had the experiences they need or who just aren't developing as quickly as their peers is to help them have experiences that push their thinking both socially and academically. These experiences need to be within a support system and accompanied by reflection. The key is to design experiences that will help the children see different perspectives and make connections. I may challenge my son's thinking about the moon following him, for example, by asking questions about the moon that don't work with his theory. I may get out a model of the moon and the Earth and show him how it works. I will also remember that even with this support and these experiences, he will understand when he is ready, and that is OK.

The information I had about Ben told me that his issue was developmental and not cognitive, cultural, or environmental. His behavior, physical attributes, and ideas all told me that his mind and body just hadn't developed at the same rate as his peers. In addition, I did some **conservation tasks** (Labinowicz, 1980) with him to help me understand his thinking and found that he wasn't conserving yet and was probably still preoperational (see Table 7.1).

TABLE 7.1   Piaget's Levels of Development

	Description of Level:	What You Can Do to Support Them:
Preoperational: Approximately 2–7 years of age	• Strongly influenced by appearances. If there are two dimensions, such as height and width, this child will focus on one. • Unable to envision going back to an original state. For example, if we change a ball of clay into a long snake, this child won't be able to "see" the clay going back to a ball mentally. He or she would need to experience it. • Only able to sort or order objects in one category, such as color or size. • Cannot take another person's point of view. • May talk at friends instead of with them. • Able to walk somewhere he or she has been before but is unable to represent the path he or she took on a physical model. • Play revolves around reality. • Believe that rules to games cannot be changed because they come from authorities. • Actions are based on immediate interest. What is pleasant to this child is what it means to be good.	• Provide experiences that challenge this child's ideas. • Allow this child to use physical materials to help him or her understand his or her experiences. • Provide opportunities for singing, drawing, reading aloud, manipulating, and working with peers.
Concrete Operational: Approximately 7–11 years of age	• Able to hold two dimensions at a time. • Able to mentally reverse actions. • Able to sort in multiple categories but needs concrete objects to do so. • Cannot solve ordering problems when they are presented orally. • Increased ability to see another person's perspective. • Able to represent something with a model but may not have accurate distances. • Realizes that rules can be changed as long as everyone agrees to them. • Moral actions are living up to expectations of a significant group.	• Provide time for reflection, either written, oral, or pictorially. • Allow peer interaction through games and assignments. • Provide opportunities for concrete experiences with objects.
Formal Operational: Approximately 11–adult	• Able to envision ideas that are not concrete, such as energy. • Able to classify and reclassify in different ways without objects. • Able to compare classification systems mentally. • Can solve "if . . . then" problems mentally. • Can engage in hypothetical thinking. • Can adopt another person's point of view and sees own point of view as one of many. • Self-conscious of physical changes. • Able to create 2-D or 3-D models or maps with more abstract representations of reality. • Understands that values are relative.	• Provide opportunities for abstract thinking and creativity. • Allow self-regulation and assessment opportunities. • Provide time for action/reflection/action.

Source: Adapted from Labinowicz, 1980.

This told me that some of the tasks I was asking him to do weren't appropriate for him and that I needed to look at what I was asking him to do and get him some support. If a baby isn't walking yet, we don't try to make him walk by putting him in situations where he will fall and hurt himself. We help the baby by giving him a tool like a walker, and we hold his tiny fingers and hunch over while walking around with him so his legs and body can experience walking. What did I do for Ben? I made sure he did activities that were appropriate for him in ways that didn't separate him from the rest of the class. I worked within class meetings to encourage appropriate behavior. I sent Ben to the kindergarten room to help smaller children so he could gain a sense of responsibility and pride. I could have made Ben do activities he wasn't ready for without the support, but he wouldn't have learned much, except that he couldn't do them. Finally, I was not afraid of his behaviors and knew that he didn't behave the way he did because he was naughty. His behaviors had a purpose.

Development is a tricky idea when thinking about classroom management. Now, more than ever, we are moving skills once expected in a higher grade down several levels. In addition, many people advocate early-as-possible intervention for children who need it. While I agree with early intervention, it is vital to think about the implications of a special-education label necessary for a child to receive services. That label doesn't go away and can be detrimental to children if they come to believe that the expectations are low for them. I believe it is important to look at development as a potential issue instead of moving directly to a label.

Physical and Mental Disabilities

Ben wasn't as physically and cognitively developed as his peers. As he grew and gained some experiences, he would eventually catch up. If he did not, his teachers could then consider another possibility, such as a **learning disability**. Some children you will work with, however, may have cognitive disabilities or gifts that may be improved but never go away. I had a fifth-grade student named Danielle in my room one year. Very quiet and struggling in all subjects, Danielle wasn't conserving yet, something that typically happens around age 7 or 8. She was, however, very social and happy. She worked tremendously hard but could not keep up with the curricular expectations even with support. She needed special-education support.

At some time or another, a child or children in your room will need support from a special educator. The student may need accommodations throughout the day, or he or she may need very specific services, such as speech/language therapy, physical therapy, or accommodations for a specific subject like reading or mathematics. You may teach a child with severe behavioral issues, who is autistic, or who is blind or deaf. Management within classrooms where there are children with mental or physical disabilities continues to revolve around autonomy, belonging, competency, and motivation. What you need to do to meet these needs, however, may be a bit different.

Students with special needs still need autonomy. "Many children with special needs have things done for them, rather than initiate activities on their own in response to inner wishes. Because a child's own desires and interests are a critical part of who she is, caregivers seem to do best when they can entice a child to use her own initiative and desires to practice some of the necessary skills" (Greenspan & Wieder, 1998, p. 14). A child who doesn't read well may be willing to work on reading if it involves something that interests him. A student who has to work hard to write or make graphs may find it easier and more enjoyable if she can use the computer. Traci, a special-education teacher, once showed me two graphs. One was made by hand and looked very rough and inaccurate. The other, made on the computer, was very well done. Interestingly, the same student with a learning disability made both graphs. The student happened to be interested in computers and was better able to make his graphs with that medium. Students with mental or physical disabilities need to have choices just like any other student.

Children with mental and physical disabilities must belong to the whole group. Sometimes leaving students out of whole group activities is tempting because it is easier. Rae and her fourth-grade students make a life-sized model of a whale in the gym every year. One year she was concerned about a special-needs student in her room. He had behavior issues, and she wondered how he would do in a large gym with an activity as big as making a whale. Instead of being afraid and "accommodating" him out of the activity, she worked to find a way to involve him and decided to make him in charge of the tape. He had to give tape to those who needed it. As a result of this important job, the student did great. Of course, Rae could have given him the job, and he still could have struggled. What could she have done next for him if this were the case?

Children with mental and physical disabilities must feel competent. Indeed, it is easy to have low expectations for children with special needs. You may feel sorry for them or not want to deal with the consequences of asking them to tackle difficult tasks. In addition, disabilities can hide strengths. A child with a physical disability may be very intelligent but lack the speech and language abilities to demonstrate that intelligence. The point is not to make such children do things that are so far beyond their reach they could never succeed. Helping them move toward their individual goals, however, is important. For example, if a student will not make eye contact with you and that is a goal for that child, it is important that you work to make eye contact with him or her, which may be a bit uncomfortable. Just letting the child go on without making eye contact may be easier but won't help him or her. Instead, playfully try to get the child to work on a goal through games or within topics or tasks that he or she likes.

Competency continues to be important for children with mental or physical disabilities even though it may look different. Sometimes we try to accommodate students with special needs by drilling them on academic skills when really we should be working on skills that will allow them to be competent. Such skills as self-regulation, interest in the world, complex communication, and emotional thinking may be more important than the rote academic skills we often push students with mental or physical disabilities to do (Greenspan & Wieder, 1998). My friend and colleague Cheryl tutors a student named Holly who has been labeled ADHD and is struggling academically. Instead of working with Holly on complex communication, memory, thinking, and organization skills, her teachers try to get her to memorize multiplication facts. While memorizing multiplication tables may be important for students her age, the skill will not help Holly. First, she doesn't understand numbers well enough to understand multiplication. Second, that time could be used for helping Holly learn to reflect or to organize. What should Holly be doing during multiplication at school? Maybe she could do multiplication facts by organizing and counting manipulatives into groups of five, seven, or other numbers. After she is finished, the teacher could ask her what she did and talk about what worked and didn't work.

Thinking about making a classroom fit every child's needs, especially a child with very specific needs, is a bit daunting. It is important to think about individualization not always as making up several activities for each concept (although you can do that at times within workshops). Instead, think about how activities can provide opportunities for all. If an activity is broad enough, it can accommodate many different objectives. For example, if the academic objective is to measure and the social objective is to communicate effectively with a partner, the problem might involve having teams of students use blocks to represent the length of the largest and smallest birds, bugs, mammals, amphibians, and so on. Special-needs students could work on many different skills while doing the same activity. For example, if a student is working on counting, you could have him count how many blocks fit a particular size of animal. If a student is working on motor skills, she could hand the blocks to her team. If a student might throw blocks, his or her team could use tape or something else that wouldn't be a throwing hazard. In other words, you can adapt good activities so everyone can participate. Students with strengths in some areas can be in charge of those jobs within small-group workshops.

Danielle was mildly mentally handicapped, and her parents, her special-education teacher, and I created an IEP (individual education plan) for her that would allow her to work on appropriate goals while still in the classroom. I knew Danielle liked to draw and was very social, so group work was ideal for her. I challenged her to do math problems that were somewhat easier than those her peers were doing by drawing pictures and using manipulatives. During reading workshop, Danielle read books that she chose with the help of tape recordings made by a parent volunteer or me. During writer's workshop, Danielle wrote about ponies and drew rainbows all over her paper. The students as peer editors helped her fix her spelling, and I had her read her writing aloud so she could hear how it sounded. In other words, Danielle did everything her peers did, just in different ways and with different goals.

If a child has mental or physical disabilities, collaboration with special-education teachers and therapists will be important. It is also important for you to help each student with his or her needs. This means working to individualize what students are asked to do as much as possible. "Many school programs are not sufficiently individualized. They expect the child to adapt to the program, rather than the program to adapt to the child. The child with special needs does not necessarily have the flexibility to adapt because she hasn't yet developed the skills to do so" (Greenspan & Wieder, 1998, p. 404).

Cultural Differences and English-Language Learners

As I write this book, I am getting ready to send my son to kindergarten. Most likely he will have an easy transition to school (cross your fingers!). In any case, he will know the language that is spoken, understand the verbal cues his teacher relays to the students, and look and sound like most of his peers in the classroom. Although he may have some anxiety about going to kindergarten for the first time, other cultural issues will not be a factor. I cannot say the same for many of the children who enter school each year at various grade levels.

While observing a student teacher as a semester began in January, a new student who spoke very little English came into the classroom. The child clung to his mother, who didn't speak English either, and cried. Although the teacher herself didn't know languages other than English, some of the other children in the classroom did, and they helped the teacher communicate with the new family. The teacher talked to the mother through the translation and mostly reassured her that she would take good care of the boy. Then they peeled the young boy off of his mother, and she left. Although a classroom of students was waiting, the teacher took time to hold the child and hug him until he was ready to sit with the group. As I observed, I reflected on how frightening it must be for a young child to go to a place where he couldn't understand what was happening and where other children knew. Cultural differences would make school not only frightening but also difficult at times. Children who don't speak English; who are different physically; or who don't have the same customs, habits, celebrations, and so on, can find themselves in trouble behaviorally and behind academically if they do not have a teacher who cares to understand the differences. Make no mistake: Children with cultural differences aren't in this chapter because they have mental or physical disabilities but because they may need accommodations to help them succeed in the classroom.

It is certainly easy to take for granted how coming to school feels for different children. Just as we must consider our own prior experiences as we teach, we must also recognize that students' prior experiences outside of school will influence their academic and social abilities

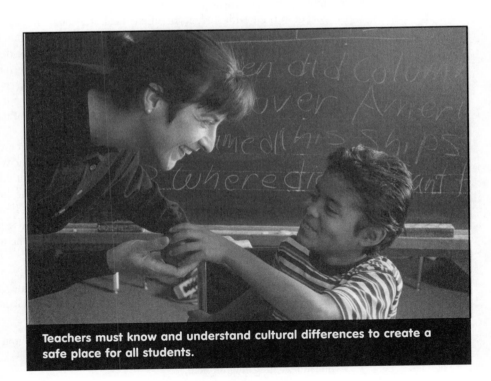

Teachers must know and understand cultural differences to create a safe place for all students.

in school. Behaviors that look naughty may have a cultural influence. For example, students who do not rise to expectations of individual competition are not necessarily unmotivated. They may just be culturally cued to demonstrate motivation in other ways, such as in cooperative group arrangements (Gay, 2000). In other words, we cannot rely on assumptions to truly understand behaviors. We need to care enough about the students to research, investigate, understand the behaviors they exhibit and work to help them. Developing relationships with students and learning about their culture is vital. Just the attempt to learn about different cultures can go a long way in developing a sense of trust among culturally diverse students, their parents, and you. "People in the community know if you are trying to understand their culture. Students also see it. Becoming involved shows people that here is a teacher who is trying to learn about our culture" (Parkay, 2006, p. 155).

Caring alone may not be enough, however. Gay (2000) believes that teachers must be caring but also "**culturally competent**" (p. 70). This does not mean learning the customs and languages of every culture but doing some investigating before and during your work with culturally diverse students. It means reflecting before you ever meet the child and then while you work with the child about things he or she may need. Doing so may prevent problems before they occur. In some cultures, looking an adult in the eye is impolite. Knowing this may alleviate tension in the classroom because you will understand rather than question actions. If a child is not participating in class very much, he or she may be worried about sounding different or not knowing the language well enough to participate. Knowing the individual student as well as being culturally competent will help you manage a classroom with a diverse population.

The goal of working with students of different cultures should not be to strip them of their culture. Helping students learn about each other and celebrating differences will create opportunities to learn about different cultures, as well as to show pride in one's own. "Informed, sensitive, and caring teachers can play an important role in helping all students develop to their full potential. Such teachers realize the importance of recognizing diverse perspectives, and they create inclusive classroom environments that encourage students to respect differences among themselves and others and to see the contributions that persons from all groups have made to society" (Parkay, 2006, p. 162).

Creating an inclusive classroom may mean gathering materials that are free from any forms of racism or stereotyping. It may mean adding pieces of literature, activities, and ideas from various cultures. "To create classrooms that are truly multicultural, teachers must select instructional materials that are sensitive, accurately portray the contributions of ethnic groups, and reflect diverse points of view" (Parkay, 2006, p. 152). I might argue that even when you aren't teaching in a diverse classroom, it is important to use multicultural materials. In addition, Ernst, Castle, and Frostad (1992) recommend the following when working with culturally diverse students:

1. Whenever possible, try to use a variety of formats that go beyond the traditional lecture format. This will enable you to target different learning styles in your classroom.

2. Organize, when possible, cooperative learning activities. Small groups give second-language learners a chance to use their second-language skills in a non-threatening environment.

3. The use of videos films, drama/role plays, manipulatives, pictures, artifacts, posters, music, nursery rhymes, games, filmstrips, maps, charts, and fieldtrips can enhance teaching and learning.

4. Your school ESL specialist is a wonderful source of knowledge and information about what to do and what materials to use with your LEP (limited English proficiency) students.

5. Encourage students to indicate when they are confused or do not understand. Students may feel more comfortable indicating understanding rather than acknowledging confusion.

6. When testing we need to be sensitive to students' cultural background. Culturally biased tests are a major hurdle for second-language learners. Standardized tests can be a common culprit. Misinterpreting terms, directions, or situational cues can cause your students' tests performance to drop drastically.

7. When planning lessons or assignments, think about the following questions: What background knowledge do students have? Will the assignment use academic language or critical thinking skills unfamiliar to your students?

8. Restate, rephrase, summarize, and review frequently. (pp. 14–15)

Remember Emzie from Chapter 1? He was the boy from Nigeria who always fought at recess. I wasn't very culturally competent and didn't do a very good job of bringing in multicultural materials. I knew nothing about Nigeria and didn't work hard enough to get to know Emzie. It was difficult because he was very quiet and introverted. In retrospect, I think if I had held class meetings or had a lunch or two with him, things might have turned out better. You never know, and I did the best I could at that time. I hope you will remember Emzie, however, as you work with students of different cultures. You can do better than I did.

Environmental

One of the districts I taught for was in a very affluent neighborhood. Most likely, if you came to the school, you would think the children who went there had perfect families and the perfect environment in which to grow and learn. Indeed, many of the children had an environment during and after school that helped them be able to focus and learn, handle issues that came up, and enjoy being in school. However, as with *any* class in *any* school district, some children's environments weren't conducive to learning. "Thinking of vulnerable children as poor or ghetto children not only ignores the many non-poor children who suffer deprivations at home; it discounts these circumstances in the larger world that affect children of every race and class. Getting beyond divisive stereotypes and understanding the true nature of childhood vulnerability means looking closely at these circumstances" (Weissbourd, 1996, p. 27). Once again, as teachers, we come to a point where we must look at the individuals and not the group to which they supposedly belong. Just as the previous paragraphs encouraged knowing children when they are developmentally behind their peers, when they are physically or mentally disabled, or when they come from a different culture, we must know their environments as well.

Knowing an environment means having a general sense of what happens to children when they aren't with you. Are they being fed? Are they staying up very late because a parent works long hours? Is physical or mental abuse taking place in their homes? Are their parents going through a divorce? Are children supervising themselves? Is substance abuse taking place in the home? The point is not to judge families or pity children but to be aware of influencing factors when problems creep up during the school year and to work to solve problems before they happen. Many times, vulnerable children who grow up in very stressful homes aren't assisted until there is a crisis (Weissbourd, 1996). Noticing problems, wondering what is going on, and working to help children is vital. In fact, many studies on resilient children show that just one adult's interest in helping a child heading toward crisis can make a huge difference (Doll, Zucker, & Brehm, 2004; Dorn, 2006). Although you may not be able to fix every child's environmental problems, you may be able to keep from adding to the problems and make school a safe place.

Sometimes, for whatever reason, parents aren't able to organize and keep track of what their children need for school. They may not help students bring homework or the necessary

This young girl looks very tired. She may be just having a tired day, but it is a good idea to find out if something is keeping her from resting at home.

supplies. You may think it is the students' job to manage their supplies and homework, but remember that these are the last things students dealing with stress in the home are worried about. They may not be able to get what they need for school. Helping them will *not* make them irresponsible but worthy and more apt to help others. Mary Jo, for example, worked with a student whose mother filled out forms from year to year with different birthdates for her son. On the student's birthday, verified by his birth certificate, Mary Jo brought treats to the classroom just in case he didn't get to celebrate at home. Indeed, the student came to school on his birthday without treats and appreciated his teacher's gesture. He knew she cared about him. These details in children' lives that seem trivial often mean a lot to them. Helping children save face or giving them something that allows them to participate are gifts to students whose environmental needs are not met. Many teachers make sure to have extra school supplies, clothing, and snacks, just in case.

Sometimes issues involving children's outside environments are not trivial at all. Children may come to school from abusive homes, and it is the law for you to report anything suspicious to authorities. Paying attention to students' behaviors, physical appearance, drawings, and writing is an important way to help children who are vulnerable due to abuse or neglect. It is not your job to counsel or determine what needs to happen with the child after abuse is reported. Your job is to notice, report, understand, and make the classroom as safe for the child as possible. Read Chapter 9 for more about resources for abused or neglected children.

Many children in your classroom will come from homes with severe poverty. Parents, in this case, may not be abusive but may be unable to care for their child's basic needs. Students may be hungry or very tired, may not have appropriate clothing for the weather, may not have the right supplies or be able to pay for field trips, and may arrive to school very early and leave very late. All of these things will affect children's stress levels and ability to perform in school. Creating relationships with students and their parents will help you understand their needs and help them find resources for help. Although you will not necessarily be able to fix the situation these children live in, you will be able to help them be a part of the classroom community that will support their learning and hopefully support them in staying in school. How can you manage the classroom so such items as supplies, clothes, and money aren't issues? One idea is to have community supplies in your room. In other words, students put all of their markers, crayons, pencils, and so on, into a tub shared by everyone in the classroom or everyone at a table. Can you think of others?

So far, we have talked about the home environment affecting students' work in school. Sometimes, however, the school environment itself creates, or at least adds to, problems for students. Students who are different due to any of the issues above may experience **bullying** in school. Once again, it does not matter what school system you teach for or how poor or rich the students are in your class; you will need to be aware of bullying at all different levels. Bullying can be everything from teasing to taking possessions to beating up to sexually molesting. Students who are bullied day after day in bathrooms, lunchrooms, and playgrounds are often withdrawn, do poorly in school, and may rebel. In some cases, they may bring weapons to school to protect themselves (Dorn, 2006). When children are being bullied, it must be stopped immediately. If you suspect someone or a group of students is being bullied, get help from resources in your school, but don't rely on others for help. If one resource isn't working, find another. Make sure you support students as well.

Dorn (2006) talks about how we often leave children alone for long periods and allow bullying to take place. Bathrooms, hallways, and playgrounds must be monitored. Students, through class meetings, data collection, and individual conferences, should also have a sense that they can bring up bullying issues without being identified. My student, Zach, who had Asperger's syndrome was often teased at school. To help him, we had a group of students be his guardians. They were in charge of making sure that Zach was not teased in line before coming to school in the morning and that he was included in games. They were wonderful children who were given permission and expectations to help, and we made sure to place them in the same classroom with Zach throughout his years in elementary school. Although something like this may not be possible, there are many ways to keep children safe from bullies. Once again, you must think outside the box and keep limitations from clouding your actions.

Please note that the information above is only a dusting of information about possible issues for special-needs children. You will want to do further reading and reflecting on experiences to best help students with special needs. Most important, however, is that you be aware of issues affecting students in the classroom and work to come up with the best ways to help them.

The Teacher's Role

Beyond awareness and recognizing when behaviors or schoolwork is being affected by something beyond students' control, it is important that you play an active role in the classroom. How can you help students with needs that require special accommodations in the classroom?

Be There

You must be in the school and in the classroom both mentally and physically every day. As we all have our own issues outside of school, sometimes this may be difficult. Taking good care of yourself is key, as is getting out from behind your desk and sitting, talking, and working with the students. Being there means making sure that children are not alone for long periods and that they have a safe place to be when they need one. It means taking extra time to work with families in respectful and thoughtful ways. For one of my students, being there meant walking out to his car with him after school to talk to his mother about the week. The family did not have a phone, and I could not count on notes getting home. There are many ways to be there for students. You need to figure out the best ways for you and your students each year.

Reflect Toward the Future

For material related to this concept, go to Clip 7.1 on the Web-based Student Study Site.

You have probably been reflecting about your past quite a bit. Reflection about past experiences, as well as during experiences, is vital to learning. As a teacher working with special-needs children, however, it is important that you reflect toward the future as well. This means using what you know about individual children or past experiences with children to think about what might happen and working on preventative measures. If you know that a student has problems with loud noises, reflect toward the future about common loud noises that he or she will encounter and work to help the child. This may mean taking a child out of the building when you know this is going to happen or at least talking to him or her about the upcoming noise. If a child won't sit with the whole group during a lesson, reflect toward the future about how you might help him or her join the group. If you know a child will have trouble sitting on a gym floor during a long assembly, bring a chair.

Accommodate Individuals

Accommodation for individual students is key in providing the best environment for every child. Accommodation can be a lot of different things for different students. Some students may need physical accommodations, like standing on a balance board that helps their bodies move or sitting on a bouncy cushion rather than a chair. These kinds of accommodations help students meet their physical needs while allowing them to be a part of the classroom. Some students may need work accommodations. For example, if a student is not conserving numbers, doing 30 problems of two-digit addition isn't appropriate. This student may need to do five problems but use manipulatives and pictures with each. Some students may need accommodations in the daily schedule—for example, to have a rest time built into the day or a time when they go to a special-education room to be away from the busyness of a classroom. Accommodation for some might be assistance with organization, using a checklist or a timeline showing what will come next. Whatever the accommodation, you must be willing to help students. It will make management easier and students more successful in school. Instead of trying to stuff a round peg into a square hole, make the hole round!

Sometimes issues of accommodation bring up the word *fair*: "It isn't fair that some children get to sit on bouncy seats." "It isn't fair that some children only do five problems or get to take a rest during the day." I don't know who said this first, but I think it is an important phrase when working with special-needs students: "Fair doesn't mean equal." Children often came to me and told me that something was unfair. I didn't argue with them. I merely told them that they didn't need whatever I had done for the other student. That usually worked. If not, the student and I talked together about things he or she needed and tried to get the focus away from the other student.

Another common reason teachers don't always accommodate students as they should is that they think students will toughen up or benefit from the struggle. Be mindful that the brain can only take a limited amount of stress (Sousa, 2001). A child who is bullied or whose brain isn't developed enough to understand something won't toughen up but will shut down. Accommodations must be used so children with special needs have the opportunity to struggle with support, not torture.

Accommodating doesn't mean accepting inappropriate behavior. Students with special needs need to be a part of creating a safe classroom like everyone else. Sousa (2001) recommends making sure students understand classroom expectations and consequences, avoiding confrontational techniques and power struggles, designating a cooling-off location in the classroom, and speaking privately to the student about inappropriate behavior (p. 213). While you cannot accept inappropriate behavior, you can understand it. Keep in mind that misbehavior may be unintentional.

Advocate

There will be many different opinions on how to best meet the needs of students who require accommodations—a good thing most of the time. Make sure, however, that you are an advocate for all students in the classroom. Beyond their parents, you will know them as well as anyone else. It is easy to get caught up in "expert" opinions and forget what you know about the student and your classroom. If you believe students need special services or need to get services in the classroom or no services at all, use your voice to help make it happen. Of course, it must be an educated voice, and you must be an educated advocate. Sometimes you will need to advocate for nonservice items, such as eyeglasses or a coat. Sometimes you will have to advocate for students' need to use manipulatives, a computer, or something else that makes their learning easier. Whatever you are advocating, make sure that you have done your homework, that you have discussed it with parents, and that you go through the proper channels.

Collaborate

When working with special-needs students, you will most likely be working with other teachers, administrators, and therapists. I can't emphasize enough that your ability to collaborate with them is vital to the well-being of special-needs students. Invite them with open arms into your classroom, learn with and from them, and involve them in your decision-making processes and planning sessions. At times, this will be difficult. Sometimes you might disagree about how to best serve a particular child. If you can work to bring many ideas to the table and then determine what would work best, however, the child will benefit.

You will also find yourself working with staff in the form of teachers' aides or **para-professionals**. These people are indispensable, and you need to work with them as colleagues rather than subordinates. Be specific about what you need them to do as they work with children, but be open to listening to their ideas and input. I would advise that, unless they have difficulty working with students, you use them in a role that allows them to work with students in the classroom. Having them do paperwork may be tempting, but good aides and para-professionals can be the difference between keeping a student in the regular classroom with support and needing him or her to go to a special room.

In addition to collaborating with school personnel, you also need to collaborate with parents. Be sure that they are as involved as possible when decisions concerning their children are made. At times, judging parents as not qualified to make decisions for their children is easy. No matter what, however, they know their child better than you. Do your best to involve them in the decision-making process through strong communication.

Be Creative/Be a Learner

It is very easy to get into a school district and follow its policies and procedures for special-needs students without much thought. I urge you, however, to be creative when working with all children. Sometimes students don't need what the procedures tell us to do. They may need something that isn't written in a policy. It is important to think beyond what has already occurred. Many times, we keep doing the same things for students even when they haven't worked before. Some of you may think you aren't creative, but I think being creative is more about gathering resources than creating new ideas. My friend and early-childhood special-education teacher Sue is always reading a book about different strategies. She will say to me, "There is a child with _____ in my class this year, and we need something special to help him be successful." Sue was not willing to use the same ideas and structures year after year. She was creative and continued to learn from resources. Gathering new ideas and structures has become quite easy. You can look on the Internet, look in books, and ask other teachers. Some may call it stealing, but I call it being resourceful. Be sure to make the resources you gather fit individual students. Feel free to "steal" the ideas below!

Structures and Tools for Struggling Children

Perhaps one way to make working with special-needs children fun instead of frightening is to use exciting structures and tools. If you are not excited about what you are trying with special-needs students, chances are they aren't excited either. Structures and tools that provide special-needs students something to care about, peer interactions, technology, and movement are just some ways to bring energy into school for students with special needs. Of course, not all students will need the same things. As students show signs that they need something special, try some of the ideas below, make them "fit" the student, and then brainstorm some more.

Something to Care About

Create opportunities for special-needs students to study topics of interest. You have read about studying ideas that interest students in some of the other chapters, and it bears repeating here. If special-needs students get to study something that they care about and that interests them, they will be more motivated to learn. We often do the opposite with special-needs students. If they are unable to read, we have them work on skills with no context. If they struggle in math, we have them memorize facts that aren't meaningful. You may think special-needs students need to work on skills where they lack ability. This may be true, but why can't they learn the skills within topics that interest them or about which they care? If they need to learn sounds, find poems or stories with sounds in them. If they need to learn numbers, find a game or a topic like baseball or baking where numbers are used. Through workshops, thinking routines, and whole group activities, you should be able to include special-needs students in interesting units and engaging topics of study. Be sure to make time for students to share their projects and what they have learned with the class.

Create opportunities for students to care about an animal or a plant in the classroom. Sometimes students may benefit from caring for something beyond their schoolwork, such as an animal or a plant (Beck & Katcher, 1983; Davis, 1986; Nebbe, 1991; Trainin, Wilson, Wickless, & Brooks, 2005). Sheri, a principal I know, often brings her dog Reece to school so children can read to him or just have time to talk with him about their troubles. School counselor Linda Nebbe (1991) writes about a child named Rodney who, when he was having a bad day, would not talk to anyone or move. He became motionless, and no one except Nebbe's dog could get through to him. When the dog came into the room, Rodney put his arms around him and sobbed into his coat of fur until he was ready to go back into the classroom. Indeed, caring about an animal or a plant can be helpful for many different reasons.

> A friendly puppy, kitten, or dog gives the child with low self-esteem a boost. The aggressive child can experience being gentle with a nonthreatening and accepting recipient. These skills can be transferred. Social skills can be taught and accepted with a friendly animal. Touch is easily accepted and given even by children who have little experience with people-touch or who find touching with people threatening. A child can experience control while walking a dog or having it do special tricks. Trust can be demonstrated by giving a child responsibilities, such as feeding the fish or staying with the dog. Feelings and fears are easily projected to an animal as a person identifies with the perceived feelings of the animal. Role-playing with an animal or observation of the child's behavior with an animal often gives insights into a child's personality. The list of possibilities is endless. (Nebbe, 1991, p. 370)

If you decide that an animal or a plant would be good for your classroom, be sure to think about how you will care for it at night, on weekends, and during breaks. Some teachers

Abigail reads to Zoey the dog, building her confidence and having fun!

ask for parent volunteers to "adopt" the animal on weekends and during breaks. This may not be an option if the care won't be adequate. For the most part, the animal or plant will be your responsibility, and if you don't want that responsibility, don't get one.

Other alternatives, however, can be effective in helping special-needs students care for animals and plants. For example, you may be able to bring an animal into your room once in a while rather than full-time. You can do this through zoo exchange programs, your own animals, or the Humane Society. When I first started teaching, I was single and lived in an apartment that didn't allow animals. It was not possible for me to care for an animal in the classroom. Instead, I worked with a woman from a local wildlife rescue organization who came in and taught the children how to care for wildlife in our area. She brought in many animals that had been hurt and let the children help her care for them. We also had many plants around the room, and the children named and took care of them. Finally, we took care of little animals when we studied insects (mealworms, crickets, milkweed bugs). Although they were not warm and fuzzy like a dog or a cat, the children took very good care of them and rushed in each morning to make sure they were well. Make sure your principal accepts these kinds of programs and that your students aren't allergic to certain creatures.

If you cannot have animals or plants in your room for any reason, some other alternatives will work as well. Webkinz are stuffed animals with an Internet link that requires you to take care of them virtually. Many teachers I know have purchased Webkinz as class pets and had students take care of them. If you have a specific student who really needs to care for something, you may want to make him or her in charge of the animal. Students can also make human connections through animals. For example, my students did a butterfly migration project where we made and sent monarch butterflies to children in Mexico, and then butterflies from Mexico "migrated" back to us in the spring along with notes of friendship. For more information, type "Journey North" into your favorite search engine. Finally, you might also work to invite animals to your school. Plant a butterfly garden or make squirrel or bird feeders to put around the school. All of these things will help children care about animals and feel good about school and themselves.

Peer Interactions

For material related to this concept, go to Clip 7.2 on the Web-based Student Study Site.

Create opportunities for students of different age and experience levels to work together. Students who are struggling academically or socially may benefit from connections with their peers (Sousa, 2001). Building in times when students can get help from someone more experienced, as well as give expert help, can be worthwhile for students with special needs. This kind of peer tutoring can benefit students' self-worth, skill development, and motivation in school (Greenwood, Arreaga-Mayer, Utley, Gavin, & Terry, 2001; Miller & Kohler, 1993). Peer tutoring can be done with an older or a younger buddy class or just on a one-to-one basis with children you believe need help or would benefit from giving help. This kind of peer tutoring will require you to collaborate with teachers in your school. For example, I collaborated with a preschool teacher in our district so my children could create and give puppet shows to her students. Another time, we made counting and ABC books for the students in her room. I also collaborated with a fifth-grade teacher to have several of her students who needed a boost come down to read with my second graders who needed some help with their reading. In other words, the whole class didn't have a buddy every time. Another time, I had high school students in a journalism class come to our room and help us make a class newspaper. The activity itself was fun, and the interaction among students was cool, too.

Create opportunities for severely at-risk students to have an older friend. In some cases, students may not need peer tutoring, but they may just need a friend. I once had a student, for example, who had trouble with behaviors in the classroom. He was unkind to the other children, and they had a hard time befriending him. I teamed up with a high school counselor in my district who sent a high school student willing to come and "hang out" with the student for about an hour each week. The high school student didn't tutor or work to counsel my student but instead just came to play with him. They played basketball, drew pictures, blew bubbles, and so on, and my student gained something to care about and someone to count on. The next year, my whole school participated in a friends program, and we selected 10 students to participate who needed some interaction with a trusted friend. The high school students were hand chosen as those who would be dependable, who would not try to teach the students, and who would be caring toward them. It worked very well, and even though I have been away from the school where it was started for almost 10 years, the program continues today. If high school students don't work, try recruiting some retired teachers or others to come in and do different projects with children.

Technology

Create opportunities for students to use technology to assist their learning. I once worked with a teacher of middle-school special-education students. She told me stories of children who helped her program her cell phone and could use all kinds of technology but didn't do well in school. She began to incorporate technology into everything they did with great success. Shown to be a helpful supplement for students with special needs (Christmann, Badgett, & Lucking, 1997; Sharp, 2002; Sousa, 2001), technology is a tool you can use in your room to help manage students' academic and behavioral goals.

One way to support special-needs students with technology is through **computer-assisted instruction**, which allows for individual pacing and can allow students to participate in activities that might otherwise be difficult. Students who are unable to perform tasks that require fine motor skills can use software that operates with single-switch technology (Christmann & Christmann, 2003). Many Web sites will provide needed materials for students. For example, Recording for the Blind & Dyslexic records books for students who are blind or unable to read, and its Web site (www.rfbd.org) contains recordings and computer-compatible resources to promote learning through listening for all ages (Koehler, 2007). Another particularly useful Web site, www.marcopolo-education.org, has all kinds of lessons and ideas to differentiate for students with special needs. You can look up any level or subject you want. In addition, you can download games and visuals for free. You can also find good sites with a search engine or by asking other teachers or children.

Computer software, smart boards, **assistive communication devices**, and digital cameras can also help and motivate special-needs children. Dan, a middle-school teacher, worked with students in his room to create projects around a social studies topic using technology. Students who had traditionally struggled in his class found new motivation in using technology and

LETTER FROM A MASTER TEACHER 7.2

Knowing All Students

In my 22 years in the classroom, teaching all levels from kindergarten to eighth grade, I have had the opportunity to work with all types of students: low and high socioeconomic levels, disabled, challenged, learning impaired, speech and language impaired, English-language learner, any "label" used to classify students. If you are a teacher, you try to make a difference in the lives of *all* students placed in your care.

I truly believe the key for a teacher to make that difference is to form relationships with your students. This can take a lot of energy in class sizes of 30 "average" students. But I also have learned that forming relationships with 15 students in an inner-city poverty-level school or 5 in a special-needs classroom can take as much if not more energy. Having your students take an interest inventory or create a poster "All About Me" does not build these relationships alone. These relationships are proven by time, research, trying new approaches, fielding frustrations, and, yes, even your financial resources. You may need to give up your lunchtime to eat with students one-on-one. You do whatever it takes to help the students succeed. You show them that they are important to you and that you care about them.

I can pick up a book and read how to help students with a "label." There is a myriad of literature on how to help these students learn and succeed. The problem with set prescriptions for each type of learner is that no two students will ever be alike. The relationship you foster helps guide you to success with a student. Use whatever resource you can to know your students well and help them connect their learning to their interests and background knowledge. If a student loves basketball, use that tool to help him connect with math. This is a small example, but knowing the student well helps you find the keys to unlocking his or her connections. Without connections to a student's world, learning cannot take place. John Dewey (1938) calls it a student's "own personal power."

Will you ever have a student you won't be able to reach? I cannot answer that question. I can only tell you that if you approach each student, no matter where he or she comes from, with a resolve to help that student personally succeed, grow, and reach, you will succeed. A basic human need is to be affirmed for who you are. From the minute a student enters your presence, you are building that relationship. My principal said yesterday in our first staff meeting of the new year to new teachers and veterans, "They won't care what you know, unless they know that you care." The place to begin is just to get to know your students.

—Deanna Adams
Fifth-Grade Teacher

made a phenomenal video presentation. Working on the computer or with a camera may be easier for some students and allow their true abilities to come through. If our goal is to include special-needs students in the classroom, we should use whatever tools we have available to allow them to participate rather than just be in the room (Frattura & Capper, 2006). I certainly have not given you all of the possibilities for using technology in this short section. I hope that you are aware of what technology can provide for special-needs students and that you will continue to gather resources as you work to help all students become successful learners.

Movement

For material related to this concept, go to Clip 7.3 on the Web-based Student Study Site.

We often ask children to sit for long periods, and for most it is not impossible . . . or fun. For some, sitting still is impossible. For others, sitting for long periods creates a severe lack of attention. The movement ideas in Chapter 3 included doing brain exercises and just stretching. Go back to those and resee them for children with special needs. Some children may need even more movement. They may benefit from a balance board or sitting on a chair with tennis balls on three of its legs so it tips quietly back and forth. A cushion that rocks back and forth may work for others. Sometimes, the movement can be as minor as holding a Koosh ball or another squeezable ball.

When students need to go to assemblies or sit on the floor in other classrooms, find a good spot for them to stand and show them how to rock back and forth on their heels or stand with weight on one foot more than the other and then switch. Be sure to teach them these strategies before you go so you don't have to pull them out in front of everyone.

As I sit here thinking about an ending to this chapter, I can't help but go back to the metaphor from the beginning. What if I had just tried to make the last play during the basketball game or to run the last leg of the relay? Looking back, I would not have failed because I would have tried. You will not fail the special-needs children in your room either; all you have to do is try.

So . . . What?

We are often afraid of disruptions and of children who seem different. We must get rid of those fears and create places where they are welcomed, wanted, and even loved. To help special-needs children become successful academically and socially, our first job is to learn about them.

Begin by asking: Is this a development issue? Is this a physical or mental disability? Is this a cultural issue? Is this an environmental issue?

In the classroom and out: Be there, reflect toward the future, be an advocate, be a collaborator, accommodate for individuals, be creative, and be a learner.

Create something special that makes participation in school a wonderful experience, such as something to care about (topics of study, animals and plants), peer interactions, technology, and movement.

Don't be afraid of failing. You won't if you just try.

Get Ready For . . .

We worked in this chapter to know special-needs students and ways to meet their needs. One way, language and literature, deserves a whole chapter. The words we use and the stories we tell and help students create are powerful ways to help all students make meaning about the world in which they live. We say a lot about autonomy, belonging, and competency with the language and literature we use in the classroom, so get ready for some Jedi mind tricks!

Activities to Try

- Review this chapter and select three or four of the students who were mentioned. Alone or with a group, brainstorm what you could do to accommodate their needs in your classroom beyond the items already mentioned.

- There is so much information about special-needs students! Pick some of the resources used in this chapter and read further. I especially recommend *Weakfish* by Michael Dorn (2006), *The Vulnerable Child* by Richard Weissbourd (1996), and "The Human-Animal Bond and the Elementary School Counselor" by Linda Nebbe (1991). I can't even begin to tell their stories adequately.

- **Make a collection!** Take some time to go on the Internet and find Web sites to use with children. There are some great ones out there!

- **Conduct action research!** Interview a special educator. Be sure to ask him why he became a special educator and why he loves it. Ask him to tell you stories of his students.

Student Study Site

The companion Web site for *Elementary Classroom Management* can be found at www.sagepub.com/kwilliamsstudy.

Visit the Web-based student study site to enhance your understanding of the chapter content. The study materials include video clips, practice tests, flashcards, suggested readings, and Web resources.

CHAPTER 8

Language and Literature as Classroom Management Tools

My husband is a pilot for the Air National Guard. He grew up in an Air Force family with no teachers, and other than going to school, he really hadn't thought much about classrooms or education in general—that is, until he met me. Since then, he has listened to me, as well as the many other members of my family who are teachers, talk about schools, curriculum, pedagogy, and so on, almost every day. Don't feel sorry for him. I have listened to numerous airplane stories as well! When we first got married, however, much of what I talked about evidently didn't soak into his brain, and I was able to covertly practice using language as a management tool on him. For example, I would say, "Do you want to do the dishes or fold the laundry?" He would choose, and we would go on with life. After a few months, however, we were sitting at the dinner table, I asked him if he wanted to clear the table or wash the pans, and he got a funny look on his face. He paused and then, with an air of disbelief, said, "Don't use those Jedi mind tricks with me! You're talking to me like your second graders!" We laughed and laughed, and then I said, "Honey, I have been doing that for a while now. It works well!"

My husband, of course, was referring to the *Star Wars* movie where the characters are able to get their enemies to do something just by suggesting it. Although I am certainly not suggesting mind control, the language you use and the stories you tell are excellent tools when

195

Jesse Keifer

One benefit of using language that creates opportunities for autonomy, belonging, and competency is that the students start to use the language too.

working with all children. "In fact, language can be a powerful vehicle for activating thought, and as teachers we need to be aware of the role it is playing" (Ritchhart, 2002, p. 116). If we are working to help all students gain autonomy, belonging, and competency in the classroom; to develop democratic communities; and to help children develop academically and socially, how we use language and literature matters.

In the last chapter, we talked about children with special needs. The language and literature in this chapter will be another tool to help you meet their needs. Remember that some children, for a variety of reasons, will have special needs on a day-to-day basis. These children do not qualify for special services but may need our attention at times during the school year. Students may have a bad day, temporary circumstances that interrupt their learning for a few days or weeks, difficult temperaments, or a hard time relating to others. This chapter is about language and literature tools that will help all children with social issues in the classroom. It is about tools that will help children work through a tough situation without power struggles and with a sense of dignity. It is about learning rather than punishing and students controlling themselves rather than teachers controlling them. The tools in this chapter are not Jedi mind tricks, as my husband called them, but just one more way to help all children develop autonomy, belonging, and competency in the classroom.

By the end of this chapter, I hope you have:

- An understanding that the kinds of language you use affect students' autonomy, belonging, and competency

- Some strategies for using language that promote choice and decision-making skills

- A beginning collection of children's literature that will help children solve problems, develop different perspectives, and become introspective

- The ability to help children begin to meet their social goals by writing stories with them

Although language and literature might seem like a small detail of classroom management at first, it is really a very important key to all you have read so far. Children cannot gain autonomy, belonging, and competency if the language they hear is controlling. You cannot have a democratic community in a classroom if your language is directive and punishing. Motivation will not be high if damaging words dangle in the air. Punitive language will erase all the effects of workshops, thinking routines, class meetings, data collection, and brain exercises.

Managing With Language (and I Don't Mean Swearing!)

You can really take two different routes with the language you choose to use in the classroom: language of power and control or language of respect and facilitation. Think about this for a minute in a context outside of school. If I had started my marriage as a dictator with statements like "You need to do the dishes every night," my husband and I would have seriously conflicted. No one likes to be spoken to in a way that takes away their opportunities to be autonomous. Of course, I still expect my husband to help around the house, but we get the work done in a much happier way if we negotiate and treat each other with respect. He is much more willing to do his share if he is in on the decision making and feels I listen to his perspective. I bet you feel the same way.

Perhaps you think marriage is a different situation because the parties involved are both adults. An interaction between two adults is certainly different from an interaction between a teacher and students; however, if you speak to children like they are worthy of respect and yet convey your expectations, you will be able to form partnerships and work on problems together rather than struggle against one another. How can students learn to be respectful if they don't see or hear respect? For example, let's say a child is yelling at you and is really upset. You have some choices as a teacher. You can say, "You'd better not talk to me like that, or you will have to leave the room." Or you can say, "I can tell that you're angry right now, and when you're able to cool down a bit and aren't yelling, we can talk about why you're upset." In both cases, you are conveying the message that yelling isn't OK. The first choice, however, doesn't acknowledge the student, creates opportunities for a power struggle, and results in no learning. The second choice helps the child know you see the anger, provides time for cooling down, and creates opportunities for the child to learn what to do when he or she is angry.

Although teachers don't always have time to consciously consider the kinds of language they will use when a situation arises, I suggest you begin thinking about how language can help you manage different situations in the classroom by creating choices for yourself and practicing when you have opportunities (maybe on your husband!). The language you use probably won't always fit nicely into two categories, but the dichotomy of language presented below will help you start thinking about language as a management tool. Remember that we are talking about management that promotes academic and social learning, community, and self-worth. In classrooms where management is about controlling students' behavior, the language used doesn't really matter.

Questions Versus Statements

For material related to this concept, go to Clip 8.1 on the Web-based Student Study Site.

We often think of questions as a good strategy for promoting academic learning. Questions are valuable for social learning as well. Whenever you can ask students a question rather than give them a statement, you will help them think, make choices, and solve problems. You will help them learn how to handle situations in respectful ways and with dignity. Statements require no thinking on students' part and teach children to behave in certain ways because the teacher said so rather than because it is the right thing to do. Questions can help children feel capable and competent while teaching them why certain behaviors are expected. In addition, good questions relate that we care about students and their perspective because (hopefully) we will take the time to listen to their answers. Fay and Funk (1995) recommend using several questions to help children think about their behaviors and decisions:

- What would you like to happen?
- Would you like my thinking on that?
- Is it possible that . . . ?
- How do you feel about . . . ?
- Is there any chance that . . . ?
- How do you suppose that might work out?
- What do you think I think?
- On a scale of 1–10, how good a decision do you think that is?
- Would you like to hear what others have tried? (p. 179)

I also recommend using questions that help children understand that they have choices. For example, don't say, "You need to go to the office and cool down." Instead, ask, "Where would be a good place for you to cool down?" If a student is having trouble paying attention from where he or she is sitting, you could ask, "Where would be a good place for you to sit so you can be the best learner possible?" Then ask, "How will I know it is working for you?" Sometimes it works well to give them specific choices, such as "Would you like to work with the group, or would it be better for you to work alone right now?" All of these questions give the decisions back to the children, require them to think about themselves and others, and help them learn to self-regulate.

It is important to make sure you are asking questions that are legitimate, not rhetorical, and not phrased as put-downs (Fay & Funk, 1995). For example, don't ask students where they would like to cool down if you won't really let them go there. If there really isn't a choice, don't make it seem like there is one. Sometimes it is easy to get so mad that it is difficult to ask questions and really care about the answers. If a situation has escalated to a point where you can see the red in your eyes and can't think straight, the children will know that you really don't want to know their answers. In this case, stopping for a minute might be necessary. You can say, "I am so mad right now that I need to calm down a bit before we talk." Not only will this help children see that walking away when you are mad is a good thing, but it will also give them time to think about what happened and put it into perspective. They may be able to figure out a solution before you come back to ask questions. We often think we have to respond right away to problems, and in cases where children are in danger, you must. Allowing a student time to think about the issue for a few minutes, however, often benefits all parties (Fay & Funk, 1995).

Questioning rather than stating can be difficult at times. We aren't used to using questions. My suggestions?

- Go into stressful situations with two words circling in your head: *calm* and *curious.* Then try to live those two words. You need to start wondering aloud why a student is acting the way he or she is and really want to know the answers.

- Practice some key questions that you can use in many situations.

- If you ask a question and know it wasn't the "right" one, keep trying.

When I was student teaching, one of my goals was to use questions rather than statements. I wasn't very good at it, but I didn't give up. I remember one time a student was tapping his pencil on his desk, poking others with it, and just really having a hard time using it. I went up to him, kneeled down, and said, "Would you like to put the pencil away?" Of course, he said, "No." Wrong question . . . try again. "Is that pencil helping you learn?" He said, "No." Another question that didn't work . . . try again. After about five tries and the child looking at me like I was crazy, I finally got one that worked. I asked, "Would you like to put that pencil in your desk or on mine?" He quickly put the pencil away, and I walked away relieved (which I think the child felt too!). Although the question wasn't very deep and maybe not the best one I could have asked, I gave the child an opportunity to think and make a decision about his pencil. What questions might have been better? As with all learning, there are many "right" answers and, in this case, questions (see Table 8.1).

You don't always have to use questions as ways to solve particular problems. Sometimes simply being calm and curious may be necessary to figure out what the problem is and to acknowledge how children are feeling. Asking questions like the following may be good when you sense that a child isn't doing his or her very best:

- "Are you feeling OK today?"

- "What happened that is making you angry?"

- "Is there something I can do to help you today?"

TABLE 8.1 **Questioning Cases**

Look at the following cases and list as many helpful questions as you can. If you have partners to try the questions with, give them the scenario and ask them to be as awful as they possibly can so you can practice question after question. Remember that you aren't necessarily trying to get them to do what you want them to do. You may need to learn what the child needs instead. Remember also that there isn't just one but rather many "right" questions.

Case 1:	You are teaching first grade, and you want all of the students to come to the floor to listen to a story. One child will not come to the floor. What questions could you use to help him or her?
Case 2:	You are teaching eighth grade, and a student comes into your room with a hat and coat on even though the school policy is that hats and coats must not be worn in the classroom for security reasons. What questions could you use to help him or her?
Case 3:	You are teaching fifth grade and notice that a child is stealing items from the classroom. What questions could you use to help him or her?
Case 4:	You are teaching first grade, and a child is calling others names at recess. What questions could you use to help him or her?
Case 5:	You are teaching sixth grade, and the whole class is loud and horsing around. What questions could you use to help your students?

Although you may have to intervene in other ways, asking a beginning question that simply shows the child that you noticed he or she was struggling and that you care can be helpful in itself. If children don't respond to questions, just acknowledging that they are having trouble rather than dismissing it can be very helpful (Faber & Mazlish, 1995). For example, if a child says, "I hate reading," instead of telling him he has to read anyway, you might say, "I know what you mean. Sometimes I would rather go outside and play too." Take some time to think about how you can acknowledge students' feelings in the classroom.

Stories Versus Lectures

Classroom happenings can sometimes tempt teachers to give lectures about what should be happening or what the expectations are in class. Ask any teacher, and he or she could probably come up with standard lectures he or she gives each year. Ask any student, and he or she could probably tell you there were lectures but not remember the contents. For example, I work with groups of 50 teachers working to get master's degrees. Each year, my colleagues and I try to help them to get to know rather than judge their students. We have even lectured the teachers about this at times, explaining that it is important to know students and that they may not know what the students are going through. They usually nod their heads and agree, but I doubt it has had much impact. One year, however, after we had listened to teachers talk about how students weren't handing in homework, weren't motivated, and came to school without any values, Sheri (my colleague and elementary principal) stopped the group and began telling them a story about a child in her building. The child's mother was going to prison in a few weeks and came into Sheri's office to be sure the child would be OK. Sheri talked about how she hoped the child just made it to school every day, as well as how important it would be to help that child feel welcome even if she came late or without supplies or homework. Sheri ended the story by urging the teachers to "know students' stories." After she finished the story, all 50 teachers were silent. How do I know the story stuck with them? A year later, when we met with these same teachers, many stated that they had either reached their goals of knowing students' stories or made it a goal for that year. The lectures given previously had evoked little action on the teachers' part, but Sheri's simple, powerful story had stayed with them.

Stories can be powerful tools in the classroom as well. Telling a story can create opportunities for discussion, help students understand situations from different perspectives, and provide a more compelling reason for students to listen and think about issues in the classroom. One year, for example, I had a group of students who, for whatever reason, liked to launch classroom items into the air. Staples, pencils and erasers, often flew around the room. I don't think the students were trying to hurt anyone, but they didn't seem to realize what might happen if the launching continued. Instead of warning them not to do it for fear of a consequence like staying in for recess, I told them a story about one of my sixth-grade classmates. Someone in my class was playing around, shot a piece of lead out of a mechanical pencil, and hit a boy named Dustin in the eye. After a minute of gasping and asking questions about what happened, the students and I talked about why it would be important not to launch anything around the room. Most of the students were able to internalize the story and think ahead about the consequences of something so dangerous. Sometimes, when students engage in dangerous, annoying, or otherwise disruptive behaviors, they aren't aware of others' perspectives or able to think beyond what is happening in the moment. Stories that provide a glimpse into the future or help spur conversations about others' perspectives are very helpful in these cases.

As always, there are some cautions about using stories as vehicles for language in a classroom. Just as lecturing over and over may cause children to tune out what is being said, too many stories can have a similar effect. Save storytelling for when you have a really good story to tell, when it fits well with the issue in the classroom, and when you haven't told one in a while. Be sure to tell stories that are true; made-up stories are easily spotted and won't have the same effect. The story about Dustin really happened, as did all of the stories in this book. If you don't have a good story of your own, get a children's literature book about the topic (see below). Stories don't always have to be sad. Sometimes funny stories can liven a class discussion or make a point just as well. Finally, you don't always have to tell stories to the whole class. Sometimes working stories into conversations with small groups or individuals can have the biggest impact.

Empathy Versus Anger

"Isn't it great to watch a master at work? The masters always make things look so easy. They stay calm. They avoid taking on ownership of another person's problem. They set firm limits without waging war" (Fay & Funk, 1995, p. 3). One of the hardest things to do in a classroom, at least from my perspective, is to be empathetic rather than angry. Taking poor behaviors and giving them back to the students to solve rather than making them your own is hard. It can be difficult not to take poor behaviors personally, but helping children take ownership of their behaviors, as well as their plans for correcting them, is better for the children and better for you. Children will become autonomous and competent only if we allow them to think through their actions and work to create solutions of their own. Children will have a sense of belonging if we are empathetic, rather than angry, when they work through their behaviors and solutions.

How does empathy look and sound in the classroom? It may look like a straight face rather than an angry face, an understanding nod or a hand on a child's shoulder, or kneeling down so you can be on the students' level rather than towering above them. Sounding empathetic may include speaking quietly enough about a problem so other children can't hear the conversation. It may be saying, "It seems like you have a problem. How can I help you?" rather than "You are having a problem. Get out of here." Empathy in a classroom may be taking the time to listen rather than jumping to conclusions.

I had computers and magnets in my classroom each year I taught. Although my students and I always talked about not putting the magnets near the computers, one child, Kristin, held a wand magnet up to each computer screen until there were large, multicolored rings all over it. I was really angry. I also feared that my entire paycheck would be swallowed up by the fee for the monitors. Instead of getting angry at Kristin, however, I turned my empathy on full force. I said, "Oh, gosh. This is a big, big problem. What are you going to do?" Keep in mind that I said it without sarcasm and that I sincerely felt bad for her. I was just glad *she* would have to tell the technology support person and not me! Kristin cried for a while. Then we sat down and talked about what she was going to do. She decided that she would need to get some help for the computers and follow directions more carefully in the future, and she ended up calling and finding out what to do for the computers. Luckily, it was just a matter of turning the computers on and off multiple times until the screens reset themselves. Kristin then decided to turn them on and off during class. I empathetically noted that I cared too much about her for her to miss class and asked her if she had any other ideas. She decided to come in from recess to do the work and even recruited some of her loyal community members to help her. For the next week, students came in with Kristin and turned the computers on and off. It would have been really easy for me to get angry at Kristin, give her a consequence, and fix the computers myself. By being empathetic and firm in my decision that she would need to fix the problem, however, Kristin learned a lot and kept her dignity. In fact, I think Kristin felt a greater sense of belonging because her classmates offered to help her. My hair didn't turn gray with worry, and everything got fixed.

I realize that Kristin's situation was a fairly easy example to share. A child wasn't hurt, and the computers got fixed. Sometimes, though, hiding your anger will not be possible. Indeed, there have been plenty of times when I couldn't hide my anger, so I am not asking you to leave your true emotions behind. Working to look at problem behaviors as opportunities for learning and putting the ownership back on the children, however, is very helpful in teaching them to learn from mistakes, come up with ways to solve problems, and understand why their inappropriate behaviors can't exist in classrooms. This may take a lot of reflection and time to think before you interact with children. Remember, when you are angry with children, you are teaching them to be angry when solving problems. I took a plane ride with my son when he was 2, for example, and he screamed for most of the flight. The flight attendant came back and angrily told me to keep him quiet and that the other passengers didn't deserve to listen to his screaming. In that moment, I didn't become a better parent. Her anger didn't help the situation at all. In fact, it made me feel tense and upset and thus made my son more upset. The problem would have been solved much more quickly and without so much strife if she had offered her help and empathized with my situation. Children will not become better learners if we are angry with them. They will not behave better or learn more content. They will only wish they weren't in the classroom.

Empathy to some may seem like giving in to students' inappropriate behaviors, but this is not the case. "To internalize the lessons of life, children need to experience the consequences of their behavior. The application of consequences with empathy rather than anger tends to speed up the internalization" (Fay & Funk, 1995, p. 110). Children may need to have consequences for behaviors. Kristin definitely had a consequence. Students must understand, however, that those consequences are because of their decisions and not because their teacher is angry. Being empathetic doesn't mean you can't show emotions, however. Telling children you are upset or showing sadness when they make poor decisions is good. It helps children understand that those emotions are OK. Using anger as a way to punish children (waging war), however, doesn't help anyone.

Assessment Versus Evaluation

Once again we have arrived at a topic that is often seen as an academic issue when really it is a learning issue. During a social learning situation, language that facilitates assessment will be more helpful than evaluative language. Remember from Chapter 3 that assessment is what's right, what's wrong, and how to fix it (Lockett, 2006). **Evaluation** is merely what is wrong. When we assess other people or ourselves, whether it is an academic or a social issue, our goal should be to help them or ourselves get better. The language we use helps others understand our intentions. We are often very evaluative in schools when it comes to behavior. For instance, teachers say things like "Stop talking," "You need to show some respect," or "You can't talk out of turn in class." All of these statements might be legitimate evaluations, but they don't help the student know how to fix the problem. Before reading on, take a minute to think about how you could change these evaluative statements into assessment questions or statements.

Why is assessment versus evaluation so important? You must be very clear about and define your expectations. For example, respect has many different definitions, especially if we are defining how it looks and sounds. Although evaluative statements may give children a sense of what you want them to do, telling or asking them how to fix the behavior creates a sense that everyone is on the same page. Let's say a child is blurting out answers during a class discussion. I could say to that child, "You're not taking turns talking in class." For some that may help; however, the problem may be easier for a child to fix if I say, "If you have an answer, what could you do?" In a sense, this helps children figure out what to do instead of what not to do. It also helps teachers figure out what the child is thinking and what he or she understands about his or her behaviors. Students from different backgrounds or cultures may not have the same idea of what it means to be respectful, how to gain attention, and so on.

You can use assessment questions and statements in a variety of ways. If you are in the middle of something and need a quick solution to a problem, you could quickly advise a student how to fix it. For example, if a child is running around the classroom, you could say, "You will need to walk." Later, when you have a moment, you could sit with the child and ask him or her some questions about running in a classroom. If you see one child calling another child names, you may need to have a more extensive conversation. For example, you might need to tell the child what you saw and ask him or her what was going on and how he or she could fix the problem. Planning for a solution to a problem rather than just discussing what happened is important.

As with all of the suggestions in this chapter for using language that will help children learn about their social goals, I realize it isn't always possible to say what you want to say when you want to say it. Sometimes, in the moment, remembering to ask questions, tell stories, be empathetic, and use assessing comments rather than evaluative statements is difficult. If you think about this kind of language as a bull's-eye that you are targeting, keep practicing, and reflect on conversations you have with children to determine how close or far away you were from the bull's-eye, it will get easier to automatically use language as a tool.

Times to Be Directive

When a child is being hurt, you need to use directive language. Most of the time, you will want to use language that is full of questions, stories, empathy, and assessment. Sometimes, however, you should use directive language. For example, when children are being hurt, it is not a good idea to ask the child who is hurting them what to do. It is not a good idea tell a story. Save those things for later when no danger is present. If one child is hurting another, be directive. Tell him or her to stop or go to the office, another part of the building, or up against a wall if you are outside. After you have helped the hurt child, begin talking to the other child with some of the suggestions given above.

You also need to be directive if a child is in danger. If a child is about to do something dangerous, like go out in the street, or if your children are outside and it begins to storm, tell them exactly what to do or not do. Use a firm, loud voice that sounds different from the one you regularly use.

Remember that being directive is most effective when it is used for extreme situations. I would not suggest doing this all or even some of the time. If a group of students is bullying other children or engaging in illegal behavior, you will need to be direct with them and more than likely utilize resources that your school and community provides (see Chapter 9).

Effective Single Words

Another use of language that is effective in helping children learn about classrooms and social situations is single-word reminders. Even though you may use questions, stories, empathy, and assessment language, children may relapse. Instead of revisiting the stories and ideas over and over again, coming up with one-word reminders that help children remember those other conversations may be a good idea. For example, when my students were mean to each other with unkind words or deeds, I often said, "Kindness." The children automatically knew the word *kindness* meant that I had assessed their behavior and that they needed to come up with a plan for being kind. I didn't discuss this word with them ahead of time, but they quickly figured it out. I believe I said that word so often that, when I was out in a group of adults, I had to keep myself from saying it!

Another word that I find helpful in managing a classroom is *and*. It may sound crazy, but that little word really helps when you are working with a child on a social goal. For example, if a child is messing around when he is supposed to be reading, I might go over to him, get down at his level, and quietly say, "What are you supposed to be doing?" He would tell me he is supposed to be reading. I might say, "Why is it important to be reading right now?" Then I would proceed to listen to his ideas, and every time he came up with one, I would say, "And …" until he had exhausted all possibilities. That little word *and* helps students come up with multiple reasons for doing things, verbalize those reasons, and …

Finally, a fun management tool for the students may be helping you come up with single words that have secret meaning to only their class. For fun, instead of saying, "Quiet" or turning out the lights, my students would come up with a single word that anyone in the class could say if he or she needed everyone's attention. It was a classic moment when, one day, I happened to say, "Loogie" just as the principal came in the room. The good news is that everyone got quiet (OK, there were a few giggles).

Body Language

For material related to this concept, go to Clip 8.2 on the Web-based Student Study Site.

Sometimes your body language can help you communicate with students more effectively than oral language. Giving the "evil eye" or shaking your head can help students know that what they are doing is inappropriate. In addition, this kind of body language can quickly and without interruption help children get back to what they need to be doing. Sometimes, if a specific child needed a certain cue often, the child and I would come up with a signal that only he or she understood. For example, some students may have behaviors that are distracting to others but that they are unaware of, such as humming during class. To help them stop humming without singling them out of the group, you might come up with a physical signal that would let them know they need to stop. Sometimes proximity alone can help struggling children. If students are doing things they shouldn't be, try standing next to them.

Children can also use body language to help you manage the classroom. You can make up signals that students can show you when they need something. For example, I once knew a teacher who had a student who never raised her hand to answer questions or give ideas. After getting to know the student a little better and talking to her about her participation, the teacher found out that the student was afraid of answering incorrectly. So together they came up with the idea that she would raise her right hand if she knew the answer and her left hand if she didn't know the answer. The teacher told the student that she would only call on her if her right hand was raised. In that way, the student felt better about participating in front of her peers.

Language is a powerful management tool. Throughout this book, I have given you some ideas about classroom management. Unfortunately or fortunately, I cannot give you a program of things to say or do in your classroom. It is up to you to plan for, use, and reflect on language that will help you create the best environment for children and their learning. Just like any other tool, you will need to practice using language so it will be easy when situations are difficult and emotional. Just like any other tool, when language is used effectively, children will respond positively.

LETTER FROM A MASTER TEACHER 8.1

Understanding Children's Language

Sometimes, as teachers, we get caught up in our own language. However, we must also consider the language *children* use in the classroom. It is our responsibility to take the time to listen to our students, to know them, and to understand what they are saying.

This past year, I had a student named Jack who was having a difficult time entering established playgroups. Rather than asking if he could join, he would either take a dinosaur and "crash" into the group or tap a group member on the head or back and then run away. These attempts only led to frustration on the part of the children in the group, and as a result, Jack was not invited to play. I used every "technique" that I had learned to try to get Jack to verbalize what he was feeling to no avail.

After a few weeks, we happened to be journaling one day with the topic, "My wish would be _____." When I got to Jack, he had drawn a lot of faces on his paper. I read the lead sentence and paused. He finished the sentence with "that my friends would like me." Jack was able to verbalize that he thought his classmates thought he was "yucky" and that was why they would not let him play with them. What a perfect opportunity to read my favorite book, *Charlie the Caterpillar* by Dom DeLuise. Charlie is a caterpillar who makes numerous attempts to play with other characters. Each attempt fails as the other characters call him ugly and tell him they don't want to play with him. As each page details another negative social interaction, the students are able to discuss more appropriate ways for the other characters to interact with Charlie. On one page, two rabbits are playing tennis. When Charlie asks if he can join, they tell him no because he is an ugly caterpillar. In our discussions, we talk about other ways the rabbits might talk to Charlie. One student said, "They should tell Charlie that he doesn't have big enough hands, so he can't play tennis with them because he can't hold the racket, but he could be the score taker or the cheerleader." Another said, "They should tell Charlie that only two can play tennis, and he can have a turn on the next game." The students can empathize with Charlie and understand how the hurtful words affect him. What a wonderful way to help Jack's situation.

Social disputes and emotional insecurities have such underlying effects on your day-to-day environment. When children are given the opportunity to work out their disputes or feelings of insecurities with the support of a caring teacher, they will be able to apply what they have learned in these instances to events that may happen later in life.

—Lisa Meyer
Preschool Director

Management With Children's Literature

Another great way to use language as a management tool is with literature. Sometimes a good book can speak to children in ways that adults can't.

> When books are shared in the classroom, the characters and stories become part of that learning community. We can use those trade books to start discussions, to pique children's interest in a subject to be explored, to answer some questions and to pose new ones. We identify with characters, recognizing others or ourselves in some of the feelings and reactions we get from reading the stories, and we get life lessons from the lives we glimpse in those stories. (Hurst, 2000, p. 1)

Indeed, using literature in a classroom to help children understand or deal with social issues is easy and effective. Hundreds of books have social messages and can either highlight or help solve a problem in the classroom. Whether you are working to help children see others' perspectives, make friends, understand someone different, or deal with a problem behavior, someone has probably written a children's book about it.

There are some great ways to use books to help children learn both socially and academically.

What's a Good Book?

Since we are talking about using literature for social goals in the classroom, it may be tempting to look for books that are clearly "values literature." Be cautious, however, when using books written specifically to teach a lesson. There are exceptions—such as Dr. Seuss or Leo Lionni books—but for the most part, books with a clear social lesson aren't the best to use. Hurst (2000) recommends looking for literature that can spark a conversation or activity surrounding a social goal rather than literature clearly written to teach a behavior lesson: "We need books that have been written because the author had a story to tell, not because he or she had a lesson to teach" (p. 2). Books should have believable characters and interesting plots.

Choose books that you love, and be purposeful about the times you use them. For example, I love *The Lion's Bed* by Diane Redfield Massie. It is about a group of animals who live peacefully in the jungle and find out that a lion is coming to live in their part of the jungle. Frightened, they panic and begin contemplating moving. Instead, however, they work as a team; each animal uses its own strengths to convince the lion he doesn't want to live there. I read this book at the beginning of many school years in many grade levels because I loved it, but it also sparked great discussions about community, working together, and individual talents. Once in a while, when we were having trouble working together, I got the book back out and reread it without any discussion ahead of time about why. Most of the time, students figured it out, and it was a nice reminder without any lecturing from me. If you don't love a book, it may be hard to use it effectively.

Choose books that will be useful in several different areas. Good books usually have more than one topic that can be explored. For example, in *All the Places to Love* by Patricia MacLachlan, all of the characters' favorite places are discussed and illustrated. Getting to know students' favorite places can be something very important in creating a community. The book, however, is also about a brother getting a new sister and could provide opportunities for children to uncover their thoughts about family. Academically, this book could be used to learn about different places in the world. You see, good books provide children with opportunities to go wherever their minds need to go at that moment.

How to Use Literature as a Management Tool

Of course, there are many, many ways to use literature in your classroom. As you become more familiar with children's literature, it will be easy to come up with ways to use it to help children think about and achieve social goals. These are just some of the ways that I have either tried or borrowed from other teachers. As always, you will need to make these ideas your own.

Literature can be used to help children move toward meeting general social goals. You will want to uncover some topics each year. For example, no matter what group of children you have, you will want to help them become a community and think about friendships, respect, working together, and differences among others. Children's literature can foster a beginning conversation about these topics, as well as give you ideas for activities to use with them. My very favorite book ever is *The Big Orange Splot* by Daniel Pinkwater. It is about a man who lives on a street where all the houses are the same. One day, a seagull drops a bucket of orange paint on his house, and his neighbors get really mad at him because it has made his house different. In the end, all the neighbors end up with houses that represent their dreams. I used this book every year to talk about how being different is a good thing. The students sometimes made dream houses (where we incorporated lessons on perimeter and area), and sometimes we just read and talked about the book. These kinds of social goals are easily planned because you will want to do them with each group of students you teach. Another teacher I know, Connie, uses *No, David!* by David Shannon to talk about classroom expectations, and then each student writes a *Yes, David!* book about what they want their classroom to be like.

Sometimes situations will arise that you will need to address with certain groups of students. In other words, one group of students may have specific social goals that need addressing, but another group may not. For example, I once had a group of students who really struggled with group work. Not all of them struggled, but teaching the class how to work together was especially difficult that year because personalities were so different. To get conversations going about working together, I read *Chester's Way* by Kevin Henkes. It is about Chester the mouse who has a mind of his own and who likes to do things in a specific way. He and his friend Wilson get along famously because they have similar perspectives. Lily moves into the neighborhood, however, and creates some tension due to her exuberance and risk taking. In the end, they all learn from each other and become fast friends. *Chester's Way* is a good book to read before working in groups or when groups are having trouble getting started on a project. In this case, you may not know very far ahead of time that you want to use this book or one like it, and thus it is good to know some children's literature books that you can use for a variety of purposes. The teacher next door to me, my friend Cheryl, was a magnificent resource for literature. I could go into her room at the last minute and say, "I need a book about _____" and she would get me one. You can use your librarian, other teachers, Web sites, and so on, to help you look for good books. Be sure to read them for yourself before you use them, however, because they may not end up as you expected.

Literature can also be used with individuals or small groups of students who are struggling with a social issue. In this case, you may not want to take class time to work on a small number of students' social goals. In my classroom, for example, I once had two boys who could not get along. They got in trouble every day at recess for fighting, and finally the teachers on the playground told me the boys would need to work things out before they could come back to the playground. So they came into my room the next day for recess and were required to read Dr. Seuss's *The Butter Battle Book* aloud to each other. *The Butter Battle Book* is about two towns that butter their bread on different sides, and the fight over how to butter bread escalates from throwing stones to getting fences to making bigger and better war machines. It is one of my favorite books for children because it shows how fighting really doesn't solve anything, as well as how silly the beginnings of our fights can be. At first, the boys wouldn't read the book. After a while, however, they figured out that they weren't going back on the playground until they read the book and worked out their problems. The two boys begrudgingly sat near each other and began taking turns reading aloud. They laughed and talked about the book and then let me know they were finished. The book had helped them put things into perspective and relax a bit, and they were ready to talk about the issues surrounding their own fights. Certainly, not every issue can be worked out with literature. When it can help solve a problem, however, literature is a very powerful tool. By the way, *The Butter Battle Book* has many different uses. Seventh-grade teacher Tom Roff, for example, uses it to help students understand the Cold War in his history class.

Hurst (2000) recommends waiting to use children's literature until directly after a trau-matic experience. They believe that children who have recently had a troubling life experi-ence should not be offered a book about whatever is troubling them. For example, giving a child whose dog just died a book like *Old Yeller* in which the dog is put to sleep at the end probably isn't the best idea to help the child grieve. Weeks or months after the event, however, the child might be ready for a book, but "usually at the moment of trauma and for awhile after they need our open arms and hearts to talk, to listen and to mourn" (Hurst, 2000, p. 4).

Another thing to think about when using children's literature as a classroom manage-ment tool is the kind of conversations you want to have about the chosen book. Be sure to think carefully about the questions you will ask and how you will handle children's responses. They may be willing to share with other students more than you want them to. Consider having them write in a journal or draw a picture about the book before discussing it aloud. In addition, you will want to have a conversation, not a question and answer session, surrounding the children's literature that you choose. This may take practice on your part, as well as repetition. Modeling can also be very helpful. For example, if you are having a con-versation with children about *The Big Orange Splot,* you might tell them what the book made you think about and then ask them what it made them think about. If you are reading *The Butter Battle Book,* you might ask the children to connect that book to the classroom. Use some thinking routines to help you. Think-pair-share is a great way to start conversations about books because students have the opportunity to share their ideas with one person before sharing them with the whole group.

When sharing books to spark activities or conversations surrounding social goals, it is wise to have a purpose for using the book. Also remember that the children might get something different from your aim, and that is OK. Learning never ends. All learning, even social learning, is about making connections between past, present, and future experiences. The children may not have the same experiences as you do and therefore may not make the same connections.

Books to Use and How to Find More

For the most part, finding good literature to use in the classroom is about asking, searching, and experimenting. Ask the teachers at your school what literature their children love, and be sure to ask your school media specialist. I did some asking for you as well: I asked all the teachers I know about books they use in the classroom. Table 8.2 shows what they came up with. I didn't put a difficulty level on the books because I want to encourage you to look at them before planning to use them, and I hope you will use books of all levels in your class-room. Obviously, you probably can't read a long chapter book to a group of kindergartners, but many other books can be read to many different groups. For example, fifth-grade teacher Jennifer Bell recommends using *The Little Engine That Could* and *I Knew You Could,* both of which I have read to my young sons. She uses them to help children get off on the right track and then think about what they have accomplished at the end of the year. Several of the teachers on the list are high school teachers who use picture books in their classrooms because they are so powerful.

TABLE 8.2   Recommended Children's Literature

These books were recommended by teachers at all grade levels just for you.

Title	Author	Social Topic	Recommended By
Mr. Mole's Stove	Laura Appleton-Smith	Being a helpful friend	Vicki Brabec
Crow Boy	Taro Yashima	Being different in school	Vicki Brabec
Loudmouth George and the Sixth-Grade Bully	Nancy Carlson	Being a bully	Vicki Brabec
Tight Times	Barbara Shook Hazen	Father losing a job	Connie Hammond-Scheer
The Great Fuzz Frenzy	Janet Stevens & Susan Stevens Crummel	Building community, sticking together	Terri Ross
Mr. Peabody's Apples	Madonna	The power of words and rumors	Pam O'Mara
Ian's Walk	Laurie Lears	Why children with autism look normal but act differently	Sonja Ford
No, David!	David Shannon	Rules and consequences	Danielle Cassell
A Frog Thing	Eric Drachman	Motivation, setting goals, getting help from others	Mary Trehearn
The Recess Queen	Alexis O'Neill	Bullies	Terri Ross
The Little Engine That Could	Watty Piper	Trying your best	Jennifer Bell
The Missing Piece Meets the Big O	Shel Silverstein	Self-reliance	Regina Guinn
I Knew You Could!	Craig Dorfman	Making good choices	Jennifer Bell
A Bad Case of Tattle Tongue	Julia Cook	Tattling	Tara Camp
My Mouth Is a Volcano	Julia Cook	Taking turns when talking, interrupting	Tara Camp
How to Lose All Your Friends	Nancy Carlson	Being nice, sharing with others, friendship	Tara Camp
Mr. Lincoln's Way	Patricia Polacco	Bullies, diversity	Leah Fischer
The Tale of Depereaux	Kate DiCamillo	Forgiveness, love, hope	Laura Blumenthal

(Continued)

TABLE 8.2 (Continued)

Title	Author	Social Topic	Recommended By
The Hundred Dresses	Eleanor Estes	Differences, speaking a different language	Barb Kruid
Oh, The Places You'll Go!	Dr. Seuss	Going off into the world with good and bad times	Sarah Rogers Smith
Did You Carry the Flag Today, Charley?	Rebecca Caudill	Being helpful	Robbyn Schultz
You Are Special	Max Lucado	Tolerance and cooperation	Shanon Wilmott
If Only I Had a Green Nose	Max Lucado	Tolerance and cooperation	Shanon Wilmott
Stand Tall, Molly Lou Melon	Patty Lovell	Tolerance and cooperation	Shanon Wilmott
Feathers and Fools	Mem Fox	Tolerance and cooperation	Shanon Wilmott
Ellison the Elephant	Eric Drachman	Tolerance and cooperation	Shanon Wilmott
Chicken Soup for the Kid's Soul	Jack Canfield, Mark Victor Hansen, Patty Hansen, Irene Dunlap	Social skills	Jamie Badstieber
Wemberly Worried	Kevin Henkes	Worries about school	Katie Stratman
The Meanies Came to School	Joy Cowley	How to behave at school	Christine Goetzinger
Chicken Sunday	Patricia Polacco	Persistence, problem solving, earning something	Kerry Williams
Friends	Helme Heine	Sometimes friends need some time alone	Kerry Williams
The Library Lion	Michelle Knudsen	Sometimes it's OK to break the rules	Kerry Williams
The Big Orange Splot	Daniel Pinkwater	Differences are good	Kevin Kraus
A Bad Case of Stripes	David Shannon	Being yourself	Megan White

Title	Author	Social Topic	Recommended By
The Hole in the Dike	Norma B. Green	Contribution to community	Cheryl Larmore
The Empty Pot	Demi	Honesty	Cheryl Larmore
Amazing Grace	Mary Hoffman	Autonomy	Cheryl Larmore
Drummer Hoff	Barbara and Ed Emberley	Diversity	Cheryl Larmore
Town Mouse, Country Mouse	Jan Brett	Choice	Cheryl Larmore
Foolish Rabbit's Big Mistake	Rafe Martin	Communication	Cheryl Larmore
Dandelions	Eve Bunting	Autonomy, belonging, competency	Cheryl Larmore
Fly Away Home	Eve Bunting	Acceptance, differences	Cheryl Larmore
The Wednesday Surprise	Eve Bunting	Accomplishment	Cheryl Larmore
The Important Book	Margaret Wise Brown	Autonomy, having voice	Cheryl Larmore
Lucy's Picture	Nicola Moon	Diversity	Cheryl Larmore
If You're Not From the Prairie	David Bouchard	Belonging	Cheryl Larmore
Molly's Pilgrim	Barbara Cohen	Cultural diversity	Cheryl Larmore
I'm in Charge of Celebrations	Byrd Baylor	Competency, voice	Cheryl Larmore
I Want to Be	Thylias Moss	Competency	Cheryl Larmore
Alexander and the Terrible, Horrible, No Good, Very Bad Day	Judith Viorst	Adversity	Cheryl Larmore
The Relatives Came	Cynthia Rylant	Diversity, belonging	Cheryl Larmore
Crickwing	Janell Cannon	Bullying, teamwork	Brian Johnson
Pinduli	Janell Cannon	Name calling	Brian Johnson

For material related to this concept, go to Clip 8.3 on the Web-based Student Study Site.

The second thing to do when looking for good literature is to search. Use the Internet and teaching magazines, sit in the library and peruse books, or go to bookstores to see the latest books. Some great sites on the Internet are meant to help teachers find books. I used www.carolhurst.com when writing this book, but there are many others. In addition, teaching magazines often support good literature. For example, *School Library Journal* is a great resource for reviewed books. The longer you teach, the more literature you will know and use from your own collection. Be sure, however, to continue to look for new books and ideas at your school or local library and bookstores. Although I couldn't buy as many as I wanted, I bought a few each year, and when parents asked what to get for end-of-school-year gifts, I always mentioned books.

Finally, the only way to find good literature is to try it. When you find a book that you and the children love, you'll know, and you'll look forward to reading it each year. These kinds of books will give you other ideas for books as well. For example, I found that I really love Jan Brett books, so every time she came out with a new book, I sought it out and read it. First, I found *Trouble with Trolls.* I like that book because the girl in the story solves problems with ingenuity rather than force. Lately, I found *Honey . . . Honey . . . Lion!* fabulous because it is a really neat story about sharing. Check them out! The key to using literature to help children meet social goals is using it.

Writing Stories Together

Although children's literature can be very helpful in planting seeds for conversations about social goals, books may be too far removed from the situation for some children to make connections. Instead of just planting seeds, we may need to give these children the actual flower. We may need to be very specific about what we want them to do. Ironically, just telling children what to do doesn't always do the job. They may need visuals or a specific context that really allows them to think and reflect about their actions. In this case, writing a story with the child about the behavior we want to influence meets those needs while still providing opportunities for choice, voice, and getting to know what the student understands. Stories that they have helped write help children predict the actions of others, as well as the routine. In addition, they describe a situation in detail, give direct contact with social information, and give the child an opportunity to practice the skill on his or her terms (Haggerty, Black, & Smith, 2005).

When to Write a Story

For the most part, writing a story with a child who is struggling with a social goal will be up to your intuition, as well as timing. It is important to think of writing a story with a child as a tool to help him or her learn. If you believe a child knows the appropriate behavior and just isn't motivated to act on it, writing a story with him or her may not be helpful, and in fact, the child may have difficulty writing a good story. If a child doesn't seem to understand any other way to react to stress or a social situation, writing a story about alternatives may be very helpful. For example, if children throw tantrums when they don't get their way or hit as a reaction when something goes wrong with a classmate, they may not know what else to do or be acting on impulse. Writing a story about what they can do often helps curb the behavior and also provides something tangible for them to reread if they have a setback. Researchers have successfully used child-written stories to decrease socially unacceptable behavior, including tantrums, inappropriate sharing, poor eating manners, and verbal assaults. In addition, researchers have observed an increase in empathy and a decrease in undesirable behavior, such as shouting and physical assault, when writing stories with children (Ivey, Heflin, & Alberto, 2004).

Writing a Story With a Child

For material related to this concept, go to Clip 8.4 on the Web-based Student Study Site.

When you decide that you have a situation involving a child who might benefit from taking the time to write a story, get some paper, take the child aside, and invite him or her to write a story with you. Since the goal is learning and not punishment, you might be wise to wait for a calm moment. Although you may have to remove the child from the situation to begin with, he or she won't learn much if you write a story with him or her while he or she is angry. Sometimes I even waited until my students were having writer's workshop time so writing a story wouldn't be different from what the other children were doing.

If you have a calm child and a bit of time, you can make the story-writing experience into an entire writing-process event. Be very specific in the goal of the story, and ask the child to be a part of it. For example, if a child is hitting in situations where other children are causing stress, tell him you want to write a story that will help children know what to do when someone takes their pencil (or whatever else the child was mad about). I know that sounds very specific and unusable for other times when the child is hitting, but in cases where children don't understand social situations, this is necessary. Depending on the child, you may need to write several stories together before the behavior disappears.

Next, work with the student to come up with the beginning of the story. While he tells you, write down the child's version of what happened without using other children's names.

1. Be sure to ask how the child felt when this happened.
   You might write: *When somebody takes his pencil, Jim gets mad.*

2. Then ask the student what happened next, but change it into the opposite when you write it.
   You might write: *Jim won't cry or get on the floor anymore when someone takes his pencil.*

3. Ask the student what he thinks he could do to solve the problem. Offer suggestions if needed.
   You might write: *If his pencil gets taken, Jim will ask the other student for his pencil. Jim could also ask Mrs. Williams for help.*

4. Finally, talk with the student about how he will feel if he gets his pencil back.
   You might write: *Jim will feel happy if he gets his pencil back and doesn't cry or get on the floor.*

As you can see, the stories don't have to be long or complex. Have the child illustrate the story and read it aloud to you. If you have access to a camera, have the child take photographs

LETTER FROM A MASTER TEACHER 8.2

Writing Stories to Help Children Socially

I have had great success using short stories that describe school and social situations with simple terms and pictures.

These stories work especially well for my students because they are able to see a particular situation from the perspective of others. Kindergartners tend to dislike surprises and respond well to repetition. I use these stories to describe a social setting or situation, to describe step-by-step directions for completing an activity, and to reinforce school rules and manners.

Sentences within these stories are stated in positive terms. Incorporating phrases like "I can try" or "This will make my class happy" help children hear specific emotional cues.

Pictures within the story play a big part in the child's comprehension. These picture cues work well for my non-English-speaking students. Another wonderful thing about these stories is that they can be used for multiple readings when the need arises—for the whole group or for an individual student.

—Jenny Meyer
Kindergarten Teacher

and add them to the book. Then you can bind it and put it in a place where the student has access to it.

Sometimes, you won't have time to write a complete story but will still want the child to understand some options for behavior. In this case, you might sit with the child for a few minutes and just draw quick stick pictures of what he or she is and is not going to do. I often drew a picture with a "no" line over it to help the child visualize the unacceptable behavior.

Sometimes it might be advisable to have the whole class create stories with social messages. For example, you might do a playground behavior book with the whole class where each child makes a page of things that are allowed on the playground. Again, taking pictures that go along with the pages would be fun, although children's illustrations are great too. I suggest this kind of thing as a way to help children proactively rather than after the fact, but you can always reread the book when needed.

Writing stories with children can be a great way to learn about social behaviors. They don't take very long to make, they are effective, and children like to make them. I have merely scratched the surface when it comes to writing stories with children. If you are interested in finding out more, the creator of Social Stories, Carol Gray, is a great resource. Check out her Web site at www.thegraycenter.org.

Language and literature are simple ways to change the tone of your classroom from controlling to cooperative. Because, for the most part, we have not experienced classrooms like this, it may be difficult to implement at first. In addition, during stressful moments, it may be easy to revert back to controlling rather than facilitating. I hope you will continue to shoot for the bull's-eye even if you don't hit it every time, and I hope you will think of language and literature as Jedi mind tricks only inasmuch as they help children relax and let their guard down long enough to begin to learn.

So . . . What?

Safe classroom has become a buzzword. Whenever I ask teachers what students need, they always mention a safe classroom. But what does it mean to have one? Specifically, what kinds of language promote safety in classrooms? What kinds of tools do the teachers use when a child is struggling? Although this may seem like a small detail when thinking about all of the other things that go into classroom management, it may be one of the most critical. Pay attention to the language you use in the classroom and work to improve it. Pay attention to how you teach social goals in the classroom and work to make them about learning rather than punishments. The ideas in this chapter will be a great start. Remember to try to:

Use questions more than statements. Make statements about acknowledging students' ideas and feelings.

Use stories more than lectures. Stories will stick with children more effectively than lectures.

Use empathy more than anger. Work to help both you and the children stay calm, and work on problems together rather than "waging war" on students.

Use assessment more than evaluation. If children know you are in the business of helping rather than judging them, classroom management will take on a more "safe" tone.

Use a directive tone when children are being hurt or are in danger.

Use single words like *and* to help children think further or as reminders for social goals.

Use body language for quick, effective communication without talking.

Children's literature can be a great tool for teaching social goals. Remember to choose books with good stories rather than merely a "values" message, books that you love, books that have a lot of uses, and books that spark great conversations about social topics. If a child needs more than a subtle hint, try writing a story with him or her that specifically addresses his or her needs.

Get Ready For . . .

Have you ever had a nightmare about children noisily laughing and talking, throwing paper airplanes, and climbing out of windows? I have. It's scary. Most of the time, these children exist only in our nightmares. Just in case you have a child or children with extreme classroom issues and so you can feel better about helping all children, however, the next chapter is about resources you can use when you need help. No teacher should be expected to be isolated in a classroom without any help.

Activities to Try

- Ask a child you know to write a story with you about a social situation. Even though he or she may not have an issue with social behaviors, practice helping him or her think about the many "right" ways to handle problems.

- Take some time to think about the many different questions you could ask students who struggle. Although you will not have a script to follow in the classroom, reflecting about possible questions will help awaken them in your mind.

- Practice reading some of the literature that you may use in the classroom aloud to someone else. Brainstorm some activities that may help children further reflect on the messages in the books.

- **Make a collection!** Start looking for more children's literature and begin to organize it so you can easily find the book you need.

- **Conduct action research!** Observe in a classroom for a couple of hours. Keep track of how many questions are asked, as well as statements made in the classroom. If you can, keep track of which questions were used for social goals and which for academic goals.

Student Study Site

The companion Web site for *Elementary Classroom Management* can be found at www.sagepub.com/kwilliamsstudy.
   Visit the Web-based student study site to enhance your understanding of the chapter content. The study materials include video clips, practice tests, flashcards, suggested readings, and Web resources.

CHAPTER 9

Asking Students, Parents, and School Resources for Help

Each year as I readied the classroom for incoming students, I made a sign that said, "Help Wanted." I then put as many dots as I had students all around the sign along with descriptions of different things the students could do to help. Each student had a clothespin with his or her name on it that connected to a dot and therefore a job. All of the children took turns throughout the year helping in different ways. For example, some children were in charge of taking the lunch count. Others were meteorologists or delivered the mail. Do you have any ideas about why I made this sign and had children help do these kinds of jobs? If you think these jobs help children develop a sense of community or learn responsibility, you have come up with some of the many right answers to that question. One of the right answers, however, isn't directly related to children but has to do with me, the teacher. I put the sign on the wall because I really did need help. I didn't want to spend the morning taking lunch count. Instead, I stood at the door and welcomed everyone or talked to children informally about happenings in their lives. I wanted to be able to observe and think about really good, juicy questions rather than think about the weather that day or pass out the mail.

One reason teachers—and especially new teachers—struggle in the classroom is the workload that teaching requires (McCann & Johannessen, 2004). Getting to know students, creating meaningful lessons, and meeting the needs of individual learners while keeping up with paperwork and meetings and having a life outside of teaching is time-consuming and difficult. You will need to think about the important pieces of classroom management and then determine how to balance those things with other requirements. One way to find a balance is to ask for help.

Classroom management is another aspect of teaching that can cause teachers stress. I hope this book will help alleviate classroom management as a stress maker; however, my experience as a classroom teacher keeps me grounded in the fact that some management situations will be difficult to resolve even if you use this book's structures and tools perfectly every day. Although teachers have a great deal of information and ideas about management, they often keep their ideas in the classroom rather than share them when another person needs them (Johnson & Donaldson, 2007). Once again, asking for help will allow you to benefit from the resources right in your building.

Take a moment to think about all of the roles a teacher must play in the classroom. There are so many, yet teachers often do not have the expertise to effectively fulfill them. For example, some children come to school with mental illnesses. Rae, a fourth-grade teacher, had a student in her room diagnosed with bipolar disorder. Although Rae is an outstanding teacher with all kinds of experiences and education, she is not a physician and thus has little knowledge about bipolar disorder. Rae knows, however, how to use resources inside and outside of her school. She knows how to gain access to them and how to collaborate to best help children she can't help on her own. Although it may seem easier to just get through a year with a child who struggles with something you don't understand, you must be an advocate for this type of child. One way to do this is to ask for the kinds of help the child needs.

I've often said that teaching is a thinking profession. To teach well, you must do a great deal of thinking about the content, the children, and the structures, strategies, and language you will use. You must continue to think and learn as long as you teach because each new school year will bring a new set of students with unique individual needs. I also believe that teaching is a collaborative profession, or at least it should be. I watched a lady on television this morning talking about ways to discipline children. I paid especially close attention both for this book and for my own children. I thought, "Maybe she'll tell me how to motivate my son to set the table!" As she began to talk, however, a sadness came over me. Her advice consisted mainly of quick fixes for children. She even got out a shredder and advised shredding children's movies or CDs right in front of them as punishment. There was no listening or questioning. There was no empathy. There were no structures that might help children learn about behaviors. Yes, we live in a quick-fix society, and I suppose shredding a beloved item might do the trick to force a child to do something, but at what cost? Children should not be quick fixes. Instead of trying to "fix" a child with a gimmick or a trick, when you have run out of ideas, patience, or time to listen, ask for help. Think of it as an imaginary "help wanted" sign that you post outside your room. A lot of people both inside and outside your school will gladly place their clothespin on your sign.

By the end of this chapter, I hope you have:

- Tools that will invite children to participate in the work of running a democratic classroom

- An understanding of parent needs so they will be able to participate in all kinds of classroom happenings

- Resources that you can find and access inside your school

- Resources that you can find and access outside of your school

Lauren is excited to be the helper of the day in her classroom.

Help Wanted: Children Who Help in the Classroom

For material related to this concept, go to Clip 9.1 on the Web-based Student Study Site.

Your contract as a teacher will probably say that you need to be in the classroom half an hour before the children arrive at school and maybe an hour after they leave. It will also have the number of contracted days you will be teaching and going to inservices for the year. Those hours and days, however, are just the beginning. I don't know a single teacher who teaches, plans, or reads, only during the specified hours on his or her contract. I do know teachers who get to school early, work through lunch, leave school at 7 or 7:30 p.m., and then take classes all summer. While you need to put in extra time and effort to be a great teacher, working so hard that you get burned out is not optimum. Having children take responsibility for themselves and their classroom helps them develop autonomy, belonging, and competency and makes it easier for you to have a life as well.

Children Can Help You With Jobs Around the Room

Students are capable of doing many jobs around the room that will leave you extra time to do other things. Take a minute to think about some of the jobs that children can do around the room. Use the chart in Table 9.1 to help you organize and manage the jobs. After you've made

TABLE 9.1 **Assigning Jobs in the Classroom**

Take some time to brainstorm different jobs you might want students to do in the classroom.

Job	When It Needs to Be Done	How Many Children	What They Will Learn
Changing the calendar	Once a month	2 or 3	How to set up a calendar, number order, month order

a list, start to think about how you will assign them. For example, teachers I worked with took a night after school each month to update the class calendar. Not only using valuable planning, thinking, or meeting time to put up the calendar, they were taking a valuable learning opportunity away from children. I've said it before, and I'll say it again: The person doing the doing is doing the learning! I asked for volunteers in the classroom to change my calendar. Among other jobs, children watered the plants for me, erased the boards, cleaned the sink, and hung up student work on the bulletin boards. In addition to teaching some valuable lessons that helped them feel competent, doing the jobs also helped them take ownership of the classroom. If they made a mess, they cleaned it up. If they wanted to hang something in the room, they hung it. This approach had one limitation: My room wasn't the prettiest. The calendar wasn't always straight, and sometimes when the students sat in front of it, they noticed mistakes. We learned a lot, though, and I didn't spend hours taking care of the students' classroom by myself.

Having children help you in their classroom does require some organization. You have to know the jobs and how you will assign them to children. For example, some of the jobs in the classroom need to be done every day. If you have children be librarians, they will need to make sure books are back in the appropriate places every day, not just once a week. It is the same with taking lunch count, taking notes to the office, and doing the weather. You might put these jobs on a help-wanted sign and rotate them every so often so all of the children have the opportunity to do them. Some jobs might work better once a week or once a month. For example, watering plants, changing bulletin boards, and cleaning shelves might not need to be done every day. You can come up with another sign for those jobs or incorporate them into the same sign. I chose to have one sign for all of the jobs, and we changed the helpers weekly. Sometimes the children had jobs that required work every day. Sometimes they were assigned jobs that they only had to do once that week. Children volunteered for jobs that were more sporadic. There are so many ways to have children help around the classroom. Use a plan that works well for you.

Children Can Help With Assessments

I know teachers who spend hours after school grading and looking at projects and papers. Indeed, assessing student work throughout the year is important for learning and developing feelings of competency; however, it is also vital that children have opportunities to self-assess and set goals. Feedback from the teacher should be given quickly and provide information for improvement rather than merely a judgment (McTighe & O'Connor, 2005). If the teacher does all of the assessing and takes three weeks to get the feedback to students, not much learning will take place. Creating assessment techniques to help students assess their own work, to provide immediate feedback, and to help students see their growth over time is key in promoting autonomy, belonging, and competency. It can also help you lighten the assessment workload. The following few ideas are meant to help you start thinking about how to involve children in assessing their assignments.

One way to provide immediate feedback, as well as to get students involved with assessing, is using double-sided answer sheets (Lockett, 2006). For example, when you give a spelling test or another kind of quick-answer celebration of knowledge, have the children write their answers twice (see Table 9.2). Then have them hand in one set of answers to you and check the other themselves. That way, students get immediate feedback, you get to see students' needs right away, and you get an original copy that you can refer to if needed. For younger students who may have a hard time writing answers two times, get carbon paper so they only have to write once. Printing stores often throw away this kind of paper. Find such a store in your area and ask if you can have the carbon paper for school.

Cooperative workshops (Chapter 4) can also help you develop time for meaningful conversations about students' progress. For example, if you are doing workshops with different stations, make one an assessment station where you sit and have children do math problems, set up a science experiment, or write a short letter. You can take some excellent observational notes during this time, as well as ask students individualized questions. Once again, students get immediate feedback, you can help them learn to think about their own progress, and you don't have to take that particular assessment home.

You may want to keep a portfolio of students' work throughout the year to show growth over time. Keeping track of 25 to 30 student portfolios is a lot of work, however, and often keeps teachers from using this valuable tool. I recommend having the students (even kindergarteners) take care of their own portfolios. Set up folders for each child in a place to which the students and the teacher have access. That way, you can both add meaningful

TABLE 9.2   Double-Sided Answer Sheet

Name:

1.	1.
2.	2.
3.	3.
4.	4.
5.	5.
6.	6.
7.	7.
8.	8.
9.	9.
10.	10.

items to the portfolios. Teach students how to put the date on their work and to write why they put each particular item in their folder. Then, at the end of each month, take a few minutes to have them go through and organize their work. This is a great thing to do for several reasons: It allows students to see their work and actually notice their own progress rather than rely on a teacher's assessment, allows them to create goals for themselves and celebrate their progress, creates opportunities for both teacher and student input into portfolios, and teaches students to organize and become more metacognitive about their schoolwork. Finally, having students help manage their own portfolios decreases the workload for you.

Preparing report cards and getting ready for parent/teacher/student conferences should also be a team effort. Students need to be a part of sharing their progress, as well as areas they need to improve. Even young students can look through their work and determine their stars and wishes for school. Students are typically portrayed as dreading conferences, but in my room, they were very excited about sharing their work because it was a celebration of their learning. Dan's mother, for example, told me he pestered her all day about conferences; he was excited to share his work and celebrate his growth. Certainly, parents will want some specific feedback from you. Pairing a teacher report with students' work and ideas of their progress, however, provides a bigger picture.

Children Can Help You Communicate With Parents

Parent communication, a very important area in teaching, can take a lot of time. The next section of this chapter will deal more closely with parent involvement, but for now let's look at how you can encourage your students to communicate with their parents. Once again, the help you receive will benefit the students and increase your time for other

Savannah gets out her portfolio so she can put a piece of writing inside.

aspects of teaching. After all, if you can get parents and their children communicating, everyone will benefit.

Some forms of communication don't require you to make phone calls or write individual notes. For example, if you want parents to come into your room for an event, have students make the invitations. It is a good opportunity to teach them about invitations, writing, dates and times, and so on. If you want to send a newsletter of happenings in the classroom to parents, have your students make one. You can have a newsletter committee once a week or maybe once a month, write it as a whole group, or have individual students write letters to parents about happenings. Writing a newsletter will help students review the week or month of learning, provide an authentic writing experience, and perhaps provide an opportunity to use technology to complete a project.

It may seem as though I am suggesting looking for ways to get out of the work of being a teacher, and in some ways that is true. I see teachers working so hard that they do not enjoy teaching any longer or choose to quit. I see children with no sense of ownership of what happens in their classrooms. The most important reason for giving children the opportunity to participate in classroom management goes back to the idea of autonomy, belonging, and competency. Students need to experience taking care of themselves, one another, and their classrooms. Teachers need more time to think, reflect, create, and understand. Both can be achieved if you are willing to ask for help.

Parents can be great sources of help inside and outside of the classroom. It is important to create opportunities for parents to come to school.

Help Wanted: Involved Parents/Caregivers

The master's students I work with often tease me about being the parent of a kindergartener. They say, for example, "I wouldn't want to teach your child. I wouldn't want to have you as a parent!" I can't imagine why they say this! I think I will be a great resource for help in the classroom, I suppose they say this because parents who have been or are teachers are especially difficult because they bring some knowledge to the process. Some parents can be a bit intimidating, some gruff, and others nonexistent. No matter their limitations, however, all parents bring some positives to the classroom and are important in their child's learning experience. Parents shape children's values and expectations for behaviors. They are the child's first teachers. Asking parents for insights, ideas, and help in the classroom is wise because their involvement in the school experience affects students' learning (Christenson & Sheridan, 2001; Fan & Chen, 2001). Remember, though, that asking parents for help doesn't always mean asking them to do things for you. Sometimes parent help comes in the form of the insights they have about their children; sometimes it comes in the form of support and the influence they have on their children; certainly, it comes in the form of classroom participation. Asking parents for help requires some of the same key ingredients as working with children. Forming relationships, providing meaningful tasks, and offering a variety of invitations to be involved are all important aspects of asking parents for help.

Good Relationships With Parents Provide Opportunities for Help in the Classroom

We have talked a lot in this book about knowing students, but being willing to get to know students' families and caregivers is equally important. These people who know their children better than you ever will can be fantastic resources in promoting learning. They can give you insight into how a child learns and behaves in the classroom. Remember that students come to school with prior experiences that have shaped who they are and thus what they understand about the world. Parents and caregivers have their own strengths, issues, and priorities that can ooze into a child's experience at school. Knowing parents is like getting clues to a puzzle.

At times, getting to know and forming a relationship with parents is about listening. I taught in a school near a military base for a year, for example, and had a student named Brianna in my room. Brianna struggled in school but was personable, outgoing, and friendly. Before our first parent/teacher conferences, we invited parents into our room to share projects about the human body. Some children studied the heart and used liter bottles, piping, and colored water to demonstrate how the heart pumps blood; others made posters; and Brianna's group made a skeleton out of different kinds of pasta showing all of the bones and their names. After the presentations, Brianna's mom came to me and wanted to schedule a conference. We did, and on the day she came, she was very upset. She believed Brianna needed a more structured environment and a strict homework schedule. She wanted Brianna to sit in a desk, with her hands folded in front of her, listening to the teacher. She told me the presentations were terrible and couldn't believe I would let the children move around the classroom. Finally, she said, "Brianna can memorize every word of every song she hears, but she can't seem to memorize words to help her read." Through all of this, I just listened. What did I learn? Brianna's mom was worried about her child and needed to voice her frustrations. She wasn't mad at me. She wanted to help her child but only knew one way. She needed someone to listen.

Although it took me a few days to get over the sting of what Brianna's mom had said, I finally felt ready to work with her to find a way that we could help Brianna together. She listened to me talk about why Brianna might be able to remember song lyrics and not site words. I listened to her talk about why Brianna needed specific homework every day. I think, however, that we listened to each other only because she had been given time to vent. The classroom environment did not change after our visit; however, I sent Brianna home with textbooks and daily assignments that corresponded with whatever we were studying. You might wonder how this qualifies as "parent help" when I ended up with more work that only impacted one child. The relationship I formed with Brianna's mom by listening and taking into account what she knew about her daughter helped me provide an easier experience for all of us. At the end of the year, Brianna's mom sent me a card. Inside, she wrote that though she didn't always agree with my methods, she was so glad Brianna had someone who cared about her and gave extra time to help her.

Blaming parents for issues in the classroom may be easy. Indeed, sometimes parents don't always make the best decisions when it comes to their children. A very wise man, my dad, always says that people do the best they can at any moment in time. We can't change their parenting or how they live their lives. We can, however, work to create good relationships with them. Listen to parents even when you are in a hurry or if you disagree with what they say. Let them know that they are always welcome in the classroom without appointments or prior notice. Communicate that you know the parent's child both socially and academically. Remember that one way parents can help is to be an advocate for their child. Working with parents who aren't involved is much harder than working with parents who are advocating for their child. Parents who feel insignificant, apathetic, or afraid won't be willing to seize the many opportunities to help children inside and outside of the classroom. We need to work to make sure we aren't contributing to those kinds of feelings.

Sometimes parents may seem uninvolved or unwilling to help their children because of cultural differences. Copeland (2007) found that parents from different countries have different views about their role in school. Sometimes we assume that everyone sees parent involvement in the same way. Some parents, however, may not think it is appropriate to come into the classroom, just as they would not go into surgery to help a surgeon. "With heightened awareness, teachers can recognize cultural differences and address parents' reactions in ways that may help smooth students' adjustment to practices in a U.S. classroom" (Copeland, 2007, p. 67).

Relationships with parents are not always easy. If you do what you can to have a good relationship with parents but they are abusive in their conversations with you or have other issues that keep you from having a good relationship, be sure to have another staff member, your guidance counselor, or your administrator sit in on meetings you have with the parent. You don't have to deal with abusive situations on your own. For example, I had a parent come to conferences intoxicated. She ranted and raved over inappropriate things while her fifth-grade daughter sat on my lap. I called the office, and my administrator came down to help. She got the family a cab to go home, and we rescheduled the conference. Every other time I met with that parent, another person sat in with me, and I worked with the counselor to get the family some much-needed help. This example is very extreme, but the same is true for any parent who makes you uncomfortable.

Good relationships with parents, even those who seem difficult, require good communication. Parents want to know what is going on with their child, whether the information is good, bad, or neutral. Take some time to consider different ways you can communicate happenings with parents (see Table 9.3). Be sure to think about benefits and limitations for each kind of communication tool. Notes and newsletters, phone calls, and folders (sometimes called "Friday Folders") that contain upcoming events, student work, and maybe a sticky note or two about the individual child are all traditional ways of communicating with parents, and remember that children can help you with these kinds of communication tools. Be sure to think outside the box, however. Some schools, relying more and more on technology to aid in communication, give parents anytime Internet access to information they need to track their child's progress and opportunities to make an impact on their child's learning growth (Bird, 2006). As a parent of a child who comes home and answers, "Nothing," when asked what he did in school that day, I believe a Web site sharing what happened so I could ask more specific questions about his day would be very helpful. In addition, merely sending parents e-mails in addition to a few newsletters saves a great deal of time.

TABLE 9.3   **Parent Communication Possibilities**

Take some time to think about different ways to communicate with parents. Be sure to consider the benefits and limitations of each.

Type of Communication	Possible Timeline for Use	Benefits	Limitations
E-mail	Once a week and as needed for individual students and special reminders	• Quick • Reach a lot of parents at one time • Can attach samples of student work	• Can be impersonal • May be misinterpreted • Not all parents have access

Sometimes, talking to the parent in person will be the best thing to do. After Ehren cut his bangs off with a pair of scissors during a bathroom break, for example, I walked with him out to his car after school. A note probably wouldn't have been good enough. Luckily, his mom laughed, and Ehren came to school with a buzz cut the next day. I also walked children who were struggling with behaviors out to their families both on good days and on bad days just to touch base. I realize not every child is picked up after school. For those who are, however, this is a good opportunity to communicate. If this isn't possible and you need to have an ongoing conversation with a parent, try sending a notebook back and forth to school.

Listening, understanding background and cultural differences, and communicating with parents are important anchors in forming relationships with parents and involving them in school activities. Relationships, you could say, provide the glue for your help-wanted sign, without which parents won't have anywhere to hang their clothespin.

Jesse Keifer

After you start thinking about it, you will find many ways adults can help in the classroom.

Help Parents Feel They Can Contribute

Although it may seem easiest to have parents file, do bulletin boards, or stay out of the class-room altogether, unless they are hurting students or doing inappropriate things, I recommend having them do tasks that directly affect students. For example, during writer's workshop in my classroom, students had their own dictionaries, and when they needed a word spelled, they had someone who knew how to spell the word put it in their dictionary. That way, they didn't have to ask over and over again how to spell the same word. It became a bit difficult, however, when many students needed words spelled. Having parents come in during writer's workshop and help children with many things, including spelling words in dictionaries, was heaven, and I think the parents felt needed and appreciated. As you get to know parents, you will be able to determine what jobs would suit them. In addition, I encourage you to ask them what they would like to do.

When parents come into the classroom to volunteer for a special project, make sure they have a specific role. Many parents take off work to come in for special projects and need to feel it was a worthwhile choice. We made taffy a couple of times in second grade because it was a great way to see the changes in solids, liquids, and gases. Unless I had some parent volunteers to help, however, I could only demonstrate the process without involving the children. Instead, only the parents and I knew what we would make; I kept it a secret from the children, which the parents enjoyed. When they came to volunteer, I gave them directions, a group of students that included their son or daughter, and materials. They became the guides for the lesson.

Indeed, some parents won't be able to help in the classroom, but they can still be involved in meaningful tasks. I've had parents collect paper towel tubes or milk jugs for projects. For the taffy, parents sent pans, spoons, measuring cups, and so on, even if they couldn't come for the surprise. Parents could also send pictures or souvenirs from trips so all of the children would have a chance to experience another culture or place.

Sometimes parents can provide the most meaningful help at home. Helping with homework or reading to children are both ways for parents to help teachers. Once again, though, you must know how to assist these interactions so the parents and students benefit. For example, teachers complain to me that when students ask for help with their homework, parents sometimes end up doing it for them. Assign homework that requires interaction and is not just a product so the parent must help and get to know his or her child's competency rather than just get it done. I always told parents that I wasn't going to assign much homework but that I expected the child to read or be read to every night. Notice that the parents can't just do that homework. Even if they read to their child, they are helping. Sometimes I had students ask their parents to show them another way to do a specific mathematics operation. Once again, the parent was involved, but the student had to be able to tell us about it. Be careful with homework. Many families have several commitments in the evening hours and simply don't have time to help their children with homework. In addition, some researchers question the value of homework because of its lack of effect on student achievement or responsibility (Kohn, 2006). Families need time to be together, and students need time to play and enjoy something they love that isn't offered in school. If you give homework, try to make assignments due after several days so families can choose when to complete them. If you expect students to study for a test, provide lessons on techniques for studying on their own.

In addition to meaningful tasks, be sure to recognize and show gratitude for parents' help. At the end of the year, we always had a volunteer tea in our school. We invited parent volunteers one afternoon each year and provided refreshments while they listened to children sing and teachers say thanks in a number of ways. You don't have to do something as extravagant as a tea. Sending notes of thanks or having the children make pictures for parents is another option.

Parents May Need Multiple Kinds of Invitations

No matter where you teach, some parents will be willing to help however they can, and some will stay as far away as possible. Some parents are very busy, and others may not believe they can help. These parents may need a special invitation. Keep in mind that how you invite parents to be involved in the classroom matters and often determines whether they will help (Anderson & Minke, 2007).

Offering multiple invitations may mean asking for help in many different ways throughout the school year. Some parents may want to sign up for regular volunteering sessions, like every Wednesday during math. Some parents may want to volunteer for a special project, like making taffy, or a field day. Others may need to pop in when it is convenient. Although it may seem like a challenge to have parents just dropping by, most don't, and those who do are usually very helpful. To make parents feel welcome, I always told them they could drop in anytime. They didn't have to call and schedule a visit, which served two purposes: First, parents didn't have to commit to something they couldn't always fulfill. Second, I believe they felt I wasn't hiding anything.

Some of the parents of students in my classes had special talents that fit with our studies. For example, I had a dad who was a chemist. He agreed to come in and show the children some chemical reactions when we were studying solids, liquids, and gases. This particular dad didn't come into my room any other time of the year, even for conferences, but he was willing to share his talent. His children, both of whom were in my classes over the years, really got a boost from his participation. This kind of special invitation is perfect for parents who don't naturally participate in school activities, as well as for those who do.

Sometimes, as teachers, we just assume that parents know how to help their children make progress in school when they may not have had those experiences themselves. For example, parents may not know the importance of reading to and with their child. Add an invitation to do so to a weekly newsletter with information about helping children learn at home. Jenny and her colleagues at an elementary school invited parents to hear speakers discuss different things they could do with their children at home. They had volunteer teenagers host gym time for children while the parents met, had a translator for those who didn't speak English, and had food available. I have also heard of teachers holding math night and inviting parents and students to do math together for an hour. In the beginning, such invitations may be a lot of work, but their effects will help students in the long run.

Another way to help parents become involved is to invite them to a special event at school. When we did the Body Battles play or had our publishing picnic at the end of the year, for example, we invited parents. The students made special invitations, and we tried to give presentations around lunchtime so parents could come over their lunch hour. We even made invitations for parent-teacher conferences to go with the school letter that went out twice a year. In the conference invitation, I included a form that allowed parents to write questions they wanted to be sure to ask, as well as a spot for them to write about perceived strengths and wishes for their child.

These are just a few ideas about how to engage parents in helping their child learn. There are thousands of others, and I hope you will collect them as you find them. The main idea, however, is to be open about how parents are involved. Whether they come into the classroom to volunteer, read at home with their child, fill out a conference sheet, or just read notes that come home from school, parents are involved in their child's education—and that is helpful.

Help Wanted: Resources Inside School

I have written about Josh several times in this book. He often comes to my mind even when I am not writing. I wonder how he is doing and where he ended up in life. I did the best I could for Josh, but I also wonder if I could have done more. You see, I didn't know enough about how the resources worked in my school. Specifically, I didn't know enough about the surveys teachers sometimes take to determine if a child has a behavior disorder. I didn't know how to fill it out or how sensitive it was. Instead of asking for help or at least asking questions, I filled it out the best way I could. As a result, a child who didn't need to be labeled got labeled. Indeed, this label got Josh some help in the classroom; however, to this day I am not sure it was the kind of help he really needed. I am telling you this story now because I hope it helps you feel the weight of your decisions. While I don't recommend running to someone every time a child

Carla and Sara work together as kindergarten teachers. They support one another, share ideas, and help each other with students when needed.

sneezes, be sure to stop and ask for clarification, help, and ideas when you need them. You may feel silly or incompetent, but learning something that will help you better advocate for a child's best interest will be worth it.

Sometimes, when you ask for help, you will get a shoulder to cry on or a place to vent your frustrations. You might gain insight into how the system is set up to work for children or why certain processes are in place. Other times, you may get someone to come into your classroom, observe, and make recommendations. Still other times, you may get resources that are permanently in your classroom. You can't get any of these kinds of help, however, if you don't ask or accept the help that comes with specific children.

Although school districts are different and provide unique resources, I hope this section inspires you to ask for help when you need it and creates a sense of the kinds of resources you might use in your journey as a teacher. Remember that school districts will have different processes and procedures for using these experts in your school. In my school district, for example, a teacher was expected to go through the student assistance team before referring a student to the school psychologist. Be sure to ask about your school's process.

To help you begin to think about different resources that may be available in your school district, I have listed several resource people below, as well as the areas where they may provide assistance. Certainly, I haven't named all of the available resources, as they vary from school district to school district. As you begin to interview for jobs, or if you experience a child who is struggling and don't know what to do, ask your administrators about available resources.

When Do I Ask Another Teacher for Help?

Other teachers, especially veteran teachers, are great resources as long as you have a good rapport with them and trust their advice. Sometimes schools pair new teachers with veteran teachers as mentors, and you may have a mentor teacher in the district where you teach. Be sure, however, to form relationships with other teachers as well. As you get to know them, they can help you with everything from lesson ideas to working with individual children. Certain teachers may be good to go to with specific issues. For example, if I needed help with a child who was struggling with reading or writing, I talked to Cheryl. If I needed advice about working with a particular parent, I talked to Kelly. If I wanted to add some music and movement into a unit, I talked to LeAnn. Carla helped me with the technology available in my school. Schools really are full of expert teachers. Each teacher has particular strengths, and if you ask, most will be glad to share their ideas. By the way, just because you ask doesn't mean you have to use their ideas. Asking, however, enhances the opportunity to learn something, as well as the relationships you will form with your colleagues.

Teachers who teach art, music, library, physical education can also be great resources for you. They may be able to use their classrooms to enhance a unit of study or provide resources. For example, I worked with a fantastic librarian and collaborator, Sharon, who helped me find books for units of study like space or mysteries. She allowed children to come to the library to do research, and she had great films and supplemental materials. In addition, these teachers are able to see the children in your classroom in a different light. Children who were shy in my classroom sometimes shined in music class, and my conversations with the music teacher helped me know them through a different lens.

Teachers of different grade levels are also great resources when you want to do buddy reading or other cross-grade-level activities. For example, my good relationship with Sue, an early-childhood special educator, provided opportunities for my class to create alphabet and counting books for her students. We also did puppet shows for the younger children. Other teachers, when asked, would come in for a special presentation put together by my class, and then we would go to one of theirs.

When Do I Ask a Principal for Help?

Principals and how they assist teachers will vary from school to school. Some principals are in the classroom all the time, volunteer to help with special projects, and are very much involved with the happenings of classroom life. Others are more helpful with parents, individual students, and giving suggestions for instructional improvement. When asked, however, all of the principals I worked with were receptive to listening and contemplating issues. Remember that principals are swamped with work, so giving them some notice before asking them to be involved in a project and setting up a meeting for questions may be helpful.

LETTER FROM A MASTER TEACHER 9.1

Resources for a New Teacher

As I write this letter, I think back to my first 3 years of teaching. I am reminded of my physical and emotional stress, confusion, shock, and frustration. It was 3.5 years of teaching, three facilitators, a learning community, and a master's degree that saved my career and myself from the ongoing struggle of teaching.

First and foremost, it is extremely difficult to admit to your colleagues you need additional help, but if you do not vocalize your needs, you are stuck! My first and second years of teaching, I often turned to my grade level for advice regarding discipline, curriculum, and lesson planning. Eventually, I had to ask for more help.

During my third year of teaching, I finally turned to my principal. I explained to her I needed help restructuring my entire reading block. She quickly gave me several resources, all instructors within my building, including our curriculum facilitator. My principal also suggested I coteach with our resource teacher and Title I teacher. I quickly learned my best resources were veteran colleagues.

During district meetings, I began to reach out to other teachers. I asked what they taught. Did they have any useful Web sites for math and reading? Could they suggest a book? Did they have meaningful seatwork ideas? On a volunteer basis, I also signed up for meetings regarding reading instruction.

Lastly, I reached out to my friends and colleagues in my master's program. I built a network of resources, which can be easily accomplished without a master's program. Find people in your similar teaching situation and have conversations. It is *that* easy!

Now that I am knowledgeable of my resources, teaching has become easy, if you will. My days are now filled with gratification, success, and happiness. I feel this way because I continue to use the resources available to me.

—Durkhany Bassia
Sixth-Grade Teacher

There are several examples of times when asking for help from the principal is not only wise but extremely important. If you are having trouble with a parent, if you have a child with a severe behavior problem in your classroom where other children are being hurt or bullied, or if you suspect child abuse, notify your principal right away. In addition, if you are thinking of taking a field trip or doing a project that requires something dangerous, like cooking, run it by the principal as there might be specific requirements that come with doing such projects.

You might think asking the principal for help includes sending a child to the principal's office. If you have tried some other things and are at the end of your rope, so to speak, you may need to do this; however, I recommend speaking to the principal about your options before-hand. The principal may suggest other ideas to try before sending a child to his or her office, such as a time-out room or another teacher's room. It is your job to find out the process that works in your school. If you do end up sending a child to the principal's office, make sure that it is an extreme case and that you follow up with the principal later.

Principals can also be great resources for more ideas about teaching, managing, and working with children. Try to be open to ideas that they give you, and ask for ideas if you have a specific need. Principals usually have a great deal of experience and knowledge about many different kinds of issues in education, and tapping those resources is wise. You might say, "I have a child who is _____ and am wondering if you have any resources that might help." Some principals might come in and demonstrate strategies, give you reading materi-als, or just offer suggestions. Asking a principal for help will help you gather strategies and tools to use in your classroom, as well as help you develop a positive relationship with your principal.

When Do I Ask a Secretary for Help?

In many schools, the secretary is the go-to person for questions about school happenings and procedures. Secretaries can be of great help in many ways, such as copying docu-ments, getting supplies, ordering special materials, and filling out forms. In addition, sometimes they can help with the needs of children. A secretary at my school, for example, was really good at forming relationships with children, and if they came in from the play-ground upset or hurt, she would take care of them. One of my more troubled students really liked her, so if he needed some time away from the classroom, she let him come to the office and help her work until he was ready to come back. I realize that this was not in the secretary's job description; however, her work with and without children really bene-fited the entire school.

When Do I Ask the School Nurse for Help?

You may or may not have a school nurse where you teach. In some districts, nurses travel between several schools. If you have access to a school nurse, however, take advantage of the ideas and knowledge he or she brings to your school. A school nurse may be able to help you with children who are struggling in school for medical reasons. For example, a child with ADHD may require medication, and a school nurse can help you interpret behavior, inform you about the medical information, and help you talk to parents. School nurses can also help you determine if children are having trouble with vision or hearing. In addition, school nurses are valuable resources when you have children who exhibit signs of abuse. They know what to look for and may be able to help document information that will be relevant for authori-ties. School nurses can also be helpful with finding medical resources, such as dentists and doctors, for children who need them. Finally, school nurses can help you with materials if you are required to teach health in your classroom.

When Do I Ask a Student Assistance Team for Help?

Although not all student assistance teams are called the same thing, most schools have a process where teachers can consult a team of teachers, counselors, administrators, and special-education teachers about concerns with a particular student. The teacher presents his or her observations and strategies that he or she has already tried, and then the group gives suggestions for helping the child. Student assistance teams may also recommend that a child be tested for special education or that a specialist come to the classroom to observe and make recommendations. Student assistance teams will also allow you to network with teachers with whom you may not regularly interact.

If you have a child in your room who does not receive special-education services, needs some help, and hasn't responded to academic or social strategies that you've tried, the student assistance team is a good place to start. Asking this kind of team for help does not make you a bad teacher or mean the child will automatically end up with a special-education label. The team's purpose is to provide the help and tools that the child and you need.

Even though student assistance teams are common in schools, some teachers don't utilize them. Teachers cite lack of knowledge of the student assistance team process as a reason for not using it (Rankin & Aksamit, 1994). Indeed, if you want to use this valuable resource, I suggest finding out about the process from another teacher or your administrator. You can also ask to sit in on a meeting as an observer so you can get a sense of what takes place before using the team yourself.

When Do I Ask a Special-Education Teacher for Help?

Students who already receive special-education services may be assigned to your room. In these cases, you will not need to consult the student assistant team because you will already have access to the resources of a special-education teacher, such as information about how to help students with disabilities and how to find the latest strategies and resources for children with specific issues. Be sure to ask questions and be open to new ideas so you can collaborate to help children. If your school includes special-education students in the regular education classrooms, be sure to invite the special-education teacher to come to planning sessions.

If children do not receive special-education services in your classroom but you are concerned about a specific child, you may want to ask the special-education teacher. For example, you might say, "What would you recommend for a child who_____?" Special-education teachers can help you determine if a child needs to be tested for a disability, can give you strategies to try, and may provide some insight as to why a child is struggling.

When Do I Ask a Speech Language Pathologist for Help?

Sometimes you may need advice or resources that support children who have difficulties with speech and language. A speech language pathologist can help you with those needs. When I started teaching, I had the misconception that a speech language pathologist helped children with articulation issues—e.g., saying the "r" sound. Although they do work with articulation issues, speech language pathologists also work with children who have problems communicating. So, if you have children who can listen but not comprehend what has been said or who know what is being said but can't put words together to respond, you can ask a speech language pathologist for help. Communication problems can be hidden in some cases. A child may be able to write words on a page with perfect handwriting and punctuation, but when you look closely, the words don't make sense. A child may be able to tell you a wonderful story but not be able to write it on paper. Speech language pathologists can help you with any issue dealing with oral, auditory, or written communication.

For children to receive services from a speech language pathologist, they must be tested for a disability. However, you can always ask for advice and strategies for all of your children. The speech language pathologist I worked with was always studying new techniques and ideas and willing to help me learn as well. Many of the resources speech language pathologists can give you are worthwhile for all children.

When Do I Ask a Reading Specialist for Help?

This one is obvious. Nevertheless, it is important to note that reading specialists are a great resource that will help you become a better reading teacher. Ask for help if specific children are struggling in reading, if you are not happy with your reading instruction, or if you want to try something new. Reading specialists will usually meet with you but may also conduct lessons in your room depending on your need. Sometimes districts have curriculum specialists as well. You may be able to ask these people about reading instruction or any other subject.

When Do I Ask an Occupational Therapist for Help?

An occupational therapist works to help children participate in activities as fully as possible and helps create a plan for making accommodations so children can be as independent as possible. They work with children on eye-hand coordination, perception, and manipulation skills so children can write, dress themselves, play on the playground, and so on. Occupational therapists are also experts on equipment that may assist students who struggle. If a student is struggling with manipulating a pencil or needs help coming back to school after an accident, for example, the occupational therapist in your district may be called in to assist the child or provide equipment that will help him or her function at school and at home. The occupational therapist may not be someone you contact directly; however, you should know about this available resource so you can be an effective advocate for your students.

When Do I Ask a Counselor for Help?

School counselors can help you and your students in a variety of ways. Sometimes counselors come into classrooms and teach whole group lessons on social issues. This may be a regularly scheduled event, or you may have to sign up for a visit from the counselor. Either way, I encourage you to think about a social issue that your specific class could use and ask the counselor to do a lesson on it. Counselors also pull small groups of students out of class to work on a social issue. For example, there might be a group comprising children whose parents have recently gotten divorced or a friendship group comprising children who lack friendship skills. School counselors also work with individuals who may be experiencing difficulty due to social issues or the environment in which they live. One of my students, for example, threatened suicide at home because a "girlfriend" was upset with him. Frantically trying to figure out what to do, the child's mom met with the school counselor while her son was in school, and then she, the counselor, the child, and I sat down after school and worked on some strategies for him. Luckily, he was OK, and we got him some help.

Counselors have great strategies for children who are angry, don't have friends, may be depressed or struggle behaviorally in school. They can be important resources for children who just need to talk and release their feelings. If a child comes to school upset, shows signs of anxiety and depression, or physically acts out against other students, the counselor is a good person to contact, especially if the signs persist. Contact the school counselor as well if you suspect abuse. A girl in my class one year, for example, all of a sudden started drawing pictures of children with skulls and crossbones over their genitalia. I asked the student if I could borrow the pictures for a minute and then, during a break, took them to the counselor. Why didn't I just call the parents? I could have, but I wondered if the student was being sexually abused and needed help with the process. The counselor and I looked at the pictures, and then she talked to the girl about them. We determined that we didn't think there was abuse but called the child's mom anyway. The mom came to school, we talked to her, and then we decided to keep an eye on the student for a while before proceeding. I really have no way of knowing if she was being abused. After that day, she never again showed signs of abuse. If she had been being abused, however, we would have had to follow a specific procedure. With the counselor's help, we could have gone through that procedure to help the child.

When Do I Ask a School Psychologist for Help?

School psychologists are great resources in school districts because they have a wealth of knowledge about many different topics and training in several areas that influence student learning and success in school. For example, school psychologists are knowledgeable about mental health, biological and cultural influences that affect student learning, and family systems and special-education processes, and they know statistics, research, and evaluation techniques that help shed light on students' problems (National Association of School Psychologists, 2000). Unfortunately, there usually aren't many school psychologists in a district, and therefore you may not have immediate access to one. A school psychologist may be called in if the student assistant team recommends testing or observation. If a child in your room will be tested, he or she may be pulled out of the room for a few hours a couple of days. If the school psychologist wants to observe, he or she may sit in your classroom and take observation notes.

The school psychologist will also attend any meetings you have to determine if a child qualifies for special-education services. This is a great opportunity to ask questions about the tests and recommendations for classroom modifications. Although asking questions in a meeting may seem uncomfortable, I have found that it is important. Parents always attend those meetings, and if, for example, I didn't understand a student's test results, the parents didn't usually either and appreciated that I asked. You can't provide the best help for children if you don't understand. Ask!

There are certainly other resources for you in schools. I have written about only a handful because of space and because I believe you must research your school district's available options. I hope, though, you are now aware that many different people employed by school districts provide help to teachers and students, and I hope you feel you can reach out to them whenever you need to. You don't have to struggle through problems on your own. Please remember that no matter how many years you teach, individual children will always need solutions to individual problems. Getting to know them as individuals is the first important step, but you must take the next step: collaborating with the resources around you to come up with a plan to help them. Take time now to read the cases in Table 9.4. Whom would you ask for help?

Help Wanted: Resources Outside of School

For material related to this concept, go to Clip 9.2 on the Web-based Student Study Site.

Teaching children well every day requires support, no matter your experience or ability level. Collaborating with your colleagues in school is a fantastic way to form relationships, continue to learn about teaching and learning, and get help when you need it. Just as I recommend using these resources within your school, I also recommend that you become aware of the resources outside of school that can provide services for students, families, and you. Although the resources inside the school will most likely be able to assist you in accessing outside services, it is a good idea to have a sense of what they are. Why? If you know resources are available, you may be more likely to ask about them. Second, you may be able to recommend them to parents (with the help of an administrator). Finally, having resources may contribute to a sense of hope for those children who cause you worry or stress.

Indeed, children come to school with a variety of needs. Maslow (1968) believed that all people have a hierarchy of needs where their need for survival, safety, belonging, and self-esteem must be satisfied before they can know and understand, meet aesthetic needs, and reach self-actualization. Take a minute to think about what that means for classroom management and using outside resources. For me, Maslow brings to the forefront that academic success (competency) requires more than lessons. It requires us to look at the whole child. As teachers, we must do everything in our power to make sure a child's needs are being met so he or she can begin to learn, set goals, and become independent. Sometimes meeting those needs requires us to go beyond the school walls so we can use and recommend resources that help children become autonomous, connected, and competent.

Internet Sites Can Be a Resource for You and for Children

Perhaps the easiest way to gain access to outside resources is via the Internet. Although the Internet is full of misinformation, if navigated well it can be a tremendous resource for information, ideas, and tools. The key is to know which Web sites are good and how to find more of them. To help teachers find good Web sites, some school districts put up Internet resources on their own sites. For example, one of the school districts where I used to teach now has links for teachers, parents, and children on its district Web site. There are sites for each subject area, medical Web sites for information on health, and online educational games for children to play. Table 9.5 also provides a short list of Web sites that you may find useful. Recommended

TABLE 9.4   Help-Wanted Cases

Think about the following cases and determine what resources you would use. There are no right answers, but be sure to have rationale for your choice.

Case 1:	Ryan, a fifth grader, struggles in school in all areas except physical education, music, and art. He has not been identified for special-education services, however, because the gap between his achievement tests and his IQ tests was not big enough. He is showing signs of frustration and low self-worth. What other information do you need? What do you do for Ryan? What resources do you use?
Case 2:	Adam, a second grader, gets very angry in class whenever something doesn't go his way. He breaks and throws pencils, clenches his fists, turns red, and grumbles under his breath when angry, but he hasn't ever hurt anyone and doesn't fight at recess. What other information do you need? What do you do for Adam? What resources do you use?
Case 3:	Shannon, an eighth grader, is at a school assembly put on by the police about what to do if you are being abused. You stand behind her and watch as she slumps down in her chair, pulls her hood over her head, and puts her gloves on her hands. What other information do you need? What do you do for Shannon? What resources do you use?
Case 4:	Carly, a kindergarten student, cries and clings to her mother every morning at school. You have to peel her off, which takes a lot of time away from the other children, but she is fine after her mother leaves. What other information do you need? What do you do for Carly? What resources do you use?
Case 5:	Derek, a fourth grader, suddenly refuses to go to the bathroom during school hours. He has had to change clothes several times this year, and his schoolwork is declining. What other information do you need? What do you do for Derek? What resources do you use?
Case 6:	Iman, a first grader, seems to be having trouble listening during class. She isn't following directions and bothers others when you read aloud, but she is doing grade-level work in reading and writing. What other information do you need? What do you do for Iman? What resources do you use?
Case 7:	Tyler, a seventh grader, comes to your room for a midmorning class. By the time he is there, he is tired, lethargic, and inattentive. He lives with his single mom and is often home by himself. What other information do you need? What do you do for Tyler? What resources do you use?
Case 8:	Kasey, a second grader, has cerebral palsy and is confined to a wheelchair throughout the day. This makes it hard for her to participate in some of the activities in the classroom, like energizers and brain exercises. What other information do you need? What do you do for Kasey? What resources do you use?
Case 9:	Eric, a kindergartener, stutters when he talks. The other children in the classroom, beginning to notice, ask him why he talks that way, and he participates less and less in class. What other information do you need? What do you do for Eric? What resources do you use?
Case 10:	Elizabeth, a sixth grader, seems to be stealing money and items from other children's desks. Her classmates have told you this, and you have seen her with some of they items they mentioned. What other information do you need? What do you do for Elizabeth? What resources do you use?

TABLE 9.5 **Teacher Resources on the Internet**

The Web sites below will help you start using the Internet as a resource in the classroom.

http://www.marcopoloeducation.org	Multiple lesson plans; tools and games students can use and play; content knowledge resources.
http://www.aplusmath.com	Math resources for elementary children, including games, interactive flashcards, and lesson plans.
http://www.starfall.com	Early elementary reading Web site with books for children to read electronically and games and resources for teachers and parents.
http://www.planemath.com	Math lessons, activities, and stories, all revolving around planes and plane trips.
http://www.pecentral.com	Activities and ideas for physical education; a lot of quick activities that encourage movement.
http://www.bookadventure.com	You can put in criteria, and this site creates a list of books that fit the criteria. It has great lists of books, but I recommend it only for teachers because it gives quizzes and prizes when children use it. However, teachers could use the site for finding books for individuals.
http://school.discoveryeducation.com	Sponsored by the Discovery Channel, this site has lessons and resources for multiple grade levels and subject areas.
http://www.teacherweb.com	This site is so cool! You put in the topics and grade level you want, and it gives you a list of different Web quests that you can do with children.
http://www.quest.nasa.gov	This site has lesson plans and resources, and you can sign up for online chats with astronauts!
http://www.sitesforteachers.com	This site contains a list of thousands of Web sites teachers can access, as well as direct links to the sites.

by teachers, these sites can be used for several different reasons. My favorite "teacher" Web site, www.marcopoloeducation.org, is like a mini search engine for teachers. It has all kinds of lessons, content information, and tools you can download and use for free. Sponsored by such professional organizations as the National Council of Teachers of Mathematics, the International Reading Association, and the Smithsonian Institution, this site has direct links to each of their Web sites. If you click on teacher resources and then on the lesson plan index, you can go to a page that allows you to search lesson plans according to topic, grade level, and kind of resource. For example, when I put in the topic of math for K–2 and 3–5 and that I wanted student interactives, I got 21 tools, including "marble mania," a graph creator, and "piggybanking" from that single search.

How does the Internet relate to classroom management? We have talked about pedagogy and lesson plans as key in helping children become engaged and excited about school, and Web sites may help you create those kinds of lessons. In addition, the Internet is a valuable resource for questions about a certain disability or a behavior a child is exhibiting. Remember that you can get bad information on the Internet as well. Be sure to take into account the Web site you use. For example, if you read about ADHD on the Johns Hopkins Web site, www.hop-kinschildrens.org, you will probably get good information. If you read about a remedy from a parent who has had a child with ADHD, be careful.

Professionals in Your Community Can Be a Resource for Children

Some children in your classroom may be vulnerable because they live in an environment that doesn't support their basic needs for safety or survival. These children may require the support of many professionals in the community. Weissbourd (1996) wrote about attributes of teachers who work effectively with these children:

- Effective teachers pick up on the quiet troubles that undermine children in school, such as mild hunger or wearing the same clothes day after day, and respond aggressively to these problems.

- Effective teachers know when to respond to a child's problem themselves and when a child needs to see another professional who has specialized training. (p. 183)

In other words, you must become sensitive and responsive to cues children give you. One response may be to ask for help from a professional who doesn't work within the school district. Before contacting these professionals, I suggest that you work with your administrator or counselor as a team to help the child. In addition, people at your school may have specific contacts that have helped before. One school in my area, for example, has dentists see children in the school twice a year for free. How did the staff get this to happen? They saw a need, got together and wondered what could be done, and then asked. People want to help, but you have to ask.

Sometimes such professionals as social workers, psychologists, and physicians will already be assigned to a child. In this case, your job is to collaborate with them. Call and talk to them if you are struggling with a child in their care or have questions about the care a child is receiving. In my room one year, for example, I had a child named Chelsea whose foster parents did not send her to school dressed appropriately or with supplies. At conferences, the parents were apathetic about her progress and told me they couldn't get too close to her. She wasn't being hugged or loved in any way. Another teacher who had Chelsea's sister was seeing the same thing, so we called the social worker and met with her to discuss it. Chelsea and her sister were pulled out of the home within a week. As teachers, we are with children 6 or 7 hours of their day. Professionals working with students intermittently may not be aware of important issues and happenings. Sometimes you may need to be a child's voice.

Letter From a Master Teacher 9.2

A Principal's Advice

As a first-year teacher, I remember thinking I needed to find my own answers to my many, many questions. I couldn't approach fellow teachers or my principal, not that I viewed our staff as uncooperative or unsupportive; on the contrary, they were very willing to offer their help and ideas. I thought, however, if I asked for help, they would find me in over my head and, much worse, incompetent. I was not about to expose any inadequacies to a group of professionals from whom I desperately sought approval. Fortunately for me (and, moreover, my students), my principal took the time to come to me and ask how I was doing. Of course, I lied and said, "Great!" the first few times. Finally, I realized I was not only hurting myself by not asking for help; I was ultimately not giving my students my best every day, which I had promised them from day one. After a conversation with my principal, I found that I really wasn't incompetent—or inadequate, for that matter. I just needed some affirmation that I was doing a good job and some suggestions for improvement. What I took from that day is not the strategies we discussed or the offer to observe another master teacher in the school but the unconditional support I felt from my administrator and the lines of communication that were opened.

A very wise superintendent once told me he viewed asking for help as a *strength*. He *expected* me to ask questions and seek help. Now that I am an administrator, I find myself asking teachers how they are doing and how I can help. I certainly don't have all the answers, and sometimes the best thing I can do is make myself available for questions or just "lend an ear." What I know for certain is that a question that goes unasked is a question that goes unanswered.

I have witnessed firsthand what can be accomplished when educators put their personal inhibitions and pride aside and ask for help. When given the opportunity to collaborate and share ideas, we grow as professionals and improve our schools. If teachers continue to teach behind closed doors, however, we are in danger of not moving our profession forward, and our students will suffer the most. If you never ask for help from another professional in your school or district, ask yourself, "Am I willing to leave my students' success to chance?"

—Chad Boyer
Elementary Principal

Organizations in Your Community Can Be a Resource for Children

Many organizations are willing to help children and schools when asked. Educational service units, libraries, and nonprofits like 4-H, for example, can help with resources for classrooms, and often they will have unique or expensive supplies that you can borrow, speakers willing to talk to children about a variety of topics, or programs for families that they can access for free.

Other organizations can provide items that families cannot afford, such as eyeglasses, coats, school supplies, food, and clothes. If you believe a student or students need these resources, find out from other teachers, your administrator, or your counselor who provides those kinds of items in your community. For example, my area's Lions Club often provides free eyeglasses for children, and a local television station always puts on a coat drive in the fall. It is important to keep abreast of what is happening in your community and then be willing to go through the necessary procedures to get children the items they need.

Sometimes whole families may need assistance. Some school districts contract with counseling firms to provide services for families in need. You can use these kinds of contracts, sometimes called employee assistance programs, as well. Churches also sometimes provide whole family assistance. For example, Catholic Charities provides meals, help for the homeless, clothes, and other resources to families in need. Another family resource in my area is the Child Saving Institute, which helps families in emergencies with services like babysitting and counseling. Since such resources are free, you can recommend that families contact them or contact them with questions yourself.

Other times, services will be in place for children or families if they take the time to use them. You can be of assistance in these cases as well. At one school I visited, for example, a high level of children qualified for free or reduced lunch, but many parents weren't filling out the forms correctly so they could receive this resource. The school principal and several teachers learned how to fill out the forms and checked over each one as it came in to be sure it would get through the system quickly. Helping families navigate the sometimes-complex system of forms and agencies will be a great benefit for children.

Perhaps you are thinking about the time and effort all of this takes. Perhaps you would rather not insert yourself into a family situation where your help is not wanted. Indeed, you cannot solve every problem in the world, and sometimes families will not accept your resources. I hope you are now aware, however, of ways to get help when the situation presents itself to you. Perhaps you can consider putting your clothespin on someone else's help-wanted sign every once in a while!

So . . . What?

This chapter is about awareness. Be aware that your time and energy will be limited. Be aware that classroom management isn't easy, even with helpful structures and tools. Be aware that children will have issues that require expert advice and support.

This chapter is also about awareness of resources to help you with these things if you ask. Be aware that children can help you in the classroom so your time is well spent. Not only is this kind of help good for you, but it also helps promote autonomy, belonging, and competency (Chapter 1) and democratic classrooms (Chapter 2). Be aware that parents are great resources if you do a good job of inviting their involvement within meaningful and varied tasks. Be aware that many resources inside your school are experts on different topics and can give advice, provide tools, and help children. Be aware that many resources outside you school can help you get supplies, promote health and well-being, and get children the items they need to be successful in school. Great teachers ask for help, and then they give help. Plan to make a help-wanted sign and a clothespin with your name on it so you too may give and receive help.

Get Ready For . . .

The final section! The final three chapters are about the big, little things of classroom management. Huh? After reading about democracy and community, whole group activities, and pedagogy, reading about the physical setup of the classroom, managing outside of the classroom, and how to make classroom management your own may seem small. Some of those little things mixed together, however, will be big in a creating a well-managed classroom. First, in Chapter 10, we are off to the physical classroom and how it affects management. Get your architecture lenses on!

Activities to Try

- Think about and write a short piece about a time you got picked to do a job in school. What was the job? How did you get picked? How did you feel? What did you do? What can you take away from that story that is relevant for a classroom today?

- Brainstorm and come up with names for a list of jobs you might have in the classroom. For example, instead of "weather checker," use "meteorologist."

- Create a template for a newsletter, as well as a "Friday Folder," that goes home with children each week. What kinds of information should be in both?

- **Make a collection!** Create a collection of Web sites that are good for children, parents, and you. Share them with others.

- **Conduct action research!** Interview 10 teachers about resources outside of school they have used in the past year. Why did they choose that resource? How did they find out about it?

Student Study Site

The companion Web site for *Elementary Classroom Management* can be found at www.sagepub.com/kwilliamsstudy.

Visit the Web-based student study site to enhance your understanding of the chapter content. The study materials include video clips, practice tests, flashcards, suggested readings, and Web resources.

Making a Classroom Management Plan Your Own Inside and Outside

The key to any good classroom management plan is really owning it and making it uniquely yours. I hope you will use the many structures, strategies, and tools in this book, as they will help you find success in the classroom. For these things to work, however, you have to figure out how to mold them so you believe in them and can put your heart into them. If you don't, they will just be motions that you go through, and often they won't work. This section is about transforming the classroom, the learning spaces outside the classroom, and your own learning into something that is yours. Don't get me wrong; the children are still in the forefront, but you can't put children at the forefront of anything you don't believe is good.

Chapter 10 is about the physical classroom and things to think about as you design a place where students come each day to learn. Although it may not sound directly related to classroom management, the arrangement of the classroom, the materials, and the aesthetics will greatly affect students' learning. This chapter also provides some really cool reflection tools to help you begin designing.

Chapter 11 takes us outside the classroom to explore management in spaces that aren't always considered for learning, such as the playground, the computer lab, the hallways, and even the bathroom. Get ready to take a little out-of-class vacation!

Chapter 12 is all about you, the teacher. You must think of yourself as a continual learner of classroom management, so we will return to the three things that all learners need: autonomy, belonging, and competency. This chapter explores what is necessary to be autonomous, feel a sense of belonging and support in the school building, and have the competency to create a great classroom management plan. This is the end of the book, but your adventure into managing a classroom with heart has only just begun.

CHAPTER 10

Creating a Classroom Arrangement That Promotes Autonomy, Belonging, and Competency

In the very first chapter, we talked about being "behind the scenes" of classroom management. For the most part, a teacher's role is to, from the background, ask questions, create good problems for students to ponder, accommodate individual needs, and then let the students perform (learn). For this chapter, however, you will need to come out on stage and check the props. After all, managing a classroom includes the physical environment you and your students create. What kind of setting promotes great performances?

As you begin to read this chapter on the physical arrangement of the classroom, please take some time to think about your favorite book, television show, or movie. Write or tell someone about a part you liked best. What comes to your mind: the characters, the problem, the funny parts, the setting? Though it may not be the first thing you share about a favorite book or movie, try to imagine the story without the setting. Difficult, isn't it? A horror film wouldn't be the same without the haunting music and screams. A western wouldn't be as good without the dust, old-fashioned clothes, and horses. Although we may not think of the setting at first, it is definitely integral to our feelings and ideas about the characters and the problems they encounter.

Memorable movies and books for me bring the characters, their problems, and the setting together. The same can be said for a classroom. To make learning memorable, every aspect of classroom management must be combined into experiences that move students' senses and keep their minds active. In addition to purposeful pedagogy, juicy content, community-building activities, respectful language, and accommodations for special-needs students, we need a setting that ties it all together. The environment, or setting, may not be the first thing that comes to mind when we think of classroom management, but it is indeed vital to student learning. "Physical environments influence how we feel, hear, and see. Those factors, in turn, influence cognitive and affective performance" (Jensen, 2005, p. 82). Just as you need to be purposeful as you design pedagogy, content, and community, you also need to plan an environment where children will be comfortable, learn successfully, and love to be each day. The stage is yours—start designing!

By the end of this chapter, I hope you have:

- Some ideas about how to begin designing a classroom space that promotes autonomy, belonging, competency, community, and motivation

- Some helpful hints and planning tools to help you put all of your ideas about classroom spaces together

The Classroom Setting

How would a classroom space designed to promote autonomy, belonging, competency, community, and motivation look, sound, smell, and feel? As always, there are many right answers; however, this doesn't mean you shouldn't choose a purposeful design. Placement of furniture and materials, lighting, temperature, and sounds all make a difference in student learning and therefore should be carefully considered (Jensen, 2005). Below are a few ideas to start you thinking about the physical classroom. The good news is you can easily change the setting if something doesn't work as planned or if an individual needs something different. In other words, don't be afraid to change the classroom arrangement throughout the year as needed.

We have each spent a great deal of time in different classrooms, starting when we were young. What do you remember about the classrooms in the schools you attended? I remember sitting and looking at a screen filled with notes from the overhead in some of the classrooms I attended. I can remember only desks in others. For some, I have specific memories, like my handwriting page being hung on the board, which I think I remember because it was embarrassing; I didn't have good handwriting, and my paper never ever got a "wow" sticker as others did. Take these kinds of memories into account as you begin to think about designing a classroom environment. Reflecting on how you felt about learning in a specific setting can be helpful; however, do not let your experiences completely drive how you arrange your classroom. It is easy to get stuck in a vision for a classroom that reflects your past rather than looks forward toward new information and innovative ways to create a setting that promotes learning. Just because you sat in rows facing the front of the room in eighth-grade social studies doesn't mean your students should. Looking at many different options and being aware of the implications of each is important. Remember that what worked for you may not work for all students. As you begin to read, notice that this chapter is organized by questions rather than statements. For the most part, there aren't any "right" answers. There are, however, some "right" questions to ask as you design the physical classroom.

Room Arrangement

One of the first decisions to make when designing a classroom setting is how you will arrange the room. It is important to think about an arrangement that will best help students learn and belong in a classroom community. Many factors will be out of your control within the classroom. For example, you won't be able to move cabinets, doors, chalkboards, or windows, and you may not have a choice of tables or desks. You will, however, be able to make other decisions. Here are a few things to think about as you begin to arrange your classroom. Be sure to check out the tools in the final portion of this chapter as well. They will help you put these ideas into practice.

How Many Students Will Be in This Room?

The room arrangement will look different for a class of 19 than it will for a class of 35. If you teach several groups of students each day, plan for the largest class. Having a large number of people in a small space can cause stress if it is not well managed. If you will have a large class, create as many empty spaces as you can so the classroom doesn't feel cramped and children can spread out if they feel the need. One year, I had a group of 28 students in a very small classroom. In an attempt to make things feel more open, I removed items from the walls and didn't have as many extra tables or chairs in the room. Although not ideal, we made it work.

What Will the Seating Arrangement Be?

Although you may not have control over whether you have desks or tables, how you place furniture will influence what students do in the classroom. One study showed that children sitting in a semicircle tend to ask more questions than children sitting in rows (Marx, Fuhrer, & Hartig, 1999). Grouped seating, whether at tables or with desks pushed together, fosters peer interaction while row seating promotes student focus on individual tasks (Jensen, 2005). Desks in a circle de-emphasize hierarchical relationships, or make everyone feel as though they are at the same level. Just ask any of the Knights of the Round Table! "The key, therefore, is to match the appropriate seating arrangement to the activity—for example, use a cluster arrangement when collaboration is the goal or row seating when concentrated independent learning is the goal" (Jensen, 2005, p. 83). This doesn't mean that you need to change the seating arrangement 10 times a day. Think about what the children in your room will be doing most of the time, and then change it for special occasions.

Remember that students don't always have to sit at desks. If you have the space, place some other furniture around the room to accommodate student needs. For example, if you place desks or tables in groups so students can collaborate, you may want to have other tables or desks around the room that individual students can use when they need to focus on an assignment.

LETTER FROM A MASTER TEACHER 10.1

Acceptance as an Important Piece of the Classroom Setting

As I began to prepare my letter, I thought of lots of grand examples of things you could do in your classroom to create the ideal setting for learning. The more activities I thought of, however, the more I realized that the ideas and examples won't be meaningful if a key component is missing: acceptance.

When I think back to the years in which my classroom seemed to have the "ideal" setting, it really didn't have as much to do with what was on the walls, who was sitting where, or what music was playing in the background (although those things certainly foster learning). Instead, there was a cohesive, welcoming, passionate learning environment because the students had learned to accept that they and their classmates each had specific strengths, weaknesses, and differences. Because of this acceptance, they didn't feel they had to compete against each other to be the best, behave the best, or get the best grade, but they each had something to contribute so all could improve in their learning.

Being accepting means you and your students realize that not everyone reads, solves problems, or creates models of the solar system well. Acceptance means you give the children opportunities to build on their strengths and applaud the effort when they attempt something difficult. How different would your classroom be if the children knew that Billy is not a good reader but is the go-to guy for a question in math? How about them knowing that Suzy can't walk without braces on her legs but is a human dictionary when it comes to spelling? How about them knowing that Adam has difficulty controlling his temper but takes good care of the class gerbil?

Accepting others doesn't mean you don't have expectations—quite the opposite. You expect the students not to laugh when someone makes an error when reading aloud. You expect the students to try harder, especially at something difficult. You expect all the students to participate in games, even if that means someone keeps score because he or she is physically unable to play. You expect a child with behavior issues, instead of yelling at a classmate, to give him- or herself a time-out (this is where you come into play, creating a space in your room where children who need to cool off can go).

When your classroom setting promotes acceptance, the students will use their strengths to push themselves to learn more, do better, and help others who don't have the same strengths. They won't give up or say they can't do it. In the classroom, they will be judged only by what they do to help themselves and others.

—Kelly J. Smith
Second-Grade Teacher

For material related to this concept, go to Clip 10.1 on the Web-based Student Study Site.

Do not use this kind of furniture as punishment (e.g., sending a student to the desk in the corner because he or she is talking too much) but instead as a choice for students who know they need to work alone sometimes. Since sitting in a U shape may promote asking questions, have a spot on the floor where students can sit in a U shape when you want to have this kind of session.

Sometimes you will also want to move the furniture for a special occasion. For example, when students were presenting plays, puppet shows, books, or other projects in my classroom, we often pulled our chairs into "audience" seating mode. The children knew what that was and could arrange their chairs that way quickly and easily. We also talked about how an audience looks and sounds so there were clear expectations for this kind of seating arrangement. Chapter 6 talked about class meetings and opening circles. If you use this community-building tool, you will need space for a circle, which you should consider when placing furniture around the room. One teacher, Brian, has his students sit in two rows of desks facing each other so they can work in groups and help each other. In addition, when it is time for a circle, the students in the middle can pull their desks out to the ends, connecting the outside rows together. Another teacher, Mary Jo, has her students become a train when she wants them to have a class meeting, and they pick up their chairs and follow the leader toward the insides of their desks.

The desks in this room promote group work but can also be pulled apart to create opportunities for a group circle.

For material related to this concept, go to Clip 10.2 on the Web-based Student Study Site.

Beyond Sitting at Tables or Desks, Where Will Students Be?

If you have room, you may want to have places for children to work other than their desks. Content-based stations, a library area, and/or a place for the students to come together for whole group activities are some ideas to get you started. In my second-grade classroom, I always had children sit on the floor close to me when I read them a story, gave directions, or taught a mini lesson to the whole group. We called it the front floor, and it had a different-colored rug in the area where students sat. This helped me with management when students needed to listen. If they were spread out at their desks, I had a harder time keeping their attention. I tried to make sure this area wasn't near a window or a door and was tucked in the back of the classroom to minimize distractions. I didn't want children to face the front when seated at their tables because that wouldn't facilitate group work. Sometimes, however, I needed students' attention and solved this issue by creating another area where they could focus on the speaker, whether me or another child.

I also had a library area with books, pillows, and lamps for reading. Children could choose a book and find a comfortable spot to read. How many of you read sitting straight up at a desk? Most people like to curl up on a comfy couch or chair to read. I have seen some rooms where teachers brought in couches, rocking chairs, and even a bathtub full of pillows so students could feel comfortable reading. I never had room for such large items; however, my students could grab a pillow and find a quiet spot to read. If reading with a pillow caused them problems, they came up with another place to read.

The other areas to think about when designing your classroom are based on content. Even if you don't plan on having stations in your room, it is nice to have designated areas for subjects like science, math, language arts, social studies, or computers or for specific topics if you only teach one subject. These spaces may be a place to work or to keep materials and projects. For example, I had a science area where children could look at things under a microscope, grow a plant under a sunlamp, or observe our pond. We also had a puppet show area, a computer area, and a math area. Of course, students didn't do math exclusively in the math area; however, materials were there to help them. As with all things in life, math or any other subject is connected to every other subject. If my students were working on a project in the science area that required a calculator, they knew where to find one.

What Will the Traffic Patterns Be?

Be careful to leave space for movement. Children will need to move around the room for various reasons, such as sharpening pencils, throwing trash away, going to the restroom, getting supplies and materials, and so on. Proximity is key. If you have the trash can, the supplies, and the pencil sharpener near the door, the traffic there will be considerable. To manage the traffic flow in the classroom, put less-traveled spaces between highly traveled spaces. Put areas where small numbers of children will be close to those where large numbers of children will be. For example, having the paper in a confined space near the pencil sharpener or trash can may not be wise, as lots of children will need access to these spaces. You could, however, put the paper near the computer area, as only a few students will be going there.

Also consider teacher and student movement in the classroom. As noted in Chapter 9, feedback is key in helping students learn. Your chosen room arrangement should accommodate your ability to get feedback to students quickly. You will also want to be able to quickly reach students who need your help behaviorally.

In addition, much of the recent brain research promotes movement throughout the day for children in a classroom (Jensen, 2005; Sprenger, 2007). The environment you create should facilitate this kind of movement for learning. If students are going to do brain exercises before math, they will need space to do them. If they are going to walk along a "balance beam" (i.e., a piece of tape) to their next class, they will need room to line up. If they are going to move to music, they will need space as well. Remember, if planned carefully, some spaces can be used for multiple occasions. No one has that much room!

Should Students Choose Where They Want to Sit?

Certainly there are benefits and limitations to having students choose where they want to sit in the classroom. Erwin (2004) recommends giving students a say in where they sit as long as they don't disrupt or cause others' learning to suffer. Indeed, you could argue that this would promote autonomy and belonging; however, you could also argue that the teacher should decide where students sit to meet their competency needs. Is there a way to have both? I think so. Try to see this as a yes *and* no, rather than a yes *or* no, question. Giving students some choice while encouraging meaningful learning can be fulfilled in a classroom seating structure that is flexible and full of movement. That structure should provide opportunities for children to work with all of their classmates throughout the year. At times, students should work with others who have a similar skill level. Other times, they should work with children who have a higher or lower skill level. Still other times, students should work with children who have similar interests. In other words, seating arrangements might not be permanent. How can a classroom arrangement facilitate this kind of structure?

Perhaps there should be some limits when students choose their seats!

Let's look at an example. In my classroom, I set up the tables with enough chairs around them so everyone had a seat, but I put students' names on chairs rather than on the tops of the desks. That way, students could easily move to different groupings without having to deal with others being upset about someone else sitting in their spot. I put individual supplies in cubbies, but some teachers put "book bags" on the backs of chairs as well.

Sometimes I gave students a group to sit with, and other times they chose an interest category (e.g., students who wanted to read mysteries went to the blue table). Sometimes I placed their chairs in groups before they got there, and other times they could sit wherever they wanted to. In other words, the seating arrangement depended on managing the curriculum and the learning. If we want students to learn academically and socially, the seating arrangement should support that. If students work only with their friends or never get to choose where they sit, they will miss opportunities to work on many social and academic goals. In my classroom, for example, students were required to behave in a way that helped their classmates learn. If they had trouble in a group, I talked to them about moving, and sometimes they did. Seating children in many different groupings throughout the year, however, provides management that facilitates learning and not just behavior.

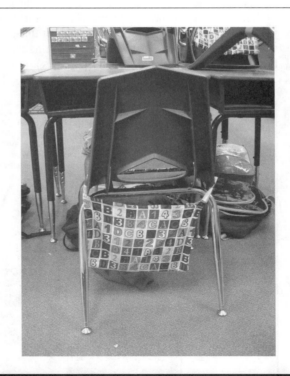

A parent made these chair book bags for the teacher in this room.

Where Will You Incorporate Individual Student Spaces Within the Classroom?

You have thought about spaces for the whole group, spaces for children working alone and in groups, and spaces for content, and next we will think about spaces for materials. Right now, however, let's think about a classroom arrangement that will incorporate space for individual students and their things. Children need a space to call their own within the classroom (Rosenfeld, 1977).

How you incorporate individual spaces will depend on your teaching assignment. For example, if you have the same class of students throughout the day, there will be quite a few ways to provide individual spaces, such as cubbies with children's names on them, individual desks, or bags on chairs. I always had mailboxes as well, in which children could keep papers and information to go home. In addition, they could mail each other letters, which promoted writing skills. If your teaching assignment requires you to teach multiple groups of students, however, individual spaces will need to be a bit different, such as folders or a spot on the wall for things that make students proud. I knew one teacher who used part of her bulletin boards for individual spaces. She took ribbon and made grids on the walls. Each child put his or her name on a square and whatever he or she wanted to in the space. Some children put ribbons from races they had won, others put papers from school, and still others posted pictures of their family and friends. Some teachers I know hang string around the room and give each student a clothespin from which to hang their things. You might also store each group's chair bags in five or six different tubs. Students could pick them up when they walk into the classroom and then put them back when they leave. These individual spaces may not seem like much, but they will help children feel connected to the classroom and take ownership of classroom activities.

Another individual space to consider is where to put ongoing projects. You might want to set aside places on shelves or use plastic tubs to store unfinished projects. Be sure to label any spaces you use for works in progress, and make the spaces safe so that work isn't harmed (Clayton & Forton, 2001).

How Will Students With Special Needs Be Accommodated?

You won't be able to answer this question completely until you meet the individual children who need specific accommodations. When designing a setting for learning, you should first spend some time analyzing children's individual needs. You won't be able to do this until you know the children and their families, and you may have to change things once you get to know a child. Some accommodations may seem obvious. For example, if you know your classroom will host a child in a wheelchair, space between furniture, time on the floor, and desks will be important ideas to consider. If you have a child with a sensory processing disorder, however, physical classroom accommodations may not be your most important consideration. Seat children who are distracted easily by physical aspects of the classroom at the end of a group so they have more room, allow them to sit on an exercise ball, cover hard surfaces with carpet or cloth, and keep sounds and smells to a minimum (Kranowitz, 2005). Getting to know children and paying attention to struggles in the classroom will help you begin to understand how changing the physical environment may help your students learn better academically and socially. The key, as always, is to recognize that sometimes children do not misbehave on purpose and may need something different from what you are providing, and sometimes that something different may be the setting.

When creating a setting for children with special needs, think next about movement in the classroom. Some students may need to move frequently, so set up places in the room where they can move even when the rest of the class isn't moving. Try providing a bouncy seat that allows them to move without leaving their seat, or have them stand on a balancing board so they will stay in one place but must move to balance the board. Some children need constant sensory stimulation. Teachers I have worked with have placed Velcro strips on the underside of students' desks, tables, or chairs so they can rub their fingers on it, removing the need to move conspicuously in the classroom. Chewing gum can also alleviate the need for constant movement. If you worry about gum being stuck on the furniture, put a piece of paper on the wall with everyone's initials and ask students to put their gum next to their initials when finished. That way, you can make sure all of the gum is thrown away.

Other children will have problems with the movement around the classroom. Children in wheelchairs or with physical disabilities may find it difficult to move to the floor or from station to station. You may need to create additional space between tables and desks to allow them room to move. You may not be able to use the floor as much if it is difficult for one child to get to the floor. One teacher I know had a student named Amanda, who was in a wheelchair. Amanda could move from the wheelchair to the floor but had a special pillow that supported her. Each time students moved to the floor, one of the children got the pillow out, and then Amanda scooted over to the floor and lay on the pillow. While this worked well, the teacher needed to create a clear path so Amanda could get to the floor, as well as a spot to store her pillow. These are easy accommodations; they just need to be planned.

Finally, thinking about the furniture arrangement is important when working with children with special needs. You will want to make sure all children can work on social and academic goals, and furniture placement can create opportunities or provide obstacles for children with special needs. For example, Logan, Bakeman, and Keefe (1997) found students with learning disabilities were more engaged in learning when working in small groups or one-on-one with an adult. Students with sensory issues, however, may need time alone to focus on academic work. In other words, you will need to accommodate several individual needs through furniture arrangement. You may need to set up an area where a student can go to be alone. You may need to put desks together in ways that allow all students to participate.

Although you want to accommodate individual students, keep your focus on social and academic goals for all children. Make sure accommodations work with the rest of the classroom setting. If they don't, you may need to think of another solution. For example, let's say a student in a wheelchair can't sit on the floor, but you want your class to have meetings in a circle on the floor. Giving up classroom meetings should not be an option; however, you may need to arrange the furniture so you don't have a floor space but a space to move chairs into a circle. If a child needs alone time when you want your students to work in groups, move the furniture to meet both needs.

Materials

Like the arrangement of a classroom, the materials and how they are organized are important aspects of designing a place where students can learn. Depending on the school where you teach, you might have many materials or very few. I will never forget moving from a school and a classroom where I had access to microscopes, math manipulatives, multiple copies of books, and a room full of paper and other supplies to a school and a classroom where I had access to textbooks and nothing else. I remember walking into the empty classroom and wondering to myself, "Where's all the stuff?" In the second classroom, I needed to work to get materials. Those children deserved microscopes and manipulatives just as any other children did. Whether you have a lot of materials or not, it is important that you begin to think about how to get appropriate materials for the students you teach, how to store them so children have access to them, and how to manage a classroom full of materials that students are using.

How Do I Find Materials for the Classroom?

If you walk into a classroom or school with relatively few materials and you don't have millions of dollars to spend, you may need to collect more and more materials each year until you have what you need rather than buy everything at once. There are ways, however, to get materials for free or with little expense to you. For example, although having math manipulatives like hundreds/tens/ones blocks is nice, pinto beans and cups are just as effective; in fact, they are sometimes even more effective because children will need to count out 10 beans and put them in the cups rather than grab a tens block. Spinners, dice, and playing cards can all be handmade, as can many other math materials. Spaghetti noodles are great for patterns and can be dyed different colors if necessary.

If you don't have many books for your classroom library, be sure to hand out book orders every once in a while. As children from your room buy books, your classroom will earn points, and you will be able to stock your library. In addition, check out books from your school library and place them in your classroom library. Garage sales are great places to find books as well. I once found a whole set of the Boxcar Children book series for a quarter at a garage sale. It also doesn't hurt to ask parents to donate books they are no longer using. Finally, be sure to make the stories your students write into books and put them in the library area, a great way to get children interested in books while promoting the need for editing and polished writing.

Sometimes you can check out materials from different organizations. I got many science materials from our educational service unit, for example. I just asked the school librarian for a catalog of the materials the organization checked out to teachers and ordered all kinds of models, microscopes, and animals (crickets, mealworms, butterflies, etc.). If you live near a university or college, go to the science department and ask to use old test tubes, Petri dishes, and lab coats. The 4-H organization may also rent you materials for a small amount of money. I got a great but inexpensive planting table with a grow light above it from 4-H, for example, and the organization even came and set it up for me.

You will want to have a lot of writing materials for children as well. I always asked wallpaper stores in my area to donate old wallpaper books, and children made book covers with the samples. You can also ask printing stores to donate paper they would normally recycle so children can have all kinds of paper to use for projects and writing. Make sure to have a variety of pens, pencils, markers, and stamps available for children to write with as well.

Technology is another material that is expensive and at times hard to care for. Most schools provide at least some access to computers, but some may not. A kindergarten teacher I once knew was not given any classroom computers because her students were so young, so she wrote grants to get computers; however, she never had to send the grant proposal in because, due to her persistence and knowledge, her district agreed to purchase computers for all of the kindergarten rooms. You may also have a computer lab in your school but not computers in the classroom. This was once the case for me. I really wanted computers in my classroom because I wanted the students to be able to use them for workshops, especially writing workshop, so I went to thrift stores and bought old computers that still worked and put them in my room. Although they didn't have Internet access, I was able to put writing software on them, and children could write and print stories. Be sure to ask your administrator if bringing in computers this way is acceptable.

Sometimes you will need reusable supplies. For example, you may want to do a cooking project, a science project, or a math project that requires materials you don't normally have in the classroom, and you may need help. Ask parents to send materials from home, such as food, candy (a great math manipulative), and recyclables like toilet paper tubes or milk jugs. Ask other staff members to save supplies like baby food jars (if they are new parents), extra scraps of material, or newspapers.

With organization like this, students can easily find materials they need.

Where Should the Materials Be Stored?

Although classrooms often have a great array of materials, teachers often place them where students can't reach them or don't have immediate access to them. Perhaps they do this to avoid management issues; however, doing so causes students to miss out on valuable opportunities for autonomy, belonging, and competency. For example, if a student is struggling with a math problem and has access to hundreds/tens/ones blocks, he or she can get them and work on fixing his or her own problem. It is an exciting day when students know there are tools in the classroom that will help them, know they need one, and then use it to help them learn, thus controlling their own learning.

Having access to materials means making sure materials are organized and within reach. Organizing materials in this way is fairly easy. Use plastic tubs, drawers, or low shelves for materials that will be used regularly and cabinets and higher shelves for materials that are unsafe without adult supervision or that aren't used regularly. As students should be responsible for taking care of materials, you should label tubs or shelves so children can put them away appropriately. For example, labeling materials with words and pictures or photographs in grades where children might not be reading yet will help them know where to put materials, as well as give them a chance to read words. At the beginning of the year, you may need to model and have discussions about how taking care of materials looks and sounds.

How Do I Manage a Class of Students Using Materials?

When asked why they don't let children use materials in the classroom, many teachers tell me they are afraid the children will just "play" with the materials. Indeed, visions of children throwing blocks or eating the chocolate bars meant to represent decimals can haunt teachers into keeping the materials to themselves. Demonstrating seems easier than actually letting children use the materials. If this sounds like something that swirls around in your head, consider a few ideas that may help manage children and materials, and remember that many children in your classroom will learn more effectively if they actually get to use materials and then connect their experiences with reflections. Materials, as you read about in Chapter 3, are quite motivational as well.

So how do you manage the classroom so children can use materials to help them learn? First, make sure the children understand that the materials in the room are tools and not toys. You might have a class meeting or two about how to use materials in the classroom, as well as how to put them away and care for them. Be sure to tell your students that the materials are there to help them learn and that they may not always need all of the tools. You might even use a story to help children understand how to use the materials in the classroom.

Remember, like any other concept, students need to learn about using materials. Take some time to make learning about the tools part of your lesson. Before using materials, give children some time to just play with and come up with different ways to use them. For the first couple of days of school, students in my room spent time finding materials around the room and presenting what they found and how they might use it to learn. It was kind of like a scavenger hunt for materials. Children learned about the materials they would use throughout the year, they began to see them as tools for learning, and we got to practice putting them away. If I introduced a new tool, students had a few minutes to figure out how to use it. Sometimes, if the material was complex enough, we had one whole lesson about using the tool. For example, before using microscopes in the room, we did a lesson where the children learned to make slides using any materials they wanted to view. After they learned that, we went on to looking at drops of water.

Although students will become accustomed to using materials in the classroom, talking about using materials before you use them, even if it is just a reminder, may be wise. Ask simple questions like "What is using these materials going to look like today?" or "What kinds of things might cause these materials to go away?" Almost every time my students played math games, for example, I gave a mini lesson where we talked about how to roll number cubes so they didn't go flying.

Another aspect of using materials ties directly to your room arrangement and the timing of the lesson. If you will be using materials that are messy or noisy or require more space, plan for that. For example, if children will be using beans and cups to add and subtract two-digit numbers, you may need to spread desks apart or move some children to the floor to allow everyone enough space to work. You may need to use noisy materials at specific times of the day so you don't bother other classes. Teach children to use messy materials in designated areas, or be sure to put newspaper or plastic down if the whole class will be using the materials.

Children who are having trouble using the tools for learning might need to put them away for a bit. Be sure to let them know that if this happens, they will always have the opportunity to use the materials again when they are ready. Sometimes, limiting access to a material for the whole class for a certain period may be necessary. For example, I know teachers who have put tools away for a day or two, had a class meeting about the tools, and then put them back out again. Once again I am reminded of teachers who tell me that "some classes can handle materials, but some can't," and once again I will argue that any class can use materials if you teach the students to use them and have clear expectations about their uses. Indeed, for whatever reason, some classes may seem difficult and others easy. I hope you think about children and what you want them to know and be able to do out in the world. You want them to be able to use and take care of materials, right?

What Materials Might Be Useful for Managing a Classroom?

Sometimes materials can be useful in the classroom as actual management tools. Materials placed in a relaxation station or a peace corner can be excellent tools for children who are upset and in a state that hinders learning. An ooze tube to look at, a Koosh ball to squeeze, or a heavy hand (a glove filled with beans and sewn shut) to put on a shoulder can all help frustrated, mad, or upset children change states fairly rapidly (Swanson, 2007). A principal I know has ooze tubes in her office, and whenever an upset child comes in, she pulls one out and has the child look at it for a few minutes before she talks with him or her. She finds this more effective than trying to talk with children while they are still in a frustrated state. You can also use these kinds of tools for children who have trouble paying attention to a speaker or while a book is being read. Help students concentrate, for example, by giving them a Koosh ball or even a sock or stuffed animal filled with beans and sewn shut to put in their laps. Teach children when to use these tools and that not everyone will need them. At first, everyone may want the tools, but after a while the novelty will wear off and students will get the tools only when they really need to.

Another material that may help you manage a classroom is music (Sprenger, 2007). Songs for beginning the day, songs signaling that work time is almost finished, and cleanup songs can be great management tools and state changers. For example, if the classroom needs to be cleaned quickly, pop in a song like the overture to *William Tell* and tell the students that the room must be cleaned by the time it is over. If you want students to work actively, put in a classical piece by Mozart or Beethoven. If you want them to feel up for a challenge, put in the theme from *Mission: Impossible* (Sprenger, 2007). Music can also help children who are distracted by any sounds around the classroom. You can soften the auditory environment by playing classical music just loud enough to cover up noises from outside or the buzzing sounds of lights (Kranowitz, 2005). You don't always have to use professionally produced music, however. Children love to sing! My son's class, for example, always ends the day with a goodbye song.

Managing the classroom may be about allowing children to choose what materials they use. At the beginning of the year, the children in my class were always so excited that they could actually use the markers they had purchased for school. In previous classes, they could use markers only for art class or special occasions. Having a choice of materials is motivating. If you want to get children writing, reading, or doing any other subject, create opportunities for choice of materials whenever you can. Indeed, some children will have an easier time and be more successful with different materials. "Provide a choice of writing implements. Some children do better with standard pencils, others with fat primary pencils; some with standard crayons, others with chubby crayons" (Kranowitz, 2005, p. 258).

Sometimes it may be nice to use some materials to help children use other materials appropriately. For example, if you are worried about children throwing number cubes all over the room, give each group a small plastic tub in which they can roll the number cube. If you want children to use only specific materials for a lesson, place the materials in baggies before the lesson and hand them out when you are ready to begin. If you want children to use math manipulatives but don't want them scattered all over the room, laminate large pieces of paper to create mats on which the manipulatives need to stay. You can even make these mats conducive to student learning by splitting them into two or three different colors: blue for ones, red for tens, green for hundreds. If children can't remember to treat materials with care, have them make a poster to remind the whole class.

Aesthetics in the Classroom

For material related to this concept, go to Clip 10.3 on the Web-based Student Study Site.

So far, we have talked about the room arrangement and the materials in the classroom setting. Another aspect of designing a setting where children are best able to learn is how the classroom feels. Is it warm and inviting or cold and sterile? When I teach college classes in different rooms, this aspect of designing a classroom setting clearly stands out because often the room to which students come for class is not exclusively ours. We cannot hang things on the walls, regulate the heating or cooling, or change the lighting in the room. Fortunately, you may be in a room for a whole school year and be able to make changes. Here are a few questions to help you begin thinking.

What's on the Walls?

The walls of the classroom can help inspire, motivate, and create community and thus help students learn. Studies have shown that students do well with an optimal view (Jensen,

2005). As you have probably noticed when visiting or attending classrooms, the walls can create an overall feeling in the room. Placing student work on the walls around the room instead of commercial posters creates a different feeling. Walls that are bulging with all kinds of papers and words give a different message than walls that are organized and clutter-free. In other words, there aren't necessarily right answers when it comes to wall space. The choices you make send clear messages to children, however, so consider them carefully.

Many teachers choose to put student work on the walls of the classroom, a great way to share work that doesn't require a great deal of time and can be motivational for students. It also allows others to see the topics you've been studying. One of my principals, Joli, often came by our room just to see what was on the walls. She came by one day to see student-made posters of the defensive body weapons, including mucus, earwax, and stomach acid, hanging in the room. She laughed and said, "Only you guys would have mucus hanging on the walls! You must be learning a lot!" Hanging student work is indeed important; however, be careful about the kind of student work you hang. Many classrooms I visit have walls filled with worksheets adorned with stickers and 100% signs. It is hard to tell what the students have learned with this kind of display, it doesn't help children continue to learn, and it de-motivates students who don't do well on "worksheet" learning. Walls shouldn't be used to compare students' learning. If you are going to hang student work, be sure to hang something from every student and only hang pieces that aren't graded. Do hang pieces done in groups or chosen by students. For example, I visited a classroom recently where students in first grade were studying farms. Children got to create a wall-size mural of a farm and then made animals to surround it. Every student had an animal hanging on the wall, and boy, was each one willing and proud to show me his or hers.

"In addition to celebrating students' learning, displays should inspire questions and exploration" (Clayton & Forton, 2001, p. 114). Clayton and Forton suggest having a question board or box where children can write questions about others' work or a display. For example, a "What do you notice?" sign near a table of student-made projects can help them connect their own project to others. You can also have a community brainstorming board where you can pose a question and give children slips of paper on which to write their thoughts. For example, you might put up a math question, collect answers for a couple of days, post the answers on the board, and then talk about them before moving on to the next question. In my classroom, I had a board on cycles that stayed up all year long. Each time a student recognized a cycle, such as the water cycle, the life cycle of an insect, or the writing cycle (process), they wrote it on a yellow circle and placed it on the wall. By the end of the year, we had many cycles on the board and were able to make some conclusions about them. Another year, a student brought in space wallpaper, and we covered our walls with it during our space unit. The children made all kinds of projects that went over the wallpaper and were very excited to come to school every day.

In some schools, teachers aren't allowed to put things on the walls in classrooms because of paint or other considerations. Other times, the space itself may not allow you much room to hang student work or topic-related displays. You may get around this, however, by hanging a string across newly painted walls, complete with clothespins for holding work. Sometimes you can hang work from the ceiling using paper clips or string. You can also buy such materials as adhesive putty that won't remove paint from walls.

This is the farm mural from Terri's class. What do you think the students learned?

As you think about what's on the walls, be sure to consider the best way to organize the items you hang. Although I certainly don't think classroom walls need to be symmetrical or perfectly straight, I do believe that walls need to be uncluttered and easy to look at. Organize wall space so it is defined in some way. For example, you might put borders on the walls to help children distinguish between different subject areas or put different colors on different spaces for organization. Split up big spaces on the walls with empty spaces. Put signs and tools, like the alphabet or number charts, where children can see and use them, most likely lower rather than high above the chalkboard.

For some children, visual stimulation can be so distracting that they won't be able to work. If you find that children in your room are having trouble concentrating due to sensory overload, you will need to reduce it. "Eliminate clutter on bulletin boards. Secure artwork, maps, and graphics on the walls so they don't flutter. Tack a sheet over open shelves to cover art materials, games, and toys that may attract a child's attention" (Kranowitz, 2005, p. 252).

What Kind of Lighting Will You Use?

Interestingly, lighting has been shown to be a hugely important factor in how well students do in school. Students in brightly lit classrooms seem to perform better compared with those in dimly lit classrooms (London, 1988). Lighting can enhance mood and therefore performance especially in the winter months (Harmatz et al., 2000). Fluorescent lights have been found to be detrimental to student performance in school, however, while natural light helps improve students' moods and performances (Jensen, 2005).

Sometimes you will need to be creative with the spaces in the classroom. Stephanie needed to hang student work on this string because of the removable wall in the room.

What does this mean for designing a classroom? First, be aware of how lighting can influence learning and behavior. If students are dragging, check the lighting in your room. In addition, you may want to take the students outside for a lesson so they can get some sunlight. Second, maintain a constant level of bright lighting in your classroom. If the lighting in your room is fluorescent, bring in lamps and turn the lights off. Limit time in a darkened room. When doing math, for example, avoid using an overhead and use a white board instead. Create opportunities for children to get natural light. Open blinds on windows, and take children outside when possible (Jensen, 2005).

How Will You Keep Classroom Noise to a Minimum?

This question is not meant to make you believe that children should be silent in the classroom all day long. Learning is a social endeavor, and children should talk to each other about what they learn. Instead, the question is about the environmental noise in the classroom and how it can affect students' states and learning. "Excessive environmental noise including traffic sounds, aircraft noise, machinery, beepers, and even casual conversation can reduce comprehension and work performance, especially in the early stages of learning a new task" (Jensen, 2005, p. 89). Noise can also affect children physiologically, such as by elevating their blood pressure, heart rates, or stress levels (Evans, Lercher, Meis, Ising, & Kofler, 2001).

To reduce environmental noise in the classroom, Jensen (2005) recommends taking stock of the noise level in the classroom. If children are straining to hear, you may need to make changes. Computers are one noisemaker that often goes unchecked, so be sure to turn them off when they are not in use. Soften the noise level in the classroom by hanging tapestries or fabrics on the wall, or mask disturbing noise with classical or environmental music. Finally, schedule reading or writing times during the quietest parts of the day. For example, if your classroom is near the cafeteria, do not schedule activities that require a quiet environment when other classes will be at lunch.

How Can You Make Children Comfortable in the Classroom?

Classroom teachers often have to make do with many aspects of the physical classroom. In most classrooms where I taught, for example, I had only one window for sunlight; in some classrooms, I had no window at all; and I often couldn't control the temperature in the room or whether or not my lights were fluorescent. It is important to remember, however, that you can work to make learning as comfortable as possible. Helping children feel comfortable really does matter. Try bringing in pillows for them to sit on while on the floor, putting plants in the room, and making the room smell good. If you can change the temperature in the room, be mindful that warm temperatures can cause stress and aggressiveness (Jensen, 2005). Cooler but not cold temperatures are better for learning than hot temperatures. If you can't control the classroom temperature with a thermostat, use fans, open windows, and encourage students to drink water.

Planning Tools for Classroom Settings

As I write Chapter 10, I look back at all of the questions and am amazed at how many decisions a teacher must make—even though I spent many years making them myself! Every aspect of teaching, including creating the setting for learning, is complex. The good news is that some of the decisions you will make throughout the years will become more and more automatic as your experiences change. Children will teach you about creating a setting as they show you what works and doesn't work. Other lessons will require deep reflection and another try. For example, you might not realize that the hum in the lights is causing a distraction until a child begins to struggle, and it may take you four or five tries to really figure out that the setting is the cause.

Reflection is key in coming up with the best possible solution for any management issue, including planning and living in the physical space of a classroom. The tools below are meant to help you reflect about classroom spaces in the future, present, and past. Why reflect toward the future? Taking time to plan a classroom space that will positively influence children's learning will be of great value and save you a lot of time in the long run. Believe me; I have spent hours moving furniture around only to look at it and move it again. If I had just taken some time to reflect on the relationships between the areas I needed and the actual space itself, I would have saved myself a lot of time—not to say that reflection ends when all of the furniture is placed. Reflection about classroom spaces also needs to be in the present. After you have placed the furniture and materials, go through the checklist below to see if the area is ready. Remember that creating a classroom space that works isn't necessarily about the "right" solution but rather about the best solution at that moment. The idea is to continue to look at the space as an influence on management. Reflecting on the classroom space in the

LETTER FROM A MASTER TEACHER 10.2

If you always do what you always did, you'll always get what you always got!

—Verne Hill

Boy, that sure describes me in my first years of teaching when it came to arranging my classroom. I had always seen the product, and it seemed to work for the role models who used it. The teacher's desk was front and center, with all of the students' desks in neatly arranged rows. The picture I saw and first used had the teacher as the leader and all the students as the followers. Wow! I wish I could go back and break up those traditional and stoic rows to spice it up with the arrangements I currently use. I truly believe I would see differences in the dynamics and interactions among the students of my past.

I can't really say when I started arranging my students' desks in horseshoes or pods or, better yet, according to their choice, so let's just say out of the 28 years I have been teaching, I can't remember when the rows still existed. I start off the new school year with the students' desks in two U shapes and my desk off to the side. I like the U pattern because it lends itself to student collaboration. Students are easily able to turn to their neighbor or pair-share to check in with one another. This room arrangement also allows the students to see one another easily, a key factor when creating community among your students. It adds excitement when we race around the U to turn papers in. "On your mark, get set . . ."

After the beginning U-shape patterns, I like to make a circle with the desks. This may be a bit more challenging, but the trust and community it nurtures negates the clumsiness of its appearance. The circle may need to have breaks in it to allow for walkways and areas that need to be visible to the students.

Our classroom is set up through class meetings. It truly is not my classroom but rather ours. At our meetings, the students and I discuss the new possibilities that we can create, and each month we select a new arrangement. So far, we have had a pumpkin, a turkey (use your imagination), and "their choice" of pods (groupings of desks, not equally arranged). It has worked better than I ever could have imagined.

If seasonal themes are on students' minds, be sensitive to all students and their backgrounds. Know your classroom community to honor all students, and encourage those with different cultural backgrounds to voice their opinions.

When a teacher shows faith and trust in his or her students by giving them ownership, the students will believe in themselves. The physical arrangement of a classroom truly sets the tone. Think about what ring you want resounding in your classroom.

Lastly, keep in mind that there are advantages and disadvantages to any seating arrangement. Jot down your reflections as you and your students experiment and see where it leads you, and possibly keep a record of what works and doesn't work as you experiment with the community dynamics in that particular class.

"I am still learning."

—Michelangelo

—Jill Niemann
Sixth-Grade Teacher

past means looking at what's happening in the classroom and wondering if things can be improved. Indeed, you do not want to constantly think about where to move the furniture; however, if an issue comes up in the classroom, consider the classroom space when you look for solutions.

Reflection Tools for the Future

Relationship Diagram

Before you begin making decisions about where furniture goes in a classroom, reflect about the relationships between the areas in the room. This will help you begin to decide what areas will be close to each other, what areas need to be far apart, and what areas might integrate well together. Architects often use a relationship diagram as they begin to come up with the best solution to the problem of creating a new building. Relationship diagrams aren't meant to help you put specific furniture in specific places in a room. Instead, they are meant to help you conceptualize what areas would work well or not so well together. Making this kind of diagram will help you reflect on important spaces you want to have in the classroom, as well as how to fit them together.

You need three things to do a relationship diagram: a pencil, a piece of paper, and a stencil with different sizes of circles. The stencil isn't absolutely necessary but can be helpful if you make circles like I do by hand! After you have these things, you can begin.

- Step 1: List all of the areas you want to have in the classroom. Remember that this is a conceptual map and doesn't involve specific items. For example, you aren't working to figure out where the big fuzzy couch goes but how the library area will interact with the computer area. Should they be close together or far apart? Could they go next to each other? Look at the catalog of possible areas in Table 10.1 to get started, but don't limit yourself to those. What areas do *you* want to have in the classroom (see Table 10.2 for an example)?

TABLE 10.1 Classroom Area Catalog

Choose as many or as few areas as you want in the classroom.

Art area	Listening/music area
Calendar area	Materials area
Coat/backpack area	Math area
Computer area	Movement area
Floor area	Peace corner
Group work area	Science area
Individual student space	Teacher area
Library area	Writing area
Lining-up area	

TABLE 10.2 **Step 1: List Areas You Want in the Classroom**

Here is a list of what I wanted in the classroom.

Front floor (calendar and sharing)
Group seating
Library
Science
Computers
Writing
Math
Individual student space

- Step 2: Prioritize your chosen areas according to amount of space needed for each (see Table 10.3). For example, the floor area in my classroom required more space than the science area because the whole class sometimes met at the floor area while only individuals or small groups needed access to the science area. I might give the floor area an 8 and the science area a 3. Remember that some areas can have the same number if they require the same amount of space.

TABLE 10.3 **Step 2: Prioritizing the Areas You Chose**

Put a number next to each chosen area according to space needed. Below is an example of my priorities.

Front floor (calendar and sharing)	2
Group seating	1
Library	3
Science	3
Computers	4
Writing	5
Math	5
Individual student space	6

- Step 3: Assign a circle to represent each area in the classroom. Choose a large circle for areas in the classroom that will take up the most space and smaller circles for areas that won't need that much space (See Table 10.4). For example, I assigned "group seating" the largest circle because all of the students will need to be there. I gave "individual student space" the smallest circle because individual students will be there. The numbers you assigned the areas in the last step will be helpful.

TABLE 10.4   Representing Numbers With Circles

Place a specific size of circle next to each number. If the science and math areas have the same number, give them the same size circle.

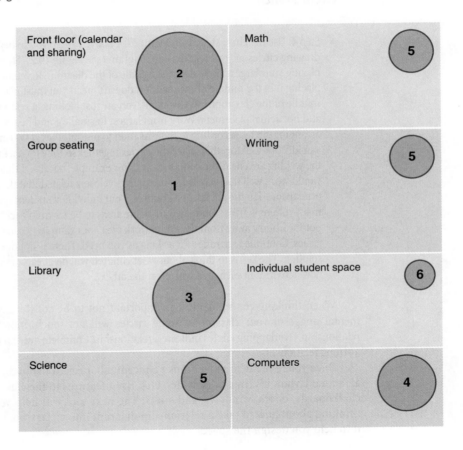

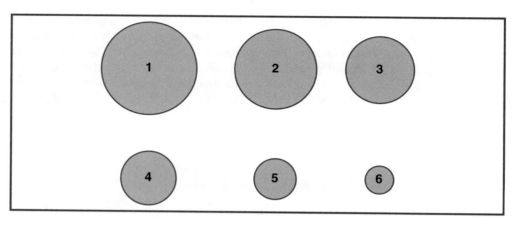

FIGURE 10.1 **Circle Stencil**

- Step 4: Use the circle stencils in Figure 10.1 above to help you to begin drawing circles in your relationship diagram (see Figure 10.2). Start by placing your largest circle near the middle of the diagram. Remember that placing it in the middle of the diagram doesn't mean you must place it in the middle of the classroom. At this point, you are just looking at relationships and not actual placement. Work from largest to smallest and begin arranging circles according to their relation to one another. If two areas would work well together, place the circles together so they touch. I placed the writing area near the computer area, for example, because I thought they would work well that way. If two areas are so closely related that they could overlap, overlap the circles. For example, I put individual student space in many different areas. You may want some areas to be far from each other. I put the library away from the group work area, for example, because of noise issues. Continue to arrange for as long as you need. There is not one "right" solution. The key is to think about what children will do at each area and how activities in each area will affect the others.

When thinking conceptually, it is important not to be constrained by the mental image of your classroom. Some circles will not touch, indicating no relationship. Overlapping circles indicate a relationship. Complete overlap indicates a strong relationship.

Once you're ready to move from a conceptual or relationship diagram to an actual layout, it's time to consider such fixed features in the classroom as chalkboards, doors, windows, and sinks. The next tool will help you begin thinking about how to take a relationship diagram into a classroom and use it to help you design the space.

FIGURE 10.2 **Making Your Relationship Diagram**

I made this relationship diagram based on what I wanted for my classroom and to help me determine where to place areas therein. What do you notice about the placement of areas in the diagram? Why would I place the circles there?

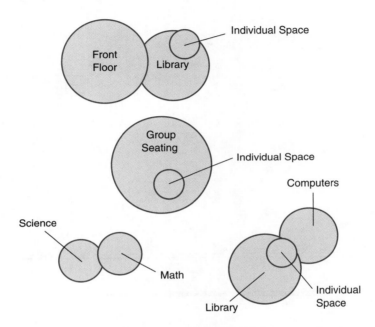

Note: It is important when thinking conceptually to not be constrained by the mental image of your classroom. Some circles will not touch indicating no relationship. Overlap indicates a relationship. Complete overlap indicates a strong relationship.

Classroom Sketch

Classroom spaces can be very different, even within the same school. Some have windows, some are large, some don't have many walls, and so on. This makes it difficult to plan a classroom setting before you see the actual classroom you will use. When you do have access to a classroom and have done a relationship diagram, take some time to sketch the classroom so you can get an idea of where things might go before you begin moving furniture. For practice reflecting and thinking, consider the several different classrooms in Figure 10.3, and then use the relationship diagram to place specific furniture in the rooms. Although you may not have the furniture you want when you get to your classroom, taking a relationship diagram and transferring it to a classroom outline will be beneficial.

a.

b.

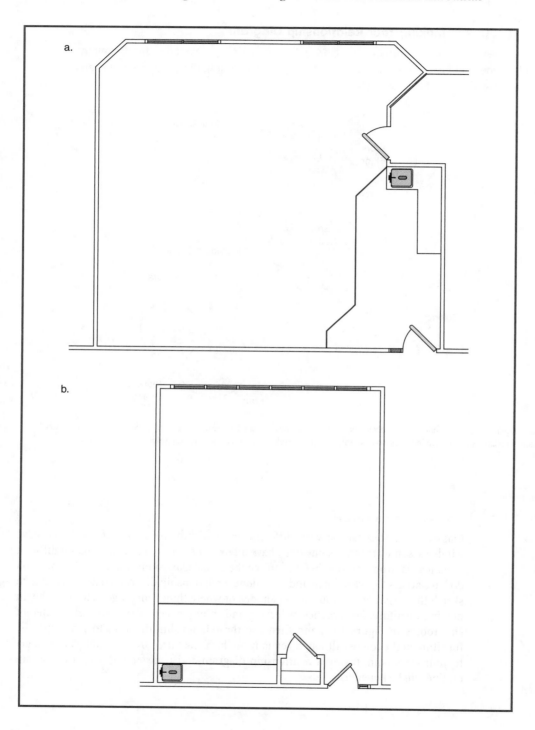

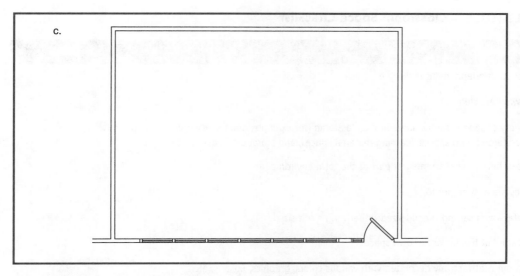

FIGURE 10.3   Classroom Drawing

Take some time to sketch desks, individual spaces, and so on, on the three different classroom blueprints. Figures a, b, and c, give you different layout options to use.

Reflection Tool for the Present

Classroom Checklist

Once you have reflected about possibilities for a classroom arrangement and have actually set up a classroom, reflect on the present to make sure you have met all of your goals. With all of the decisions to be made, having a checklist to help you remember them is sometimes nice. I have included a checklist with this book, as well as a few blank spots so you can add what you want to remember (see Table 10.5).

As you either check or don't check the boxes next to each item, think about how to improve the room. For example, if you didn't check the box about bright lighting, bring in some lamps. As always, the classroom setting is a work in progress. As you change units of study, get to know your students better, and "live" in the classroom for a while, continue to reflect about what has happened in the room and how you can make changes.

Reflection Tools for the Past

Student Classroom Setting Survey

For the most part, this chapter has revolved around the teacher and the decisions that he or she makes when creating a classroom setting. It is important to note, however, that students should have a voice in the way a classroom is arranged. Some teachers even have students

TABLE 10.5 **Classroom Space Checklist**

Arrangement	Check
The seating arrangement is flexible.	
Pathways are clear.	
A variety of spaces are available in the classroom (for example, quiet spaces, small group spaces, large group spaces, learning material spaces, and storage spaces).	
The teacher's area is an integral part of the total environment.	
Spaces are easy to get to.	
The classroom setting is child-sized rather than adult-sized.	
Each student has his or her own space.	
The room is attractively decorated with various colors, graphics, posters, etc.	
The room is comfortable and inviting.	
Traffic patterns promote teacher proximity and feedback for students.	
The room promotes content learning.	
Materials are accessible to students.	
There are places for movement in the classroom.	
There are materials and space for special-needs students.	
Unsafe materials are stored out of reach of children.	
Lighting is bright.	

come up with and then vote on arrangements for the room. Try this after the class has become a community with which you can have conversations about important ideas in learning and working together.

You can also involve children in making decisions about the classroom environment by doing a student survey. This is the same process you read about in Chapter 6, except it is focused on the physical environment (see Table 10.6 for an example). Use the information to reflect on how children feel about the environment, and tailor the questions to get at specific aspects. You can also share the data with children and have them help you come up with solutions to issues you find therein.

TABLE 10.6   Sample Survey

I wrote this sample survey to help you get started; however, you will need to design a survey that fits the needs of your students' grade level and situation.

Our Classroom Environment		
I am comfortable when I am sitting at the front floor.		
Always	Sometimes	Never
I can get my work done while I'm sitting at my desk.		
Always	Sometimes	Never
My teacher sees me when I need help.		
Always	Sometimes	Never
I can find the materials I need.		
Always	Sometimes	Never
I like where I sit in the classroom.		
Always	Sometimes	Never

Self-Reflection

There is no fancy tool for self-reflection. Some people write in journals, others use calendars to write happenings each day, and still others talk to colleagues or loved ones about their classrooms. The point is not how you reflect but that you reflect. After you "live" in the classroom for a few months, take some time to reflect on happenings in the classroom and determine if the environment is causing any problems or could be changed to help a struggling child. For example, if a child is depressed, what could you do to the environment to help that child? If a child isn't able to sit in his or her seat, what could you do to the environment to help that child? If a child isn't able to concentrate on work, what could you do to the environment to help that child? You can easily change the setting to accommodate children's needs; however, you must reflect on what is really happening and think through ways to make the setting work for all of the children working to give their best performance.

So...What?

There are many decisions to make as you create a positive classroom environment. Teachers often forget how important the physical aspects of the classroom are to students and their learning. Seemingly minor details can prove very important to students' access to learning. I hope this chapter has given you some information and tools that will help you create a wonderful space for students to grow academically and socially in their year with you.

We started this chapter by reflecting on our past experiences as students in classrooms, and we ended the chapter with reflection tools to help you think outside the box and create a classroom environment that meets all students' needs.

When you're thinking about designing a classroom, take into account:

- How many students you have

- The seating arrangement and how it is affected by traffic patterns, activities, and student choices

- Individual student spaces

- Accommodations for children with special needs

When you're thinking about putting materials into a classroom, take into account:

- What kinds of materials you will need and how you will get them

- How materials can be stored so students have access to them

- How you can manage student use of materials

- Materials that can be helpful for classroom management purposes

- Materials for children with special needs

When you're thinking about the aesthetics in the classroom, take into account:

- What's on the walls that will help children learn

- How the lighting affects students' learning

- How to keep distracting noise out of the classroom

- Children's comfort level

Use reflection tools that will help you plan and create in the future, present, and past.

Get Ready For . . .

We've spent a great deal of time inside the classroom, and now we're headed out! Teaching and thus classroom management doesn't occur only in the classroom, so we're going on a field trip, so to speak, to the playground, the cafeteria, the computer lab, and the bus stop.

Activities to Try

✎   Practice using the relationship diagram and the classroom sketches.

✎   Throughout the book, we have talked about how children need autonomy, belonging, and competency to succeed in school. Go back through the chapter and find specific instances where the setting would promote these three important aspects of classroom management.

✎   *Make a collection.* Make a collection of music that you would like to use in the classroom for a variety of reasons.

✎   **Make another collection!** Make a "dream" list of materials you would like to have in the classroom. Go back and prioritize them based on importance.

✎   **Conduct action research!** Interview students from a variety of grade levels. Ask them to talk about important aspects of the classroom. Compile the things they mention and determine if anything is important across grade levels.

Student Study Site

The companion Web site for *Elementary Classroom Management* can be found at www.sagepub.com/kwilliamsstudy.

Visit the Web-based student study site to enhance your understanding of the chapter content. The study materials include video clips, practice tests, flashcards, suggested readings, and Web resources.

CHAPTER 11

Managing Beyond the Boundaries of the Classroom

W e're on Chapter 11 now, and I thought it would be fun to go on a little trip. You get to decide where you want to go. Some of you might want to go to a warm location, like a tropical island. Others may want to go to the mountains or even a different country. Did you choose? Now shut your eyes (but not for long because you have to keep reading!) and imagine going to that place. What did you see when you shut your eyes on your mini faux vacation courtesy of me?

Believe me; I went on a few mini faux vacations while writing this book, usually to Hawaii. I imagined the beach, beautiful flowers, a catamaran ride, macadamia nut pancakes, and warm weather. I didn't imagine the inside of the hotel room. Don't get me wrong; it was probably really nice and comfortable, but when you go on vacation, the hotel room is only one of the places on your itinerary. Would it be fun to go to the mountains, to an island, or on a cruise and only stay in the room? In most cases, it seems to me that venturing outside of the room and exploring the attractions are much more fun.

For this chapter, I want you to go on another mini faux vacation in your mind, this time outside of the classroom. Classrooms, when managed well, are exciting and all-around great places to be. Children don't spend all of their time inside the classroom, however, so you must be ready to manage their adventures outside of the classroom boundaries as well. In fact, I encourage you to purposefully take "vacations" outside of the classroom every once in a while. Everyone deserves a change of scenery. Your job as a teacher requires you to manage inside and outside of the classroom.

By the end of this chapter, I hope you have:

- Some tools and structures that will help you manage situations where children are outside of the classroom but still in the building

- Some tools and structures that will help you manage situations where children are outside of the building but still on school grounds

- Some tools and structures that will help you manage situations where children are outside of the school and off school grounds

Although many of the aspects of classroom management we've already discussed still apply, situations outside of the classroom present unique issues that require planning on your part. Planning ahead of time and being familiar with situations outside of the classroom, creating boundaries where there aren't any, and teaching children how to handle adventures outside the classroom are all ways to manage these "trips."

Managing Adventures Inside the School Building

Technology

For material related to this concept, go to Clip 11.1 on the Web-based Student Study Site.

I was talking to a new teacher the other day about a project where students wrote letters to the editors of newspapers in all 50 states asking readers to send them something that represented the state. As I told her about the project, I could tell her mind had stopped when I mentioned "letters to the editor." I paused, and she asked, "The children wrote to newspapers?" And I said, "Yes, Molly, we didn't have Internet then." Yikes, am I that old? Don't answer that. The world of teaching and the boundaries of a classroom have been forever changed by the use of technology. Children can get on a computer now and go anywhere in the world they want—even back in history. As Molly wondered, why would students take the time to write to newspapers when they could contact people from different states much quicker via the Internet? In fact, Molly's class is working on a project where her students contact students from Costa Rica to learn the culture and language. Technology can indeed provide great opportunities for learning and motivate students (Li, 2007). Although technology may not require you to leave the classroom in all cases, it can definitely take students beyond the classroom walls without actually leaving the school building. Technology presents some unique management issues worthy of careful planning and thought. How will you manage the use of technology in your classroom?

First, familiarize yourself with technology and be open to the idea that technology is a great tool for learning. Even if you use technology frequently in your personal life, you will need to resee technology as a tool for the classroom. Many kinds of technology are great tools for learning. Digital cameras, video cameras, televisions, DVDs, computers, and SMART Boards are among the technologies that may be available at your school. As you begin to get a sense of the technologies available, take some time to find out how they work and how you could use them to help students learn. To familiarize yourself with technology in your school:

- Find out what is available to use with students.

- Locate and find out how to access the technology. This may mean signing up for a lab, checking out a camera, or ordering equipment from a central location in your district. Your media specialist will be a great resource for these kinds of questions.

- Play with the technology to figure out how it works. In some cases, this will take more than a bit of time. If you will need extensive instruction on how to use pieces of technology, you may want to sign up for a class or ask a technology coordinator in your district to help you get started.

- Find out what programs you have access to on computers.

- Read your school's technology policy to get an idea of the expectations already in place and how you can help children understand and follow them. Check out the other policies that will help you manage places outside the classroom as well. (See Table 11.1.)

- Ask special-education teachers if there are technologies available for children with special needs.

TABLE 11.1 School Policy Checklist

School districts have policies about many aspects of school life. Be sure to look into each of the policies below so you know what your school district expects.

Policy	Check	What I found out:
Computer use		
Field trips		
Students traveling in hallways alone		
Fighting		
Medical emergencies		
Playground incidents		

Familiarizing yourself with technology may also mean reseeing your curriculum. What are the possibilities for integrating technology into math, reading, writing, social studies, and science? Integrating technology into other subjects helps students learn not only the topic but also technology skills. For example, in my classroom, second graders who had written stories, edited them, and were ready to "publish" had the option of typing them on the computer and printing them or creating PowerPoint slide shows of their stories. The students learned writing skills and how to use two different programs on the computer. Although you don't have to incorporate technology into every lesson, finding key places to use it will benefit students. "A general rule of thumb suggests that a technology included in a lesson should make it possible for something that was done before to be done better or make it possible for something that couldn't have been done before to happen" (Duffy, McDonald, & Mizell, 2005, p. 63).

Along with finding places in the curriculum that will work well with technology, familiarize yourself with ways to incorporate technology into the pedagogy (or instructional strategies) that you use. What kinds of instructional strategies lend themselves to integration of technology? There are many; however, I suggest you start with cooperative workshops, activities that require daily routines and whole group projects. Using cooperative workshops is a great strategy for integrating technology, especially if you have technology in your classroom. Handing each group a camera to take pictures of growing/changing insects, making a computer program one of the stations in math, or writing other students via the Internet about books they are reading (Curtiss & Curtiss, 1995), for example, can be highly motivational and provide opportunities to learn content and technology simultaneously. Such activities as checking attendance on the computer, taking pictures of the weather, or writing can be done each day and provide a routine for children who haven't used much technology. Whole group projects also lend themselves to technology because you can set aside a larger amount of time for students to work with computers in a lab or process pictures or videotapes. For example, you could assign a technology-based project, like creating a slide show to share their understanding, to students learning about the Holocaust during a month-long study. Younger children could use technology to make a page for a class book.

You may wonder how anyone has time to learn about technology and how to integrate it into different subjects while continuing to teach and lead a classroom. Familiarizing yourself with technology doesn't mean you have to learn it and do it all at once. Instead, create technology goals for yourself and the classroom. Find key lessons that would work well with technology and make them happen. Ask other teachers how they use technology in their classrooms, and ask them for help. Familiarize yourself with your students' understanding and abilities, and create opportunities for them to use technology with which they are already familiar. Students can also help teach other students how to use technology if you create opportunities for them to do so.

Create boundaries where there aren't any. Technology is wonderful because it allows children to "go" places that they couldn't ordinarily. Yet allowing children to go in a million different directions also presents some management issues for teachers—that is, keeping track of many students' technology adventures can be difficult! The benefits outweigh the limitations, however, and working to create some boundaries will help you and your students use technology productively. Remember to make students a part of these conversations about

Students are often motivated to use technology. Just make sure they understand the boundaries that surround technology at school.

boundaries. Giving them a chance to talk about why boundaries are needed when using technology will help them understand and be willing to use technology safely.

Technology will require you to create physical boundaries together as a class. Just as we discussed in the materials section of Chapter 10, students need access to technological materials, yet there are some special concerns when working with them. Cameras, SMART Boards, calculators, and computers are expensive tools that you may need to monitor more closely than materials like paper, buttons, and math manipulatives. How can you make technology accessible to children yet safe?

- Talk with children about the need for special care with technology.

- Teach children how to use the technology.

- Store easily breakable items in places where children can see them but may have to ask for access.

- Be around children using technology rather than behind your desk.

- Make sure children understand that you would like them to tell you if something goes wrong with a piece of technology.

Computers pose an especially important need for planning and boundaries. In some schools, teachers and students have access to computer labs, other schools have small computer stations in common areas of each grade level, and still others have computers in all of the classrooms. Depending on the setup in your school, you can determine how to manage projects and lessons. If you have access to a lab, you may need to plan lessons that move between working on the computer and working without one. For example, students might spend time in the classroom designing a commercial for a genre of books they are reading and then have time in a computer lab to put the commercial together. If computers are out in a common area near your room, you might give children a pass to work there for a certain amount of time. Using an egg timer may help you remember when they need to return to the room. You and your students will need to come up with a list of expectations for working in this kind of setting because you will not be able to monitor them at all times. Parent volunteers and aides can assist if necessary. If computers are in the classroom, make sure students have equal opportunities to use them. My students and I solved this problem with a paperclip and list of names by each computer: Whoever had the paperclip by his or her name each day could use the computer or choose someone else to use it. Computers in the classroom also work nicely for stations. Headphones hooked up to computers will help alleviate any unwanted computer noise.

The Internet is full of possibilities for learning yet requires teachers to help manage it. Not all Web sites are created equally, and creating boundaries for students' use of them is important. Your school may already have limits in place via technology. For example, your school may have blocked certain Web sites. If not, there are several ways to create boundaries on your own. The key is coming up with ways to create boundaries that don't completely eliminate children's ability to be creative:

- Talk to the children about Internet safety. Help them understand the importance of not divulging their names, addresses, or even their school online.

- Ask the children if they know what kinds of things are inappropriate on the Internet. You don't have to go into excruciating details or even ask for a list. Just ask them if they know. For the most part, children will know if they get to an inappropriate Web site.

- Give them the following rule: "If you go on the Internet and get to an inappropriate place, turn the computer off immediately and tell the teacher. If you don't, you will need to stop using the Internet." As you can probably tell from this book, I don't normally create rules for children on my own except when it comes to safety. If children understand the seriousness of your rule, they will most likely follow it.

- Set up classroom computers so students can only access Web sites that you have placed in their "favorites" section. Ask for help from a district technology specialist if needed. Your school may have a filtering program already in place.

- Find child-friendly search engines. Yahoo! Kids is a great way for students to search the Web because it brings up appropriate sites for children. For example, if you type "ladybugs" into any other search engine, you may get some nasty results. Within Yahoo! Kids, however, the sites for ladybugs are actually about ladybugs! Other great search engines for children include Ask for Kids at http://www.askkids.com and KidsClick! at http://www.kids click.org.

- Ask children to work on the Internet in small groups, and designate one of the group members as Internet monitor.

Although boundaries are important in using technology, don't let the thought of students crossing those boundaries scare you out of using these valuable tools for learning. Plan ahead, be clear about expectations, and pay attention to what students are doing.

Learn how to use technology together. Many teachers scoff at the idea of infusing technology into learning, often because they don't know how to use technology themselves. Some people might argue that teachers must be trained to use technology or that they need more time to play with technology. I agree with that to some degree. If teachers wait to use technology until they are fully trained, however, they will never use it. Instead, teachers should familiarize themselves with technology, as I suggested before, and then learn with and from the students. When I started teaching, I didn't know how to use HyperStudio® (which has been replaced by PowerPoint). Instead of learning everything about the program, I played with it for an hour or so until I knew how to get students started, and then the children and I learned together. By the end of our first session, children were coming up to me excited that they had learned how to make a button or record their voices. They would show me, and I would show them. They weren't going to hurt the program or the computers by trying new things. If they locked the computer up, we turned it off and started again. If I had spent time learning every aspect of HyperStudio, I still wouldn't be using it with children. I still advise you to do some work ahead of time to know the programs; I am just not sure you have to know everything before you use technology in a lesson.

Ask for help when using technology. If you want to use specific programs or technology for a lesson, contact the technology director in your district, your media specialist, or another teacher. Such an expert can help you decide what technology would best meet your needs and get you started using it. For example, Rachel, a first-grade teacher, wanted to share student work with parents. She contacted her technology director, and he recommended that she develop a Web page and use podcasts to allow parents to hear their children. He helped her get started, and the project took off. Just the other day, she let me listen to her first graders sing a song on a podcast from her Web site. Although Rachel probably couldn't have accomplished that by herself, she was willing to ask for help, and now she will be a great resource for others. I bet Rachel will not add any more technology to her repertoire this year, but I am excited to hear about her goal for next year.

For material related to this concept, go to Clip 11.2 on the Web-based Student Study Site.

In the Hallways

Although the label "classroom management" suggests merely managing the classroom, many places within the school require a management plan and, if not managed well, will inevitably influence what happens inside the classroom. The classic example of this is school hallways.

Happenings in hallways can help prepare students for learning or create situations where students have trouble focusing in the classroom. Of course, you will want to facilitate the former. Although you may not be able to keep every issue from creeping into the classroom, planning hallway management may enable students to enter the classroom ready to learn. Hallway management may also improve your relationships with other staff and teachers.

Stand outside of the classroom as students come and go throughout the day. Depending on your assignment, you may only do this as children come to school and go home. This kind of management isn't very difficult and can go a long way in helping students feel welcome and in developing a good relationship with them no matter what happens during the day. My students could choose a hug or a high-five as they left the classroom. If students in your school move rooms between class periods, standing in the hallway as they come and go can help prevent fights and bullying, allow you to build relationships with children, and help you understand why a child may come into the classroom upset or angry. Being aware of issues in the hallway will help you prevent problems inside the classroom. For example, if you see a child get shoved in the hallway and he or she comes into the classroom upset, you can offer a tool, such as a Koosh ball or an ooze tube, to help him or her calm down. Sometimes management is about understanding why a child acts the way he or she does. Standing in the hallway can sometimes give you insight that you wouldn't get otherwise.

Have a plan for helping children walk in hallways as a whole group. Some teaching assignments, such as music, physical education, art, or computers, will require you to lead children down hallways to other classrooms. Noise and making sure all of the children go where they need to go can be problematic if you don't plan ahead. Be sure to create expectations for walking down the hall together with the students. For example, you might have a class meeting where children decide the best way to walk down the hall (in a single-file line, in pairs, etc.). At this kind of meeting, you can also ask them to talk about why it is important to walk quietly down the hall rather than run noisily. Your position in walking down the hallways is also important. Take some time to think about the benefits and limitations of walking at the front of the line, in the middle, or at the end.

Using brain exercises can be a great tool in helping children make it down the hallways of a school. Children who are walking down the hallway and thinking about moving their left thumb up and their right index finger out and then switching them as quickly as they can will have a harder time talking or bothering another student.

You can also have children follow a leader down the hall without talking. If your school allows it, place different-colored tape in the hallways so children can walk along the "balance beam" to their destination. Such activities will help children make it down the hall successfully, as well as engage their brains. What other brain exercises could children do as they travel outside of the classroom?

Have a system in place for children who need to go outside of the classroom by themselves. Sometimes individual students will need to go to the office, the bathroom, the nurse's office, or the guidance counselor, and you will not be able to go with them. Your school may have a policy regarding this kind of travel, so be sure to check that out before school starts. In addition, talk with students about expectations for leaving the classroom. You may

LETTER FROM A MASTER TEACHER 11.1

Helping Students Generalize Responsible Behaviors Outside the Classroom

It is common knowledge among teachers that encouraging students to behave responsibly within the classroom setting is a top priority. But what about those places and situations outside of the classroom where responsible behavior is equally important? More often than not, students see the playground, a field trip, or the computer lab as an opportunity to "forget" about behaving responsibly. When students are away from their structured and predictable classroom setting where the expectations have been discussed and practiced every day, it is imperative that they recognize the necessity in behaving responsibly elsewhere. So how can we help students generalize their responsible behaviors across multiple educational settings?

Remember to prepare children well in advance for the change in venue. If you introduce it before it actually happens, this will give the students time to process and discuss the desired responsible behaviors with peers, teachers, and family.

Help students visualize the new setting by showing pictures and maps. Familiarizing students with the location removes anxiety about the unknown and alleviates undesirable behaviors.

Engage in classroom discussions about the expectations that will apply to the new educational setting and role-play the responsible behaviors that will be used to follow those rules. Remember to clarify *why* these rules are important to follow in this particular situation.

Link irresponsible choices to natural consequences. Students understand that their failure to behave responsibly influences how they view themselves and their relationships with others. For instance, a student who chooses to go down the slide head first will get hurt because the act will cause him or her to hit his or her head on the ground and miss recess time as he or she recovers from the injury and explains his or her choice to the teacher, and peers may notice his or her choice and prefer to play with those who are behaving responsibly. The student will then come to the conclusion that following the slide rule will gain him or her extra time for recess activities and more opportunities to spend time with peers.

Offering learning opportunities in alternative educational settings supports best-practice teaching. Students who behave responsibly outside of the classroom setting do so because they have engaged in authentic and purposeful discussions regarding the expectations prior to these new experiences. Consequently, their learning will be rich, engaging, and meaningful.

—Carla Farley
Kindergarten Teacher

Grace and Anna demonstrate the finger brain exercise.

want to create procedures for traveling in the hallways as a class. For example, you might develop a sign-out sheet or passes for hallway use. Be careful to emphasize that these kinds of procedures are put in place for safety reasons rather than to belittle students. Today, even teachers and visitors must have ID badges when in schools for safety's sake. Try not to hinder children's autonomy by limiting their mobility. If a child needs to go to the guidance counselor, let him or her go. If it becomes a problem, work with that child individually to come up with a solution rather than limit everyone.

Plan for problems that occur in the hallways. Hopefully, there will not be many fights or problems in the hallways where you teach, but it is always good to plan ahead. Once again, I encourage you to ask your administrator for the policy regarding fighting both verbally and physically in school, as well as regarding medical emergencies. For example, if students get into a fight outside of the classroom, what should you do? Should you call for help? Should you intervene? In addition, be sure to talk to teachers around you about their plans for helping students in need in the hallways. You might discuss a designated signal or sound that indicates a teacher needs help. You might create a plan for handling a medical emergency if your school does not have one already in place, as well as for how to monitor the other children in the classrooms. This kind of planning will help you and the other teachers work together to handle problems that may occur.

In and Out of the Bathrooms

Wait a minute! Wasn't this supposed to be the vacation chapter? Do we have to go on a mini faux vacation to the bathroom? Ewwww! You might be surprised at how many management issues originate in the bathrooms, or maybe you wouldn't. In any case, we have to go there. Take some time to think about a plan for managing bathroom breaks, as well as individuals who need to go to the restroom. This small bit of planning will prevent problems and help children feel comfortable in the classroom.

For material related to this concept, go to Clip 11.3 on the Web-based Student Study Site.

As you have probably experienced, teachers provide bathroom breaks in many different ways. Each has benefits and limitations and is based on things like schedules, location of the restroom, and student needs. Some teachers designate times for the whole class to take a bathroom break. Everyone lines up, goes out of the classroom to the bathroom, and takes turns while the others wait. In addition to bathroom use, children are usually permitted to get a drink. This kind of break is usually scheduled around a trip, like on the way back from music class or on the way in from recess. Benefits include the teacher's ability to monitor the break and limited interruptions during class; however, this kind of break requires monitoring students who are waiting for others to use the restroom, which can be a limitation. If the bathroom is a good distance from the classroom or if the students are younger, this may be a good plan with some modifications for waiting in line.

Some teachers allow students to use the restroom when they need to use it as long as it won't interrupt someone else's presentation. In my son's preschool class, for example, the teacher has created a hand signal that the children use when they need to use the restroom, and she nods at them if it is an appropriate time to go. This helps students who may worry that they won't be able to wait to use the restroom until a designated time and doesn't require lining up or waiting for each child. The bathroom at my son's school, however, is built within the classroom. You will need to consider location of the classroom and maturity level of students before you choose this plan. In addition, hand signals, sign-out sheets, and bathroom passes require some level of teaching. If you choose this way to manage bathroom breaks, be sure to discuss your expectations or write a story to help children understand what to do. Another limitation with this kind of plan is that you won't be able to monitor problems like bullying if you stay in the classroom. Even if you only send one child to the restroom at a time, children from other classrooms may be there at the same time. Be sure to consider this aspect of bathroom breaks when devising your plan.

Indeed, a combination of these two or something completely different may work well for you and your students. As with all of the management plans you will make, please consider students' autonomy, belonging, and competency as you think about bathroom breaks. Making a child wait to go to the restroom can be devastating if he or she has an accident in front of his or her peers. Paying attention to what children say and how they act after bathroom breaks is also vital. If a student refuses to go into the restroom or if a parent mentions a child not wanting to go to the restroom at school, don't ignore it. Ask the student what is happening, give a class survey on bathroom breaks, or ask the counselor for help if needed. Finally, if there is a problem in the restroom, whether it is bullying, making messes, or flushing dice down the toilet (which happened to me), acting quickly is important. Create another plan or work with individual students to solve rather than ignore the problem.

In the Cafeteria

In most schools, teachers do not have lunch-room duty because they are eating lunch as well. At some schools, however, teachers do monitor the cafeteria. Although procedures will already be in place at your school, making suggestions or implementing new ideas may be valuable if you do have cafeteria duty. You never know; the school might catch on. In addition, if you don't have cafeteria duty, I encourage you to eat in the cafeteria sometimes. The children will think it is fabulous, and you will get some insight into cafeteria happenings.

Most children really like to go to lunch, so motivation isn't a problem; however, eating may be. The biggest management issues in the cafeteria are usually too much noise and not eating in the allotted time. Empathizing with students is easy in both cases. After all, teachers like to chat with friends while they eat and can be distracted from their eating duties, too, right? It is easy to have an hour for lunch but not finish eating when you are with friends. Unfortunately, children in school don't have an hour for lunch and need to eat so they have energy for the afternoon—a source of frustration for anyone managing the cafeteria. Many times, this leads to teachers making children sit away from their friends, yelling at them, or making them eat silently. There are things you can do to help children eat and make lunchtime pleasurable, however. Helping children use their lunchtime for eating and quiet conversation may require you to think outside the box. Here are some suggestions to keep the noise level to a dull roar and help children eat:

- Educate children about the importance of eating and speaking in an inside voice. Practice the difference while in the cafeteria.

- Play music in the cafeteria.

- Play trivia games using a microphone, or start a "gossip" statement at one end of the room and see what it has turned into by the time it reaches the other end.

- Ask children who have finished eating to pick up others' trays or wash tables.

- Make a large "noise monitor" or bring in an actual decibel meter so the children can see the actual noise level.

- After a table or group is finished eating, let the students sing karaoke or tell a joke to the whole group.

All of these suggestions will depend on the situation at your school. You don't have to do these things every day, but having fun with cafeteria duty will make it easier for you and the children. If children struggle with individual issues, work with them individually. Remember to treat children how you would want to be treated at lunchtime.

Assemblies

I feel compelled to put a part in this book about assemblies, even if it is only a paragraph or two, because I remember being blindsided by my first assembly. I actually knew there was an assembly that day. The circus bears came early, though, and I needed to get my class to the gymnasium in a hurry without much teaching ahead of time. Assemblies are often scheduled at inconvenient times of day, and students are often very excited about them. Some assemblies keep students' attention, and others are so slow or hard to hear that it is difficult to keep children focused. That's why having time before an assembly to talk about expectations and create specific places for children to sit is so important.

Before an assembly, talk with students about being an audience even when they might not enjoy the performance:

- Ask them how an audience looks and sounds.

- Ask them what they like an audience to do when they perform. Ask them the difference between a game and an assembly and how the audience acts in both cases.

- Work with children to think about who they might sit next to in order to be a good audience member.

- After the assembly, debrief what happened. Ask the students how they liked the assembly and how polite they were as an audience.

Individual students may need special accommodations during assemblies. This may be as easy as having these students sit near you or bringing them a small ball to squeeze during the performance. It may require you to ask a special educator or teacher's aide to come to the assembly with you. Make a plan with another teacher who will be at the assembly to monitor your students if you need to leave, and vice versa. Whatever accommodations you make, I encourage you to sit with your students so you have access to any children who need help. Sitting with my students on the hard gymnasium floor watching bears dance for an hour taught me that sitting still for that long is not easy!

Managing Adventures Outside the School Building

The Playground

Managing a playground is unlike any other management situation you will encounter. There are usually a large number of children on the playground with no routine or boundaries to help teachers. Don't get me wrong; recesses are highly valuable for children in school, providing students time to move freely, rest their minds, and socialize and build relationships with friends. Like many other aspects of school life, however, teachers often send children to the playground, wait for problems to occur, and then punish students for causing problems. Instead, let's examine possible playground issues and come up with ways to help children solve them before they happen. This doesn't mean creating routines and boundaries so rigid that they keep children from benefiting from this free time. It means providing opportunities for children to engage in fun, loosely structured activities; creating processes that will help

Although you may not think you need to consider the playground when planning for classroom management, issues on the playground very much affect life in the classroom.

children work through problems that occur; and being aware of what happens on the playground whether you are there or not.

Before we begin, take a minute to think about recess and what children might learn during this time. Even though recess provides a break for children from academic learning, it is still a learning time. What do children learn about themselves, their peers, and their ability to solve problems during recess? Helping children enjoy recess will not only make managing students on the playground easier but also help them come in from the playground ready to learn.

The first aspect of playground management doesn't occur on the playground itself. It may occur before the school year even begins as you work with other staff members to determine what games are available for children to play outside. It may occur inside the classroom during class meetings or with small groups of children who struggle on the playground. "It is not enough to place students together without also providing them with enjoyable and relevant activities to do. Boring playgrounds can create conflicts within peer groups" (Doll,

Zucker, & Brehm, 2004, p. 21). In other words, if your school's playground has only one structure to play on, you will notice children beginning to create activities that aren't so fun. For example, some children may throw rocks or chase and push each other. Others may just wander the playground by themselves. If, on the other hand, you meet with the children to determine what games are available for them to play on the playground or even to teach them some games as a class each week, they will have some ideas of fun things to do. Painting four-square boxes, ordering jump ropes, or providing sidewalk chalk doesn't cost very much and can make a world of difference. Be sure to check with your administrator before doing so, however. The physical education teacher may also have great ideas for games children can play.

Sometimes individual children will struggle on the playground. They may bully or be bullied, have trouble joining a game, or play so rough that others get hurt. Students who struggle on the playground may not have the social skills needed to engage in free activities with other children, or they may be struggling with an issue outside of school. As Doll, Zucker, and Brehm (2004) advise, "Incidental activities are as effective or more effective in fostering friendships as are activities with the explicit purpose of teaching social skills" (p. 21). In other words, working to create opportunities for children to engage in fun activities is more effective than trying to teach them canned social skills. Doll, in a lecture to graduate students, told a story about a group of children she tried to teach how to join games on the playground. Teachers had identified these children as alone on the playground, and Doll worked hard to teach them the language she thought they needed to engage with other students. Then, one day, it snowed, and the children began building a big snowman. Doll watched as all of the children packed snow onto the snowman; determined that the right activity makes it much easier for them to learn social skills; and thus began looking for activities that would help foster friendships rather than social skills. This is an important story for all teachers who teach on the playground. What kinds of activities provide opportunities for every child with every level of skill to participate?

The next aspect of managing a playground doesn't occur on the playground either. It occurs in the classroom during class meetings and data collection opportunities. Unless you know the problems on the playground, rectifying them will be difficult. If you are not on the playground after lunch but notice that children are upset when they come inside, come up with a survey that might help you determine why children are struggling and then help them come up with solutions. Many times, issues on the playground are about children not being able to determine the rules to games, being left out of games, and determining teams for games. To help children who want to play soccer, for example, determine playground rules for soccer that they can agree upon. You may think this will take away some class time for academic learning, but I bet trying to sort out why children are mad and why someone is in the office for fighting would take a lot more time than preventing problems with student-made solutions.

In addition to creating opportunities for engaged play, you will likely need to come up with a plan for problems that occur when you are actually outside on the playground. Although you can avoid many issues with fun activities, class meetings, and class surveys, isolated incidents may occur every now and then. The first part of your plan needs to include being aware of happenings on the playground. Thinking of playground duty as a time for you to vegetate is easy; however, coming up with a way to stay "awake" on the playground will help prevent fights from escalating and injuries from happening. Wandering around the playground rather than standing in one place is a great way to be visible and will help you hear and see happenings.

The second part of your plan needs to be about helping children who need to get away from a situation on the playground. For example, if a child is teasing another child or is climbing on the monkey bars in an unsafe way, you will need to have a plan for that child. Refer to Chapter 8 for some questions and choices. In addition, make a plan for how you will remove the child from the situation. Will he or she need to go to the office? Will he or she need to stay outside but play a different game? Will he or she need to stand by you for the rest of the recess? Of course, each situation is different, but thinking about possibilities will be helpful.

Finally, some children on the playground will most certainly need to go inside before the rest of the class. Children may need to use the restroom, take medicine, treat an injury, or get a coat. Part of your playground management plan should include a conversation with your administrator about how to handle this kind of issue. Should you send the child in by him- or herself or with a buddy? Should you take the whole class back inside the building? Is there a signal that would inform the office you need assistance? Whatever the answer, be sure to know it before you take a group of students outside. For children's safety, leaving them outside alone without an adult is not an acceptable plan.

Outside Lessons

It doesn't matter if it is freezing cold, rainy, or very hot: Children love to go outside! The outdoors has a tremendous amount of potential for learning even if you just take the children to the playground area of the school. You may envision taking children outside and having them read or having a classroom circle outside as a change of pace or motivator. Although those are excellent reasons to take children outside to learn, the great outdoors is also full of learning opportunities that go beyond motivation.

Jesse Keifer

Learning outside can motivate both teachers and students.

Plan outside lessons for all subjects. Science is the most obvious subject for learning outside. Children in my room went outside, for example, to count the number of insects in a Hula-Hoop, check for erosion, find evidence of different animals on the playground, collect rocks, play camouflage games, and check out how our bodies keep us warm in the cold if we are standing still. That last one about temperature was so funny! I had the children go out in the cold Nebraska winter without their coats for one minute. First, I asked them to move around, and the second time we went outside, I asked them to stand still. They thought it was hilarious that I took them out without their coats, and I doubt they will ever forget their goose bumps!

Math and writing are also great outside subjects. In math, you can measure the playground and make a scale model of it; find shapes; play on sidewalk chalk number lines for multiplication, addition, and subtraction; count about anything outside; compare sizes; or find patterns. For writing, you can look for topics and, weather permitting, even write outside. I am certain you can come up with better and more ideas. Think "outside" the classroom!

If you are going to take the students outside for a lesson, you will need to think about management in a unique way. Taking students outside creates issues that you may not have to worry about inside. For example, inside there are probably four walls and not many places for students to be "lost." Taking children outside, however, means no walls and not many physical boundaries. Inside, there are clocks and visual reminders of when time is running out. Outside, there aren't these kinds of cues, and you may need to rely on another kind of signal. Inside, children have easy access to supplies, bathrooms, and so on, that may be needed outside as well. Finally, inside you can count on a regulated temperature, and outside weather may influence student learning and behavior.

To ensure children's safety and that learning actually takes place during a lesson outside, you will need to do an "outside learning" lesson before your planned adventure. If I were you, I would do this every time rather than just once at the beginning of the year. Within the "outside learning" lesson, while you are still inside the classroom, you might:

- Tell children the directions for the lesson. "You will be going outside to collect different sizes of rocks. Try to find each size that we studied, including sand, gravel, pebbles, and boulders."

- Talk to the children about the boundaries of the activity. "Where might the boundaries be for this activity?" Then clarify this expectation in simple, easy-to-remember terms. "Stay in the back of the schoolyard where you can still see the teacher. Do not go in the street."

- Talk to the children about materials. "What materials do you think you will need?" Then clarify the ideas with the children. "Take only a ruler and a paper sack with you."

- Talk to the children about how they will know it is time to finish and come in. "When you hear the whistle, time is up, and you need to meet me by the swings."

- Talk to the children about safety. "Be sure to stay with your group at all times. Do not go where you cannot see the teacher."

- Talk to the children about what will happen if the expectations aren't followed. "Going outside is a very exciting thing. If you can't follow these guidelines, the class will need to stay inside for lessons."

Having this kind of a conversation won't take long and will make children aware of expectations each time, and you will have opportunities to answer questions or address concerns children may have while you're inside.

In addition to making expectations clear for children, you will want to let others know you are going outside. Tell your administrator when you are taking the children outside for a learning experience, and ask a parent volunteer or two to come with you if possible. If you are just going to be outside on school grounds, you may not need permission. If you are walking around the neighborhood or going to a nearby pond (as I had access to when I taught), however, be sure to ask if you need to get parent permission. If you have a cell phone,

Students are often willing to help each other when going outside for a special project.

take one outside with you just in case something happens or the school needs to call you back to the building.

Plan for children with special needs when taking your class outside for a learning experience. If a child won't be able to engage in an outside activity due to allergies or a physical disability, don't take the other children outside either. *No activity is valuable enough to leave a child out.* If a child can engage in the activity but will need accommodations, be sure to plan for those well in advance. Ask a special educator to attend the outside activity, put together groups of students who will be able to help each other, or rearrange the activity so all can participate. For example, if you ask students to collect rocks, assign jobs like measurer or carrier. That way, if a child is in a wheelchair, he or she can have a job or role too. You could also assign students to different areas of the playground and that group in particular to an area with wheelchair access. If a child has behavior concerns, assign him or her to a group that will be helpful, and make one of the roles in each group checking in with the teacher every so often. You can make many accommodations for each individual child. Plan ahead and be creative. How could you change the rock-collecting activity for a child who is blind, hearing impaired, diagnosed with ADHD, or autistic?

Sending Students Home

Organizing going-home time can be chaotic if not managed well, especially at the beginning of the school year. Be sure to create a routine for most days of school so children will know what to do and feel more secure. One aspect of an end-of-the-day routine may be a process for gathering coats, backpacks, and materials that need to go home. For example, you might have all of the girls get their backpacks and sit them on their chairs, and then have the boys repeat the activity. You might assign a mailbox to each child so, as they walk out the door, you can remind your students to pick up their mail and put it in their backpacks. Whatever routine you devise, make it as calm and repetitive as possible because children will be anxious to get out of school and a "leaving school" routine will alleviate many problems. Other end-of-the-day routines include singing a goodbye song or a closing circle where everyone tells a good thing about his or her day.

If you work with young students or have concerns about getting children home safely, plan a management strategy for getting students on the right bus or van, to their cars, walking or biking home, or staying at school for aftercare. Your plan might include having students line up in separate lines depending on how they will get home. For the first couple days of school, you might also ask each student as he or she leaves how he or she is getting home or to another kind of care. If the student doesn't know, make sure you keep him or her with you until you figure out for sure where he or she should go. If you work with older or younger students, it is a good idea to follow them outside and monitor happenings as they disperse throughout the school grounds. Being outside for a few moments after school will help you see any possible issues between students, enable you to chat with parents, and help you keep track of students leaving school grounds.

LETTER FROM A MASTER TEACHER 11.2

Providing Expectations Inside and Outside of the Classroom

Congratulations and welcome to a career that is both challenging and rewarding at the same time. The one great thing about teaching is that no two days are alike! For instance, you may have the best lesson plan and your whole day mapped out perfectly, but in the middle of your lesson two of your students are checking out. One student has a dentist appointment, the other just came back from the nurse, and both have requested make-up work. To please everyone, you try to get your students working independently as quickly as possible, only to find out that you have another parent in the doorway wanting to discuss an upcoming field trip. Yes, you will have days like this. But don't let that discourage you because, after finally finishing your lesson, little Susie, who has been having trouble understanding the concept, has an "aha" moment. She jumps out of her seat, gives you the biggest hug, and says, "Thank you for teaching me!"

I would like to give you just a few suggestions to try in your classroom to help with classroom management both in- and outside of the classroom. First of all, this chapter talked a lot about expectations, and you must set high expectations for all your students, both academically and socially. It is important to set those expectations so all members of your class know exactly what they are. Some ways to do this include having a classroom meeting to discuss them and writing them down so they are not forgotten. You may even have to refer to them so they are remembered. In my experience, the more the students take part in making the expectations, the more they abide by them.

You may also want to try typing procedures the students come up with for behavior in the halls, in the lunchroom, in the bathroom, and on field trips and give each of your students a copy or hang one in the room. If you have one or a couple of students who do not follow a certain procedure, have them identify what part of the procedure they did not follow.

One more thing to think about has to do with the scenario above, and that is to find an easy yet efficient way to have make-up work ready for students who miss school or who check out early. If parents know that their child is checking out early for an appointment, you may want to put in your handbook to have them write a letter so you are aware of this ahead of time. This will save you from scrambling around trying to get make-up work together and managing the rest of your students at the same time.

Good luck and best wishes! You have entered into the most important occupation ever.

—Deann Hunt
Special-Education Teacher

Managing Adventures Off School Grounds

Field Trips

Field trips are a great way to create meaningful experiences for children. Attending a play, going to a nature center or zoo, visiting a planetarium, or listening to an orchestra all have a great impact on students, yet many of the students you work with won't have the opportunity to do so except through school. If your school district provides funds for field trips, take advantage of this resource. Whether you take children in the beginning, middle, or end of a unit of study, I suggest you plan field trips that are connected in some way to what you are studying. While just going on field trips is good, they can be much more meaningful if the children can connect them to something. For example, if you go to the planetarium but haven't studied and don't plan on studying anything related to space, students won't make many connections. If you live in a sparsely populated area and don't have access to field trips like those mentioned above, you can take students to businesses around town, such as the post office or bank, and get the "behind the scenes" look at those important parts of a community.

Just as you did when planning outside lessons, you will need to plan for management on a field trip. I was in New York City on the subway one time and saw a teacher and her 20-some students get on the subway for a field trip. To me, that was the epitome of a well-planned field trip! The students were together, were all very calm, and seemed intent on what they needed to do. Here are some things to think about when planning a field trip:

- Plan for the transportation you will need. Whether you are going by subway, bus, or any other mode of transportation, you will need to help children understand the expectations for getting to the destination. You might need to discuss voice level, staying in their seats, and procedures for emergencies. If the ride will be long, give students things to do on the way, such as tic-tac-toe sheets or math puzzles to do with a partner. Another thing that may help keep noise down on the bus is music. When we drove to the planetarium on the bus, for example, my second graders listened to "space" music from the movie *Space Jam*.

- Plan for the actual event. Different field trips will require different plans. If you are going to a zoo, to a museum, or somewhere the children will move around, create an accountability tool. I am not necessarily in favor of sheets on which children have to answer certain questions because that can make a trip more about collecting right answers than taking in the sights. Having children fill out a sheet with something they saw or learned in specific museum rooms or zoo exhibits, however, makes students accountable while still providing them a chance to see what interests them. If you are going to a play or an orchestra performance, children will be sitting for a long time. You will not need to plan for accountability in this case, but you may need to discuss appropriate etiquette in a theater.

- Plan for adults to come on the trip. It is a good idea to invite several parents to join you on field trips. If not many parents are able to attend functions during the day, ask your principal, aide, guidance counselor, and so on.

- Plan for permission slips. To go on field trips, you will need to have parent permission. Create a letter that tells parents specifically what you will do and how you will get there and that invites them to participate. Have a plan for those students who are unable to attend the field trip.

Field trips can be wonderfully engaging experiences for children. They can help children connect with what they already know, help them become motivated for a new topic, and provide excellent opportunities for experiences they may never have otherwise. Although things may happen that are out of your control, planning field trips carefully will help them go smoothly. What unplanned events might happen on a field trip? What would you do if a child got sick on a trip? What would you do if a child required medicine during school hours? What would you do if the trip went long and you didn't get children back to school before the ending bell?

So ... What?

It is important to think about management plans that include times when children are outside as well as inside of the classroom. Although the first nine chapters gave you some valuable tools and structures to manage situations of all kinds, remember that experiences outside of the classroom often require some unique strategies. Whether you are using technology or sending children to the restroom, to the cafeteria, to the playground, or on a field trip, think about a plan that will help you be familiar with places outside of the classroom, create boundaries where there aren't any, and teach children how to handle such situations. Each place where children have adventures outside of the classroom may not seem like a vacation to you but will be much easier to manage if you shut your eyes and venture out with your students.

Get Ready For ...

The final chapter! An important one, it's all about you and making classroom management your own. I certainly hope you will take the suggestions, ideas, and structures from the first 11 chapters and use, use, use them. I also know, however, that if teaching were as easy as following a recipe, there would be a lot more great teachers in the world. Chapter 12 is designed to help you create your own philosophy of classroom management by stirring what you believe about learning, children, and yourself into a plan that will fit only you.

Activities to Try

- Look through curriculum materials for one subject that you teach or that you borrow from another teacher to find places where you could incorporate technology, outside lessons, or field trips.

- Plan an outdoor lesson using the lesson plan from Chapter 4.

- Write a letter to parents describing the technology policy you will use.

- **Make a collection.** Make a collection of possible field trips available in your area.

- **Conduct action research.** Spend a few hours on a playground (with permission), and keep track of the issues that teachers deal with for each grade level.

Student Study Site

The companion Web site for *Elementary Classroom Management* can be found at www.sagepub.com/kwilliamsstudy.

Visit the Web-based student study site to enhance your understanding of the chapter content. The study materials include video clips, practice tests, flashcards, suggested readings, and Web resources.

CHAPTER **12**

Making the
Classroom Your Own

A Beginning

I didn't know my grandmother very well because she died when I was just 6 years old. I do remember that she sang to me while she pushed me on the swings, she always had a dish of candy out when I came over, and she made unbelievably great pie crust. I have her recipe for pie crust that she gave to my mother and my mother gave to me. Although the recipe gives the exact amounts of flour and butter and has the correct temperature setting, it is incomplete. There are processes that my grandmother used when making the crust that aren't written in the recipe. For example, according to my mother, at one point the crust is supposed to feel like peas. Does that mean the crust should be broken up into small balls? Does it mean it should feel smooth? Hopefully, it doesn't mean it should be green! Even though the recipe is seemingly incomplete, my mother still makes excellent pie crust. Why? It is excellent because she has taken the key ingredients that my grandmother gave her and put them together in a way that works for her. She doesn't always make great pie crust. In fact, my mother tells all kinds of funny stories about hitting the pie crust with her rolling pin and throwing it up against the wall. My mom needed to tweak, change, and reread the recipe. She needed to make the recipe her own. If I want to make good pie crust, I will need to use the ingredients and ideas passed down to me and make them my own. And, knowing how well I bake, the most important ingredient might be a lot of reflection and redoing!

In a sense, the ideas in this book can be thought of as a recipe for classroom management. It is being "handed down" to you from great current and past researchers and the literature they created about classroom management, as well as from master teachers' experience and stories. Just like my grandmother's pie crust recipe, however, this classroom management "recipe" isn't meant to be precise. Instead, it is meant to give you a way into your own beliefs about classroom management so you can discover what works well for you and for the students you teach. Although there are such key ingredients as autonomy, belonging, competency, motivation, resources, reflection tools, and structures to try, you will need to think and reflect on the experience that it takes to create a successful classroom. You will need to try things more than once and work to make them better each time based on your experience. You will need to listen to the different children in the classroom each year, with all of their different needs, and make adjustments. You will need to come up with your own philosophy of classroom management that is flexible yet always goes back to your core beliefs about how children learn academically and socially. In a sense, this last chapter is really a beginning. It is the beginning of you taking all of the ideas in this book and making them your own.

As with any kind of learning, making a pie crust requires autonomy, belonging, and competency. One needs autonomy to make decisions based on the current situation. What is the oven like? How about the humidity? One needs belonging to ask for help and share successes and failures. In the beginning, I will need support from other pie crust makers so I don't become too frustrated. Finally, I will need competency to put in the necessary ingredients, taste the pie, and assess any needs for next time. Learning classroom management requires autonomy, belonging, and competency as well. We have talked a lot about creating a classroom environment that helps children gain autonomy, belonging, and competency, but you will need some too. I hope this chapter will help you see yourself as a learner of classroom management who needs to experience and reflect, who needs to celebrate and perhaps to cry, and who needs autonomy, belonging, and competency like every other learner you will encounter.

By the end of this chapter, I hope you understand and begin to have:

- Classroom management autonomy

- Classroom management belonging

- Classroom management competency

Making a pie crust would certainly be easier if you could just follow the directions and everything would come out beautifully. Now that I think about it, you could—with a premade pie crust. Classroom management would certainly be easier if I could just tell you how to do it. In this world, however, we don't need premade teachers. We need caring, competent, reflective, and flexible teacher-learners who make their own decisions based on what they understand about learning and what individual students need.

LETTER FROM A MASTER TEACHER 12.1

Interview Questions About Classroom Management

Forgive me, but I must start this letter with a question. How important is it to be knowledgeable about classroom management strategies? To help answer this question, I will attempt to paint a picture of an experience many of you have had or will have in the near future.

Let me set the stage: You are being interviewed for a teaching position. This is your dream job, and you have one chance to impress. The request comes: "Please tell me about the classroom management strategies you incorporate in your classroom and which methods you find most beneficial."

When you hear this, you begin filtering your memory for what you've read, been told, and been taught. This is the moment of truth where all those years of schooling in management strategies will pay off. But what answer to give? So many flood your brain. Does the interviewer want to hear rewards, punishments, think-time, time-out, love and logic, or something else? You begin to question yourself. Will all of them work in this instance? Is there one that will leave a better impression? Is there something she wants to hear? Remember, your answer could be the difference between being hired and a simple "Thank you for your time."

The real answer is somewhere in between, not a fix-all or universal system but a system in which great teachers see, hear, listen to, and understand the situation. What are my students telling me? What do they need? What type of management does this situation warrant? The real answer varies like the children in your room. Each of them needs something unique, something special, something designed just for him or her. Is this easier than implementing a policy that has been handed down by administration? No, but the benefits of a management plan created by thoughtful teachers who know their students will lead to a body of students who not only believe their teachers care for them but also strive to be self-reliant within their classroom community.

Having recently become a father, I can tell you that people are all too quick to offer you advice on how to raise your child. Odds are that the advice they give has worked for each and every one of those who have offered, but that doesn't mean it will work for me. Fatherhood is a journey much like teaching: One size doesn't fit all.

So how will you respond to that interview request?

—Josh Snyder
High-Ability Learner Coordinator

Classroom Management Autonomy

Costa wrote, "Meaning making is not a spectator sport. It is an engagement of the mind that transforms the mind" (York-Barr, Sommers, Ghere, & Montie, 2006, p. xv). I might suggest that classroom management making isn't a spectator sport either. You must do the thinking. You must do the creating. It must be yours. Making a classroom management plan your own doesn't necessarily mean you must come up with every process and structure on your own, which would make this book and the ideas here meaningless. On the contrary, I hope you use all of the processes in this book and tell others to use them as well. Making a classroom management plan your own *does* mean having some autonomy to take others' structures, tools, and ideas and mold them into your own plan. Below are a few areas of classroom management that require autonomous thinking. After you read them, reflect on the previous chapters of this book, as well as on your previous experiences and beliefs. Take some time to write about each of the areas, realizing that your ideas may change with time and experience.

What Are Your Core Beliefs About Classroom Management?

Over the years, I have observed teacher after teacher get really excited about a new strategy or tool and then put it back on the shelf when it does not meet expectations. They do not reflect on why it isn't working or try to change it a bit so it might work. Instead, they go on to the next strategy, never really stopping to figure out what they believe about classroom management. The tools and structures you choose must align with what you believe about how children learn academically and socially. So this piece of autonomy is about determining your core beliefs regarding classroom management.

My core beliefs about classroom management are easy to find in this book. I am certain, if you go back through it, you will find them. For example, one of my core beliefs is that classrooms need to be democratic in nature. Since that is a core belief of mine, the structures and tools I choose to use all align with democracy. Cooperative workshops, class meetings, classroom arrangement, and so on, are all tools that support this core belief, and even when they don't work just right, I am able to reflect and tweak them rather than put them on the shelf. Because I have this core belief, I can keep aiming for it even if I don't hit the bull's-eye every time. Has this core belief been tested? Absolutely. One time, for example, 50 of my graduate students were to meet one weekend when it snowed heavily, and a decision needed to be made about whether or not to cancel class. In keeping with my democracy belief, I asked them to decide what to do. It was awful. E-mails were going back and forth, people were unhappy, and we didn't make a decision until too late for many people. Do I still believe in democratic classrooms? Yes. Will I do that differently next time? Yes. My core belief hasn't changed. I just know that I will need to handle the structure of it differently than I did before. I will still aim for democracy but perhaps from a different angle or with different tools.

You have hopefully already begun to think about your own core beliefs regarding classroom management. If you haven't already, however, take some time to write a few "I believe" statements now (see Table 12.1). Your beliefs may not be the same as mine, and that is OK. The good news is you can still use the tools and structures in this book. You will just need to alter them so they align with your core beliefs, just as one might tweak a recipe to meet his or her own tastes and needs. For example, let's say one of your core beliefs is that teachers need to model all aspects of learning for students. If this is the case, you can add modeling pieces into the structures and tools within this book. Cooperative workshop planning may include a time when you show children how to do the activity. Classroom meetings can be modeled by the teacher. Movement in the classroom can be done so the children follow the teacher's lead. Remember that your core beliefs may change as time goes on and as you learn more and experience more. They aren't set in stone.

How will thinking about core beliefs help you have classroom management autonomy? I hope, if you have these statements, understand what they mean to you, and believe in them, you will be able to make decisions about what tools and structures you use in the classroom, as well as tailor other tools and structures to truly fit you and your students.

I recently had a conversation with a teacher named Beth about a writing program she was trying for the first time. She told me that she was putting the new writing program away for a while until later in the school year. When I asked her why she had chosen that path, Beth told me that the program jumped right into writing and that her children needed some time to draw pictures and feel comfortable at school first. I don't know this, but I suspect one of Beth's core beliefs is that her kindergarteners need to feel successful. She ended up using the program later but had changed it a bit so it would work for the students in her room and fit with her beliefs. Beth has classroom management autonomy. She listens to her core beliefs, as well as her students' needs, and molds the classroom management tools she uses to meet those needs.

Having a set of core beliefs, rather than following structures that may or may not work, will create opportunities for positive classroom management and successful students.

TABLE 12.1 What Are My Core Beliefs?

Take some time to think about your current core beliefs.

My Core Beliefs . . . So Far
1.
2.
3.
4.
5.
6.

What Is "Out of Bounds"?

Along the same lines but in a different direction, classroom management autonomy requires you to know what is absolutely "out of bounds" in the classroom both for you and for students. It's like knowing that you would never put pickles in a pie crust. You might try whole wheat flour or even use Crisco® instead of butter, but you would never, ever put pickles in it. Well, *you* might, but that, to me, is out of bounds! It is the same with classroom management. You need to have a sense of where your boundaries exist. If you don't know your boundaries, you may end up doing things to children and letting children do things that aren't acceptable during hard times.

Recognizing my boundaries within this book may be harder than recognizing my core beliefs. You may have some sense of my boundaries, but for the most part, I have tried to give you the "good" ingredients rather than the stuff I don't suggest. Perhaps some of the stories have suggested a big boundary for me is shaming learners. That is a line I work extremely hard not to cross. I also work hard not to use physical rewards, such as tokens or candy. These boundaries are mine because of what I have experienced and read. They might not be your boundaries, but do take some time to think about what your boundaries are. Make a list for yourself, and think about why you have these boundaries (see Table 12.2).

As you create these management boundaries, know that they might change and that you may cross them in some moments of teaching. If you have reflected on them and know what they are, however, you will also know when you have crossed them. This will allow you to step back and reevaluate what needs to change. Knowing your boundaries and why they exist is also important when working with others. Knowing will help you articulate what you do and don't do in the classroom and will help others trust that you are doing the best things for children. For example, every other teacher in one of the buildings where I taught gave stars to children doing "good" things. One of my core beliefs is that children need to do things because they are the right things to do, and one of my boundaries is giving physical rewards. Parents and administrators questioned me about this, but I when I explained why these were my beliefs, they understood and sometimes agreed with my position. When I came across a child who really tempted me to give him rewards because I couldn't get anything else to work, I had that boundary there to remind me to look a little harder and ask for help. I am not suggesting you adopt this or any of my boundaries. Instead, think about your own boundaries and adapt your classroom management plan to meet those needs.

It is also important for you to know ahead of time what is absolutely out of bounds for children in the classroom. You don't have to make a sign in the room that lists these things because the children will find out quickly. For example, in my teacher's heart, I knew I would not tolerate children being unkind to one another. It didn't matter if they didn't choose it as one of their values or if the room was in utter chaos otherwise. They would not be mean to each other. This was a priority for me.

You will need to be passionate about these "out of bounds" kinds of behaviors. If you are not, the students will not hear it in your voice, and they will not see it in consistent actions. In other words, don't choose unkind behaviors as your top priority because it says in this book that it was important to me, the author. Having an "out of bounds" idea in your head doesn't mean that you stop teaching. When children were mean to each other, I didn't start screaming at them and kick them out of the classroom. This is not something that enables you to shame a child. It is merely an idea in the back of your head when you walk into a classroom that keeps you focused on what is truly important.

How does knowing boundaries help you have autonomy within classroom management? If structures and tools in this book or any other resource ask you to cross a boundary line, you must be able to fix them so they work for you. This doesn't necessarily mean tossing the structure or tool. It may mean thinking about how to change it so it does work for you. My school administrator insisted that I hand out stars to children even though he knew I didn't believe it was the right thing to do. One of his core beliefs resided within consistency, and I was not being consistent with the rest of the teachers in that building. Instead of throwing out the structure I was supposed to use or crossing my boundary, I compromised and had the children give each other stars. We celebrated the stars rather than handing out a prize for them, and I had classroom management autonomy that fit my administrator's expectations.

TABLE 12.2   What Is "Out of Bounds"?

Take some time to think about what is currently "out of bounds" for you and your students.

These Things Are Out of Bounds for Me
1.
2.
3.
4.
5.

These Things Are Out of Bounds for Students in the Classroom
1.
2.
3.
4.
5.

Withitness

The two sections prior to this one required some thinking outside of the classroom. To gain classroom management autonomy, however, you will need to think a lot inside the classroom as well. To have classroom management autonomy, you must know what is happening in the classroom. "Kounin discovered that teachers very good in classroom control seem to have the proverbial eyes in the back of the head and know what is going on in all areas of the

Carla knows what is happening in the classroom because she works at tables with her students rather than sits at her desk.

classroom at all times. He called this awareness withitness and considered it the factor that most clearly differentiated between effective and ineffective teachers" (Charles, 1999, p. 37). As evidenced by the quote from Charles, withitness is often seen as a way to keep track of naughty children so you can prevent bad behaviors and be in control. I believe withitness is important to classroom management as well, but for a different reason. Withitness, to me, is important because it provides you opportunities for thinking and reflecting about what is happening in the classroom. Return to the pie crust for a minute. If you have a supposedly fantastic pie crust recipe but you follow it aimlessly without being in the moment, you may miss a telltale sign like the pie crust being too sticky or flaky. To have an effective classroom management plan, you must be in each moment, listen and see, feel and understand, and be "with it." You want to have eyes in the back of your head so you can assess situations and tweak your plan to help children learn academically and socially.

One of the tools that you read about in Chapter 6 was a classroom meeting, which is great for helping children work through issues and celebrating successes. This tool is useless, however, if you don't realize it is needed or wanted. It is the same with all of the resources from Chapter 9. If you don't notice a student is struggling, choosing a resource that may be able to assist him or her will be difficult. In addition, it will be difficult to know how to tailor a structure or tool to meet a certain student's need or an entire group's need if you don't really know what the issue is.

Several tools and structures within this book will help you gain withitness in the classroom. In addition to others, building relationships with children, collecting data from surveys, and even watching how children participate in brain exercises can help you get a sense of what is happening in the classroom. Standing outside of the classroom as children walk in can help you see what they might need that day. For example, if a child throws his books into his locker and slams it shut, you may need to get a brain tool for him to use. Certainly, these tools and others will help you prevent problems in the classroom and, in the process, do the autonomous thinking about what your classroom management plan needs.

How does being "with it" help you develop classroom management autonomy? Really knowing what is going on in the classroom will help you tweak, fix, add to, and take away from any structures you plan to use. It will allow you to change at a moment's notice and work with the students rather than against them. I recently visited a preschool whose playground equipment is being replaced with a more natural playground, including a treehouse and butterfly garden. While observing the class's circle time, a large bulldozer drove back and forth repeatedly by the window. Lisa, the teacher, was very much aware of the students' excitement and wonder and had all of the students go over to the window and observe the bulldozer. "With it" enough to feel the students' excitement, she chose not to continue with her preplanned lesson. Instead, she used her classroom management autonomy and changed plans, most likely preventing some attention issues at circle time. Withitness allows a teacher to make management decisions based on needs and with thought rather than reaction.

Jesse Keifer

Making the classroom your own doesn't mean owning it. Students should have ownership of the classroom as well.

Making Classroom Procedures Your Own

Classroom procedures, such as planning, time management, giving directions, and gaining attention, will be important in organizing yourself, the students, and the classroom events. Going into a classroom and using the same procedures as the other teachers rather than figuring out what works best for you may be tempting. Trying to use a procedure that doesn't make sense to you or that you haven't been involved in creating can be difficult, however. It is important to have some autonomy within this area of classroom management. Once again, this doesn't mean completely reinventing the wheel but instead thinking about existing procedures and making them work for you and your students. For example, every teacher I had ever been around planned within small boxes spread across a planning book and covered an entire week at one glance. You have probably seen one of these and may want to use one to plan your days, but it didn't work for me. I wanted to have a list of supplies I needed, a list of children I wanted to have conferences with, and specific procedures for some subjects. I didn't want to have to rewrite the procedures that would happen routinely each day over and over again. So, rather than trying to cram all of the things that worked for me into small boxes, I made my own planning notebook using a template for each day with blanks for specific items (see Table 12.3). Don't be afraid to try something different.

The key to having autonomy in classroom procedures is taking the time to think about each procedure and define needs, possibilities, and tools that will help you. Remember that procedures will evolve as needed or perhaps even change completely. In fact, you may end up wanting to use the same procedures as other teachers. Autonomy isn't doing something just to do it differently. It is about really knowing what you and your students need. Here are some procedures to think about as you begin to create a classroom management plan.

Think about how to organize the order of events each day. Although this sounds simple, it can be quite complex. If you teach in a self-contained classroom, you will need to decide when you will teach each topic or subject, working around things like lunch, recess, and such subjects as art, music, and physical education where children will leave the classroom. You may need to work around the schedule of a special educator as well. For example, if you have a child who will receive special-education services for reading, you will need to schedule your reading time when the special educator can help the child. Time of day can be an important factor to consider as well. If you find that the students in your room are tired in the morning and struggle to get going, you might want to plan more physically active topics during the morning. You may also want to make decisions about scheduling based on how the subjects fit together or what children will be expected to do. For example, reading and writing might transition well from one to the other. On the other hand, I liked having writing workshop right after lunch because the children knew exactly what to do and could get started without any direction from me. This saved a lot of time settling children down from recess so they could listen to directions. They just came in, got their writing folders out, and started. Finally, you might also consider any preparations you might have when you schedule the events of the day. I usually needed time, for example, to get science supplies ready. I scheduled science time right after the children went to music, art, or physical education because that allowed me the time I needed. Whatever schedule you choose, remember that it needs to be a routine so children know what is coming yet flexible enough to be changed when needed. Use Table 12.4 on page 316 to help you plan.

TABLE 12.3   Plan Book

This is how my plan book looked, just one example of how I made procedures of teaching my own. What will yours include?

Date: _____

8:20–8:45:   Opening (Students come in and do their jobs and calendar routine.)

8:45–9:45:   Reading Workshop (half reading to self, half working on projects or shared reading)

               Conferences:

               Mini Lesson:

9:45–10:30:   Writing Workshop (Children are writing, editing, conferencing, illustrating, and publishing.)

               Conferences:

               Mini Lesson:

10:30–10:40:   Novel:

10:40–11:35:   Math

               Plan: I Need:

11:35–12:15:   Lunch and Recess

12:15–1:00:   Science

               Plan: I Need:

1:00–2:00:   Specials and Spelling

1:00–2:00:   Mondays: Music/Library; Tuesdays: Spelling/P.E.; Wednesdays: Spelling/Music; Thursdays: Recess/P.E.; Fridays: Art

2:00–3:00:   Plan-Do-Review (Children plan in their notebooks and then do their plan. At 2:40, they go back to their seats to review and then share at the front floor.)

3:00–3:15:   Closing

If you teach a single subject to many groups of students, your schedule will be a bit more limited; however, you will still need to organize the agenda for each day. In this case, you may want to develop a flexible daily routine. Your routine might include what students do when they first come in the room and so on. Some teachers write a daily agenda on a board so students know what is coming. Since novelty helps the brain learn, mix it up every once in a while, and be sure your routine includes some movement and opportunities for children to change states.

TABLE 12.4 Order of Classroom Events

The order of events in the classroom is key in classroom management.

Instructions: Choose a grade level and use the tool below to start thinking about the order of events. Put each of the subjects at the left into time slots (either by drawing a line or cutting them out and laying them on the slots or just writing them in the time slots). The empty boxes are for you to add events, such as recess, plan-do-review time, or other extras you may want to include. Class starts at 8:00 and ends at 3:00. Be sure to have rationale for why you put events where you did.

Math	8:00–_____
Science	_____–_____
Social Studies	_____–_____
Writing Workshop	_____–_____
Reading	_____–_____
Lunch	_____–_____
Specials	_____–_____
	_____–_____
	_____–_____
	_____–_____

For material related to this concept, go to Clip 12.1 on the Web-based Student Study Site.

For material related to this concept, go to Clip 12.2 on the Web-based Student Study Site.

Come up with procedures for gaining attention in the classroom. Some teachers turn the lights off, clap, or ring a bell; others have a secret word that indicates attention is needed; and some have hand signals that students replicate until everyone is attentive. I have seen many teachers use songs to get children's attention, as well as give them directions for where to go next. You may want to use more than one procedure for different things. For example, you may want to sing a song to get children into a circle and ring a bell when time is up. I wasn't always that creative. Most of the time, I just turned off the lights and gave students the next direction. I have observed teachers who skillfully used attention-getting tools effectively. Take some time to think about what you have observed and how you might want to handle this procedure.

Giving directions is an important procedure to consider. Although it may seem simple enough, giving good directions is not easy. You must consider the cognitive level of the students and the directions themselves. Some projects may have multiple steps, and you will need to think about how to break them up so children won't get lost in the middle. Writing directions where children can see them may be important. You may want to create opportunities for children to talk about the directions with partners or you to make sure they understand. Using key words or short phrases to sum up lengthy directions can help children remember them. For example, let's say the directions are to get into small groups, create a poster that represents the stages in an insect's life, and hang it on the science board. After you say those directions, you might end with, "Group, create poster, hang up." Combinations of giving directions work well. Try some different strategies or come up with your own to see what works best.

Plan for transition times and times when children finish early or late. Just as you needed to think about managing places outside of the classroom in Chapter 11, you will also need to plan for times outside of specific subject times. What will you expect children to do when they finish earlier than others? How will you get children to the next topic or classroom without wasting too much time? You will want to have these ideas ready so you can pull them out as needed. Sometimes, an activity you think will last for a half-hour will only take children 15 minutes, and vice versa. As you plan activities, you will also want to plan for what's next. It is often tempting to tell children to read or help a classmate over and over again. These are good solutions, but you will want to have more options so these things don't become tedious. At the same time, you don't want children to rush through the next activity to get to the next best thing. Extension activities work well, especially for children who need a challenge. For example, if children are figuring out the number of ways to make a certain amount of money, you can give them a different, harder amount to try when they have exhausted all possibilities. Another suggestion for this example is to have some money games available for children to play or a sheet with money amounts for each letter so they can figure out the value of different words. Transition times can work similarly. If you are studying the states, while students move from their desks to line up, have them tell you one state and its capital or sing a states and capitals song.

Classroom management autonomy requires the ability to develop procedures that help children learn and keep the classroom running smoothly. It is important to create procedures that work for you and the students you teach and to know when something isn't working and change it. Knowing you have the ability to change something that isn't working will help alleviate any out-of-control feelings you might have. There are always ways to make classroom procedures work better.

Creating core belief statements, deciding what is out of bounds, working to be "with it" in the classroom, and developing classroom procedures that work for you are all ways to have autonomy in the classroom. Remember that having autonomy doesn't mean you are unwilling to try new things or you won't listen to others' suggestions. Having autonomy means taking all that you have experienced and learned from others and molding it into something that works for you. Without autonomy, teachers become preprogrammed robots or worse: premade pie crust teachers! With autonomy, teachers become creative and flexible facilitators of students' needs.

Classroom Management Belonging

When I first started teaching, I figured that classroom management would get easier with each year I taught, and in some ways, it did. My autonomy and ability to reflect improved year by year, I had more strategies to choose from, and I felt more confident in my decisions. Inevitably each year, however, something would put a new kink in my plan and cause me stress. A tool I thought I had mastered would be tested by a child with different needs, or a structure would not support a group of students as I had planned. In those instances, it was easy to feel as though I was the worst teacher in the world. It didn't matter if it was my first year of teaching, my sixth year, or just yesterday. Teaching is indeed a roller coaster of

LETTER FROM A MASTER TEACHER 12.2

Things That Make the Classroom Your Own

I have learned through my years of teaching what works for me and what does not. I am fortunate to work in a district that doesn't require me to implement consequences or procedures that I don't believe in. I know not every teacher is this fortunate. The important thing to remember is no matter what is expected of you, you have to make it your own. It needs to reflect what you believe in as a teacher. One of my core beliefs about learning is that it should be student-centered. Therefore, posting the rules and consequences doesn't work for me. Telling students what they can't do and what will happen to them if they do it puts all the power in the teacher's hands. It teaches the children what is important to the teacher and what they need to do to survive in that classroom. I don't believe it encourages growth toward taking ownership of their choices and behavior. Setting high expectations, even when it seemed like the students would never reach the ultimate goal, has saved my classroom community many times.

Making your classroom your own involves so many things. Just last week, for example, I asked for student input on a new seating arrangement. They threw out some ideas, and Anna said, "I've seen this one seating arrangement on TV where all the desks are lined up straight, except there is space in between all of them." I tried to keep my amusement silenced as I realized what she meant: traditional rows! Another example of personalizing your classroom is what you choose to hang on your walls. While my room is covered in a theme of "hands" and color-coordinated borders, my brother, an excellent teacher, takes a more simple approach. The birthday bulletin board that his students signed themselves is as good as aesthetically pleasing gets in his room, but I guarantee his students barely notice. What they do notice is that it is as unique as their teacher.

Getting to know yourself as a teacher is one of the biggest challenges of the job. Getting to know your students each year and then conquering the curriculum in a way that connects them to not only what they are learning but also to you and each other is a process in itself. Making your classroom your own is hard, can be disappointing, and is most of the time unnoticed by visitors. But when you and your students can feel it, you'll know why you work so hard at creating it.

—Mary Jo Kraus
Fifth-Grade Teacher

emotions. In all its ups and downs, it is important to feel support from those around you so you can continue to learn.

Taking different structures and tools and creating your own classroom management plan requires a great deal of thinking and decision making. It also requires that you have support when something doesn't work and celebration when something does. We talked a great deal about building relationships with children and facilitating their sense of belonging in previous chapters of this book. Now it is time to think about your own need for belonging as you continue to learn as a teacher. Even veteran teachers need support in the form of feedback, a safe place to voice concerns, and people who will celebrate successes with them. Building relationships and having a sense of belonging will grant you the support you need to feel confident about the decisions you make and the thinking you do. It will also make your job a lot more enjoyable.

Frank Smith (1998) wrote, "You learn from the company you keep" (p. 9) and talked about this kind of company as "learning clubs." I don't think he meant that we should all go out and join book clubs or study groups. He was talking about how we learn vicariously from the people we are around. As you continue to read this chapter, I hope you will consider the "clubs" in and out of your school that will help shape how you teach, as well as your perception of how well you teach. Some of the "clubs" you will have an opportunity to belong to will help you pursue a classroom management plan that is uniquely yours through support, feedback, questions, and perhaps just a listening ear. Others will not. If indeed we do learn from the company we keep, as Smith suggests, an important task will be to find the company that best supports your learning. Remember that supporting your learning and helping you make a classroom management plan that works for you does not necessarily mean agreeing with every decision you make. Ideally, you want to find a group of people who will support you but also push you to continue to learn. You can find these kinds of "clubs" at school, as well as at home and within friendships.

Colleagues

The teachers you work with can often be your best source of support and belonging. Colleagues in your building will know the children and families in the classrooms, know building procedures, and be in the trenches with you each day. They will understand the hard work teachers do and may often have resources and suggestions to move you forward. You will want to work to create good relationships with the teachers around you.

How do you belong to a colleague "club?" In some cases, this will be an easy task, and in others, it may be more difficult. In some buildings, relationships happen naturally because of the way teams are set up or because the administration knows the importance of it and works to create community just as a teacher would in the classroom. For example, some groups of teachers are given time to work and plan together during the school day, making it easy for them to share ideas and support each other. In other buildings, teachers can be isolated because of physical constraints or time issues. For example, I taught one year in portable classroom outside of the school building. It was difficult to belong there due to the lack of proximity to other teachers. It was sometimes easier just to get my work done and go home than trek into the building. I encourage you to build relationships with colleagues, whatever the circumstance in the building where you teach. So the first key ingredient in developing a sense of belonging is to make a conscious effort to build relationships, even if it requires some work.

It is important to be proactive when building relationships with colleagues. In other words, don't wait for someone to support you. Instead, ask for help, ideas, and suggestions. You may believe that other teachers will think you are incompetent and question your ability to teach; however, for most teachers, the opposite is true. Teachers like to be recognized as a source of help, and most will bend over backward to help you. In the process, you will be creating a relationship and a source of support. In addition, talk to teachers about topics other than school. Ask them about their children, vacation, or hobbies. Take the time to stop and talk to other teachers even if you're busy. Ask for advice about things other than school, such as where they get haircuts or cars fixed. Go out with groups of teachers on a Friday sometimes. If you find the right teacher or teachers, play a joke on them sometimes! These things may sound small, but getting to know your colleagues will make a big difference in how you view your job and your school and thus how well you teach.

Another key (and maybe the most important key) is to figure out which colleagues will best support your sense of belonging. You may find that some teachers in your building are unable or unwilling to be a part of that "club." As in any aspect of life, some people connect better than others, and you will want to find those people who connect with you. Remember that you can build relationships around many different ideas. "Clubs" can be formed around topics, such as technology or literature; problems to solve; or just people having fun. Figure out which people you can support, which people will support you, which people are good to go to with questions, and which people will have fun with you. Indeed, these may be the same people in some cases, but be sure to expand your "club" every chance you get.

The final key in benefiting from "learning clubs" with colleagues is being a professional. Even when you disagree with someone, when it might seem interesting to gossip, or when someone is not professional to you, you must be a professional educator. This means that you keep conversations about children to yourself, that you don't spread rumors, and that you are polite, calm, and curious when disagreements occur. It is important for teachers to have conversations about children and sometimes even about their families to get support. It is vital, however, that these conversations be professional. In addition, being a professional means taking care of your own work. Don't expect someone to do work for you. If you are planning as a team, be sure you are prepared to contribute. If you need an idea for a lesson, ask for one, but don't expect someone to do all of your lesson planning. Do what you say you are going to do. If you say you will get busses for the next field trip, be sure that you do. If you say you are going to rotate to another classroom at a certain time, be ready at that time.

Stop reading for a minute, and take some time to think about what all of this means for classroom management and making a "recipe." How does building a sense of belonging among colleagues transfer into a classroom management plan? In simplest terms, if you have that sense of belonging, that sense that the teachers, cooks, custodians, secretaries, and para-educators in your building are on your side and willing to support your ideas, it will be easier to stick to your core beliefs and boundaries, have withitness, use procedures that work, take thoughtful risks, and ask for help when needed. Developing a sense of belonging in a school building is not something often taught during methods classes or student teaching. Belonging is vital to learning, however, and therefore vital to you as you learn within your own classroom management plan.

Friends and Family

Teaching, fortunately or unfortunately, is not just a job. The weight of your responsibility, as well as the joy of helping a child learn, can sometimes feel enormous or overwhelming. You cannot leave this job at the office and come back to it the next morning. It will seep into your thoughts during the weekend and your dreams at night. It will tag along even on vacations and during the summer months when you are supposed to be relaxing. I will never forget the look on my husband's face when I made him stop alongside the road each time we came to a different state on a long road trip so I could collect dirt (I wanted the children to see the differences in soils)! I still think about children I had in class more than 10 years ago, wondering how they are doing and if they are safe. So this job requires you to belong to a friends-and-family "club" that understands that passion and responsibility. At times, your friends and family will be better than a "club" of educators because, during hard times, you will not feel judged and, during wonderful times, you will be able to celebrate without feeling like you're bragging.

Finding a support system outside of the school building will help you put happenings and new ideas into perspective. Friends and family may have helpful ideas and suggestions as well. I counted on my friends and family so much and still do. They help me be a better teacher each day because they support me unconditionally. My friend Sue used to listen to me, on the treadmill every night, talking about the classroom. Just discussing my ideas aloud helped me think them through. My husband reads this book and gives me suggestions. His perspective is valuable because he is not an educator; if he gets it, there is a better chance that others will. My family, including my mom, dad, and sister Jennifer, even volunteered in the classroom when they could. It felt good to have them enjoy the children and the classroom. In addition, they were able to see long-term changes that I couldn't see because I was with the students each day and they were not. I don't know how your support system outside of the school building will look, and really there are many right answers. But I urge you to have people you can trust who aren't connected to your school in your belonging "club" so you can lean on and celebrate with them when needed.

Because teaching is a job that elicits such commitment and responsibility, it is important to be able to get away from it every now and then. Your friends-and-family "club" will be a great asset for this as well. It is easy, especially but not exclusively as a new teacher, to stay at school working late. Your friends and family can help you get away from school and have some fun. I know; I know: What does having fun have to do with making a classroom management plan your own? Sometimes, you can get into such deep thought about a situation or plan that you get lost along the way. In other words, you can't see the forest for the trees. Making a management plan your own may mean stepping away from it for a while and coming back to it with fresh insight or a rested eye. Be sure to find ways to relax that work for you. Friends and family can help.

Children

I often hear veteran teachers telling novice teachers they shouldn't care if the children like them or not and they shouldn't be the students' friend. Instead, they urge the new teachers to work to be respected. I understand this comment. It is easy to go in as a new teacher and base all of your classroom management structures and tools on whether the children are having fun and be more concerned about whether they like you than about what they are learning. Our need for belonging doesn't just extend to the teachers or to friends and family. It is natural to want students to enjoy class and like their teacher. Rather than seeing classroom management as a way to get children to like or respect you, however, work to create an environment that builds *mutual* respect and opportunities to learn *together*. In the process, you will feel a sense of belonging, of being a part of the learning community.

Some of the same things you do to develop relationships with children will help you gain a sense of belonging in your own classroom. Why? If children feel like you will listen to their needs, like you care about them, and like they belong, they will be more likely to do the same for you. You don't have to make them like you by giving prizes or having low expectations. They will like you because you like them and because you care about their learning. You don't

Having a sense of belonging in a classroom means creating respectful, caring relationships with students.

have to make them respect you by being controlling or harsh to those who make mistakes. They will respect you because you have expectations for learning and because you respect them. You don't have to make children learn by threatening bad grades or a phone call home. They will learn because you set up opportunities for individuals to learn, listen to their feedback, and learn enthusiastically with them. A sense of belonging comes in a classroom when everyone works together to achieve a goal. In the classroom, that goal is learning.

It may sound funny to think about working to have a sense of belonging in your own classroom. That's the key, though. It isn't your own classroom; it's your students' and your classroom, and if you are an outsider looking in or a leader with no followers, classroom management will be harder, and you may feel isolated. Smile a lot. Have some fun. Let the students take the lead. Help the students get to know you, and get to know them. Have high expectations for learning. If you do, you will belong to a great learning "club" that will stay with you for a very long time.

Classroom Management Competency

Competency is the last thing on my list to write about for this book. There is no way to get around it. You can have all of the autonomy and belonging in the world, but if you don't understand why you are doing what you do, classroom management will be a struggle. Just as you must be competent about what ingredients go into a pie crust, to have a classroom management plan that is yours and that works well, you must be and feel competent about teaching and learning.

Competency itself is a noun, but I want you to think of it like a verb. Your competency about classroom management and teaching in general should be growing constantly rather than coming to an end. Competency in the area of classroom management requires continual reflection on experience, reading new classroom management literature, and trying new things. The knowledge you have in your second year of teaching should exceed the knowledge you had as a first-year teacher, and so on. Three areas of focus are vital to classroom management competency: knowledge of children and how they learn, knowledge of the content you teach, and knowledge of your strengths as a teacher. These very broad areas of study make it possible to grow in ways that are meaningful to you. It doesn't matter which way you grow or move in your career, only that you continue to do so, making competency a verb.

Knowing How Children Learn

It seems to me, in many cases in schools today, teachers are so bombarded with helping children pass tests and getting a certain number of topics covered that they aren't even thinking about how children learn. Certainly, this is not a shortcoming of the teachers themselves but instead a product of the educational system where they happen to teach. I hope, however, you will develop competency about how children learn as you begin to create a classroom management plan. How do children's minds work? What do they understand? What don't they understand? If we want children who are self-directed, active, creative learners, we will need to figure out how they will best learn those things.

According to Labinowicz (1980), children learn because they develop cognitively, have opportunities for social interaction, and are actively engaged in their learning with their bodies and minds. Classroom management should contain structures and tools that enhance those opportunities. Take a minute to think about development, social interaction, and active learning. What do you know about each of them?

Why should you understand child development, and how will that knowledge influence classroom management? You may have taken an educational psychology class and learned about Jean Piaget's stages of cognitive development, including sensory motor, preoperational, concrete operational, and formal operational. This kind of information is certainly good to know and understand. Have you considered, however, what those stages have to do with learning, teaching, or classroom management? Let's look at an example of how cognitive development influences learning. Children (approximately ages 2–7) in the preoperational stage of cognitive development have difficulty seeing things from another person's perspective. In fact, if you put some objects on a table and ask them to draw the table as if they were sitting in the chair across from them, they are often unable to do it. This kind of competency will influence how you handle such a situation. If you understand that children at this age may not be able to take another person's point of view, it will help you solve the problem in a productive way. Knowing that students don't yet think in a certain way should not keep you from creating experiences to help them get there. If you want children to begin to see different perspectives,

What structures and tools will help these individual students learn?

create opportunities for them to do so in the classroom, but know that it may be difficult for them and why. "Children's sense-making activities can be seen as efforts to achieve the best understanding they can with the intellectual capacities they possess at a given stage of development" (Katz & Chard, 1989, p. 21). Being competent in child development will help you be aware of why things may be happening and help you create lessons that will be effective at helping children move forward. I hope this example shows the importance of being competent in the area of child development from a management point of view. This, of course, is only one example among thousands of others. Remember that competency within the area of child development does not replace knowing individual students' development. You must be competent about individual students as well. Knowing the basics and connecting them to classroom management will give you a great base from which to start.

Why should you understand social interaction, and how will that knowledge influence classroom management? Fortunately, teachers don't have to rely only on cognitive development to help children learn. According to Lev Vygotsky, learning takes place within a social context, and knowledge is mutually built and constructed (Santrock, 2000). In other words, we can influence learning by giving children opportunities for interaction with adults and their peers. "Most of what humans learn is acquired through discourse and interactions with others" (Pellegrino, Chudowsky, Glaser, & National Research Council, 2001, p. 88). Unfortunately, children are often discouraged from interacting with others in the classroom. Teachers want quiet classrooms with busy students who learn material on their own.

Vygotsky also theorized that language and culture play a large role in students' learning (Berk & Winsler, 1995). Often we neglect the effects of culture on learning, forgetting that there are many different cultures even within one society, each culture emphasizing learning differently. While students in one culture learn to use a computer, students in another culture learn to hunt for food or build a home. Culture plays a critical role in what is viewed as important for children to learn and how they learn it. If students come in with different experiences, recognizing that will be important when dealing with classroom management issues.

Take some time to think about how these ideas would influence your classroom management plan. How will social interaction look in the classroom? How will you manage it? If students learn by engaging in conversations together and with you, wouldn't it be important to create opportunities to do so? If you go back through this book, you will find many structures that will help students learn in this way. For example, in Chapter 5, we talked about thinking routines, such as think-pair-share. This simple thinking routine provides students with opportunities to interact socially, enabling them to learn from their peers. In Chapter 8, we talked about the stories and language you can use to help children learn. These kinds of things will help children construct knowledge about social situations through social interactions. Can you find other examples? What else do you want to know about social interaction?

Why should you understand active learning, and how will that knowledge influence classroom management? John Dewey (1964) wrote, "Of course intellectual learning includes the amassing and retention of information. But information is an undigested burden unless it is understood. It is knowledge only as its material is comprehended. Education consists of wide-awake, careful, thorough habits of thinking" (p. 249). The words *wide awake* describe quite well the state of a true learner. We cannot pour knowledge into children's heads. Instead, they must actively construct it with their minds and hands. Active learning, then, means giving children opportunities to manipulate objects, words, or their bodies to experience something new and then reflecting on that experience so connections take place. "There should be brief intervals of time for quiet reflection provided for even the young. But they are periods of genuine reflection only when they follow after times of more overt action and are used to organize what has been gained in periods of activity in which the hands and other parts of the body beside the brain are used" (Dewey, 1938, p. 63). Providing active learning opportunities means helping children have the richest, most thoughtful experience possible.

How will competency about active learning influence classroom management? If children will be actively engaged in the classroom, classroom management structures and tools must support that notion. There must be opportunities for hands-on activities and reflection. For example, we talked earlier in this chapter about coming up with a schedule or an agenda. You must build in time for active experiences and reflection if they are to take place. We talked about managing materials in Chapter 10. Students must have access to materials if they are to have active experiences.

I have chosen to write about Piaget, Vygotsky, and Dewey to get you thinking about learning. There are many theories, however, about how children learn. I have not written here about B. F. Skinner, Abraham Maslow, or any of the information-processing theories of learning. You may want to read about those as well. As you go back and forth between theories of learning and your own experiences, I hope you will continue to connect them to classroom management. Being competent in how students learn should influence your classroom management plan, as well as make it stronger.

Knowing the Content

For the most part, this book has been about competency in the area of pedagogical knowledge. Indeed, knowing pedagogy (the strategies and structures of helping children learn) is a must for any teacher. You must know what kinds of activities, questions, and management will best help children understand a topic. You mustn't forget, however, that content knowledge (the ideas and facts of the subject matter you teach) is also vital in managing a classroom well. Teachers' personal understandings of the subject matter they teach have a powerful influence on their instructional practice (Ball, 1988). Content knowledge determines teachers' explanations, demonstrations, diagnosis of misconceptions, acceptance of students' own methods, and curriculum decisions (Ernest, 1989). Teachers without much content knowledge avoid answering student questions and limit verbal participation (Stoddart, Connell, Stofflett, & Peck, 1993). Making the connection between these things and classroom management is not difficult. We talked about how juicy problems are important for motivation, about creating engaging experiences within workshops, and about asking good questions and providing opportunities for children to think. All of these things are impossible if you do not have content knowledge.

There is a lot to learn; I know. The good news is that content competency doesn't have to happen exclusively outside of the classroom. Instead, I suggest you learn concept knowledge before you teach a topic and then learn some of the content with the children. Let me explain.

Clark (2002) defines a concept as "a big idea that helps us make sense of, or connect, lots of little ideas" (p. 94). If you are teaching fractions, you will want to learn about fraction concepts, such as why we use them, how they are related to other math concepts, and what children might learn before and after fractions. If you know these big ideas, you can begin to explore the procedures and ways of manipulating fractions with the children. This may sound risky, and I am not implying that you go into a topic of study without knowing where you are headed; however, it's good to explore ideas with the children as well. If you do, rather than showing them the "right" way, you will better enable them to construct ideas about a topic.

If knowing content is both gathering information before you teach and being open to learning with the students, you will need some resources. Your textbooks, the Internet, magazines, and books are great sources for information. In addition, I always learned a lot just trying to find an innovative lesson for a specific topic. For example, I found a lesson on making a pond in the classroom for the topic of habitats in a teacher magazine. I learned by reading the article that the big concepts included a habitat's need for sun, producers, consumers, and decomposers. Finally, ask such experts as scientists, authors, and mathematicians to help you learn content knowledge. One year, for example, my students wondered why two negative numbers equal a positive number when multiplied. They knew the rule but wanted to know why. I didn't know. I called a mathematician at a local university, and he helped me understand so I could help my students move toward understanding it.

Modeling as a pedagogical tool is tricky because you always run the risk of limiting children to doing whatever they learn in only your way, requiring very little thinking. I believe, however, that learning content is one exception. Modeling learning new concepts and content is a valuable classroom management tool. Be sure to learn aloud for all to hear.

Knowing Yourself as a Teacher

The final bit of competency that will serve you well as you create a classroom management plan is knowing yourself as a teacher. Don't worry. This requires you to do only one thing: reflect. We have talked about reflecting throughout the entire book, and now we will end with it. Knowing what you believe about teaching requires you to reflect on where you have been, what you are doing now, and where you want to go. "Experience needs to be coupled with substantive reflection to have an impact on practice" (Zembal-Saul, Blumenfeld, & Krajcik, 2000, p. 320).

Reflecting on your past experiences will help you create a better classroom management plan. Personal histories, experiences, and beliefs greatly influence how and what teachers teach. In fact, Stoddart, Connell, Stofflett, and Peck (1993) found that teachers tend to teach the way they were taught. This means that you may gravitate toward structures and tools that worked for you as a learner rather than think about what works for your students. Although previous experiences can have a positive influence on instruction, sometimes these experiences can keep you from finding more effective ways to teach. I am not asking you to throw away all of your previous experiences to move forward. Instead, reflect on them so you are aware that they are there.

Reflecting on your present experiences will help you create a better classroom management plan. Earlier in this chapter, we talked about withitness. Knowing yourself as a teacher means knowing and reflecting about what happens in the classroom each day. You don't necessarily have to reflect on every tiny thing; however, if something intriguing happens or something doesn't work well, take some time to think about why it happened and what should happen next. You can do this in the form of writing, just thinking on the way home, or talking to someone who cares. If you do not reflect on present happenings, it will be easy to continue to do things that aren't working rather than move forward.

Reflecting on your future will help you create a better classroom management plan. This is the part where you get to make goals. Knowing yourself as a teacher means knowing where you want to improve your management strategies. This may not be a priority at first, but as you gain experience, it will be important to set goals for yourself so you continue to learn and grow. The goals you set could include planning goals, such as incorporating more activities for children to do on the playground. You might also set personal teaching goals, like asking more questions during lessons. Teachers always have a lot to learn. It is important not to lose sight of the fact that you don't have to do everything at once. Add a little bit here and a little bit there, and have new goals in the wings.

The End?

Here we are at the end of this book that is really the beginning. I hope it is the beginning in the sense that you will go into a classroom with a sense of your management plan and work forward from there, molding it and adding new ingredients until you stop teaching. I hope it is the beginning in the sense that you will refer to the ideas in this book again and again when you need support or when an experience connects you to a certain part. I hope it is the beginning of your own stories and joyous experiences in the classroom.

Some people think we can create perfect classrooms and perfect learning by directing teachers through the use of scripts and foolproof lessons, like premade pie crusts. Learning isn't perfect, though, and there isn't any such thing as a perfect pie crust or a perfect classroom. Really great classrooms are made with heartfelt hard work and love, just like my grandma's pie crust. Thanks for reading!

So . . . What?

As you begin to create a classroom management plan, be sure to think about your own needs as a learner. Just as your students need autonomy, belonging, and competency, so do you. To have classroom management autonomy, create a list of your core beliefs and a list of boundaries not to be crossed. Make sure you are "with it" in the classroom, and make the procedures you use your own. To have classroom management belonging, make an effort to get to know your colleagues, rely on your friends and family for support, and make the classroom a place of mutual respect between you and the students. To have classroom management competency, work to gain competency about how children learn, including how they develop, the importance of social interaction, and active learning. Competency in the classroom must also include content and concept knowledge and a willingness to continue to learn. Finally, you must reflect on your past, present, and future so you can continue to improve your classroom management plan. No premade teachers here!

Activities to Try

🖎   Ask several teachers to show you the order of events in their classrooms. Be sure to ask them why they order the events this way.

🖎   Make your own template for a planning book.

🖎   After defining your core beliefs and boundaries, write a philosophy statement describing what you believe about classroom management.

🖎   **Make a collection!** Make a collection of "clubs" that will help support you in your quest to create a great classroom.

🖎   **Conduct action research!** Find a classroom where you believe there is a great deal of social interaction and active learning. Record ways teachers provide these opportunities.

Student Study Site

The companion Web site for *Elementary Classroom Management* can be found at www.sagepub.com/kwilliamsstudy.

Visit the Web-based student study site to enhance your understanding of the chapter content. The study materials include video clips, practice tests, flashcards, suggested readings, and Web resources.

Glossary

Abilities: One of three qualities that represent intelligence (e.g., knowledge, memory, creativity, physical ability, artistic ability, and musical ability)

Accommodations: Changes in classroom activities and assignments that allow children who otherwise might not be able to participate to do so

Assessment: Helping a child understand what is right about a task he or she has completed, what is wrong about it, and how to fix it

Assistive communication devices: Electronic or non-electronic devices that help children who have difficulty speaking or writing communicate more effectively

Attention-deficit/hyperactivity disorder (ADHD): A physician-diagnosed condition that interferes with a child's ability to stay focused on meaningful tasks, control his or her impulses, and regulate his or her activity level and whose main symptoms include hyperactivity, inattention, and impulsivity

Attribution: Who or what a child believes caused or was in control of a good or bad performance

Authentic: Relevant, real, and valued by the students (e.g., authentic tasks)

Autocratic environment: A classroom where the teacher has absolute power and voice in decision making

Autonomy: A sense of independence that allows people to make decisions, be self-reliant, and be able to think for themselves

Belonging: A sense that one is accepted or is not alone

Bullying: Intentionally causing another person unhappiness by hurting him or her physically, mentally, or through coercion or harassment

Child-centered: A classroom with a focus on the needs and abilities of students and on the topics that are relevant to the students' lives, needs, and interests and in which the teacher shares control of the classroom and students are allowed to explore, experiment, and discover

Class meetings: Meetings where students either discuss issues and problems they are having in the classroom or other areas of the school, such as the playground, or celebrate what they have learned

Classroom management: Promoting learning with the use of tools that help students develop cognitively and socially in a setting together

Classroom management structures: Routines, plans, problems, questions, furniture, and materials that promote learning

Collection: A system for keeping lesson plan ideas, computer Web sites, literature, and so on, that will be helpful in managing a child-centered classroom

Competency: A sense that one understands or is knowledgeable about a specific subject or in general

Computer-assisted instruction: Drill and practice, tutorial, or simulation activities on the computer that supplement regular teacher instruction

Conceptual understanding: When a person has a functional grasp of ideas that is more than knowing isolated facts or procedures

Conservation tasks: Problems created by Jean Piaget to determine if a child understands that changing the form of a substance or an object does not change its amount, overall volume, or mass

Contagion: A harmful influence

Continuity of learning: Dewey's idea that learning does not happen linearly or in a specific order but that connections are made continually to experiences from the past, present, and future

Cooperative learning: A structure that puts students together to work on problems and projects that promote social and academic learning, interdependence, and individual accountability

Cooperative workshops: A structure that provides opportunities for students to work together or independently on tasks that promote individualized learning and social goals

Culturally competent: Understanding or working to understand the customs, traditions, values, and role of the school in cultures other than your own

Data: Numbers or statements purposefully collected to make sense of something happening in or outside of the classroom

Democratic classroom: A classroom where the teacher and the students share decision making

Democratic environment: An environment in which the teacher and the students have equal power and voice in decision making

Differentiate: To adjust the teaching process according to needs of the learners by adjusting the product, the task itself, or the amount of support

Effortful strategy: A recommended way of completing a task or changing a behavior other than just telling a student to try harder

Energizer: A short activity that helps students move to a state of awareness and energy (e.g., a short game, a song, a drink of water, or walking around the room)

Evaluation: A judgment of another person's work

5-minute writes: A short writing activity where students respond to a question that the teacher poses to better understand what is happening inside or outside the classroom or what students know about a topic of study

Freedom: Students having voice and choice in what happens in the classroom but not necessarily getting to do whatever they want

General education classrooms: Classrooms where all students participate in learning, not where only special-needs students learn

Inclinations: One of three qualities that represent intelligence (e.g., having the desire to continue to learn despite obstacles, addressing problems, and seeking out help when needed)

Individual accountability: A role or structure that encourages a student to take responsibility for his or her own actions in support of a group project or goal

Inquirer: Someone who wonders, ask questions, and looks for the next right answer

Interdependence: A role or structure that encourages a student to rely on others in his or her group

Learning disability: A disorder manifested by significant difficulties in the acquisition and use of listening, speaking, reading, writing, reasoning, or mathematical abilities but not low intelligence

Mastery goals: Goals that encourage learners to develop new skills, try to understand their work, and improve their level of competence and that are based on where the individual learner begins

Metacognitive knowledge: A student's ability to reflect on his or her own thinking and realize when something doesn't make sense

Motivation: The desires, goals, and needs that determine our behaviors

Paradox: A contradictory statement that may be true

Para-professional: A person hired by a school district who assists a teacher with various activities in the classroom

Pedagogical structures: Techniques, routines, games, questions, and so on, that help students learn and help the teacher teach a whole group of students effectively

Pedagogy: The activities of educating or instructing; the "how" in teaching

Performance goals: Competitive goals that encourage students to focus on their ability by outperforming others in achievements or grades

Permissive environment: A classroom where students do whatever they want even if it hinders others' learning or their own

Plan-do-review: A thinking routine where students make a plan, do it, and then spend time reviewing what happened

Portfolio: A collection of materials that represent students' work and show examples of their growth in different subject areas

Positive affect: Feeling that life is good and enjoyable overall

Reflection: Thinking about, learning from, and making connections to happenings in the past, present, and future

Relatedness: A sense that you are connected to others in some way

Resiliency: The positive ability of a child to cope with stress and hardship, indicating his or her ability to resist future negative events

Rewards: Something given to a person for worthy behavior or reaching a goal

Scaffolding: A form of assistance provided by a teacher that includes knowing where a student is in his or her understanding of a topic and then using language tools, peers, and visuals, among other tools, to help him or her move forward in his or her understanding

Self-efficacy: A person's judgment (which may be different from task to task and topic to topic) about how well he or she feels he or she will perform on a task

Self-regulation: The ability to take responsibility for and direct one's own actions

Sensitivities: One of three qualities that represent intelligence; the ability to notice that there is a problem or an issue

Service learning: A project where students complete a task that helps others in some way and that provides opportunities for them to learn about different subjects, topics, or themselves

Special-needs students: Students who require a unique tool, structure, or strategy or language assistance to be successful in the classroom

Stimulus-response: A cause and effect link between an event and the action that follows

Tally chart: A table or display that shows the frequency of a specific occurrence

Teacher-centered: Classrooms where the teacher gives knowledge and expects the students to take and remember that knowledge

Thinking routine: A teaching strategy consisting of a few memorable steps that are accessible to all learners, are easy to teach and learn, and get used repeatedly to help students think deeply about different topics and problems

Vision: A picture or an image of what one would like to create

Vulnerable: A child who is more likely than other children, for a variety of reasons, to be hurt emotionally or physically, to be behind in the classroom, or to need assistance

Zone of proximal development (ZPD): A term used by Lev Vygotsky describing an area in which an individual student will best be able to learn and in which the material is not too hard and not too easy

References

Abernathy, T. V., & Obenchain, K. M. (2001). Student ownership of service-learning projects: Including ourselves in our community. *Intervention in School and Clinic, 37*(2), 86–95.

Albert, L. (1996). *Cooperative discipline.* Circle Pines, MN: American Guidance Service.

Alberto, P., & Troutman, A. (2003). *Applied behavior analysis for teachers* (6th ed.). Upper Saddle River, NJ: Merrill/Prentice Hall.

Amabile, T. M. (1985). Motivation and creativity: Effects of motivational orientation on creative writers. *Journal of Personality and Social Psychology, 48,* 393–399.

Ames, C. (1992). Classrooms: Goals, structures, and student motivation. *Journal of Educational Psychology, 84,* 261–271.

Anderson, K. J., & Minke, K. M. (2007). Parent involvement in education: Toward an understanding of parents' decision making. *Journal of Educational Research, 100*(5), 311–323.

Arlin, P. K. (1990). Wisdom: The art of problem finding. In R. S. Sternberg (Ed.), *Wisdom: Its nature, origins, and development* (pp. 230–243). New York: Cambridge University Press.

Assor, A., Kaplan, H., & Roth, G. (2002). Choice is good, but relevance is excellent: Autonomy-enhancing and suppressing teacher behaviors predicting students' engagement in schoolwork. *British Journal of Educational Psychology, 72,* 261–278.

Avery, C. (1993). *. . . And with a light touch: Learning about reading, writing, and teaching with first graders.* Portsmouth, NH: Heinemann.

Baker, J., & Zigmond, N. (1995). The meaning and practice of inclusion for students with learning disabilities: Themes and implications from five cases. *The Journal of Special Education, 29,* 163–180.

Ball, D. L. (1988). Unlearning to teach mathematics. *For the Learning of Mathematics, 8*(1), 40–48.

Ball, D. L. (2000). Bridging practices: Intertwining content and pedagogy in teaching and learning to teach. *Journal of Teacher Education, 51*(3), 241–247.

Bandura, A. (1977). Self-efficacy: Toward a unifying theory of behavioral change. *Psychological Review, 84,* 191–215.

Bandura, A. (1993). Perceived self-efficacy in cognitive development and functioning. *Educational Psychologist, 28,* 117–148.

Beck, A., & Katcher, A. (1983). *Between pets and people.* New York: G. P. Putnam's Sons.

Beck, M., & Malley, J. (1998). A pedagogy of belonging. *Reclaiming Children and Youth, 7*(3), 133–137.

Bee, H. L., & Boyd, D. (2007). *The developing child* (11th ed.). Boston: Pearson Education.

Benard, B. (2004). *Resiliency: What we have learned.* San Francisco: WestEd.

Bergman, R. (2004). Caring for the ethical ideal: Nel Noddings on moral education. *Journal of Moral Education, 33*(2), 149–162.

Berk, L. E., & Winsler, A. (1995). *Scaffolding children's learning: Vygotsky and early childhood education (Vol. 7).* Washington, DC: National Association for the Education of Young Children.

Berndt, T. J. (1999). Friends' influence on students' adjustment to school. *Educational Psychologist, 34,* 15–29.

Bird, K. (2006). Student Information Systems: How do you spell parental involvement? S-I-S. *T.H.E. Journal, 33*(7), 38–42.

Black, A. E., & Deci, E. L. (2000). The effects of instructors' autonomy support and students' autonomous motivation on learning organic chemistry: A self-determination theory perspective. *Science Education, 84,* 740–756.

Blum, R. W. (2005). A case for school connectedness. *Educational Leadership, 62*(7), 16–20.

Boggiano, A. K., Flink, C., Shields, A., Seelbach, A., & Barrett, M. (1993). Use of techniques promoting students' self-determination: Effects on students' analytic problem-solving skills. *Motivation and Emotion, 17,* 319–336.

Boggiano, A. K., Main, D. S., & Katz, P. A. (1988). Children's preference for challenge: The role of perceived competence and control. *Journal of Personality and Social Psychology, 54,* 134–141.

Bogner, K., Raphael, L. M., & Pressley, M. (2002). How grade-1 teachers motivate literate activity by their students. *Scientific Studies of Reading, 6,* 135–165.

Bridge, H. (2001). Increasing parental involvement in the preschool. *International Journal of Early Years Education, 9*(1), 5–21.

Briggs, D. (1996). Turning conflicts into learning experiences. *Educational Leadership, 54*(1), 60–63.

Bronfenbrenner, U. (1991). What do families do? *Institute for American Values,* Winter/Spring, 2.

Brooks, J. G. (2002). *Schooling for life: Reclaiming the essence of learning.* Alexandria, VA: Association for Supervision and Curriculum Development.

Brothers, L. (1997). *Friday's footprint.* New York: Oxford University Press.

Bruer, J. T. (1998). Brain science, brain fiction. *Educational Leadership, 56*(3), 14–19.

Bruning, R., Schraw, G., & Ronning, R. (1999). *Cognitive psychology and instruction* (3rd ed.). Upper Saddle River, NJ: Prentice Hall.

Burnett, G., & Walz, C. (1994). *Gangs in the schools.* New York: ERIC Clearinghouse on Counseling and Student Services (ERIC Document Reproduction Service No. PD 372 175).

Cacioppo, J. T., & Petty, R. E. (1982). The need for cognition. *Journal of Personality and Social Psychology, 42*(1), 116–131.

Cacioppo, J. T., Petty, R. E., Feinstein, J. A., & Jarvis, W. B. G. (1996). Dispositional differences in cognitive motivation: The life and times of individuals varying in need for cognition. *Psychological Bulletin, 119,* 197–253.

Cameron, J., Banko, K. M., & Pierce, W. D. (2001). Pervasive negative effects of rewards on intrinsic motivation: The myth continues. *The Behavior Analyst, 24,* 1–44.

Canella, G. S., & Reiff, J. C. (1994). Individual constructivist teacher education: Teachers as empowered learners. *Teacher Education Quarterly, 21*(3), 27–38.

Carbo, M. (2007). *Becoming a great teacher of reading: Achieving high rapid reading gains with powerful, differentiated strategies.* Thousand Oaks, CA: Corwin Press.

Carper, J. (2000). *Your miracle brain.* New York: HarperCollins.

Carr, M., Borkowski, J. G., & Maxwell, S. E. (1991). Motivational components of underachievement. *Developmental Psychology, 27,* 108–118.

Center, D., Deitz, S. M., & Kaufman, M. E. (1982). Student ability, task difficulty, and inappropriate classroom behavior: A study of children with behavior disorders. *Behavior Modifications, 6,* 355–374.

Charles, C. M. (1999). *Building Classroom Discipline* (8th ed.). Boston: Pearson Education.

Chipman, S. F., Segal, J. W., & Glaser, R. (1993). *Thinking and learning skills, vol. 2: Research and open questions.* Hillsdale, NJ: Lawrence Erlbaum Associates.

Christenson, S., & Sheridan, S. (2001). *Schools and families: Creating essential connections for learning.* New York: Guilford Press.

Christmann, E. P., Badgett, J. L., & Lucking, R. (1997). The effectiveness of microcomputer-based computer-assisted instruction on differing subject areas: A statistical deduction. *Journal of Educational Computing Research, 16*(3), 281–296.

Christmann, E. P., & Christmann, R. R. (2003). Technologies for special needs students. *Science Scope, 26*(7), 50–53.

Clark, A. (1997). *Being there.* Cambridge, MA: MIT/Bradford.

Clark, E. T. (2002). *Designing & implementing an integrated curriculum: A student centered approach.* Brandon, VT: Holistic Education Press.

Clark, M. L. (1991). Social identity, peer relations and academic competence of African-American adolescents. *Education and Urban Society, 24,* 41–52.

Clark, R. (2004). *The excellent 11: Qualities teachers and parents use to motivate, inspire, and educate children.* New York: Hyperion Books.

Clayton, M. K., & Forton, M. B. (2001). *Classroom spaces that work.* Turners Falls, MA: Northeast Foundation for Children.

Collins, M. (1992). *Ordinary children, extraordinary teachers.* Charlottesville, VA: Hampton Roads.

Colvin, G. (2004). *Managing the cycle of acting-out behavior in the classroom.* Eugene, OR: Behavior Associates.

Cook, B. G., Cameron, D. L., & Tankersley, M. (2007). Inclusive teachers' attitudinal ratings of their students with disabilities. *The Journal of Special Education, 40*(4), 230–238.

Copeland, A. P. (2007). Welcoming international parents to your classroom. *Kappa Delta Pi Record, 43*(2), 66–70.

Cordova, D. I., & Lepper, M. R. (1996). Intrinsic motivation and the process of learning: Beneficial effects of contextualization, personalization, and choice. *Journal of Educational Psychology, 88,* 715–730.

Coulter, B. (2004). Learning science by serving others. *Connect Magazine, 17*(3), 20–21.

Covington, M. (1984). The self-worth theory of achievement motivation: Findings and implications. *Elementary School Journal, 85,* 5–20.

Crandall, J. (1981). *Theory and measurement of social interest.* New York: Columbia University Press.

Cruickshank, D. R. (1985). Uses and benefits of reflective teaching. *Phi Delta Kappan, 66,* 704–706.

Curtiss, K. E., & Curtiss, P. M. (1998). Learning about community: What second graders can teach us. *Teaching and Change, 98*(5), 154–169.

Curtiss, P. M., & Curtiss, K. E. (1995). What 2nd graders taught college students and vice versa. *Educational Leadership, 53*(2), 60–63.

Dake, J. A., Price, J. H., & Telljohann, S. K. (2003). The nature and extent of bullying in school. *Journal of School Health, 73*(5), 173–180.

Darling-Hammond, L. (1997). *The right to learn: A blueprint for creating schools that work.* San Francisco: Jossey-Bass.

Davis, B. (1996). *Teaching mathematics towards a sound alternative.* New York: Garland Publishing.

Davis, H. A. (2003). Conceptualizing the role and influence of student-teacher relationships on children's social and cognitive development. *Educational Psychologist, 38*(4), 207–234.

Davis, J. H. (1986). Children and pets: A therapeutic connection. *The Latham Letter, 7*(4), 1.

Deal, T. E., & Peterson, K. D. (1999). *Shaping school culture: The heart of leadership.* San Francisco: Jossey-Bass.

Deci, E. L., Koestner, R., & Ryan, R. M. (1999). A meta-analytic review of experiments examining the effects of extrinsic rewards on intrinsic motivation. *Psychological Bulletin, 125,* 627–668.

Deci, E. L., Nezlek, J., & Sheinman, L. (1981). Characteristics of the rewarder and intrinsic motivation of the rewardee. *Journal of Personality and Social Psychology, 40,* 1–10.

Deci, E. L., & Ryan, R. M. (1985). *Intrinsic motivation and self-determination in human behavior.* New York: Plenum.

Dennison, P. E., & Dennison, G. E. (1994). *Brain gym: Teacher's edition revised.* Ventura, CA: Edu-Kinesthetics.

Dewey, J. (1933). *How we think: A restatement of the relation of reflective thinking to the educative process.* Boston: D. C. Heath.

Dewey, J. (1934). *Art as experience*. New York: The Berkley Publishing Group.

Dewey, J. (1938). *Experience & education*. New York: Touchstone.

Dewey, J. (1964). *John Dewey on education; selected writings*. New York: Modern Library.

Dolezal, S. E., Mohan Welsh, L., Pressley, M., & Vincent, M. M. (2003). How nine third-grade teachers motivate student academic engagement. *The Elementary School Journal, 103*(3), 239–267.

Doll, B., Zucker, S., & Brehm, K. (2004). *Resilient classrooms: Creating healthy environments for learning*. New York: Guilford Press.

Dorn, M. (2006). *Weakfish: Bullying through the eyes of a child* (2nd ed.). Macon, GA: Safe Havens International.

Duckworth, E. (1996). *The having of wonderful ideas and other essays on teaching and learning* (2nd ed.). New York: Teachers College Press.

Dweck, C. (1986). Motivation processes affecting learning. *American Psychologist, 41*, 1040–1048.

Dweck, C., & Leggett, E. (1988). A social-cognitive approach to motivation and personality, *Psychological Review, 95*, 265–273.

Dwyer, T., Sallis, J., Blizzard, L., Lazarus, R., & Dean, K. (2001). Relation of academic performance to physical activity and fitness in children. *Pediatric Exercise Science, 13*, 225–237.

Ebby, C. B. (2000). Learning to teach mathematics differently: The interaction between coursework and fieldwork for preservice teachers. *Journal of Mathematics Teacher Education, 3*(1), 69–97.

Eccles, J., Wigfield, A., Harold, R., & Blumenfeld, P. (1993). Age and gender differences in children's self- and task perceptions during elementary school. *Child Development, 64*, 830–847.

Elias, M. J. (2003). *Academic and social-emotional learning*. Brussels, Belgium: International Academy of Education.

Elkind, D. (1981). *Children and adolescents* (3rd ed.). New York: Oxford University Press.

Ernest, P. (1989). The knowledge, beliefs and attitudes of the mathematics teacher: A model. *Journal of Education for Teaching, 15*(1), 13–33.

Ernst, G., Castle, M., & Frostad, L. C. (1992). Teaching in multilingual/multicultural settings: Strategies for supporting second-language learners. *Curriculum in Context, 20*(2), 13–15.

Erwin, J. C. (2004). *The classroom of choice: Giving students what they need and getting what you want*. Alexandria, VA: Association for Supervision and Curriculum Development.

Esquith, R. (2007). *Teach like your hair's on fire*. New York: Viking.

Evans, G. W., Lercher, P., Meis, M., Ising, H., & Kofler, W. W. (2001). Community noise exposure and stress in children. *Journal of the Acoustical Society of America, 109*(3), 1023–1027.

Faber, A., & Mazlish, E. (1995). *How to talk so kids can learn*. New York: Fireside.

Fabes, R. A., Fultz, J., Eisenberg, N., May-Plumlee, T., & Christopher, F. S. (1989). Effects of rewards on children's prosocial motivation: A socialization study. *Developmental Psychology, 25*, 509–515.

Fahey, J. A. (2000). Water, water everywhere. *Educational Leadership, 57*(6), 60–61.

Fan, X., & Chen, M. (2001). Parental involvement and students' academic achievement: A meta-analysis. *Educational Psychology Review, 13*, 1–22.

Fay, J., & Funk, D. (1995). *Teaching with love and logic: Taking control of the classroom*. Golden, CO: The Love and Logic Press.

Feeney, T., & Ylvisaker, M. (2006). Context-sensitive cognitive-behavioral supports for young children with TBI: A replication study. *Brain Injury, 20*(6), 629–645.

Fogarty, R. (2001). *Brain-compatible classrooms* (3rd ed.). Thousand Oaks, CA: Corwin Press.

Frattura, E., & Capper, C. A. (2006). Segregated programs versus integrated comprehensive service delivery for all learners: Assessing the differences. *Remedial and Special Education, 27*(6), 355–364.

Freeman, W. (1995) *Societies of brains*. Hillsdale, NJ: Lawrence Erlbaum Associates.

Frey, A., & Doyle, H. D. (2001). Classroom meetings: A program model. *Children & Schools, 23(4),* 212–222.

Furrer, C., & Skinner, E. A. (2003). Sense of relatedness as a factor in children's academic engagement and performance. *Journal of Educational Psychology, 95,* 148–162.

Gambrell, L. B., Codling, R. M., & Palmer, B. M. (1996). *Elementary students' motivation to read (research report).* College Park, MD, and Athens, GA: National Reading Research Center, Universities of Maryland and Georgia.

Gay, G. (2000). *Culturally responsive teaching: Theory, research, & practice.* New York: Teachers College Press.

Gelman, R. G. (1992). *Body Battles.* New York: Scholastic.

Gettinger, M., & Kohler, K. M. (2006). Behavioral approaches to classroom management. In C. M. Evertson & C. S. Weinstein (Eds.), *Handbook of classroom management.* Mahwah, NJ: Lawrence Erlbaum Associates.

Gibbs, J. (2006). *Reaching all by creating tribes learning communities.* Windsor, CA: CenterSource Systems.

Gillies, R. M. (2006). Teachers and students' verbal behaviors during cooperative and small-group learning. *British Journal of Educational Psychology, 76,* 271–287.

Glasser, W. (1986). *Control theory in the classroom.* New York: Harper & Row.

Glasser, W. (1989). Quality: The key to the disciplines. *Phi Kappa Phi, 69*(1), 36–38.

Glasson, G. E., & Lalik, R. V. (1993). Reinterpreting the learning cycle from a social constructivist perspective: A qualitative study of teacher's beliefs and practices. *Journal of Research in Science Teaching, 30*(2), 187–207.

Glickman, C. D., Gordon, S. P., & Ross-Gordon, J. M. (1998). *Supervision of instruction: A developmental approach* (4th ed.). Needham Heights, MA: Allyn & Bacon.

Good, T., & Brophy, J. (2000). *Looking in classrooms* (8th ed.). New York: Longman.

Goodenow, C. (1993). The psychological sense of school membership among adolescents. *Psychology in the Schools, 10*(1), 79–90.

Gore, J. M. (1987). Potpourri: Reflecting on reflective teaching. *Journal of Teacher Education, 38*(2): 33–39.

Gorrell, J., & Keel, L. (1986). A field study of helping relationships in a cross-age tutoring program. *Elementary School Guidance and Counseling, 20,* 268–276.

Goswami, U. (2004). Neuroscience, education, and special education. *British Journal of Special Education, 31*(4), 175–183.

Greenspan, S. I., & Wieder, S. (1998). *The child with special needs.* Cambridge, MA: Da Capo Press.

Greenwood, C. R., Arreaga-Mayer, C., Utley, C., Gavin, K., & Terry, B. (2001). Class wide peer tutoring learning management system: Application with elementary-level English language learners. *Remedial and Special Education, 22,* 34–47.

Greenwood, C. R., Carta, J. J., and Hall, V. (1988). The uses of peer tutoring strategies in classroom management and educational instruction. *School Psychology Review, 12*(2), 258–275.

Gregory, G. H., & Chapman, C. (2002). *Differentiated instructional strategies.* Thousand Oaks, CA: Corwin Press.

Grolnick, W. S., Ryan, R. M., & Deci, E. L. (1987). Autonomy in children's learning: An experimental and individual difference investigation. *Journal of Personality and Social Psychology, 52,* 977–1077.

Grusec, J. E. (1991). Socializing concern for others in the home. *Developmental Psychology, 27,* 338–342.

Guthrie, J. T., & Wigfield, A. (2000). Engagement and motivation in reading. In M. L. Kamil, P. B. Mosenthal, P. D. Pearson, & R. Barr (Eds.), *Handbook of reading research* (Vol. 3, pp. 403–422). Mahwah, NJ: Lawrence Erlbaum Associates.

Haberman, M. (1995). *STAR Teachers of Children in POVERTY.* West Lafayette, IN: Kappa Delta Pi.

Haggerty, N., Black, R., & Smith, G. (2005). Increasing self-managed coping skills through social stories and apron storytelling. *Teaching Exceptional Children, 37*(4), 41–42.

Hahn, C. (1998). *Becoming political: Comparative perspectives on citizenship education.* Albany: State University of New York Press.

Halonen, A., Aunola, K., Ahonen, T., & Nurmi, J. (2006). The role of learning to read in the development of problem behavior: A cross-lagged longitudinal study. *British Journal of Educational Psychology, 76,* 517–534.

Hamby Towns, M. (1998). How do I get my students to work together? Getting cooperative learning started. *Journal of Chemical Education, 75,* 67–69.

Hannaford, C. (1995). *Smart moves: Why learning is not all in your head* (2nd ed.). Salt Lake City, UT: Great River Books.

Harmatz, M. G., Well, A. D., Overtree, C. E., Kawamura, K. Y., Rosal, M., & Ockene, I. S. (2000). Seasonal variation of depression and other moods: A longitudinal approach. *Journal of Biological Rhythms, 15*(4), 344–350.

Harriott, W. A., & Martin, S. S. (2004). Using culturally responsive activities to promote social competence and classroom community. *Teaching Exceptional Children, 37*(1), 48–54.

Hausfather, S. J. (1996). Vygotsky and schooling: Creating a social context for learning. *Action in Teacher Education, 18*(2), 1–10.

Henniger, M. L. (1987). Learning mathematics and science through play. *Childhood Education, 63*(3), 167–171.

Hinshaw, S. P. (1992). Academic underachievement, attention deficits, and aggression: Comorbidity and implications for intervention. *Journal of Consulting and Clinical Psychology, 60*(6), 893–903.

Hinshaw, S. P. (1992). Externalizing behavior problems and academic underachievement in childhood and adolescence: Causal relationships and underlying mechanisms. *Psychological Bulletin, 111,* 127–155.

Hochschild, J. L., & Scovronick, N. (2000). Democratic education and the American Dream. In L. McDonnell, P. M. Timpane, & R. Benjamin (Eds.), *Rediscovering the democratic purposes of education* (pp. 209–242). Lawrence: University Press of Kansas.

Hohmann, M., & Weikart, D. P. (1995). *Educating young children.* Ypsilanti, MI: High/Scope Press.

Holt-Reynolds, D. (1992). Personal history-based beliefs as relevant prior knowledge in course work. *American Educational Research Journal, 29*(2), 325–349.

Hurst, C. O. (2000). *Friends and relations: Using literature with social themes grades 3–5.* Turners Falls, MA: Northeast Foundation for Children.

Ivey, M., Heflin, J., & Alberto, P. (2004). The use of social stories to promote independent behaviors in novel events for children with PDD-NOS. *Focus on Autism and Other Developmental Disabilities, 19*(3), 164–176.

Jay, J. K. (2002). Capturing complexity: A typology of reflective practice for teacher education. *Teaching and Teacher Education, 18*(1), 733–785.

Jeanpierre, B. J. (2004). Two urban elementary science classrooms: The interplay between student interactions and classroom management practices. *Education, 124*(4), 664–676.

Jensen, E. (2000). *Brain based learning.* San Diego, CA: The Brain Store.

Jensen, E. (2005). *Teaching with the brain in mind* (2nd ed.). Alexandria, VA: Association for Supervision and Curriculum Development.

Johnson, D. W., & Johnson, R. T. (1987). *Learning together and alone: Cooperative, competitive and individualistic learning* (2nd ed.). Englewood Cliffs, NJ: Prentice Hall.

Johnson, D. W., Johnson, R. T., & Holubec, E. J. (1991). *Cooperation in the classroom.* Edina, MN: Interaction Book Company.

Johnson, S. M., & Donaldson, M. L. (2007). Overcoming the obstacles to leadership. *Educational Leadership, 65*(1), 8–13.

Jolivette, K., Wehby, J. H., Canale, J., & Massey, N. (2001). Effects of choice-making opportunities on the behavior of students with emotional and behavioral disorders. *Behavioral Disorders, 26*(2), 131–145.

Kaff, M. S., Zabel, R. H., & Milham, M. (2007). Revisiting cost-benefit relationships of behavior management strategies: What special educators say about usefulness, intensity, and effectiveness. *Preventing School Failure, 51*(2), 35–45.

Kamii, C. (2000). *Young children reinvent arithmetic: Implications of Piaget's theory* (2nd ed.). New York: Teachers College Press.

Katz, L. G., & Chard, S. C. (1989). *Engaging children's minds: The project approach.* Norwood, NJ: Ablex.

Kauffman, J. M., & Davis, C. P. (2001). Self-concept, higher-order thinking and teaching: Commentary on the findings of two meta-analyses. *Elementary School Journal, 101*(3), 355–358.

Kauffman, J. M., Mostert, M. P., Trent, S. C., & Pullen, P. L. (2006). *Managing classroom behavior: A reflective case-based approach* (4th ed.). Boston: Allyn & Bacon.

Killion, J. P., & Simmons, L. A. (1992). The zen of facilitation. *Journal of Staff Development, 13*(3), 2–5.

Kliebard, H. M. (1995). *The struggle for the American curriculum* (2nd ed.). New York: Routledge.

Knowles, J. G., & Holt-Reynolds, D. (1991). Shaping pedagogies through personal histories in preservice teacher education. *Teachers College Record, 93*(1), 87–111.

Koehler, L. (2007). 50 essential Web sites for teachers of students with mild or moderate disabilities. *Communications Disorders Quarterly, 42*(5), 285–289.

Koestner, R., Ryan, R. M., Bernieri, F., & Holt, K. (1984). Setting limits on children's behavior: The differential effects of controlling versus informational styles on intrinsic motivation and creativity. *Journal of Personality, 52*, 233–248.

Kohn, A. (1993). *Punished by rewards: The trouble with gold stars, incentive plans, A's, praise, and other bribes.* Boston: Houghton Mifflin.

Kohn, A. (1995). The risk of rewards. *Brown University Child & Adolescent Behavior Letter, 11*(2), 8–11.

Kohn, A. (1996). *Beyond discipline, from compliance to community.* Alexandria, VA: Association for Supervision and Curriculum Development.

Kohn, A. (1998a). *What to look for in classrooms.* San Francisco: Jossey-Bass.

Kohn, A. (1998b). Only for my kid: How privileged parents undermine school reform. *Phi Delta Kappan, 79*(8), 568–577.

Kohn, A. (2004). *What does it mean to be well educated? And more essays on standards, grading, and other follies.* Boston: Beacon Press.

Kohn, A. (2006). Abusing research: The study of homework & other examples. *Phi Delta Kappan, 88*(1), 9–22.

Kolb, D. A. (1984). *Experiential learning: Experience as the source of learning and development.* Englewood Cliffs, NJ: Prentice Hall.

Kounin, J. S. (1970). *Discipline and group management in classrooms.* New York: Holt, Rinehart & Winston.

Kranowitz, C. A. (2005). *The out-of-sync child: Reorganizing and coping with sensory processing disorder.* New York: The Berkley Publishing Group.

Kraus, S., & Butler, K. (2000, Februrary). *Reflection is not description: Cultivating reflection with preservice teachers.* Paper presented at the American Association of Colleges for Teacher Education, Chicago, IL.

Kriete, R., & Bechtel, L. (2002). *The morning meeting book* (2nd ed.). Strategies for Teachers Series. Greenfield, MA: Northeast Foundation for Children.

Labinowicz, E. (1980). *The Piagetian primer.* Menlo Park, CA: Addison-Wesley.

Ladd, G. W., & Price, J. M. (1987). Predicting children's social and school adjustment following the transition from preschool to kindergarten. *Child Development, 58*, 1168–1189.

Landrum, T. J., & Kauffman, J. M. (2006). Behavioral approaches to classroom management. In C. M. Evertson & C. S. Weinstein (Eds.), *Handbook of classroom management* (pp. 47–72). Mahwah, NJ: Lawrence Erlbaum Associates.

Langer, E. (1989). *Mindfulness.* Reading, MA: Addison-Wesley.

Lever-Duffy, J., McDonald, J. B., & Mizell, A. P. (2005). *Teaching and learning with technology.* San Francisco: Pearson Education.

Levine, M. (2002). *A mind at a time.* New York: Simon & Schuster.

Lewis, C. C., Schaps, E., & Watson, M. S. (1996). The caring classroom's academic edge. *Educational Leadership, 54*(1), 16–21.

Li, Q. (2007). Student and teacher views about technology: A tale of two cities? *Journal of Research on Technology in Education, 39*(4), 377–397.

Licht, B. G. (1983). Cognitive-motivational factors that contribute to the achievement of learning-disabled children. *Journal of Learning Disabilities, 16,* 83–490.

Linnenbrink, E. A., & Pintrich, P. R. (2002). Motivation as an enabler for academic success. *School Psychology Review, 31*(3), 313–327.

Littky, D. (2004). *The big picture: Education is everyone's business.* Alexandria, VA: Association for Supervision and Curriculum Development.

Logan, K., Bakeman, R., & Keefe, E. (1997). Effects of instructional variables on engaged behavior of students with disabilities in general education classrooms. *Exceptional Children, 64,* 481–497.

London, W. (1988). Brain/mind bulletin collections. *New Sense Bulletin, 13,* 7c.

Long, N. J. (1997). The therapeutic power of kindness. *Reclaiming Children and Youth, 3,* 242–246.

Lowery, N. V. (2002). Construction of teacher knowledge in context: Preparing elementary teachers to teach mathematics and science. *School Science and Mathematics, 102*(2), 68–84.

Maguire, T. (2001, May). Brain gym. *The Weekly Column,* Article 59. Retrieved January 5, 2006, from http://www.eltnews letter.com/back/May2001/art592001.htm

Marachi, R., Friedel, J., & Midgley, C. (2001, April). *"I sometimes annoy my teacher during math": Relations between student perceptions of the teacher and disruptive behavior in the classroom.* Paper presented at the Annual Conference of the American Educational Research Association, Seattle, WA.

Marx, A. Fuhrer, U., & Hartig, T. (1999). Effects of classroom seating arrangements on children's question asking. *Learning Environments Research, 2*(3), 249–263.

Maslow, A. H. (1968). *Toward a psychology of being* (2nd ed.). New York: Harper & Row.

Massachusetts School Psychologists Association, Inc. (1996). *The school psychologist: Provider of health and psychoeducational services in the school system.* Cambridge, MA: Author.

McAlpine, L., & Weston, C. (2000). Reflection: Issues related to improving professors' teaching and students' learning. *Instructional Science, 28,* 363–385.

McCann, T. M., & Johannessen, L. R. (2004). Why new teachers cry. *The Clearing House, 77*(4), 138–145.

McCloud, S. (2005). From chaos to consistency. *Educational Leadership, 62*(5), 46–49.

McGee, R., Williams, S., Share, D. L., Anderson, J., & Silva, P. A. (1986). The relationship between specific reading retardation, general reading backwardness and behavioral problems in a large sample of Dunedin boys: A longitudinal study from five to eleven years. *Journal of Child Psychology and Psychiatry, 72,* 597–610.

McKenna, M. C., Ellsworth, R. A., & Kear, D. J. (1995). Children's attitudes toward reading: A national survey. *Reading Research Quarterly, 30,* 934–956.

McTighe, J., & O'Connor, K. (2005). Seven practices for effective learning. *Educational Leadership, 63*(3), 10–17.

Miller, L., & Kohler, F. (1993). Winning with peer tutoring. *Preventing School Failure, 37*(3), 14–21.

Miserandino, M. (1996). Children who do well in school: Individual differences in perceived competence and autonomy in above average children. *Journal of Educational Psychology, 88,* 203–214.

Morgan, P. L., & Fuchs, D. (2007). Relationship between children's reading skills and reading motivation. *Exceptional Children, 73*(2), 165–183.

Murphy, P. S. (2002). *The effect of classroom meetings on the reduction of recess problems: A single case design.* Unpublished doctoral dissertation, University of Denver, Denver, CO.

National Association of School Psychologists. (2000). *Standards for training and field placement programs in school psychology.* Bethesda, MD: NASP Publications.

Pellegrino, J. W., Chudowsky, N., Glaser, R., & National Research Council (U.S.) Division of Behavioral and Social Sciences and Education Committee on the Foundations of Assessment. (2001). *Knowing what students know: The science and design of educational assessment.* Washington DC: National Academies Press.

Nebbe, L. L. (1991). The human-animal bond and the elementary school counselor. *School Counselor, 38*(5), 362–372.

Noddings, N. (1992). *The challenge to care in schools: An alternative approach to education.* New York: Teachers College Press.

Noddings, N. (1995a). *Philosophy of education.* Boulder, CO: Westview Press.

Noddings, N. (1995b). Teaching themes of caring. *Education Digest, 61*(24), 24–29.

Noddings, N. (2002). *Educating moral people.* New York: Teachers College Press.

Noddings, N. (2006). What does it mean to educate the whole child? *Educational Leadership: The Best of EL 2005–2006, 63,* 2–6.

Nolen, S. (1988). Reasons for studying: Motivational orientations and study strategies. *Cognition and Instruction, 5,* 269–287.

Obenchain, K. M., & Abernathy, T. V. (2003). Build community and empower students. *Intervention in School and Clinic, 39*(1), 55–60.

Parkay, F. W. (2006). *Social foundations for becoming a teacher.* Boston: Pearson, Allyn & Bacon.

Parker, A. R. (2006). Visiting and interviewing older adults: Service-learning in the sixth grade. *Delta Kappa Gamma Bulletin, 73*(1), 31–35.

Peck, M. S. (1987). *The different drum: Community building and peace.* New York: Simon & Schuster.

Penick, J. E., Crow, L. W., & Bonnstetter, R. J. (1996). Questions are the answers. *The Science Teacher, 63*(1), 27–29.

Perkins, D. (2004). Knowledge alive. *Educational Leadership, 62*(1), 14–18.

Perkins, D., Tishman, S., Ritchhart, R., Donis, K., & Andrade, A. (2000). Intelligence in the wild: A dispositional view of intellectual traits. *Educational Psychology Review, 12*(3), 269–293.

Peyton, L. (2005). High/Scope supporting the child, the family, the community: A report of the proceedings of the High/Scope Ireland Third Annual Conference, 12 October 2004, Newry, Northern Ireland. *Child Care in Practice, 11*(4), 433–456.

Pianta, R. C., Nimetz, S. L., & Bennett, E. (1997). Mother-child relationships, teacher-child relationships and adjustment in preschool and kindergarten. *Early Childhood Research Quarterly, 12,* 263–280.

Pianta, R. C., & Steinberg, M. (1992). Teacher-child relationships and the process of adjusting to school. In R. C. Pianta (Ed.), *Beyond the parent: The role of other adults in children's lives* (pp. 61–80). San Francisco: Jossey-Bass.

Pintrich, P. R., & Schunk, D. (2002). *Motivation in education: Theory, research, and applications* (2nd ed.). Upper Saddle River, NJ: Prentice Hall.

Pittman, T. S., Emery, J., & Boggiano, A. K. (1982). Intrinsic and extrinsic motivational orientations: Reward induced changes in preference for complexity. *Journal of Personality and Social Psychology, 42,* 789–797.

Powell, S., & Nelson, B. (1997). Effects of choosing academic assignments on a student with attention deficit hyperactivity disorder. *Journal of Applied Behavior Analysis, 30,* 181–183.

Rankin, J. L., & Aksamit, D. L. (1994). Perceptions of elementary, junior high, and high school student assistant team coordinators, team members, and teachers. *Journal of Educational and Psychological Consultation, 5*(3), 229–256.

Reay, D. (2006). "I'm not seen as one of the clever children": Consulting primary school pupils about the social conditions of learning. *Educational Review, 58*(2), 171–181.

Reeve, J. (2006). Teachers as facilitators: What autonomy-supportive teachers do and why their students benefit. *The Elementary School Journal, 106*(3), 225–236.

Reeve, J., Jang, H., Carrell, D., Barch, J., & Jeon, S. (2004). Enhancing students' engagement by increasing teachers' autonomy support. *Motivation and Emotion, 28,* 147–169.

Reynolds, D., Nicolson, R. I., & Hambly, H. (2003). Evaluation of an exercise-based treatment for children with reading difficulties. *Dyslexia, 9*(1), 48–71.

Ritchhart, R. (2002). *Intellectual character: What it is, why it matters, how to get it.* San Francisco: Jossey-Bass.

Roeser, R., Eccles, J., & Strobel, K. (1998). Linking the study of schooling and mental health: Selected issues and empirical illustrations at the level of the individual. *Educational Psychologist, 33,* 153–176.

Rosenfeld, L. B. (1977). Setting the stage for learning. *Theory Into Practice, 16*(3), 167–174.

Rowe, M. B. (1974). Wait time and rewards as instructional variables, their influence on language, logic, and fate control: Part 1: Wait time. *Journal of Research in Science Teaching, 11,* 291–308.

Ryan, R. M., & Deci, E. L. (2002). Overview of self-determination theory: An organismic dialectical perspective. In E. L. Deci & R. M. Ryan (Eds.), *Handbook of self-determination research* (pp. 3–33). Rochester, NY: University of Rochester Press.

Ryan, R. M., & Grolnick, W. S. (1986). Origins and pawns in the classroom: Self-report and projective assessments of individual differences in children's perceptions. *Journal of Personality and Social Psychology, 50,* 550–558.

Santrock, J. W. (2000). *Children* (6th ed.). Boston: McGraw-Hill Higher Education.

Sapolsky, R. (2004). *Why zebras don't get ulcers.* New York: Freeman.

Schaps, E., & Solomon, D. (1990). Schools and classrooms as caring communities. *Educational Leadership, 48,* 38–42.

Schempp, P. G., Sparkes, A. C., & Templin, T. J. (1993). The micropolitics of teacher induction. *American Educational Research Journal, 30*(3), 447–472.

Schon, D. (1987). *Educating the reflecting practitioner: Toward a new design for teaching and learning in the professions.* San Francisco: Jossey-Bass.

Schunk, D. (1984). Self-efficacy perspective on achievement. *Educational Psychologist, 19,* 48–58.

Schunk, D. H. (1987). Peer models and children's behavioral change. *Review of Educational Research, 57,* 149–174.

Schutz, A. (2001). John Dewey's conundrum: Can democratic schools empower? *Teachers College Record 103*(2), 267–302.

Schweinhart, L. J., & Weikart, D. P. (1993). Success by empowerment: The High/Scope Perry Preschool study through age 27. *Young Children, 49*(1), 54–58.

Schweinhart, L. J., & Weikart, D. P. (1997). The High/Scope preschool curriculum comparison study through age 23. *Early Childhood Research Quarterly, 12,* 117–143.

Schweinhart, L. J., & Weikart, D. P. (1998). Why curriculum matters in early childhood education. *Educational Leadership, 55*(6), 57–60.

Seifert, T. L. (1995). Characteristics of ego- and task-oriented students: A comparison of two methodologies. *British Journal of Educational Psychology, 65,* 125–138.

Seifert, T. L. (1997). Academic goals and emotions: Results of a structural equation model and cluster analysis. *British Journal of Educational Psychology, 67,* 323–338.

Seifert, T. L. (2004). Understanding student motivation. *Educational Research, 46*(2), 137–149.

Seifert, T. L., & O'Keefe, B. (2001). The relationship of work avoidance and learning goals to perceived competency, eternality and meaning. *British Journal of Educational Psychology, 71,* 81–92.

Seligman, M. (1995). *The optimistic child.* Boston: Houghton Mifflin.

Senge, P. M., Cambron-McCabe, N., Lucas, T., Smith, B., & Dutton, J. (2000). *Schools that learn.* New York: Doubleday/Currency.

Shapira, Z. (1976). Expectancy determinants of intrinsically motivated behavior. *Journal of Personality and Social Psychology, 34,* 1235–1244.

Sharp, V. (2002). *Computer education for teachers.* New York: McGraw-Hill.

Skinner, E., & Edge, K. (2002). Self-determination, coping, and development. In E. L. Deci & R. M. Ryan (Eds.), *Handbook of self-determination research* (pp. 297–337). Rochester, NY: University of Rochester Press.

Slavin, R. E. (1995). *Cooperative learning: Theory, research, and practice* (2nd ed.). Boston: Allyn & Bacon.

Smith, F. (1998). *The book of learning and forgetting.* New York: Teachers College Press.

Smith, R. W. (1991, April). *Obstacles to student teacher reflection: The role of prior school experiences as a barrier to teacher development.* Paper presented at the American Educational Research Association, Chicago.

Sorsdahl, S. N., & Sanche, R. P. (1985). The effects of classroom meetings on self-concept and behavior. *Elementary School Guidance & Counseling, 20*(1), 49–56.

Sousa, D. A. (2001). *How the special needs brain learns.* Thousand Oaks, CA: Corwin Press.

Sousa, D. A. (2006). *How the brain learns* (3rd ed). Thousand Oaks, CA: Corwin Press.

Sprenger, M. (1999). *Learning and memory: The brain in action.* Alexandria, VA: Association for Supervision and Curriculum Development.

Sprenger, M. (2007). *Becoming a "wiz" at brain-based teaching: How to make every year your best year* (2nd ed.). Thousand Oaks, CA: Corwin Press.

Sternberg, R. J. (1990). *Metaphors of mind: Conceptions of the nature of intelligence.* Cambridge, UK: Cambridge University Press.

Stiggins, R. (2005). From formative assessment to assessment for learning: A path to success in standards-based schools. *Phi Delta Kappan, 87*(4), 324–328.

Stoddart, T., Connell, M., Stofflett, R., & Peck, D. (1993). Reconstructing elementary teacher candidates' understanding of mathematics and science content. *Teacher & Teacher Education, 9*(3), 229–241.

Strachota, B. (1996). *On their side.* Greenfield, MA: Northeast Foundation for Children.

Swanson, J. J. (2007, Fall). *Untitled lecture.* Lecture presented at Wayne State College, Fremont, NE.

Tannenbaum, S. A., & Brown-Welty, S. (2006). Tandem pedagogy: Embedding service-learning into an after-school program. *Journal of Experiential Education, 29*(2), 111–125.

Tishman, S, Grotzer, T, Howick, L, Wise, D., & Project Zero. (2002). *Art works for schools.* Lincoln, MA: DeCordova Museum and Sculpture Park.

Tomlinson, C. A. (2001). *How to differentiate instruction in mixed-ability classrooms* (2nd ed.). Alexandria, VA: Association for Supervision and Curriculum Development.

Trainin, G., Wilson, K., Wickless, M., & Brooks, D. (2005). Extraordinary animals and expository writing: Zoo in the classroom. *Journal of Science Education and Technology, 14*(3), 299–304.

Traynor, P. L. (2002). A scientific evaluation of five different strategies teachers use to maintain order. *Education, 122*(3), 493–511.

Ullucci, K. (2005). Picking battles, finding joy: Creating community in the "uncontrolled" classroom. *Multicultural Education, 12,* 41.

Vallerand, R. J., Fortier, M. S., & Guay, F. (1997). Self-determination and persistence in a real-life setting: Toward a motivational model of high school dropout. *Journal of Personality and Social Psychology, 72,* 1161–1176.

Valli, L. (1997). Listening to other voices: A description of teacher reflection in the United States. *Peabody Journal of Education, 72*(1), 67–88.

Viorst, J. (1978). *Alexander, who used to be rich last Sunday.* New York: Aladdin Paperbacks.

Vogelgesang, L. J., & Alexander, W. (2000). Comparing the effects of community service and service-learning. *Michigan Journal of Community Service Learning, 7,* 25–34.

Walker, J. E., Shea, T. M., & Bauer, A. M. (2004). *Behavior management: A practical approach for educators.* Upper Saddle River, NJ: Merrill/Prentice Hall.

Wasserman, S. (1988). Play-debrief-replay: An instructional model for science. *Childhood Education, 64*(4), 232–234.

Weikart, D. P. (1988). A perspective in High/Scope's early education research. *Early Child Development and Care, 33,* 29–40.

Weikart, D. P. (1989). Hard choices in early childhood care and education: A view to the future. *Young Children, 44*(3), 25–30.

Weikart, D. P., Bond, J. T., & McNeil, J. T. (1978). *The Ypsilanti Perry Preschool project: Preschool years and longitudinal results through fourth grade.* Ypsilanti, MI: High/Scope Educational Research Foundation.

Weiner, B. (1985). An attributional theory of achievement, motivation, and emotion. *Psychological Review, 92,* 548–573.

Weissbourd, R. (1996). *The vulnerable child.* Reading, MA: Addison-Wesley.

Wentzel, K. R. (1991). Social competence at school: The relation between social responsibility and academic achievement. *Review of Educational Research, 61,* 1–24.

Wentzel, K. R., & Watkins, D. E. (2002). Peer relationships and collaborative learning as contexts for academic enablers. *School Psychology Review, 31*(3), 366–377.

Wiggins, G., & McTighe, J. (2005). *Understanding by design* (2nd ed.). Upper Saddle River, NJ: Pearson.

Williams, G. C. (2002). Improving patients' health through supporting the autonomy of patients and providers. In E. L. Deci & R. M. Ryan (Eds.), *Handbook of self-determination research* (pp. 233–254). Rochester, NY: University of Rochester Press.

Williams, K. C. (2004). *Preservice teachers' perceptions of plan-do-review: A thinking routine.* Unpublished doctoral dissertation, University of Nebraska–Lincoln.

Williams, K. C., & Veomett, G. E. (2007). *Launching learners in science: How to design standards-based experiences and engage students in classroom conversations.* Thousand Oaks, CA: Corwin Press.

Woolfolk, A. E. (1998). *Educational psychology* (7th ed.). Needham Heights, MA: Allyn & Bacon.

York-Barr, J., Sommers, W. A., Ghere, G. S., & Montie, J. K. (2006). *Reflective practice to improve schools: An action guide for educators.* Thousand Oaks, CA: Corwin Press.

Zembal-Saul, C., Blumenfeld, P., & Krajcik, J. (2000). Influence of guided cycles of planning, teaching, and reflection on prospective elementary teachers' science content representations. *Journal of Research in Science Teaching, 37*(4), 318–339.

Index

Note: In page references, f indicates figures and t indicates tables.

Abernathy, T. V., 55, 160
Abilities, 45, 73, 74, 122, 331
Abuse:
  counselors and, 239
  principals and, 235
  sexual, 239
  special-needs students and, 182, 183
Academic issues:
  belonging and, 21
  cooperative workshops and, 94, 96
  democratic classrooms and, 50
  exercise and, 66
  language and, 196, 198
  motivation and, 84
  pedagogical structures and, 116
  seating arrangements and, 256, 258
  special-needs students and, 174, 177, 192
  thinking and, 124, 136, 139
  whole groups and, 165
  See also Goals
Accommodations, 331
  assemblies and, 293
  special-needs students and, 174, 176, 178,
    179, 185, 278
Accountability, 333
  community development and, 55
  cooperative workshops and, 93, 94,
    106, 110–115

democratic classrooms and, 44
  pedagogical structures and, 116
  thinking routines and, 132, 134
Aesthetics, 263–267, 278
Ahonen, T., 26
Aksamit, D. L., 237
Albert, L., 20
Alberto, P., 6, 215
Alexander, W., 157
Amabile, T. M., 16
Ames, C., 75, 76
Anderson, J., 26
Anderson, K. J., 231
Andrade, A., 122
Anger:
  counselors and, 239
  language and, 201–203, 217
  literature and, 215
Animals, 187–188, 189
Arreaga-Mayer, C., 189
Asperger's syndrome,
  20, 171–172
  See also Special-needs students
Assemblies, 292–293
Assessments, 331
  attribution and, 76
  language and, 203–204, 217
  mastery goals and, 96

students helping with, 223–224
See also Testing
Assistive communication devices, 190, 331
Assor, A., 12, 13, 15, 16
At-risk students *See* Special-needs students
Attention-deficit/hyperactivity disorder (ADHD), 40, 171, 177, 331
See also Special-needs students
Attribution, 63, 74–76, 331
Aunola, K., 26
Autistic students *See* Special-needs students
Autocratic environment, 41–43, 42f, 43t, 49, 331
See also Classroom environments
Autonomy, 5, 11–17, 14t, 27, 28, 308–317, 331
   attribution and, 76
   belonging and, 18
   caring about students and, 31, 32, 33
   classroom environments and, 43
   community development and, 57
   competency and, 23
   cooperative workshops and, 93
   costs of, 17
   democratic classrooms and, 46, 57
   the future and, 10–11
   knowing students and, 37
   language and, 196, 197
   pedagogical structures and, 90, 92, 116
   physical environments and, 250
   prior experiences and, 14–15
   reflection and, 306
   relationships and, 77
   responsibility and, 221
   seating arrangements and, 255
   special-needs students and, 176–177
   students helping teachers and, 225
   students' perspectives and, 15–16
   teacher's perspective and, 13–14
   thinking routines and, 132
   whole groups and, 163, 165
Avery, C., 108

Badgett, J. L., 190
Bakeman, R., 258

Ball, D. L., 25, 326
Bandura, A., 73
Banko, K. M., 6
Barch, J., 16
Barrett, M., 16
Bathroom management, 291
Bechtel, L., 55
Beck, A., 187
Beck, M., 19, 20, 21
Bee, H. L., 74, 173
Behavioral disorders, 82
Behavioral issues:
   autonomy and, 16
   belonging and, 21
   competency and, 23, 26
   control and, 312
   counselors and, 239
   democratic classrooms and, 47
   exercise and, 66
   knowing students and, 35–36, 37
   language and, 198, 202, 203
   lighting and, 266, 278
   literature and, 207, 208, 215, 216
   motivation and, 62, 82
   outside of the classrooms and, 289
   relationships and, 77
   special-needs students and, 174, 176, 185
   whole groups and, 144, 146, 148, 151, 157
Belonging, 5, 17–21, 27, 28, 317–323, 331
   attribution and, 76
   caring about students and, 31, 32, 33
   classroom environments and, 43
   community development and, 56
   competency and, 23
   cooperative workshops and, 93, 102
   costs of, 21
   definition of, 19
   democratic classrooms and, 46, 57
   the future and, 10–11
   knowing students and, 37
   language and, 196, 197
   pedagogical structures and, 90, 92, 116
   physical environments and, 250

reflection and, 306
resources and, 240
responsibility and, 221
seating arrangements and, 255
special-needs students and, 176
students helping teachers and, 225
teachers and, 319, 320, 321
whole groups and, 158, 163, 165
Benard, B., 19
Bennett, E., 77
Berk, L. E., 129, 325
Berndt, T. J., 102
Bernieri, F., 16
Bird, K., 228
Black, A. E., 12, 16
Black, R., 214
Blizzard, L., 66
Blum, R. W., 21
Blumenfeld, P., 74, 327
Boggiano, A. K., 16
Bogner, K., 63
Bond, J. T., 50
Bonnstetter, R. J., 112
Books, 207–214, 211–213t, 217
Boredom, 81, 139
Borkowski, J. G., 75
Boundaries, 310–311
Boyd, D., 74, 173
Brain exercises, 192, 197, 288
Brain research:
    belonging and, 21
    competency and, 26
    emotions and, 70–71
    exercise and, 67f
    knowing students and, 38
    motivation and, 63–72, 66t
    nutrition and, 67–68
    reflection and, 68–70, 70f
    routines and, 315
    seating arrangements and, 255
Brehm, K., 32, 40, 54, 151, 153, 182, 295
Bridge, H., 132
Briggs, D., 148

Bronfenbrenner, U., 33
Brooks, D., 187
Brooks, J. G., 1, 24, 47
Brophy, J., 144
Brothers, L., 19
Brown-Welty, S., 157
Bruer, J. T., 64
Bruning, R., 91, 102, 121, 136
Bullying, 331
    hallway management and, 288
    language and, 204
    playground management and, 295
    principals and, 235
    special-needs students and, 183–184
    teasing and, 153, 296
    whole groups and, 148, 154
Burnett, G., 19
Butler, K., 7

Cacioppo, J. T., 124, 125
Cafeteria management, 292
Cambron-McCabe, N., 20, 33, 90, 92, 96, 98
Cameron, D. L., 170, 171
Cameron, J., 6
Canale, J., 82
Canella, G. S., 9
Capper, C. A., 192
Carbo, M., 108
Caregivers, 41, 226–232
    See also Parents
Caring teachers, 31–33
    knowing students and, 33–41, 307
    motivation and, 62
    relationships and, 77
Carper, J., 65
Carr, M., 75
Carrell, D., 16
Castle, M., 180
Celebrations:
    community development and, 54, 55
    democratic classrooms and, 46–47
    knowing students and, 36
    motivation and, 84

special-needs students and, 179, 183
whole groups and, 143–144, 146–147, 152, 158, 161, 165
See also Rewards
Center, D., 91
Chapman, C., 108
Chard, S. C., 325
Charles, C. M., 20, 43, 312
Chen, M., 226
Child-centered classrooms, 49, 64, 332
Chipman, S. F., 122
Choice:
community development and, 57
democratic classrooms and, 51
motivation and, 82
Christenson, S., 226
Christmann, E. P., 190
Christmann, R. R., 190
Christopher, F. S., 84
Chudowsky, N., 325
Churches, 244
Clark, A., 81
Clark, E. T., 327
Clark, M. L., 102
Clark, R., 89
Class maps, 54
Class meetings, 54, 332
core beliefs and, 308, 309
language and, 197
whole groups and, 143, 148–151, 165
Classroom environments:
belonging and, 20
caring about students and, 31, 32, 33
knowing students and, 37
motivation and, 62, 63
special-needs students and, 172, 174, 181–184
thinking routines and, 135
types of, 41–44, 42f, 43t, 49
vision and, 2
what/why questions and, 6
See also Seating arrangements
Classroom structure, 12, 16
Clayton, M. K., 264, 267
Codling, R. M., 74

Cognitive development:
belonging and, 19, 21
competency and, 324, 325
curriculum and, 50
special-needs students and, 173, 174
tasks and, 98
See also Knowledge
Cognitive disabilities, 176
See also Special-needs students
Collins, M., 89
Colvin, G., 6
Communication:
community development and, 52–53, 58
parents and, 224–225, 228–229, 229t
speech language pathologists and, 237–238
whole groups and, 148
Community development:
democratic classrooms and, 48, 51–57
physical environments and, 250
Competency, 5, 22–27, 28, 323–328, 332
attribution and, 75
caring about students and, 31, 32, 33
classroom environments and, 43
community development and, 57
content and, 326–327
cooperative workshops and, 93
costs of, 27
democratic classrooms and, 46, 57
the future and, 10–11
knowing students and, 35, 37
language and, 196, 197
meaning and, 23, 24
motivation and, 82
parents and, 231
pedagogical structures and, 90, 92, 116
physical environments and, 250
reflection and, 306
relationships and, 77
resources and, 240
responsibility and, 221
seating arrangements and, 255
special-needs students and, 176, 177
students helping teachers and, 225
whole groups and, 158, 163, 165

Comprehension:
  attribution and, 75
  competency and, 25
  cooperative workshops and, 108
Concepts:
  democratic classrooms and, 44, 45
  self-efficacy and, 74
Conceptual understanding, 16, 332
  See also Understanding
Connell, M., 326, 327
Conservation tasks, 174, 176, 332
Contagion, 19, 332
Continuity of learning, 9, 332
Control:
  autonomy and, 13, 17
  behaviors and, 312
  classroom environments and, 41, 42f
  classroom management and, 5
  community development and, 55
  cooperative workshops and, 104
  democratic classrooms and, 49
  exercise and, 66
  language and, 197
  motivation and, 62, 81
Conversations:
  knowing students and, 40
  whole groups and, 143
Cook, B. G., 170, 171
Cooperative learning, 9, 20, 54, 93,
      102, 180, 332
  belonging and, 20
  thinking routines and, 132
Cooperative workshops, 87, 93–115, 332
  core beliefs and, 308, 309
  structuring, 108
  students helping with assessments and, 223
  technology and, 284
  thinking routines and, 138
  whole groups and, 146
  See also Workshops
Copeland, A. P., 82
Cordova, D. I., 82
Core beliefs, 306, 308–309, 309t, 311
Coulter, B., 160

Counselors, 228, 237, 238–239
  resources and, 243, 244
Covington, M., 73
Crandall, J., 21
Creativity:
  autonomy and, 16
  thinking routines and, 132
  whole groups and, 144
Crow, L. W., 112
Cruickshank, D. R., 7
Cultural issues, 171, 172
  emotions and, 70
  language and, 203
  learning and, 325
  parents and, 228, 229
  psychologists and, 239
  special-needs students and, 172, 174, 178–181
  thinking routines and, 132
  whole groups and, 144
Culturally competent, 180, 181, 332
Curriculum:
  autonomy and, 16
  belonging and, 19–20
  caring about students and, 31, 32
  classroom management and, 5
  community development and, 55
  cooperative workshops and, 94
  democratic classrooms and, 49, 50, 51
  goals and, 96
  motivation and, 63
  pedagogical structures and, 91
  seating arrangements and, 256
  technology and, 284
  thinking routines and, 135
  whole groups and, 160
Curriculum Comparison Study, 49, 50
Curtiss, K. E., 48, 107, 284
Curtiss, P. M., 48, 107, 284

Dake, J. A., 148
Data, 332
  bullying and, 184
  cooperative workshops and, 110
  knowing students and, 39

language and, 197
success and, 50
whole groups and, 143, 151, 153, 154, 158, 165
Davis, B., 124
Davis, C. P., 26
Davis, H. A., 77
Davis, J. H., 187
Deal, T. E., 54
Dean, K., 66
Deci, E. L., 6, 12, 13, 16, 18
Decision making:
autonomy and, 12, 16
belonging and, 18, 317, 319
community development and, 54, 56, 57
core beliefs and, 309
democratic classrooms and, 44–45, 45,
47, 48, 51, 57
language and, 198
physical environments and, 251, 277
special-needs students and, 186
tasks and, 99
teachers and, 319
thinking and, 126
whole groups and, 144, 164
Deitz, S. M., 91
Democracy, 41–43, 42f, 43t, 44, 333
caring about students and, 33
community development and, 51–57
competency and, 26
cooperative workshops and, 93
core beliefs and, 308
creating, 51–57, 58
definition of, 44–45
language and, 196, 197
motivation and, 58
pedagogical structures and, 90, 91, 92, 116
Dennison, G. E., 67, 72
Dennison, P. E., 67, 72
Developmentally delayed, 171, 172–176, 175t
See also Special-needs students
Dewey, J., 7, 9, 23, 38, 45, 124, 130, 191, 325, 326
Diet, 67–68, 69f
Direct Instruction System for Teaching Arithmetic
and Reading (DISTAR), 49

Dolezal, S. E., 63, 65, 70, 76, 79, 83, 105
Doll, B., 28, 32, 40, 54, 151, 153, 182, 294, 295
Donaldson, M. L., 220
Donis, K., 122
Dorn, M., 182, 183, 184, 193
Doyle, H. D., 148
Drop outs, 16
Drug abuse, 182
Duckworth, E., 8, 16, 25, 69, 124
Duffy, J., 284
Dutton, J., 20, 33, 90, 92, 96, 98
Dweck, C., 73, 76
Dwyer, T., 66
Dyslexia, 66

Eccles, J., 26, 74
Edge, K., 16, 23
Effortful strategy, 75, 333
Eisenberg, N., 84
Elias, M. J., 54
Elkind, D., 124
Ellsworth, R. A., 74
Emery, J., 16
Emotional issues, 27, 71f
belonging and, 21, 317–318
brain research and, 70–71
competency and, 26
disorders and, 82
special-needs students and, 177
Empathy, 201–203, 204, 217
Energizers, 146, 161–163, 165, 333
English-Language Learners (ELL), 178–181
Environmental issue
See Classroom environments
Ernest, P., 326
Ernst, G., 180
Erwin, J. C., 255
Esquith, R., 79, 89
Ethnicity, 70, 144
Evaluations, 76, 203–204, 217, 333
See also Assessments; Testing
Evans, G. W., 266
Exercise, 66, 67f, 72, 85
brains and, 192, 197, 288

Experiences:
    competency and, 25
    cooperative workshops and, 114
    prior beliefs and, 9–10
    teachers and, 327, 328

Faber, A., 200
Fabes, R. A., 84
Fahey, J. A., 67
Failure, 27
    attribution and, 74–75, 76
    belonging and, 20
    motivation and, 85
Fan, X., 226
Fay, J., 198, 199, 201, 203
Feedback:
    attribution and, 76
    belonging and, 319, 323
Feeney, T., 132
Feinstein, J. A., 125
Field trips, 282, 301–302
Flink, C., 16
Fogarty, R., 63
Fortier, M. S., 16
Forton, M. B., 264, 267
Frattura, E., 192
Freedom, 12, 18, 43, 44, 333
Freeman, W., 26
Frey, A., 148
Friedel, J., 77
Friendships:
    belonging and, 319
    counselors and, 238–239
    literature and, 208
    playground management and, 295
    teachers and, 321
    whole groups and, 142
Frostad, L. C., 180
Fuchs, D., 65
Fuhrer, U., 251
Fultz, J., 84
Funk, D., 198, 199, 201, 203
Furniture arrangements, 250, 251, 253, 257,
    258, 267, 269, 273

Furrer, C., 19
Future needs:
    belonging and, 21
    caring about students and, 31
    competency and, 26
    See also Students' needs

Gambrell, L. B., 74
Games:
    cooperative workshops and, 106
    motivation and, 83
    playground management and, 295
    special-needs students and, 184, 190
    thinking and, 124, 134
    whole groups and, 143
Gangs, 19
Gavin, K., 189
Gay, G., 180
Gelman, R. G., 146
General education classrooms, 82, 171, 333
Ghere, G. S., 308
Gibbs, J., 54, 55, 142, 144, 161
Gifted students, 170
Gillies, R. M., 102, 112
Glaser, R., 122, 325
Glasser, W., 19, 21, 23, 24, 25
Glasson, G. E., 74, 124
Glickman, C. D., 44, 45
Goals:
    attribution and, 75, 76
    autonomy and, 12, 13, 17
    belonging and, 19, 323
    caring about students and, 31
    community development and, 53–54, 55, 57
    competency and, 23–24
    cooperative workshops and, 93, 94, 96,
        107, 108, 111, 112, 114
    democratic classrooms and, 45
    lesson plans and, 97t
    motivation and, 85
    planning and, 328
    resources and, 240
    special-needs students and, 177, 178, 192
    tasks and, 96–102, 97t

thinking routines and, 139
whole groups and, 143, 145, 157, 165
See also Mastery goals; Performance goals;
    Social issues
Good, T., 144
Goodenow, C., 21
Gordon, S. P., 44, 45
Gore, J. M., 7
Gorrell, J., 21
Goswami, U., 64, 65, 67
Grades:
    attribution and, 75
    caring about students and, 34
    competency and, 25
    mastery goals and, 96
    whole groups and, 158
Graphs:
    special-needs students and, 177
    whole groups and, 153, 154f, 158
Greenspan, S. I., 170, 171, 177, 178
Greenwood, C., 189
Gregory, G. H., 107, 108
Grolnick, W. S., 16
Grusec, J. E., 84
Guay, F., 16
Guthrie, J. T., 74

Haberman, M., 21
Haggerty, N., 214
Hallway management, 287–290
Halonen, A., 26
Hambly, H., 66
Hamby Towns, M., 57
Hannaford, C., 66, 71
Harmatz, M. G., 265
Harold, R., 74
Harriott, W. A., 55
Hartig, T., 251
Hausfather, S. J., 25, 74, 124
Heflin, J., 215
Henniger, M. L., 124
High/Scope Educational Research Foundation,
    49, 50, 93, 132, 134

Hinshaw, S. P., 26
History, Relationships, Application, Speculation,
    and Explanation (HRASE), 112–113
Hohmann, M., 66, 93, 129, 132, 174
Holt, K., 16
Holt-Reynolds, D., 9
Holubec, E. J., 110
Homework:
    democratic classrooms and, 44
    parents and, 231
    special-needs students and, 182–183
Hurst, C. O., 207, 208, 210

Inclinations, 122, 129, 139, 333
Independence:
    autonomy and, 12
    thinking routines and, 132, 135, 136
    whole groups and, 160
Individual accountability, 44, 93, 94, 110–111, 333
Individual Education Plan (IEP), 178
Inquirer, 38, 333
Interdependence, 93, 94, 110–115, 333
International Reading Association, 242
Internet:
    animals and, 189
    energizers and, 163
    learning and, 286–287
    outside of the classrooms and, 282
    resources and, 240, 242–243, 242t
    tasks and, 100, 101
    See also Technology; Web sites
Ising, H., 266
Ivey, M., 215

Jang, H., 16
Jarvis, W. B. G., 125
Jay, J. K., 7
Jefferson, T., 45
Jensen, E.:
    aesthetics and, 263
    belonging and, 20, 21
    brain research and, 63, 65, 66, 68
    comfort and, 267

competency and, 24, 25, 26
cooperative workshops and, 107
emotions and, 70, 71
knowing students and, 38
lighting and, 265, 266
motivation and, 84
noise and, 266
physical environments and, 250, 251, 255
rewards and, 84
social skills and, 19
Jeon, S., 16
Johannessen, L. R., 219
Johnson, D., 93, 110
Johnson, R., 93, 110
Johnson, S. M., 220
Jolivette, K., 82
Juicy problems:
    autonomy and, 15
    community development and, 53, 54, 55
    competency and, 24
    content and, 326
    democratic classrooms and, 44, 48, 58
    folders and, 29
    knowing students and, 36, 40
    whole groups and, 165

Kaff, M. S, 171
Kamii, C., 12, 64, 124, 174
Kaplan, H., 12, 13, 15, 16
Katcher, A., 187
Katz, L. G., 325
Katz, P. A., 16
Kauffman, J. M., 6, 26
Kaufman, M. E., 91
Kawamura, K. Y., 265
Kear, D. J., 74
Keefe, E., 258
Keel, L., 21
Killion, J. P., 55, 145
Kliebard, H. M., 131
Knowledge:
    brain research and, 71
    competency and, 325

content and, 326–327
cooperative workshops and, 114, 115
learning and, 325–326
nutrition and, 67–68
thinking and, 124, 125, 130
See also Prior knowledge
Knowles, J. G., 9
Know-Want to Know-Learned (KWL), 138, 139
Koehler, L., 190
Koestner, R., 6, 16
Kofler, W. W., 266
Kohler, F., 189
Kohn, A., 6, 13, 23, 24, 32, 44, 47, 53, 79, 81, 84, 91, 131, 231
Kolb, D. A., 131
Kounin, J. S., 311
Krajcik, J., 327
Kranowitz, C. A., 257, 263, 265
Kraus, S., 7
Kriete, R., 55

Labeled children, 171–172
    See also Special-needs students
Labinowicz, E., 64, 132, 174, 175, 324
Ladd, G. W., 102
Lalik, R. V., 74, 124
Language, 196–206
    special-needs students and, 177
Language pathologists, 237–238
Laws, 183
Lazarus, R., 66
Leadership, 45
Learning:
    attribution and, 75
    brain research and, 66, 69, 70
    classroom settings and, 267
    community development and, 55, 57
    competency and, 25, 26, 27, 324, 325, 326
    content and, 326–327
    culture and, 325
    democratic classrooms and, 44, 45, 47, 48–49
    emotions and, 70–71
    knowing students and, 38
    knowledge and, 325–326

language and, 196, 203
learner-centered, 92
lighting and, 266, 278
literature and, 215
motivation and, 62, 82
nutrition and, 67–68
pedagogical structures and, 91
playground management and, 294, 296, 297, 298
relationships and, 77, 80
seating arrangements and, 255, 256
self-efficacy and, 74
tasks and, 98
technology and, 282–287 .*See also* Technology
thinking and, 121, 126, 130, 131–132, 136
whole groups and, 143–144, 145, 150, 158, 161
See also Pedagogy
Learning clubs, 320
Learning disabilities, 173–174, 176–178, 333
seating arrangements and, 258
See also Special-needs students
Learning environments *See* Classroom environments
Learning teams, 21
Lectures, 200–201
Leggett, E., 76
Lepper, M. R., 82
Lercher, P., 266
Lesson planning:
cooperative workshops and, 87, 94, 95t, 97t, 103t, 109t
culturally diverse students and, 181
knowing students and, 38
pedagogical structures and, 90
resources and, 242
technology and, 284
See also Planning
Lever-Duffy, J., 284
Levine, M., 130
Lewis, C. C., 144, 146
Li, Q., 282
Licht, B. G., 75
Lighting, 70, 263, 265–266, 278
Limited English Proficiency (LEP), 181
Linnenbrink, E. A., 65, 73, 74, 75, 76
Listening:
belonging and, 21, 319

brain research and, 66
community development and, 52–53
democratic classrooms and, 45
knowing students and, 39, 40
language and, 198, 201
parents and, 227–228
relationships and, 78, 80
special-needs students and, 186
whole groups and, 160
Literature, 207–214, 211–213t
Littky, D., 89
Lockett, N., 21, 54, 76, 203, 223
Logan, K., 258
London, W., 265
Long, N. J., 20
Lowery, N. V., 7, 25
Lucas, T., 20, 33, 90, 92, 96, 98
Lucking, R., 190

Maguire, T., 25
Main, D. S., 16
Malley, J., 19, 20, 21
Management, 49, 63, 66
Manipulatives, 83
Marachi, R., 77
Martin, S. S., 55
Marx, A., 251
Maslow, A. H., 240, 326
Massey, N., 82
Mastery goals, 75, 76, 96, 116, 333
See also Goals
Materials, 259–263, 278
Maxwell, S. E., 75
May-Plumlee, T., 84
Mazlish, E., 200
McAlpine, L., 8
McCann, T. M., 219
McCloud, S., 91
McDonald, J. B., 284
McGee, R., 26
McKenna, M. C., 74
McNeil, J. T., 50
McTighe, J., 81, 223
Meaning, 27, 308

competency and, 23, 24, 26
cooperative workshops and, 111
field trips and, 301
motivation and, 83
thinking routines and, 136
whole groups and, 158
Meetings, 143, 165, 197
See also Class meetings
Meis, M., 266
Memory:
competency and, 23, 24, 26
pedagogical structures and, 92
special-needs students and, 177, 187
stress and, 70
tasks and, 100
thinking and, 122, 124
Mental disabilities, 171, 172, 176–178
See also Special-needs students
Mental health, 239
Mentors, 234
See also Tutoring
Metacognitive knowledge, 102, 106, 333
See also Knowledge
Midgley, C., 77
Milham, M., 171
Miller, L., 189
Minke, K. M., 231
5-Minute Write, 154–155, 156t, 333
Miserandino, M., 16
Mizell, A. P., 284
Modeling:
content and, 327
cooperative workshops and, 112, 114
core beliefs and, 309
literature and, 210
thinking and, 128
Mohan Welsh, L., 63, 65, 70, 76, 79, 83, 105
Montie, J. K., 308
Morgan, P. L., 65
Mostert, M. P., 6
Motivation, 1, 61–63, 62t, 83, 334
attribution and, 63, 74–76
brain research and, 63–65, 63–72, 66t
content and, 326

cooperative workshops and, 93, 107
curriculum and, 63
democratic classroom and, 58
exercise and, 67f
grades and, 76
language and, 197
nutrition and, 67–68
pedagogical structures and, 90, 91, 92, 116
physical environments and, 250
punishment and, 70
reflection and, 68–70, 70f
relationships and, 63, 77–80
self-efficacy and, 63, 73–74
special-needs students and, 174, 176, 180,
    187, 189, 190–192
tasks/topics and, 81–83
thinking and, 123, 136
vision and, 2
whole groups and, 144, 158
Motor skills, 190
Murphy, P. S., 54
Music, 263
brain research and, 70
knowing students and, 40
motivation and, 83
relationships and, 78, 80
whole groups and, 161

Narratives. *See* Stories
National Association of School Psychologists, 239
National Council of Teachers of Mathematics, 242
National Research Council, 325
Nebbe, L. L., 187, 188, 193
Needs *See* Students' needs
Neglect, 183
See also Abuse
Nelson, B., 237
Nezlek, J., 16
Nicolson, R. I., 66
Nimetz, S. L., 77
Noddings, N., 31, 32, 39, 47, 48, 51
Noise, 266–267, 278
Nolen, S., 76
Nurmi, J., 26

Nurses, 236
Nutrition, 67–68, 69f, 85

Obenchain, K. M., 55, 160
Occupational therapists, 238
Ockene, I. S., 265
O'Connor, K., 223
O'Keefe, B., 73, 77
Organization, 314–315
Overtree, C. E., 265

Palmer, B. M., 74
Paradox, 18, 32
Parents, 226–232
    communication and, 224–225, 228–229, 229t
    cooperative workshops and, 106–107
    democratic classrooms and, 45
    knowing students and, 41
    relationships and, 79
    resources and, 245
    special-needs students and, 178, 182–183,
        184, 186, 189
    whole groups and, 146
Parkay, F. W., 180
Parker, A. R., 159
Peck, D., 326, 327
Peck, M. S., 52, 53, 55, 157
Pedagogical structures, xvii, 89, 334
    academic issues and, 116
    accountability and, 116
    autonomy and, 90, 92, 116
    belonging and, 90, 92, 116
    competency and, 90, 92, 116
    curriculum and, 91
    democracy and, 90, 91, 92, 116
    learning and, 91
    lesson planning and, 90
    memory and, 92
    motivation and, 90, 91, 92, 116
    performance goals and, 116
    problem solving and, 91
    reflection and, 92
    self-efficacy and, 91
    social issues and, 91, 116
        struggling students and, 91
        students' needs and, 90, 92, 116
        success and, 92
        tasks and, 116
Pedagogy, 89, 90, 334
    content and, 326–327
    cooperative workshops and, 93–115. See also
        Cooperative workshops
    physical environments and, 250
    self-efficacy and, 73–74
    technology and, 284
    See also Learning
Peer tutoring See Tutoring
Pellegrino, J. W., 325
Penick, J. E., 112
Performance goals, 96, 334
    attribution and, 75, 76
    motivation and, 83, 85
    pedagogical structures and, 116
    See also Goals
Perkins, D., 122, 123, 131
Permission slips, 302
Permissive environment, 41–44, 42f, 43t, 49, 334
    See also Classroom environments
Peterson, K. D., 54
Pets, 187–188, 189
Petty, R. E., 124, 125
Peyton, L., 132
Physical disabilities, 171, 172, 176–178
    playground management and, 299
    seating arrangements and, 258
    See also Special-needs students
Physical education, 66
    See also Exercise
Piaget, J., 326, 332
Pianta, R. C., 77
Pierce, W. D., 6
Pintrich, P. R., 65, 73, 74, 75, 76, 84
Pittman, T. S., 16
Plan-do-review, 40, 129, 132–137, 139, 155, 334
Planning:
    attribution and, 75
    bathroom management and, 291
    classroom settings and, 267

community development and, 54, 55
cooperative workshops and, 107, 111, 114
democratic classrooms and, 45
goals and, 328
organization and, 314–315, 315t, 316t
outside of the classrooms and, 282
teachers and, 320
technology and, 286
thinking routines and, 133, 134, 136
transition times and, 317
whole groups and, 159, 164
See also Lesson planning
Plants, 80, 136, 189, 222, 223, 267
Playground management, 293–300
Portfolios, 39, 223–224, 334
Positive affects, 16, 334
Poverty, 172, 183, 191
Powell, S., 82
Power:
  autonomy and, 13
  classroom environments and, 41
  language and, 196, 197
Preservice teachers, xiii
Pressley, M., 63, 65, 70, 76, 79, 83, 105
Price, J. H., 148
Price, J. M., 102
Principals, 234–236
Prior knowledge, 9–10
  autonomy and, 14–15
  competency and, 24
  culturally diverse students and, 181
  knowing students and, 38
  motivation and, 85
  reflection and, 28
  special-needs students and, 179
  thinking routines and, 131, 138
Problem solving:
  autonomy and, 12, 13, 16, 17
  community development and, 53–54, 55, 56, 57
  competency and, 24
  cooperative workshops and, 93, 94, 104, 108, 111, 112
  democratic classrooms and, 44, 49
  hallway management and, 290
  knowing students and, 35, 37

language and, 198, 199, 202–203, 204
literature and, 207, 209, 210
pedagogical structures and, 91
playground management and, 295
relationships and, 79, 80
special-needs students and, 182, 184–185
tasks and, 99, 100–102
thinking and, 122, 128, 132, 134, 136, 137
whole groups and, 143–144, 148–149, 152, 153, 164
Procedures, 314–317
Psychologists, 239–240, 243
Pullen, P. L., 6
Punishment:
  autonomy and, 17
  belonging and, 17
  competency and, 22
  knowing students and, 37, 40
  language and, 197, 203
  literature and, 215
  motivation and, 62, 70
  playground management and, 293
  relationships and, 79
  seating arrangements and, 253
  struggling students and, 170
  whole groups and, 145–146, 153, 158

Questions:
  belonging and, 319
  cooperative workshops and, 111, 112–114, 115
  language and, 198–200, 200t, 204
  success and, 245
  thinking and, 122, 125, 126, 127, 129
  whole groups and, 148, 155, 161–162

Racism, 180
Rankin, J. L., 237
Raphael, L. M., 63
Reading:
  cooperative workshops and, 93, 107, 108
  special-needs students and, 173, 176, 177
  technology and, 284
Reading Specialists, 238
Reay, D., 151

Reeve, J., 13, 14, 16
Reflection, 7f, 28, 306, 334
    attribution and, 75
    brain research and, 68–70, 70f
    classroom settings and, 267, 269–277
    community development and, 55
    competency and, 25
    cooperative workshops and, 111, 114
    democratic classrooms and, 51
    experience and, 8
    the future and, 10–11
    language and, 197, 202–203
    learning and, 325–326, 326
    literature and, 214
    motivation and, 85
    pedagogical structures and, 92
    prior beliefs and, 9–10, 28
    special-needs students and, 174, 180,
        184–185, 192
    students helping teachers and, 225
    success and, 6–7
    tasks and, 100, 101
    teachers and, 327, 328
    thinking and, 129, 133, 138
    whole groups and, 145, 150, 154
    See also Thinking routines
Reich, R., 142
Reiff, J. C., 9
Relatedness, 18, 334
Relationships:
    attribution and, 76
    belonging and, 20, 21, 318–319, 322
    caring about students and, 32
    community development and, 54
    cooperative workshops and, 113
    knowing students and, 33–41
    motivation and, 63, 77–80, 85
    outside of the classrooms and, 289
    parents and, 226–232, 229t
    playground management and, 293
    seating arrangements and, 251, 269–273,
        271t, 272f, 273t
    special-needs students and, 180, 183, 191
    teachers and, 319, 320

    teachers as resources and, 234
Resiliency, 19, 132
Respect:
    belonging and, 322–323
    language and, 197, 198, 203
    literature and, 208
    whole groups and, 146, 149, 150
Responsibility:
    teachers and, 321
    thinking routines and, 132
Restroom management, 291
Rewards, 334
    autonomy and, 17
    boundaries and, 310
    motivation and, 63, 83–84, 85
    thinking and, 123, 124
    whole groups and, 145–146, 153, 158
    See also Celebrations
Reynolds, D., 66
Ritchhart, R., xvii, 120, 122, 125, 130, 135,
        138, 139, 196
Roeser, R., 26
Ronning, R., 91, 102, 121, 136
Rosal, M., 265
Rosenfeld, L. B., 257
Ross-Gordon, J. M., 44, 45
Roth, G., 12, 13, 15, 16
Routines See Thinking routines
Rubrics, 115
Ryan, R. M., 6, 12, 13, 16, 18

Safety:
    community development and, 55
    Internet and, 286
    playground management and, 298
    resources and, 240
    sending students home and, 299
    special-needs students and, 182, 183, 184, 185
    whole groups and, 148, 149, 163
Sallis, J., 66
Sanche, R. P., 148
Santrock, J. W., 25, 325
Sapolsky, R., 19, 63, 70
Scaffolding, 334

academic goals and, 96
   competency and, 25–26
   cooperative workshops and, 112
   knowing students and, 38
   motivation and, 81, 85
   self-efficacy and, 74
Schaps, E., 19, 21, 144, 146
Schempp, P. G., 9
Schon, D., 7
Schraw, G., 91, 102, 121, 136
Schunk, D. H., 65, 73, 76, 84, 102
Schutz, A., 38, 45
Schweinhart, L. J., 49, 50
Seating arrangements, 251–258, 268, 269t, 270t,
   271t, 272ft, 276t, 277t, 278
   furniture arrangements and, 250, 251, 253, 257,
     258, 267, 269, 273
   learning disabilities and, 258
   sketch of, 274f, 275f
   See also Classroom environments
Seelbach, A., 16
Segal, J. W., 122
Seifert, T., 73, 75, 76, 77, 83
Self-confidence, 21, 132
Self-efficacy, 334
   motivation and, 63, 73–74, 85
   pedagogical structures and, 91
   relationships and, 79
Self-esteem:
   resources and, 240
   self-efficacy and, 73
   special-needs students and, 188
Self-worth:
   language and, 198
   motivation and, 85
   relationships and, 79
   special-needs students and, 174, 189
   thinking routines and, 134
Seligman, M., 19
Senge, P. M., 20, 33, 90, 92, 96, 98
Sensitivities, 122–123, 129, 132, 139, 335
Service learning, 157, 158–159, 165
Sexual abuse, 239
Shame, 144, 310–311

Shapira, Z., 16
Share, D. L., 26
Sharp, V., 190
Sheinman, L., 16
Sheridan, S., 226
Shields, A., 16
Silva, P. A., 26
Simmons, L. A., 55, 145
Skills:
   attribution and, 75
   caring about students and, 31
   cooperative workshops and, 108
   democratic classrooms and, 45
   self-efficacy and, 74
   special-needs students and, 176–177, 178,
     187, 188, 189
   thinking and, 125
Skinner, B. F., 326
Skinner, E., 16, 19, 23
Slavin, R. E., 102
Smith, B., 20, 33, 90, 92, 96, 98
Smith, F., 81, 82, 319
Smith, G., 214
Smith, R. W., 9
Smithsonian Institution, 242
Social issues:
   belonging and, 19–20
   competency and, 324, 325
   cooperative workshops and, 94, 96, 102, 104,
     106, 108, 115
   counselors and, 238–239
   curriculum and, 50
   democratic classrooms and, 51
   language and, 196, 198, 204, 205
   literature and, 207, 208–210, 214, 215, 216, 217
   pedagogical structures and, 91, 116
   playground management and, 295
   relationships and, 77, 79
   seating arrangements and, 256, 258
   special-needs students and, 173, 174,
     178, 188, 192
   thinking and, 129, 132, 134, 139
   whole groups and, 144, 146, 153, 157, 159, 162, 164
Social studies, 106, 137, 284

Social workers, 243
Solomon, D., 19, 21
Sommers, W. A., 308
Sorsdahl, S. N., 148
Sousa, D. A., 21, 185, 189, 190
Sparkes, A. C., 9
Special-education, 237, 239
Special-needs students, 170, 171–192, **335**
   accommodations for, 257–258
   creating opportunities for, 190
   exercise and, 66
   language and, 196
   motivation and, 83
   playground management and, 299
   See also Struggling students
Speech abilities, 177
Speech language pathologists, 237–238
Sprenger, M., 19, 21, 63, 64, 65, 66, 255, **263**
Standards:
   attribution and, 76
   autonomy and, 15
   goals and, 96
   thinking routines and, 135
   whole groups and, 145
Steinberg, M., 77
Stereotyping, 181
Sternberg, R. J., 122
Sticky notes, 137, 150, 151
Stiggins, R., 38
Stimulus-response, 61, 335
Stoddart, T., 326, 327
Stofflett, R., 326, 327
Stories:
   language and, 200–201, 204
   literature and, 207, 208
   writing and, 214–216
Strachota, B., 13, 15, 24, 79
Stress, 220
   belonging and, 20, 21
   brain research and, 70
   comfort and, 267
   competency and, 26
   emotions and, 70
   exercise and, 72

   literature and, 214, 216
   motivation and, 85
   noise and, 266
   room arrangements and, 251
   special-needs students and, 182–183
Strobel, K., 26
Structures:
   autonomy and, 311
   competency and, 324
   core beliefs and, 308–309
   flexible, 120
   special-needs students and, 187–192
   whole groups and, 142
Struggling students, 170
   attribution and, 75
   knowing students and, 38
   pedagogical structures and, 91
   playground management and, 295
   thinking and, 129, 137
   whole groups and, 146
   See also Special-needs students
Student assistant teams, 237, 239
Students' needs, 2
   belonging and, 19
   caring about students and, 31, 32, 33
   cooperative workshops and, 94
   goals and, 96
   pedagogical structures and, 90, 92, 116
   seating arrangements and, 251, 253
   special-needs students and, 183
   tasks and, 99
   thinking routines and, 139
   See also Future needs
Substance abuse, 182
Success, 27
   attribution and, 74–75, 76
   autonomy and, 16
   belonging and, 19, 21
   cooperative workshops and, 102, 104, 105, 107, 110
   data and, 50
   democratic classrooms and, 47
   the future and, 10–11
   motivation and, 62, 63, 67, 84, 85
   pedagogical structures and, 92

questions and, 245
reflection and, 6–7
resources and, 240
special-needs students and, 177, 179, 190, 191, 192
tasks and, 99
thinking routines and, 136
vision and, 1
whole groups and, 150, 151, 164
Support:
belonging and, 19, 20
community development and, 55–56
competency and, 25
cooperative workshops and, 111
democratic classrooms and, 51
language and, 206
literature and, 214
motivation and, 82
relationships and, 77
resources and, 243
self-efficacy and, 74
special-needs students and, 176, 183, 185
teachers and, 319, 320, 321
thinking and, 125, 129, 130
whole groups and, 142, 143–144, 145
Surveys:
classroom settings and, 275–276, 277t
playground management and, 295
whole groups and, 151, 153, 154f
Swanson, J. J., 70, 262

Tally charts, 155–156, 157t, 335
Tankersley, M., 170, 171
Tannenbaum, S. A., 157
Tasks:
attribution and, 75
brain research and, 66
competency and, 24, 25, 26
cooperative workshops and, 104, 108, 110, 112
motivation and, 81–83
pedagogical structures and, 116
thinking routines and, 130
Teacher-centered classrooms, 64, 92, 335
Teachers' needs, 94
Teasing, 153, 296

See also Bullying
Technology, 260
motivation and, 83
outside of the classrooms
and, 282–287
special-needs students and, 187, 190
whole groups and, 143
See also Internet
Telljohann, S. K., 148
Templin, T. J., 9
Terry, B., 189
Testing:
culturally diverse students and, 181
parents and, 231
psychologists and, 239
thinking and, 122
whole groups and, 158
See also Assessments
Therapy, 176, 178
Thinking routines, 40, 129–139, 335
accountability and, 132, 134
autonomy and, 132
classroom environments and, 135
cooperative learning and, 132
cooperative workshops and, 138
creativity and, 132
cultural issues and, 132
curriculum and, 135
goals and, 139
independence and, 132, 135, 136
meaning and, 136
planning and, 133, 134, 136
prior knowledge and, 131, 138
responsibility and, 132
self-worth and, 134
standards and, 135
students' needs and, 139
success and, 136
tasks and, 130
topics and, 138
See also Reflection
Think-pair-share, 20, 137–138, 139
Tishman, S., 122, 133
Tomlinson, C. A., 108

Tools:
  autonomy and, 312–313
  competency and, 324
  cooperative workshops and, 108
  core beliefs and, 308–309
  special-needs students and, 187–192
  thinking and, 127–130, 139
  whole groups and, 143, 147–163
Topics:
  brain research and, 66
  competency and, 323
  content and, 326–327
  democratic classrooms and, 45
  knowing students and, 37
  literature and, 208
  motivation and, 63, 81–83
  relationships and, 77
  self-efficacy and, 73
  special-needs students and, 187, 192
  teachers and, 320
  thinking routines and, 138
Trainin, G., 187
Traynor, P. L., 26
Trent, S. C., 6
Tribes activities, 54
Troutman, A., 6
Trust:
  belonging and, 21
  relationships and, 78–79, 80
  special-needs students and, 188, 190
  teachers as resources and, 234
  whole groups and, 148, 155
Tutoring:
  belonging and, 21
  cooperative workshops and, 102
  mentors and, 234
  special-needs students and, 189–192

Understanding:
  attribution and, 75
  competency and, 23, 25, 26
  conceptual, 16, 332
  cooperative workshops and, 105
  democratic classrooms and, 44

  nutrition and, 67–68
  thinking and, 124, 131
  whole groups and, 157
Utley, C., 189

Vallerand, R. J., 16
Valli, L., 7
Values:
  autonomy and, 16
  belonging and, 21
  community development and, 57
  democratic classrooms and, 44, 45, 48, 51, 57
  knowing students and, 36
Veomett, G. E., 54, 111, 130
Verbal skills, 132
Vincent, M. M., 63, 65, 70, 76, 79, 83, 105
Viorst, J., 112, 213
Vision, 335
  learning environment and, 2
  motivation and, 2
  success and, 1
  whole groups and, 149–151, 164
Vision statement, 150, 151
Vogelgesang, L. J., 157
Vulnerable children, 171, 181, 182, 183, 243, 335
Vygotsky, L., 74, 129, 325, 326

Walz, C., 19
Wasserman, S., 132
Watkins, D., 54
Watson, M. S., 144, 146
Web sites:
  elementary classroom management and, 29
  learning and, 286–287
  literature and, 214, 216
  prior experiences and, 10
  resources and, 240, 242–243, 242t
  special-needs students and, 190
  student study site and, xviii
  tasks and, 101
  See also Internet
Wehby, J. H., 82
Weikart, D. P., 16, 49, 50, 66, 93, 129, 132, 174

Weiner, B., 75
Weissbourd, R., 172, 181, 182, 193, 243
Well, A. D., 265
Welsh, L., 63, 65, 70, 76, 79, 83, 105
Wentzel, K. R, 54, 102
Weston, C., 8
Whole-class service activities, 54
Wickless, M., 187
Wieder, S., 170, 171, 177, 178
Wigfield, A., 74
Wiggins, G., 81
Williams, K. C., 40, 54, 111
Williams, S., 16, 26
Wilson, K., 187
Winsler, A., 129, 325
Woolfolk, A. E., 67, 70, 75
Workshops, 87, 93–115
    belonging and, 20

content and, 326
language and, 197
parents and, 230
special-needs students and, 178, 187
See also Cooperative workshops
Writing:
    cooperative workshops and, 93, 107
    stories and, 214–216
    technology and, 284

Ylvisaker, M., 132
York-Barr, J., 308

Zabel, R. H., 171
Zembal-Saul, C., 327
Zone of Proximal Development (ZPD),
    74, 85, 335
Zucker, S., 32, 40, 54, 151, 153, 182, 295

About the Author

Kerry Curtiss Williams taught elementary and middle school in the public school systems of Nebraska and Iowa. Her recent activities include mentoring and teaching undergraduate- and graduate-level students. She currently works with teachers pursuing their master's degrees in curriculum and instruction within a learning community format at Wayne State College in Nebraska. In addition, she teaches undergraduate courses in child development.

Williams earned her bachelor's degree from the University of Nebraska–Lincoln in the Extended Elementary Teacher Education Program (EETEP), a select experimental group. Named one of the college's "Ninety Notables," Williams has presented at national conferences about math education and thinking routines in undergraduate teacher education courses. She earned a master's degree in leadership and adult development from Drake University and a PhD in administration, curriculum, and instruction from the University of Nebraska–Lincoln. Her published works include journal articles and a text titled *Launching Learners in Science Pre-K–5*. Williams conducts workshops for undergraduate and inservice teachers on pedagogical structures, classroom management, and science education. She lives with her husband and two sons in Omaha, Nebraska.

Dr. Williams can be reached at kewilli2@wsc.edu.